Lecture Notes in Computer Science 8790

Commenced Publication in 1973
Founding and Former Series Editors:
Gerhard Goos, Juris Hartmanis, and Jan van Leeuwen

Editorial Board

More information about this series at http://www.springer.com/series/8851

Ngoc Thanh Nguyen · Ryszard Kowalczyk
Ana Fred · Filipe Joaquim (Eds.)

Transactions on Computational Collective Intelligence XVII

 Springer

Editor-in-Chief

Ngoc Thanh Nguyen
Istitute of Informatics
Wrocław University of Technology
Wrocław
Poland

Co-editor-in-Chief

Ryszard Kowalczyk
Swinburne University of Technology
Melbourne
Australia

and

Polish Academy of Sciences
Warsaw
Poland

Guest Editors

Ana Fred
Technical University of Lisbon
Lisbon
Portugal

Filipe Joaquim
Polytechnic Institute of Sétubal
Sétubal
Portugal

ISSN 0302-9743 ISSN 1611-3349 (electronic)
Lecture Notes in Computer Science
ISBN 978-3-662-44993-6 ISBN 978-3-662-44994-3 (eBook)
DOI 10.1007/978-3-662-44994-3

Library of Congress Control Number: 2014956231

Springer Heidelberg New York Dordrecht London

Printed on acid-free paper

Springer-Verlag GmbH Berlin Heidelberg is part of Springer Science+Business Media
(www.springer.com)

Preface

The present special issue of the Journal Transactions on Computational Collective Intelligence (TCCI) includes extended and revised versions of a set of selected papers from the International Joint Conference on Computational Intelligence – IJCCI 2012 – and from the International Conference on Agents and Artificial Intelligence – ICAART 2013.

The interdisciplinary areas of Intelligent Agents, Artificial Intelligence, and Computational Intelligence involve a large number of researchers who devote themselves to study theoretical and practical issues related to areas such as multi-agent systems, software platforms, distributed problem solving, distributed AI in general, knowledge representation, planning, learning, scheduling, perception reactive AI systems, fuzzy systems, neural networks, evolutionary computing, and other related topics.

This special issue presents 15 research papers with novel concepts and applications in the aforementioned areas.

The first nine papers are revised and extended versions of papers presented at ICAART 2013, focusing on theoretical and practical applications of agent and multi-agent systems, including the behavior of financial trading agents (Steve Stotter et al.), multi-agent methodology applied to supply chain management (by Borja Ponte et al.), distributed evacuation route planning using mobile agents (by Alejandro Aviles et al.), and agent-based approach to accident analysis in safety critical domains (by Tibor Bosse and Nataliya M. Mogles). Some other papers focused on more theoretical aspects, namely on the importance of interdisciplinary research relating agent systems, learning models, and formal languages (by Leonor Becerra-Bonache and Dolores Jiménez-López), the contribution of unsupervised learning and regular grammatical inference to identify profiles of elderly people and their development over time in order to evaluate care needs (by Catherine Combes and Jean Azema), and computational and formal linguistics to find good mathematical and computational models to describe linguistic phenomena (by Benedek Nagy and László Kovács). Finally, we included two papers that discuss situation theory, situated information, and situated agents (by Roussanka Loukanova), and conditional preference networks support multi-issue negotiations with mediator (by Ghosh et al.).

The other six papers are revised and extended versions of papers presented at IJCCI 2012, ranging from evolutionary computing, such as hybrid schemas using the genetic algorithm and firefly algorithm (by Olympia Roeva) and a subset-based ant colony optimization with tournament path selection for high-dimensional problems (by Emmanuel Sapin and Ed Keedwell), to neural computing, including a paper on color quantization with magnitude sensitive competitive learning algorithm (by Enrique Pelayo et al.) and another on the analysis of the local optima storage capacity of Hopfield network-based fitness function models (by Kevin Swingler and Leslie Smith) and two application-oriented papers, one on the synthesis of multicomponent reuse water networks by pso approach (by Ravagnani et al.) and the other on the Alzheimer disease diagnosis: automatic spontaneous speech analysis (by Lopez-de-Ipiña et al.).

We believe that all papers presented in this special issue will serve as a reference for students, researchers, and practitioners who research on the areas of agent technology, evolutionary computing or neural networks, or whose work is related to interdisciplinary area of computational intelligence. We hope that the readers will find new inspiration for their research and may join the ICAART or IJCCI communities in the future.

We would like to thank all the authors for their contributions and to the reviewers who have helped ensuring the quality of this publication. Finally, we would also like to express our gratitude to the LNCS editorial staff of Springer, in particular to Prof. Ryszard Kowalczyk for all his patience and availability during this process.

We hope you enjoy this special issue.

July 2014   Ana Fred
                                                                          Joaquim Filipe

Transactions on Computational Collective Intelligence

This Springer journal focuses on research on the applications of computerbased methods of computational collective intelligence (CCI) and their applications in a wide range of fields such as the Semantic Web, social networks, and multi-agent systems. It aims to provide a forum for the presentation of scientific research and technological achievements accomplished by the international community.

The topics addressed by this journal include all solutions to real-life problems, for which it is necessary to use CCI technologies to achieve effective results.

The emphasis of the papers is on novel and original research and technological advancements. Special features on specific topics are welcome.

Tadeusz Szuba — AGH University of Science and Technology, Poland

Kristinn R. Thorisson — Reykjavík University, Iceland

Gloria Phillips-Wren — Loyola University Maryland, USA

Sławomir Zadrożny — Institute of Research Systems, PAS, Poland

Bernadetta Maleszka — Assistant Editor, Wrocław University of Technology, Poland

Contents

Multiagent Methodology to Reduce the Bullwhip Effect in a Supply Chain

Borja Ponte[⊠], Raúl Pino, and David de la Fuente

Polytechnic School of Engineering, University of Oviedo, Gijón, Spain
{uol83377,pino,david}@uniovi.es

Abstract. There are several circumstances which, in recent decades, have granted the supply chain management a strategic role in the search for competitive advantage. One of the goals is, undoubtedly, the reduction of Bullwhip Effect, which is generated by the amplification of the variability of orders along the chain, from the customer to the factory. This paper applies multiagent methodology for reducing Bullwhip Effect. To do this, it considers the supply chain as a global multiagent system, formed in turn by four multiagent subsystems. Each one of them represents one of the four levels of the traditional linear supply chain (Shop Retailer, Retailer, Wholesaler and Factory), and it coordinates various intelligent agents with different objectives. Thus, each level has its own capacity of decision and it seeks to optimize the supply chain management. The problem is analyzed both from a non collaborative approach, where each level seeks the optimal forecasting methodology independently of the rest, and from a collaborative approach, where each level negotiates with the rest looking for the best solution for the whole supply chain.

Keywords: Bullwhip effect · Supply chain management · Multiagent system · Time series forecasting

1 Introduction

A supply chain encompasses all participants and processes involved in satisfying customer demands around some products. Analyzing it, Forrester (1961) noted that small changes in customer demand are amplified along the supply chain, leading to larger variations in demand supported by the different levels, as they are further away from customer. This is called the Bullwhip Effect (or Forrester Effect), which, according to the subsequent research by Lee et al. (1997), is due to four main causes: demand forecastings, order batching, price fluctuations, and shortage gaming.

There have been several changes in the last two decades in the macro environment of the companies that have set up a new business perspective. From this, the production function is considered to have a strategic role as a source of competitive advantage, so that the practices related to managing the supply chain now represent one of the main concerns of business. In these circumstances, it is especially emphasized the importance of proper management of the supply chain regarding different objectives. One of them is undoubtedly reducing the Bullwhip Effect. In fact, Disney et al. (2003a, b) demonstrated that the Bullwhip effect leads the supply chain to unnecessary costs that can represent, in some cases, more than 30 % of the total costs thereof.

© Springer-Verlag Berlin Heidelberg 2014
N.T. Nguyen (Ed.): TCCI XVII 2014, LNCS 8790, pp. 1–21, 2014.
DOI: 10.1007/978-3-662-44994-3_1

In this context, this paper proposes the application of Artificial Intelligence techniques to the problematic associated with the Bullwhip Effect, in order to create a tool aimed at reducing variations in the demands transmitted along the supply chain. More specifically, Distributed Intelligence is applied to the problem through a multiagent system. It determines the optimal order policy based on the best demand forecasting method for each one of the different levels that make up the supply chain, understanding the forecasting errors as the main causes in the creation of the Bullwhip Effect.

The presented document is divided into four sections besides this introduction. Section 2 shows a review of the most relevant and recent literature in terms of reducing the Bullwhip Effect, with special emphasis on models based on Distributed Intelligence. Section 3 describes the model created with the different agents that compose it, the structure which includes them and the relationships among them, which is the way in which intelligence has been introduced to the system. Section 4 presents the results, mainly related to reducing the Bullwhip Effect, for which we have used time series data from the literature. Finally, Sect. 5 presents the conclusions according to the planned objectives.

2 Background: Reducing the Bullwhip Effect

2.1 Traditional Solutions

Each supply chain has its own characteristics, mainly conditioned by the type of product which is offered to the final consumer and by the market conditions in which it moves, and that unquestionably complicates the analysis of valid methodologies for reducing the Bullwhip Effect. However, it is possible to find some common problems to all of them, and several authors have proposed general strategies to be adapted to each particular supply chain. These traditional solutions to Bullwhip Effect are mainly based on collaboration among the various members of the supply chain, often sharing some information.

Thus, some practices that are carried out in some companies and which have been successful in reducing the Bullwhip Effect are:

- Use of Information Technology systems such as electronic data interchange (Machuca and Barajas 2004).
- Postponement, which is based on a redesign of products with the aim that the differentiation takes place in nodes near the customer. (Chen and Lee 2009).
- Efficient Consumer Response (ECR). These are associations of companies to synchronize the supply chain. (Disney et al. 2002).
- Vendor Managed Inventory (VMI). The supplier controls the inventory of the consumer, deciding on delivery times and quantities. (Holmstrom 1997).
- Collaborative Planning, Forecasting and Replenishment (CPFR). It means that members of the supply chain can develop, in a collaborative way, business plans and processes (Ji and Yang 2005).

2.2   Multiagent Systems in the Supply Chain Management

The supply chain management, including all that related to the Bullwhip Effect, is a highly complex problem, conditioned by multiple agents, each of which has to serve a large number of variables. In the last two decades, authors have looked for different ways to optimize the management by using new techniques based on Artificial Intelligence. Among these methods, there are several authors who have approached the supply chain as a network of intelligent agents. These are called multiagent systems.

Fox et al. (1993) were pioneers in the proposal of the organization of the supply chain as a network of cooperating intelligent agents. In their work, each agent executes one or more functions of the supply chain, coordinating their actions with other agents. Later, Shen et al. (1998) developed the tool MetaMorph II, which, through an agent-based architecture, integrates partners, suppliers and customers with a lead company through their respective mediators within a supply chain network via the Internet.

Kimbrough et al. (2002) studied whether a structure based on agents could be valid for the supply chain management, and they reached the conclusion that the agents were able to effectively play the well known Beer Game (Sterman 1989), reducing the Bullwhip Effect. Moyaux et al. (2004) used a multiagent system for modeling the behavior of each company in the supply chain. The paper proposes a variant of the Beer Game, which they called "Quebec Wood Supply Game".

Liang and Huang (2006) developed, based on a multiagent architecture, a model which allowed predicting the order quantity in a supply chain with several nodes, where each one of them could use a different system of inventory. De la Fuente and Lozano (2007) presented an application of Distributed Intelligence to reduce the Bullwhip Effect in a supply chain, based on a genetic algorithm. Zarandi et al. (2008) introduced Fuzzy Logic in the analysis.

Wu et al. (2011) applied the multiagent methodology to establish a supply chain model and to analyze in detail the Bullwhip Effect created along the chain, considering the non existence of information exchange among different members. One of the last studies in that regard is the one by Saberi et al. (2012), It develops a multiagent system, and which links the various agents that form it, emphasizing the collaborative aspect.

We can conclude that supply chain has become a complex system that requires modern methodologies for its analysis, seeking to optimize their management.

3   Construction of the Model

3.1   Global Multiagent System

To prepare the base model, we have considered a traditional supply chain with linear structure, which consists of five main levels: Consumer, Shop Retailer, Retailer, Wholesaler and Factory. Figure 1 shows the graphical representation of the levels, indicating the materials flow, which occurs from the top of the chain (Factory) to the lower levels (Consumer). Therefore, it is called downstream flow. The information flow is considered to be in the opposite way, which is called downstream flow.

The methodology used for the modeling and analysis in this research is based on multiagent systems. A multiagent system is a system composed of multiple intelligent

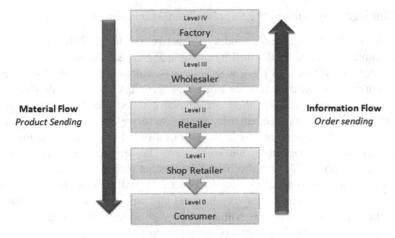

Fig. 1. Supply Chain Model.

agents, which interact among them. An agent can be defined as a computer system, which is able to perform autonomous and flexible actions that affect their environment according to certain design goals.

Thus, the behavior of each one of the main levels of the supply chain (Shop Retailer, Retailer, Wholesaler and Factory) will be simulated using a multiagent subsystem (which we will call MASS). The four multiagent subsystems form a global multiagent system (which we will call MAGS) which represents the whole supply chain. In turn, each subsystem will consist of several intelligent agents which interact among them, seeking to satisfy predefined objectives.

In our case, we consider static agents as they do not travel through the network, which have an internal symbolic reasoning model committed to the planning and negotiation for coordination with other agents. Thus, each agent has an incomplete knowledge of the problem, with decentralized data, so there is no overall control in the system.

All this means that each subsystem can represent a member of the supply chain, so that the global multiagent system has similar characteristics to the overall supply chain as:

- Autonomy: each level decides and executes without external intervention.
- Social skills: each level communicates with the other ones.
- Reactivity: each level modifies its behavior depending on the environment.

Figure 2, by way of synthesis, shows a scheme of the global multiagent system (MAGS) which simulates the supply chain, formed in turn by four local multiagent subsystems.

Thus, the supply chain management through a multiagent system allows the creation of an agile network which reacts in real-time to customer demands, compared to traditional systems, where everything is decided before the client makes the request.

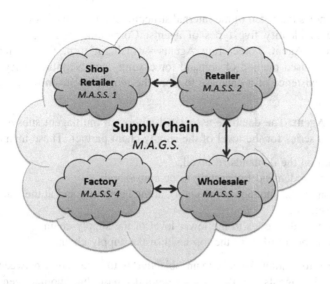

Fig. 2. General model of the global multiagent system.

3.2 Multiagent Subsystems

Each multiagent subsystem replicates the behavior of one of the levels of the supply chain. In turn, this subsystem will consist of several interconnected intelligent agents. Each multiagent subsystem will have some set goals that it will try to meet as best as possible, given certain conditions in its environment.

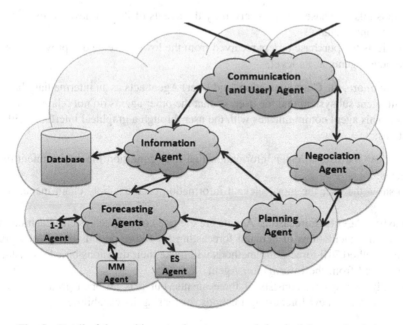

Fig. 3. Detail of the multiagent subsystem on each level of the supply chain.

Figure 3 shows the detail of the internal structure of a multiagent subsystem. There, it is possible to identify five types of agents: Communication Agent, Information Agent, Planning Agent, Forecasting Agents –which, in turn, include three agents according to the used method of demand forecasting– and Negotiation Agent. It also highlights the existence of a database to store the most relevant information for each subsystem.

Information Agent. The database associated with each multiagent subsystem store a temporary data series for the level of the supply chain partner. These mainly include:

- Information on the demands received.
- Information on demand forecasting to be considered.
- Information on the situation of inventory at the beginning and at the end of periods to be considered.
- Information on deliveries to the lower level of the supply chain.
- Information about orders to the top level of the supply chain.

Thus, the Information Agent's main objective is the mediation between the database and the other agents. So, they do not see a database, but another agent, and thus we achieve uniformity in the system. The Information Agent will only respond to requests for information from other agents and it will store the data given to him.

Communication (and User) Agent. Communication (and User) Agent will be responsible for carrying out the interactions of the multiagent subsystem with the adequate agents. It works, thus, as a spokesman. Communications among the various levels of the supply chain will be only through Communication Agents. Each one works in two ways:

- It transmits purchase orders received by the agents of its own level to the top level of the supply chain.
- It collects the purchase orders received from the lower level and it provides them to the other agents at its level.

Furthermore, the Communication (and User) Agent acts as an intermediary between the multiagent subsystem and the user, so that the other agents do not relates directly to the user. This agent communicates with the user through a graphical interface, with two objectives:

- To allow the user to enter information that may condition the environment of the agents.
- To show the user the most relevant information on the supply chain management.

Forecasting Agents. Forecasting Agents are the real core of the system. Each one will carry out the calculations of demand forecasting for future periods based on a predetermined method. All forecasting methods will make their decisions based on historical data, received from the Information Agent.

Initially, the system consists of three agents, but it is an open group, so that in future we can add new forecasting methods, increasing its capabilities.

1-1 Agent forecasts using one-one method, which is based on estimating the demand at any period as the one in the previous period. It can be expressed as follows:

$$\widehat{D}_t = D_{t-1} \tag{1}$$

Where $\widehat{D}_t$ is the forecast of demand in period t, and D_{t-1} is the demand received in period t.

MM Agent forecasts using the moving average method of order n, which estimates the demand in any period as the average of the latest n demands. It can be expressed as:

$$\widehat{D}_t = \frac{1}{n}[D_{t-1} + D_{t-2} + \ldots + D_{t-n}] \tag{2}$$

Where $\widehat{D}_t$ is the forecast of demand in period t, n is the number of periods to be considered for the moving average and D_{t-i} ($i \in [1, n]$) is the demand received in period t−i.

ES Agent, finally, determines forecasts according to the simple exponential smoothing method, which estimates the demand in any period as the weighted average of the last period demand and the forecast of demand in that period. It can be expressed as follows:

$$\widehat{D}_t = \alpha \cdot D_{t-1} + (1 - \alpha) \cdot \widehat{D}_{t-1} \tag{3}$$

Where $\widehat{D}_t$ is the forecast of demand in period t, $\widehat{D}_{t-1}$ is the forecast of demand in period t−1, D_{t-1} is the demand received in period t−1, and $\alpha \in [0, 1]$ is the exponential smoothing coefficient or weighing of the forecasting error.

MM Agent evaluates all the moving averages from n = 2 to n = 15 (for n = 1, it coincides with one-one method), selecting, on the basis of available data, the optimal moving average. The ES Agent evaluates all the forecasts for coefficients from α = 0.1 to α = 0.9, with jumps of 0.1, selecting the optimal coefficient. In both cases, we choose the optimal forecast according to the mean square error criterion, which must be minimized, expressing it as follows:

$$MSE = \frac{1}{m}\sum\nolimits_{t=1}^{m} \left(\widehat{D}_t - D_t\right)^2 \tag{4}$$

Where $\widehat{D}_t$ is the forecast of demand in period t, D_t is the real demand in period t and m is the number of available data.

Planning Agent. Planning Agent collects the forecasts made by the Forecasting Agents, and it is the responsible of deciding which one is the best, based on the Bullwhip Effect generated in the supply chain. Many authors quantify the Bullwhip Effect in supply chain as follows:

$$BW = \frac{\sigma_{df}^2}{\sigma_{dc}^2} \tag{5}$$

Where σ_{dc}^2 is the variance in consumer demand for the product, and σ_{df}^2 represents the variance in the rate of the factory production.

Likewise, the Bullwhip Effect generated at each step can be defined as the ratio of the variance in orders sent to the upper node of the supply chain, and the variance in orders received from the bottom node of the supply chain.

$$BW_i = \frac{\sigma_{out}^2}{\sigma_{in}^2} \qquad (6)$$

Where BW_i represents the Bullwhip Effect generated in the level i, σ_{out}^2 is the variance in orders sent to the upper node of the supply chain, y σ_{in}^2 represents the variance in the orders received from the lower node of the supply chain. This allows expressing the Bullwhip Effect along the chain as the product of the ratios that define the Bullwhip Effect at each level.

In these circumstances, the Planning Agent will select as the optimal forecasting method that which minimizes the effect generated in that level, seeking to reduce the effect generated in the chain, unless it is activated Negotiation Agent, in which case the selection of the optimal method is detailed later.

From there, the Planning Agent will be responsible for providing the Information Agent the necessary information on the node to complete the database. This information, for each period, includes:

- The forecast of demand $(\widehat{D}_t)$ according to the optimal method.
- The initial inventory situation (S_{It}), which is the sum of the final situation of the inventory in the previous period (S_{Ft-1}) and orders received at the beginning of the period, which, considering a unitary lead time, are assumed to have been made during the previous period (O_{t-1}).

$$S_{It} = S_{Ft-1} + O_{t-1} \qquad (7)$$

- The final situation of the inventory (S_{Ft}), which is the difference between the initial situation of the inventory (S_{It}) and the demand received in the current period (D_t), so that negative values show stock-out.

$$S_{Ft} = S_{It} - D_t \qquad (8)$$

- The deliveries to the lower level of the supply chain (Y_t), which coincides with the demand (D_t), unless it is impossible to satisfy it completely.

$$Y_t = \min\{D_t, S_{It}\} \qquad (9)$$

- The orders to be made to the upper level of the supply chain (O_{t-1}), which can be expressed as the difference between the forecast of the demand $(\widehat{D}_t)$ and the final situation of the inventory (S_{Ft}), or zero, if the above difference is negative.

$$O_t = \max\{\widehat{D}_{t+1} - S_{Ft}, 0\} \tag{10}$$

Negotiation Agent. Negotiation Agent will be activated by the user, when it is considered appropriate by the latter, from the interface of the developed tool. When it is active, it will allow the management of forecasting demand in the supply chain in a coordinated way through collaboration between Shop Retailer and Retailer, on the one hand, and Wholesaler and Factory, on the other.

Every Negotiation Agent will initiate a process of discussion with the Negotiation Agent to which it relates, through the Communication Agent. The collaborative framework is mainly based on the sharing of information between the agents with the goal of finding a balance between a forecast considered acceptable in local terms, and a forecast which is profitable to the whole system, since both terms can sometimes come into opposition.

Thus, the Negotiation Agent for each level interacts with the Planning Agent, seeking the optimal policy, which not only tries to minimize the Bullwhip Effect generated in the node, but it also seeks to minimize the global Bullwhip Effect generated in the supply chain.

3.3   Implementation of the Model

To implement the model, we have used NetLogo 5.0.1. Figure 4, by way of example, shows a screen shot of the interface of the implemented model in a particular instant of a simulation.

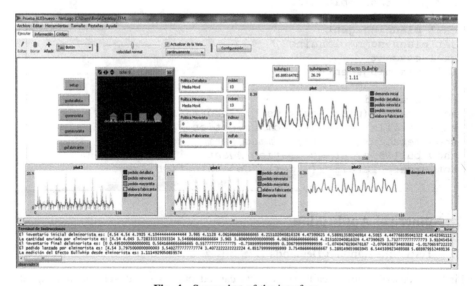

Fig. 4. Screenshot of the interface.

NetLogo is a programming environment created by Uri Wilensky (1999) and continuously developed by the Center for Connected Learning and Computer-Based Model, which allows the development of multiagent models for simulation and analysis of phenomena of a different type.

By way of example, we show below the pseoudecode of the agent "Retailer", which has identical structure as the other three. First, it is stored in the temporary variable "demand" the value of the variable "order", which contains the order issued by the previous level of the supply chain. This instruction acts as a part of Communication Agent. Later, acting as Information Agent, it is stored in the database as the demand of the level. From there, it calls the function "11agent", which makes the forecasting using the one-one method, and it performs the function "planningagent", which makes the planning around that demand and it stores in four variables (initial and final inventory, deliveries and order). Then, it repeats the same process with the other two forecast methods so that it has stored the three plannings. Then the "evaluation" function evaluates the three schedules around the minimization of the Bullwhip Effect, and it stores in the database the best planning for this level. Finally, the Communication Agent represents the demand received and transmitted by the level in the interface of the application, and also estimates the Bullwhip Effect generated, and it assigns the variable "order" the order of the level, so it is possible to use this data, as demand, in the next step of the supply chain.

```
retailer {
set demand=order ; Communication Agent
set retailer(demand)=demand ; Information Agent
call 11agent
call planningagent
set planning11=planning
call mmagent
call planningagent
set planningmm=planning
call esagent
call planningagent
set planningae=planning
call evaluation
set retailer(planning)=best ; Information Agent
show retailer(demand); Communication Agent
show retailer(order)  ; Communication Agent
show bullwhip; Communication Agent
set order= retailer(order); Communication Agent
}
```

4   Numerical Application

4.1   Tests with Random Demands

First, we describe numerically some tests carried out on the developed multiagent model, considering random demands, which follow certain statistical distributions. We have used samples with 30 and 90 temporary data.

Table 1 presents the results of the 24 tests, where the columns contain the following values: the number of the test; the statistical distribution which follows the demand, which can be normal N (μ, σ) (where μ refers to the mean demand and σ refers to its standard deviation) or Poisson P (μ) (where μ is the mean of demand); the size of the serie, the Bullwhip Effect generated if all levels of the supply use the one-one model (BW1); the Bullwhip Effect generated if all levels forecasts using a moving average of 3 periods (BW2) and the Bullwhip Effect generated by using the developed tool without activating the Agent Negotiation (BW3). In all cases, it is considered that the initial inventory at all levels of the supply chain coincides with the average of the corresponding statistical distribution.

Table 1. Results of tests with random demands.

Test	Demand	Number of data	BW1	BW2	BW3
A-1	N(100,10)	30	248,05	26,99	3,56
A-2	N(100,10)	30	331,17	18,57	2,91
A-3	N(100,10)	30	314,08	22,59	4,11
A-4	N(100,10)	90	230,48	25,38	4,67
A-5	N(100,10)	90	222,96	27,86	2,14
A-6	N(100,10)	90	209,87	15,99	3,08
A-7	N(100,1)	30	2305,30	22,13	9,17
A-8	N(100,1)	30	1705,08	22,00	5,14
A-9	N(100,1)	30	1866,49	25,79	8,30
A-10	N(100,1)	90	1994,37	25,77	3,67
A-11	N(100,1)	90	1734,57	22,66	2,87
A-12	N(100,1)	90	1750,67	26,88	9,16
A-13	P(100)	30	136,89	17,47	2,15
A-14	P(100)	30	308,45	24,61	5,98
A-15	P(100)	30	198,99	14,95	3,85
A-16	P(100)	90	215,37	26,65	6,38
A-17	P(100)	90	267,79	20,82	1,99
A-18	P(100)	90	261,21	23,11	2,07
A-19	Expo(100)	30	9078	6,70	1,59
A-20	Expo(100)	30	42,90	6,34	3,88
A-21	Expo(100)	30	81,15	7,22	2,40
A-22	Expo(100)	90	48,87	5,75	1,85
A-23	Expo(100)	90	62,36	6,34	1,51
A-24	Expo(100)	90	77,12	7,47	1,17

The results presented in Table 1 show, broadly speaking, the huge efficiency of the multiagent model developed in this paper versus one-one method. In all cases, the achieved results, in terms of Bullwhip Effect, improve the performance of the one-one model in several orders of magnitude.

In these circumstances, the shown results demonstrate the poor performance of the one-one model when the demand for a particular product can be estimated through a statistical distribution. In the case of normal distribution, the Bullwhip Effect generated along the supply chain considerably increases when the standard deviation of consumer demand decreases. In this case, the variance in orders along the supply chain will also decrease, but the variation will be smaller in relative terms.

So, with such a degree of randomness, the approximation of the demand in a certain period according to the demand in the previous period is a bad alternative. In fact, the model tends to select moving averages of a large number of periods. In the same vein, the model determines that the best solutions with exponential smoothing are offered by very low parameters, in order to minimize the effect of the latest demands in the forecast.

In the referred cases with high randomness, it is necessary to use other methods of forecasting, and a system based on intelligent agents is, in view of the data, a good way to coordinate them. The collected results show that using simple forecasting methods, such as moving averages or exponential smoothing, allows reaching great results in reducing the Bullwhip Effect.

By way of example, Figs. 6, 7 and 8 show variations of purchase orders made by the four levels of the supply chain in test A-1 in the three different cases, as well as consumer demand (Fig. 5), obtained from a normal distribution with mean 100 and standard deviation 10. It is clearly seen how the consumer demand, which is the same in both cases, is much more amplified in the case of one-one model that in the case of

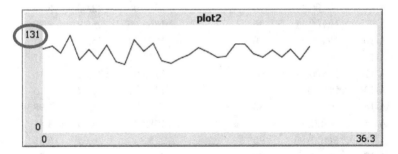

Fig. 5. Consumer demand in test A-1.

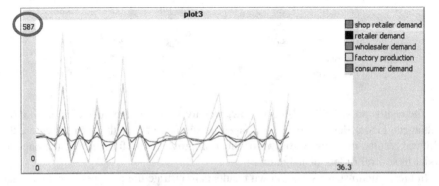

Fig. 6. Variation of orders along the supply chain in the test A-1 with One-One model.

Table 2. Optimal Policy for each level of the supply chain in test A-1.

Level	Optimal forecasting method
Shop Retailer	Exponential Smoothing with $\alpha = 0.1$
Retailer	Exponential Smoothing with $\alpha = 0.1$
Wholesaler	Moving Average with $N = 11$
Factory	Moving Average with $N = 17$

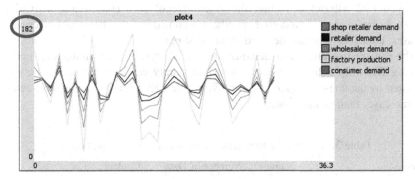

Fig. 7. Variation of orders along the supply chain in the test A-1 with Moving Average of 3 periods.

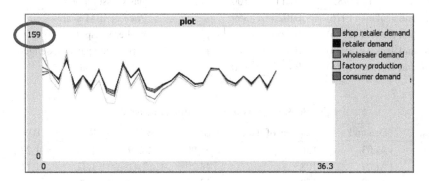

Fig. 8. Variation of oders along the supply chain in the test A-1 with the developed multiagent model.

multiagent system. Table 2 shows, in each case, the optimal policy for each level of the supply chain.

4.2 Tests with Real Demands

For further analysis, some tests with real data on the developed multiagent model will be shown. We have chosen eight time series obtained from databases commonly used for forecasting (Box and Jenkins 1970; Abraham and Ledolter 1983). Table 3 shows, for each one of the eight series, the series name; the database which contains the information; the content of the information; and the number of data which comprise the series.

Table 4 presents the results of applying the genetic algorithm on the eight series, where the columns contain the following values: the number of the test; the used series; the Bullwhip Effect generated if all levels of the supply use the one-one model (BW1); the size of the time serie, the Bullwhip Effect generated if all levels forecasts using a moving average of 3 periods (BW2) and the Bullwhip Effect generated by using the developed tool without activating the Agent Negotiation (BW3) and activating it (BW4). As in the case of random demands, it is considered that the initial inventory, in all cases, coincides with the demand of the first period.

The obtained results again demonstrate the effectiveness of multiagent model in reducing Bullwhip Effect generated along the supply chain. In all cases, the results generated by the one-one model are improved, although the difference is more relevant in some cases than in other ones.

Table 3. Data on the time series used to test the multiagent model.

Datbase	Name	Number of Data	Content
Abraham and L. (1983)	AL03	106	Electricity Consumption
Abraham and L. (1983)	AL04	108	Car sales
Abraham and L. (1983)	AL09	159	Mortgage – Loan Differences
Abraham and L. (1983)	AL11	106	Gas Consumption
Box and Jenkins (1976)	BJ02	369	Price of IBM shares
Box and Jenkins (1976)	BJ06	100	Wolfer sunspots
Box and Jenkins (1976)	BJ08	144	Airline company passengers
Box and Jenkins (1976)	BJ15	150	Warehouse sales

Table 4. Results of tests with real demands.

Test	Demand	Number of data	BW1	BW2	BW3	BW4
B-1	AL03	106	65,90	26,29	1,54	1,22
B-2	AL04	108	48,70	12,41	1,32	1,11
B-3	AL09	159	29,93	4,16	3,29	2,61
B-4	AL11	106	13,74	7,42	6,00	2,88
B-5	BJ02	369	4,20	1,21	1,12	1,05
B-6	BJ06	100	15,41	7,54	4,18	3,35
B-7	BJ08	144	12,28	3,31	1,25	1,18
B-8	BJ15	150	2,75	1,27	1,13	1,03

This situation evidences again that the use of simple forecasting methods, coordinated through a multiagent system allows a great improvement, in terms of Bullwhip Effect, comparing to the results of the one-one model. There is not clear proportionality between the result provided by the multiagent system and the result provided when all agents use the one-one model, which indicates again that the fitness of each forecasting method depends on the characteristics of the time series.

When analyzing the results, it is more appropriate to do it from a relative point of view that from an absolute one. When considering a larger number of data, and since the series in some cases have definite trends, the values of the Bullwhip Effect are significantly lower than in the cases analyzed with random demands.

AL03 time series is a clear example where the results of the multiagent system significantly improve the results of the one-one model. Without introducing Negociation Agent, the Bullwhip Effect is divided by 43 when using the model. Figures 10, 11 and 12 show variations of purchase orders made by the four levels of the supply chain in the different cases, related to the AL03 demand (Fig. 9). Comparing the vertical scale of both graphs, it is possible to see the huge difference. Table 5 shows, in each case, the optimal policy for each level of the supply chain.

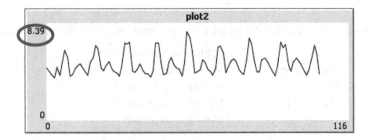

Fig. 9. Consumer demand in test B-1.

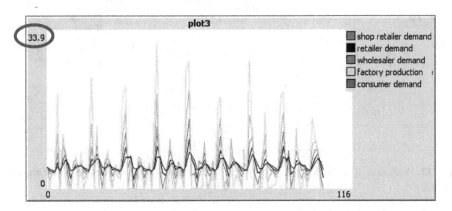

Fig. 10. Variation of orders along the supply chain in the test B-1 with One-One model.

A different situation is the one for the time series AL11 (Fig. 13). Multiagent model also allows a significant reduction in the Bullwhip Effect, as it is divided by 2.29, but not so large as in the previous case. Figures 14, 15 and 16 show the variations of purchase orders made by the four levels of the supply chain in the different situations. With these data, the multiagent system is not able to produce such a high improvement

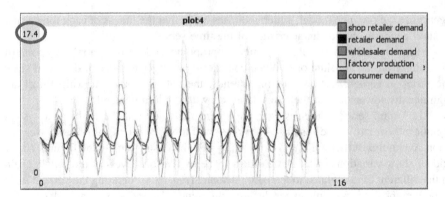

Fig. 11. Variation of orders along the supply chain in the test B-1 with Moving Average of 3 periods.

Table 5. Optimal Policy for each level of the supply chain for the AL09 series.

Level	Optimal forecasting method
Shop retailer	Moving average with $N = 2$
Retailer	Moving average with $N = 2$
Wholesaler	Moving average with $N = 14$
Factory	Moving average with $N = 14$

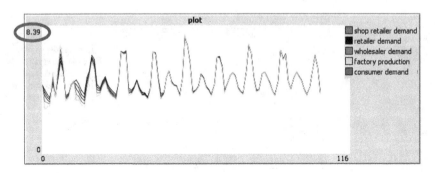

Fig. 12. Variation of oders along the supply chain in the test B-1 with the developed multiagent model.

over the one-one method, given the strongly stationary character in the series, with a high variance of orders. Table 6 shows, in each case, the optimal policy for each level of the supply chain.

The results obtained, and shown in Table 4, also show that close negotiation and collaboration in the supply chain between Factory and Wholesaler, on the one hand, and Shop Retailer and Retailer, on the other, is a very appropriate strategy for the reduction of the Bullwhip Effect. Collaboration significantly improves the performance

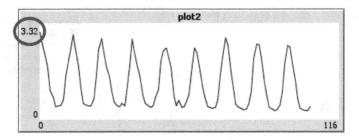

Fig. 13. Consumer demand in test B-4.

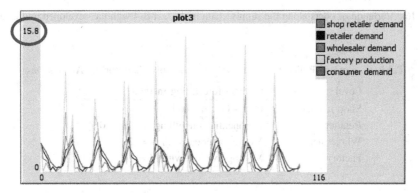

Fig. 14. Variation of orders along the supply chain in the test B-4 with One-One model.

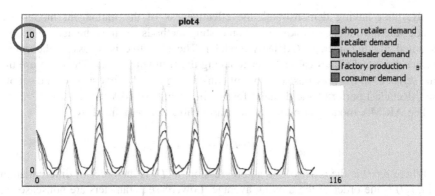

Fig. 15. Variation of orders along the supply chain in the test B-4 with Moving Average of 3 periods.

of multiagent model, achieving amazing results. Then, it is easy to justify the assumption of many authors, who advocate collaboration as one of the best solutions to the Bullwhip Effect generated in supply chains.

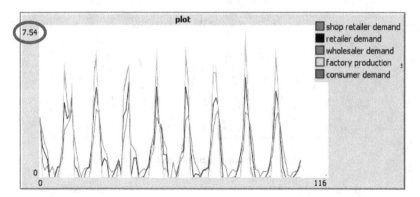

Fig. 16. Variation of oders along the supply chain in the test B-4 with the developed multiagent model.

Table 6. Optimal Policy for each level of the supply chain for the AL11 series.

Level	Optimal forecasting method
Shop retailer	One – One method
Retailer	Exponential smoothing with $\alpha = 0.9$
Wholesaler	Moving average with $N = 2$
Factory	Moving average with $N = 14$

4.3   Application of Advanced Forecasting Methods

Finally, after having demonstrated the effectiveness of the multiagent model, we consider the introduction of advanced forecasting methods, such as the autoregressive integrated moving average (ARIMA models). The objective is to assess the extent whether these techniques can help for reducing the Bullwhip Effect. Then, we use the same series as in the previous section, but considering that the first stage of the supply chain (Retailer) performs the demand forecasting using ARIMA techniques.

The ARIMA model, introducing the seasonality, can be defined by:

$$(p, d, q)(P, D, Q)_n$$

Where p (P) is the order of the autoregression, d (D) is the order of differentiation and q (Q) is the order of the moving average. Lowercase parameters are nonseasonal, while uppercase parameters are seasonal, where n is the order of seasonality.

To carry out the analysis, we used IBM SPSS Statistics 19, which contains the tool "Expert Modeler to time series". Table 7 contains the proposed model for each one of the eight time series.

Table 8 is an extension of Table 3 but adding a column with the results when considering the ARIMA models to forecast demand in the first level of the supply chain (BW5). Furthermore, we show the reduction achieved in each case.

Table 7. ARIMA models of the time series.

Database	Name	Number of data	ARIMA model
Abraham (1983)	AL03	106	$(0, 0, 1)(0, 1, 1)_{12}$
Abraham (1983)	AL04	108	$(2, 0, 0)(0, 1, 0)_{12}$
Abraham (1983)	AL09	159	$(1, 0, 0)$
Abraham (1983)	AL11	106	$(1, 0, 0)(0, 1, 1)_{12}$
Box and Jenkins (1976)	BJ02	369	$(0, 1, 0)$
Box and Jenkins (1976)	BJ06	100	$(0, 0, 2)(1, 0, 0)_{11}$
Box and Jenkins (1976)	BJ08	144	$(0, 1, 1)(0, 1, 1)_{12}$
Box and Jenkins (1976)	BJ15	150	$(1, 1, 1)$

Table 8. Results of the tests using ARIMA models.

Test	Name	Number of data	BW3	BW5	Reduction
C-1	AL03	106	1,54	1,52	1,30 %
C-2	AL04	108	1,32	1,28	3,03 %
C-3	AL09	159	3,29	2,54	22,80 %
C-4	AL11	106	6,00	3,89	35,17 %
C-5	BJ02	369	1,12	1,11	0,89 %
C-6	BJ06	100	4,18	3,45	17,46 %
C-7	BJ08	144	1,25	1,23	1,60 %
C-8	BJ15	150	1,13	1,12	0,88 %

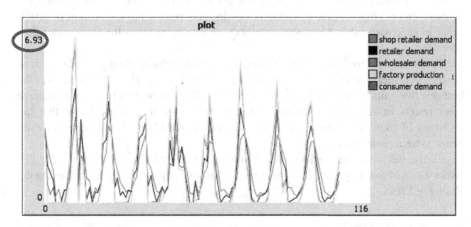

Fig. 17. Variation of oders along the supply chain in the test C-4 with the developed multiagent model using ARIMA techniques in the Shop Retailer level.

The results presented in this section show that the use of advanced forecasting methods leads to the reduction of Bullwhip Effect. Thus, the inclusion of ARIMA models at the lowest level of the supply chain provides very interesting results, and it can significantly reduce, in many cases, the Bullwhip Effect. In these circumstances, we

Table 9. Optimal Policy for each level of the supply chain for the AL11 series, using ARIMA techniques in the Shop Retailer level.

Level	Optimal forecasting method
Shop retailer	ARIMA model
Retailer	Exponential smoothing with $\alpha = 0.9$
Wholesaler	Moving average with $N = 2$
Factory	Moving average with $N = 14$

consider to incorporate them to the multiagent model, through a new agent within the Forecasting Agents.

Figure 17 depicts, by way of example, the results obtained for the serie BJ06. It is compared with Fig. 16. It is possible to see how the use of ARIMA models significantly reduces, above 35 %, the variability of orders along the supply chain. Table 9 shows, in each case, the optimal policy for each level of the supply chain.

5 Conclusions

The paper describes an application of multiagent methodology aimed at reducing the Bullwhip Effect in a supply chain. This is represented as a global multiagent system, itself composed of four subsystems multiagent. Each of them refers to one of the levels of the supply chain (Shop Retailer, Retailer, Wholesaler and Factory).

Tests performed on the raw data show that the one-one method greatly amplifies demand variability of end consumer throughout the supply chain, especially when the demands have a high degree of randomness. In this context, the application of multiagent model, with other forecasting methods, markedly reduces the Bullwhip Effect generated.

To develop the tool, we have considered only simple forecasting methods, such as moving averages and exponential smoothing, so that each level of the chain uses the best one that suits the demand it should deal with. With them, it is possible to achieve great results in reducing Bullwhip Effect. Even so, we have also shown that the inclusion of more advanced forecasting methods (ARIMA models) allows an even better system performance.

Lastly, we have analyzed the effect of negotiation and collaboration among different levels of the supply chain, verifying that it is an adequate solution in reducing the Bullwhip Effect.

References

Abraham, B., Ledolter, J.: Statistical Methods for Forecasting. Weley, New York (1983)

Box, G.E.P., Jenkins, G.M.: Time Series Analysis: Forecasting and Control. Holden Day, San Francisco (1976)

Chen, L.: Lee Hau, L.: Information Sharing and order variability control under a generalized demand model. Manage. Sci. **55**(5), 781–797 (2009)

De la Fuente, D., Lozano, J.: Application of distributed intelligence to reduce the bullwhip effect. Int. J. Prod. Res. **44**(8), 1815–1833 (2007)

Disney, S.M., Towill, D.R.: Transfer function analysis of forecasting induced bullwhip in supply chain. Int. J. Prod. Econ. **78**, 133–144 (2002)

Disney, S.M., Towill, D.R.: The effect of Vendor Managed Inventory (VMI) dynamics on the Bullwhip effect in supply chain. Int. J. Prod. Econ. **85**, 199–215 (2003a)

Disney, S.M., Towill, D.R.: On the Bullwhip and inventory variance produced by an ordering policy. Omega **31**, 157–167 (2003b)

Forrester, J.W.: Industrial dynamics. MIT Press Cambridge, MA (1961)

Fox, M.S., Chionglo, J.F., Barbuceanu, M.: The Integrated Supply Chain Management System. Internal Report, Univ. of Toronto (1993)

Holmstrom, J.: Product range management: a case study of supply chain operations in the European grocery industry. Supply Chain Manag. **2**(3), 107–115 (1997)

Ji, Y.F., Yang, H.L.: Bullwhip effect elimination in supply chain with CPFR. In: Proceedings of the 2005 International Conference on Management Science and Engineering, vol. 1–3, pp. 737–740 (2005)

Kimbrough, S.O., Wu, D.J., Zhong, F.: Computer the beer game: can artificial manage supply chains? Deci. Support Syst. **33**, 323–333 (2002)

Lee, H.L., Padmanabhan, V., Whang, S.: The bullwhip effect in supply chains. Sloan Manag. Rev. **38**(3), 93–102 (1997)

Liang, W.Y., Huang, C.C.: Agent-based demand forecast in multi-echelon supply chain. Decis. Support Syst. **42**(1), 390–407 (2006)

Machuca, J.A., Barajas, R.: The impact of electronic data interchange on reducing bullwhip effect and supply chain inventory costs. Trans. Res. Part E **40**, 209–228 (2004)

Moyaux, T., Chaib-draa, B., D'Amours, S.: An agent simulation model for the québec forest supply chain. In: Klusch, M., Ossowski, S., Kashyap, V., Unland, R. (eds.) CIA 2004. LNCS (LNAI), vol. 3191, pp. 226–241. Springer, Heidelberg (2004)

Saberi, S., Nookabadi, A.S., Hejazi, S.R.: Applying agent-based system and negotiation mechanism in improvement of inventory management and customer order fulfilment in multi echelon supply chain. Arab. J. Sci. Eng. **37**(3), 851–861 (2012)

Shen, W., Xue, D., Norrie, D.H.: An agent-based manufacturing enterprise infrastructure for distributed integrated intelligent manufacturing systems. In: Proceedings of the Practical Application of Intelligent Agents and Multi-Agent Systems PAAM'98, London, UK (1998)

Sterman, J.D.: Modelling managerial behaviour: Misperceptions of feedback in a dynamic decision making experiment. Manage. Sci. **35**(3), 321–339 (1989)

Wilensky, U.: NetLogo. Northwestern University, Evanston, IL: The Center for Connected Learning and Computer - Based Modeling (1999). http://ccl.northwestern.edu/netlogo/. Retrieved

Wu, S.N., Gan, W.H., Wei, F.M.: Analysis on the bullwhip effect based on ABMS. Procedia Eng. **15**, 4276–4281 (2011)

Zarandi, M.H., Pourakbar, M., Turksen, I.B.: A fuzzy agent-based model for reduction of bullwhip effect in supply chain systems. Expert Syst. Appl. **34**(3), 1680–1691 (2008)

Behavioural Investigations of Financial Trading Agents Using Exchange Portal (ExPo)

Steve Stotter, John Cartlidge$^{(\boxtimes)}$, and Dave Cliff

Department of Computer Science,
University of Bristol Merchant Venturers Building,
Woodland Road, Bristol BS8 1UB, UK
john@john-cartlidge.co.uk
http://www.cs.bris.ac.uk

Abstract. Some major financial markets are currently reporting that 50 % or more of all transactions are now executed by automated trading systems (ATS). To understand the impact of ATS proliferation on the global financial markets, academic studies often use standard reference strategies, such as "AA" and "ZIP", to model the behaviour of real trading systems. Disturbingly, we show that the reference algorithms presented in the literature are ambiguous, thus reducing the validity of strict comparative studies. As a remedy, we suggest disambiguated standard implementations of AA and ZIP. Using Exchange Portal (ExPo), an open-source financial exchange simulation platform designed for real-time behavioural economic experiments involving human traders and/or trader-agents, we study the effects of disambiguating AA and ZIP, before introducing a novel method of assignment-adaptation (ASAD). Experiments show that introducing ASAD agents into a market with shocks can produce counter-intuitive market dynamics.

Keywords: Software agents · Auctions · Agent-based computational economics · ACE · Agent-based modelling · ABM · Automated trading · Computational finance · ExPo · Exchange portal · Assignment adaptation

1 Introduction

In 2001, a team of researchers at IBM [9] reported on a series of experiments to test the efficiency of two adaptive trading-agent algorithms, MGD [16] and ZIP [8], when competing directly against human traders. Previous studies using homogeneous trader populations of all-humans or all-agents had indicated that, in both cases, trading interactions within the populations rapidly and robustly converged toward theoretically optimal, and stable, dynamic equilibria. IBM's results demonstrated for the first time that, in heterogeneous populations mixing human traders with trader-agents, both MGD and ZIP consistently out-performed the human traders, achieving greater efficiency by making more profitable transactions. The IBM authors concluded with a prescient statement, predicting:

© Springer-Verlag Berlin Heidelberg 2014
N.T. Nguyen (Ed.): TCCI XVII 2014, LNCS 8790, pp. 22–45, 2014.
DOI: 10.1007/978-3-662-44994-3_2

"in many real marketplaces, agents of sufficient quality will be developed such that most agents beat most humans". Hindsight shows that they were correct: in many of the world's major financial markets, transactions that used to take place between human traders are now being fulfilled electronically, at super-human speeds, by *automated trading* (AT) and *high frequency trading* (HFT) systems. AT and HFT systems are typically highly autonomous and dynamically adapt to changes in the market's prevailing conditions: for any reasonable definition of *software agent*, it is clear that AT/HFT systems can be considered as software agents, even though practitioners in the finance industry typically do not make much use of the phrase.

However, as the number of AT and HFT systems has increased, and as the billions of dollars worth of daily transaction volumes that they control has steadily risen, a worrying gap has emerged between theory and practice. Commercial deployments of AT/HFT continue to proliferate (some major financial markets are currently reporting that 50 % or more of transactions are now executed by automated agents), yet *theoretical* understanding of the impact of trading agent technologies on the system-level dynamics of financial markets is dangerously deficient. To address this problem, in 2010 the UK Government's Office for Science (UKGoS) launched a two year "Foresight" project entitled *"The Future of Computer Trading in Financial Markets"*.[1]

One report [12] commissioned by that project and published by UKGoS attempted a replication of IBM's study, but with two extensions: firstly, trading agents used the Adaptive Aggressive (AA) strategy [26], which had previously been shown to outperform both MGD and ZIP [11]; secondly, to increase the experimental "realism", order assignments to trade were continuously replenished, thus producing a continuous "drip-feed" market that more closely approximates the real world, rather than a discrete, periodic market as had been used in almost all prior experimental studies. Results showed that, under these experimental conditions, agents were *less* efficient than human traders, with slower markets hindering agent performance but enhancing human performance [12].

In this paper, we perform two sets of experiments. Firstly, we replicate the continuous replenishment experiments of [12] using ExPo: *The Exchange Portal*, an open-source platform designed to facilitate financial trading experiments between humans, agents, or both [13]. However, unlike [12], we study agent-only markets. Perhaps surprisingly, we believe that this is the first time agent-only markets have been studied using continuous replenishment of order assignments. For our trading agents, we use two well-known "reference" algorithms from the trading-agent literature, AA [26] and ZIP [8].

In our second set of experiments, we introduce "market shocks" to the system and explore a novel extension to the reference algorithms (assignment-adaptive, or ASAD, agents), designed to enable agents to take advantage of such shocks. We demonstrate that if all agents in the market are ASAD, then the market is more efficient in the presence of market shocks than if all agents are non-ASAD.

---

[1] The final report from that investigation was published in Oct. 2012, and is available at: http://bit.ly/UvGE4Q.

However, somewhat counter-intuitively, when the market is a heterogeneous mixture of ASAD and non-ASAD, non-ASAD agents outperform ASAD agents by adapting to the new price signals generated by ASAD agents.

This paper is organised as follows.[2] In Sect. 2 we review the literature on financial trading agent experiments and the agent algorithms, AA and ZIP. In Sect. 3 we introduce ExPo, our experimental platform, and describe our experimental design. In Sect. 4 we present the results from our two sets of experiments. Finally, conclusions are drawn in Sect. 5.

2   Background

2.1   The Continuous Double Auction

An auction is a mechanism whereby sellers and buyers come together and agree on a transaction price. Many auction mechanisms exist, each governed by a different set of rules. In this paper, we focus on the *Continuous Double Auction* (CDA), the most widely used auction mechanism and the one used to control all the world's major financial exchanges. The CDA enables buyers and sellers to freely and independently exchange quotes at any time. Transactions occur when a seller accepts a buyer's "bid", or when a buyer accepts a seller's "ask". Although it is possible for any seller to accept any buyer's bid, and *vice-versa*, it is in both of their interests to get the best deal possible at any point in time. Thus, transactions execute with a counter party that offers the most competitive quote.

Vernon Smith explored the dynamics of CDA markets in a series of Nobel Prize winning experiments using small groups of human participants [20]. Splitting participants evenly into a group of buyers and a group of sellers, Smith handed out a single card (an *assignment*) to each buyer and seller with a single *limit price* written on each, known only to that individual. The limit price on the card for buyers (sellers) represented the maximum (minimum) price they were willing to pay (accept) for a fictitious commodity. Participants were given strict instructions to not bid (ask) a price higher (lower) than that shown on their card, and were encouraged to bid lower (ask higher) than this price, regarding any difference between the price on the card and the price achieved in the market as profit.

Experiments were split into a number of "trading days", each typically lasting a few minutes. At any point during the trading day, a buyer or seller could raise their hand and announce a quote. When a seller and a buyer agreed on a quote, a transaction was made. At the end of each trading day, all stock (sellers assignment cards) and money (buyer assignment cards) was recalled, and then reallocated anew at the start of the next trading day. By controlling the limit prices allocated to participants, Smith was able to control the market's supply and demand schedules. Smith found that, typically after a couple of trading days, human traders achieved very close to 100 % allocative efficiency; a measure of

---

[2] For an earlier version of the work presented here, we refer the reader to [23].

the percentage of profit in relation to the maximum theoretical profit available (see Sect. 2.2). This was a significant result: few people had believed that a very small number of inexperienced, self-interested participants could effectively self-equilibrate.

2.2 Measuring Market Performance

An "ideal" market can be perfectly described by the aggregate quantity supplied by sellers and the aggregate quantity demanded by buyers at every price-point (i.e., the market's supply and demand schedules, Fig. 1). As prices increase, in general there is a tendency for supply to increase, with increased potential revenues from sales encouraging more sellers to enter the market; while, at the same time, there is a tendency for demand to decrease as buyers look to spend their money elsewhere. At some price-point, the quantity demanded will equal the quantity supplied. This is the theoretical market equilibrium. An idealised theoretical market (and many real ones) has a *market equilibrium* price and quantity (P_0, Q_0) determined by the intersection between the supply and demand schedules. The dynamics of competition in the market will tend to drive transactions toward this equilibrium point. For all prices above P_0, supply will exceed demand, forcing suppliers to reduce their prices to make a trade; whereas for all prices below P_0, demand exceeds supply, forcing buyers to increase their price to make a trade. Any quantity demanded or supplied below Q_0 is called

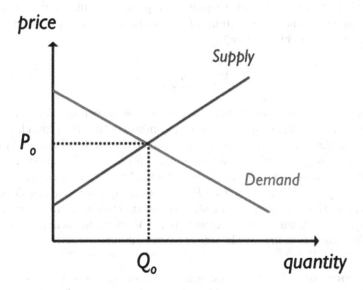

Fig. 1. Supply and Demand curves (here illustrated as straight lines) show the quantities supplied by sellers and demanded by buyers at every price-point. In general, as price increases, the quantity supplied increases and the quantity demanded falls. The point at which the two curves intersect is the theoretical equilibrium point; where Q_0 is the equilibrium quantity and P_0 is the equilibrium price.

"intra-marginal"; all quantity demanded or supplied in excess of Q_0, is called "extra-marginal". In an ideal market, all intra-marginal units and no extra-marginal units are expected to trade.

In the real world, markets are not ideal. They will always trade away from equilibrium at least some of the time. We can use metrics to calculate the "performance" of a market by how far from ideal equilibrium it trades, allowing us to compare between markets. In this report, we make use of the following metrics:

Smith's Alpha. Following Vernon Smith [20], we measure the equilibration (equilibrium-finding) behaviour of markets using the coefficient of convergence, α, defined as the root mean square difference between each of n transaction prices, p_i (for $i = 1 \ldots n$) over some period, and the P_0 value for that period, expressed as a percentage of the equilibrium price:

$$\alpha = \frac{100}{P_0} \sqrt{\frac{1}{n} \sum_{i=1}^{n} (p_i - P_0)^2}. \tag{1}$$

In essence, α captures the standard deviation of trade prices about the theoretical equilibrium. A low value of α is desirable, indicating trading close to P_0.

Allocative Efficiency. For each trader, i, the maximum theoretical profit available, π_i^*, is the difference between the price they are prepared to pay (their "limit price") and the theoretical market equilibrium price, P_0. Efficiency, E, is used to calculate the performance of a group of n traders as the mean ratio of realised profit, π_i, to theoretical profit, π_i^*:

$$E = \frac{1}{n} \sum_{i=1}^{n} \frac{\pi_i}{\pi_i^*}. \tag{2}$$

As profit values cannot go below zero (traders in these experiments are not allowed to enter into loss-making deals), a value of 1.0 indicates that the group has earned the maximum theoretical profit available, π_i^*, on all trades. A value below 1.0 indicates that some opportunities have been missed. Finally, a value above 1.0 means that additional profit has been made by taking advantage of a trading counterparty's willingness to trade away from P_0. So, for example, a group of sellers might record an allocative efficiency of 1.2 if their counterparties (a group of buyers) consistently enter into transactions at prices greater than P_0; in such a situation, the buyers' allocative efficiency would not be more than 0.8.

Profit Dispersion. Profit dispersion is a measure of the extent to which the profit/utility generated by a group of traders in the market differs from the profit that would be expected of them if all transactions took place at the equilibrium price, P_0. For a group of n traders, profit dispersion is calculated as the root mean square difference between the profits achieved, π_i, by each trader, i, and the maximum theoretical profit available, π_i^*:

$$\pi_{disp} = \sqrt{\frac{1}{n}\sum_{i=1}^{n}(\pi_i - \pi_i^*)^2}. \tag{3}$$

Low values of π_{disp} indicate that traders are extracting actual profits close to profits available when all trades take place at the equilibrium price P_0. In contrast, higher values of π_{disp} indicate that traders' profits differ from those expected at equilibrium. Since zero-sum effects between buyers and sellers do not mask profit dispersion, this statistic is attractive [17].

2.3 Algorithmic Traders

Zero-Intelligence Plus (ZIP) agents were developed by Dave Cliff [8] to overcome the provable shortcomings of Gode & Sunder's ZI-C agents [17]. ZIP agents are profit-driven traders that adapt using a simple learning mechanism: adjust profit margins based on the price of other bids and offers in the market, and decide whether to make a transaction or not. When a decision to raise or lower a ZIP trader's profit margin, $\mu_i(t)$, is taken, ZIP modifies the value using market data and an adaptation rule based on the Widrow-Hoff "delta rule" [28]:

$$\Delta_i(t) = \beta_i(\tau_i(t) - p_i(t)), \tag{4}$$

where β_i is the *learning rate*, p_i is the quote price and τ_i is the *target price* (based on the price of the last quote in the market). At time t, an update to the profit margin, μ_i, takes the form:

$$\mu_i(t+1) = \frac{p_i(t) + \Gamma_i(t+1)}{l_i - 1}, \tag{5}$$

and

$$\Gamma_i(t+1) = \gamma_i(t) + (1 - \gamma_i)\Delta_i(t), \tag{6}$$

where $\Gamma_i(t+1)$ is the amount of change on the transition from t to $t+1$, and γ_i is the *momentum* coefficient. Given the limit price, l_i, of the current assignment, ZIP then updates its profit margin, $\mu_i(t)$, based on these trading rules, where the final quote price, p_i, is given as:

$$p_i = l_i(1 + \mu(t)). \tag{7}$$

The ZIP strategy has become a popular benchmark for CDA experiments. In their IBM study, [9] concluded that ZIP was a dominant strategy, beating humans in experimental trials and matching the performance of their own modified GD [16] algorithmic trader. More recently, ZIP has again been shown to outperform humans [10,11]. However, it is no longer considered the dominant agent strategy (having been shown to be beaten by AA; see Sect. 2.3). ZIP has also been tested against humans in a continuous "drip-feed" market, where ZIP was shown to be *less* efficient than humans (a result that surprised the authors) [7,12]. However, we believe that De Luca's implementation of ZIP [18] that was used in those experiments may have played some part in this result.

The original implementation of ZIP [8] was designed to handle only one limit price, had no explicit notion of time and no persistent orders. So, when the IBM team used ZIP to conduct human vs. agent experiments, they adapted ZIP for their platform [9]. In order to handle persistent orders, a "sleep time" was introduced into ZIP, such that if no trade took place within a given time period, then the ZIP agent would automatically initiate a competitive price movement, i.e., a price movement towards the best value on the other side of the order book [ibid]. Perhaps more importantly, ZIP was further modified to have a vector of internal price variables, allowing profit to be made at different values for different assignments. These modifications were similar to an alternative implementation that had been independently proposed in a previous study [19]. Other versions of ZIP also appear in the literature. In [26], ZIP (and presumably, also AA) algorithms were forced to update only the *most profitable* bid (for buyers) or ask (for sellers) at any one time. This approach was replicated in De Luca's open-source implementation of ZIP and AA [18]. Finally, ZIP has also been adapted to enable arbitrage, by allowing an individual agent to both buy *and* sell. Initially introduced by [25], and recently adapted by [2], ZIP "arbitrageurs" contain two profit margins (buy and sell) and the price adjustment mechanism adjusts two prices each time the agent receives new market information. For this reason, ZIP arbitrageurs can be considered equivalent to two standard ZIP agents (one buyer and one seller) working as a team.

Here, we test to see whether a ZIP implementation with multiple profit margins, ZIP_M, is more efficient than a ZIP trader with a single profit margin, ZIP_S. As far as we are aware, this comparison has not been directly tested before. We use ZIP_S to describe the implementation in [26], where only the most profitable order is updated on every wakeup; and ZIP_M to denote an implementation of ZIP similar to that used in [9,19,24], such that ZIP_M is capable of updating all profit margins for all orders simultaneously. Every unique limit price received is given a new μ and γ (the values of μ and γ are decided at random when the agent is started) and all ZIP parameters are the same as those used in [8].

Adaptive-Aggressive (AA) agents were developed by Vytelingum [26] to explicitly model "aggressiveness"—trading the opportunity of extra profit for the certainty of transacting. Aggressive agents enter competitive bids (or asks) for a quick trade, while passive agents forgo the chance of a quick trade in order to hold out for greater profit. To control the level of aggressiveness, AA uses the Widrow-Hoff delta rule [28] that is also used in ZIP (Eq. 4). However, whereas ZIP uses learning to update profit margin, AA updates an aggression parameter based on previous market information. At time, t, AA estimates the competitive equilibrium price, p^*, based on a moving window of historic market transaction prices; p^* is then used in AA's long-term adaptation component, which updates θ, a property of the aggressiveness model. In this long-term adaptation component, an internal estimate of Smith's α (Eq. 1) is calculated, enabling the agent to detect and react to price volatility. AA was developed to perform well in dynamic markets. Short-term learning is used to react to the current state of the market, while long-term learning is used to react to market trends. AA has been shown to dominate other agent strategies in the literature [11, 26], however, unlike ZIP, which has been independently re-implemented by many different researchers, we believe the only replication of AA in the literature prior to this study is De Luca's OpEx implementation [18].

In Vytelingum's original AA implementation [26], it is unclear how an agent should quote when the market first opens and is empty. In De Luca's version [18], AA uses the maximum bid or ask price allowed in the market, $P_{max} = 400$, to determine an agent's initial quote price, $p_{t=0}$, such that $p_{t=0}$ is a random variable from a uniform distribution with range $[0.15P_{max}, 0.85P_{max}]$. In the absence of any "real" market data, the value $p_{t=0}$ acts as a proxy for the initial estimate of market equilibrium. But, since $p_{t=0}$ is artificially constrained by the arbitrary market value P_{max}, we believe that this method of generating $p_{t=0}$ is not domain independent and may present AA with an unfair "equilibrium finding" advantage when compared with other agent strategies, such as ZIP, which do not have access to this parameter. Moreover, for their first quote price, De Luca's OpEx agents [18] do not make use of the limit prices of their internal assignments (other than to maximally bound the quote at the bid limit and minimally bound at the ask limit). We believe this to be unrealistic. At the beginning of the market the only information agents have available for price discovery are their own personal assignments. Therefore, it is intuitive that agents should try to benefit from any information contained therein. For this reason, we introduce a modification to AA whereby agents set their own internal estimation of P_{max} such that P_{max} equals twice the maximum assignment limit price an agent holds.[3] Readers should note that agents could only submit a quote once they had received an assignment to trade.

In March 2012, an unexpected "max spread rule" in De Luca's AA code of OpEx version 1 was exposed [5]. This rule states that an agent should automatically execute against the best quote on the other side of the book if the relative spread (the difference between best quotes on either side of the book) is within a threshold, $maxSpread$ (and within limit price range).[4] Although this rule is not described in the definition of AA, we believe that it is a vestigial morph of a spread rule appearing in Risk-Based (RB) agents [27], a previous trader agent that Vytelingum eventually developed into AA [26]. The max spread rule encourages De Luca's AA agents to "jump the spread" for a quick transaction. However, in OpEx version 1, $maxSpread$ was hard-coded to a value of 15 %. Following [5], we believe that this value is unrealistically large and therefore casts a question of doubt on the validity of previous experimental results gathered using these agents.[5] In this

---

[3] We do not suggest that two is the optimum multiplier for this equation; rather we aim to investigate the effect of introducing this modification and select two as a simple heuristic estimate.

[4] For a lengthy discussion on the consequences of the max spread rule, see [5].

[5] Since this issue was raised by [5], the spread jumping rule has subsequently been classified as a bug and removed from De Luca's OpEx AA agents (http://sourceforge.net/p/open-exchange/tickets/1/).

paper, we explore the effect of the spread-jumping rule. Unless otherwise stated, we remove the $maxSpread$ condition (i.e., set $maxSpread = 0\%$ for our AA agents). All other AA parameters are set to those suggested by [26]. Following the literature, we also use the rule of updating only the *most profitable* bid (for buyers) or ask (for sellers) at any one time (similar to ZIP_S).

3   Methodology

3.1   ExPo: Exchange Portal Platform

Exchange Portal [13] is a real-time online financial trading exchange platform designed to run controlled scientific trading experiments between human traders and automated trader robots (see Fig. 2). ExPo was developed at the University of Bristol as both a teaching and research platform and has been open-sourced as a gift to the wider research community. ExPo can be run across a network (e.g., the internet), with human and/or automated trader agents messaging the exchange via HTTP. Alternatively, ExPo can be run on a single machine, with all clients running locally. For all experiments detailed in this paper, we run ExPo and the agent traders on the same physical machine. Prior to running experiments, ExPo was stress-tested through a rigorous series of agent-only experiments (see [22]).

Figures 3 and 4 show a typical set up for an auction using the admin GUI (Fig. 3) and an example of ExPo in operation (Fig. 4). The assignment sequences

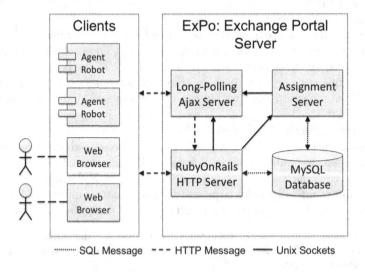

Fig. 2. ExPo architecture. The ExPo exchange is a Ruby on Rails web server application with RESTful architecture, using a MySQL database for storage. Clients (automated trader agents, or human traders using a web browser) connect and message the server using HTTP messaging. ExPo internal servers communicate via unix sockets.

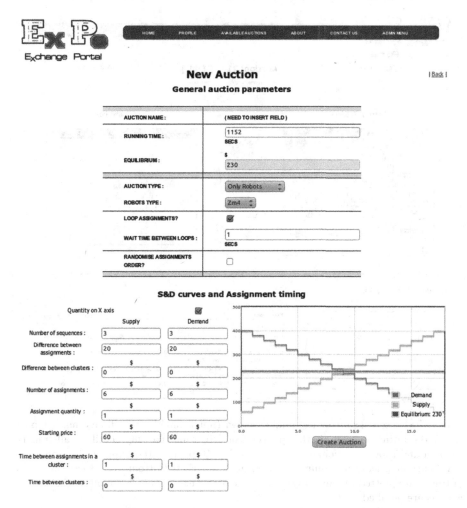

Fig. 3. Screenshot of ExPo's auction configuration GUI, used to initialise a financial trading experiment. Top: the auction parameters table is used to name a market experiment, define the market running time, set the market equilibrium price, link to the trader agent algorithm code, and select whether or not human users are able to participate. Bottom: the assignment sequences for participants are configured using the text boxes on the left, and illustrated dynamically by the graph on the right, with the blue line indicating aggregate market demand and the yellow line indicating aggregate market supply.

for participants are looped until the end of the auction. When competitors are added to an auction through the automation scripts, they are put on the same assignment sequences as already exist in the market. This is designed to avoid accidentally introducing an asymmetrical advantage for any one group.

Fig. 4. ExPo screenshot of the admin screen (not available to ordinary market participants) during an open market period. Top-left: table showing details of all traders (human and robot) participating in the market. Top-right: the public order book displays current prices and volumes quoted in the market. Bottom-left: execution prices of trades are plotted dynamically. Bottom-right: an exportable list of all market transactions are detailed.

3.2   Experiment Design

Market environments used in previous experiments typically follow the "trading day" model of Smith's original experiments (notable exceptions include [5–7, 12]). The problem with this is that it assumes traders only get new assignments at the start of each trading day—typically only one assignment each. Platforms like ExPo help to model markets in a more realistic way. By modelling a market as a continuous replenishment auction, we are able to model in *real time*, allowing assignments to drip feed into the market like they would if you were a sales trader on a financial trading desk, receiving assignments from clients throughout the day.

Each agent strategy in the market was grouped into 3 buyers and 3 sellers. The running time for each auction was 1152 s (64 assignment "loops" of 18 s each), similar to the 20 min length of time that was used in [12]. Assignments

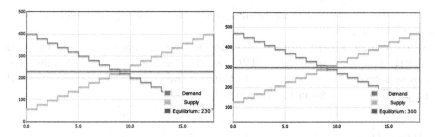

Fig. 5. Supply and demand assignment sequences used for experiments. Left: equilibrium price, $P_0 = 230$. Right: equilibrium price $P_0 = 300$. Each agent (3 buyers and 3 sellers) receives 6 assignments per assignment "loop", hence the total volume demanded and supplied per loop is 18 and $Q_0/loop = 9$. Assignments are allocated in pairs (to one seller and one buyer) every second, with each agent receiving a new assignment on average every 3 s. Assignment loops are repeated 64 times, producing a total experiment running time of 1152 s, and an equilibrium quantity $Q_0 = 64 \times 9 = 576$.

were sequentially allocated in pairs (to one buyer and one seller) every second, thus for each agent the mean time between assignments received was 3 s. Each assignment "loop" (see Fig. 5), agents each received 6 assignments with different limit prices. As assignments belonging to an agent are grouped by limit price, when an agent receives a new assignment the assignment quantity for that limit price was incremented. All agents treat current holdings of assignments as a single entity, increasing or decreasing their quote price as a group. However, one or multiple assignments may be traded from a group at any time if only a certain number are able to transact on the order book. No retraction of assignments was permitted, and once assignments were distributed, their limit prices could not be modified. For all experiments, equilibrium was set at 230 (Fig. 5, left), and raised to 300 (Fig. 5, right) when a "market shock" occurred. We do *not* use the NYSE spread-improvement rule, thus enabling traders to submit quotes at any price.

When a new assignment is provided to an agent, that agent has the ability to put it straight on the order book. Although agents can create new orders immediately, each agent can only update their orders once a sleep-time, s, has expired. While the agent is asleep (we can think of this as a "thinking" period), it is still actively able to calculate a new order price using shouts and transactions in the marketplace. Once sleep-time has elapsed, an agent is able to update their order price. The ability to put new assignments on the order book as soon as they are received is an important difference to previous implementations of sleep-time. An order placed immediately on the book is more advantageous than delaying a trade by waiting. The sleep-time of each agent was set randomly within a boundary of $\pm(0\text{-}25)\%$ of the sleep-time provided. This is the same "jitter" setting implemented in [9]. For all experiments reported here, we set sleep-time $s = 4$ s. While it is not strictly necessary to enforce a period of sleep time in agents (on the scale of human reaction times) when the market contains no humans, we do this to replicate the experimental method of [7,12]. This enables us to directly compare results, and hence challenge or confirm any of their conclusions.

All experiments were repeated 5 times and results analysed using the non-parametric Robust Rank-Order (RRO) statistical test [14,15]. The number of trials was necessarily restricted due to the real-time nature of experiments, with each run taking approximately 20 min.

4   Results

4.1   AA Modifications

Here, we present results from a series of experiments between the "reference" AA agents from the literature, and the modifications we suggested in Sect. 2.3.

The Effect of P_{max} on AA. In De Luca's implementation of AA [18], agents use the OpEx system parameter $P_{max} = 400$. For the majority of OpEx experiments, markets were engineered to have an equilibrium value of $P_0 = 200$, exactly *half* the value of P_{max}, e.g., [7,12]. We believe that the use of this system parameter by AA agents may produce artifactual dynamics and favourably bias AA agents (when compared with other agents, such as ZIP, that do *not* make use of this system parameter). Here, we test three implementations of AA to observe the effect P_{max} has on AA dynamics: AA_L, with *low* value $P_{max} = 500$; AA_H with *high* value $P_{max} = 2000$; and AA_D, with *dynamic* $P_{max} = 2 \times \max(limitPrice)$. The value used for AA_L was purposely set to be approximately twice equilibrium (set to $P_0 = 230$ in all experiments) to enable comparison with OpEx results. Note that, since limit price is exogenously assigned to agents via the supply and demand permit schedules, P_{max} will vary between AA_D agents. For example, if an agent, a, receives 2 sell assignments with limit prices 250 and 350, then $P_{max} = 700$ for that agent, a. For buy assignments, quote prices are implicitly bounded by zero.

Figure 6 displays mean Smith's α across 5 runs of homogeneous AA_L, AA_H and AA_D markets. We see that a lower value of P_{max} encourages better market equilibration by constraining the "exploration" of initial equilibrium values. This suggests that P_{max} introduces an artificial system bias. In heterogeneous markets (containing 3 AA_L and 3 AA_H on *each* side) AA_L agents gained greater efficiency in 4 of the 5 experiments. However, using Robust Rank Order (RRO) [15] this result was not statistically significant at the 10.3 % level.

Table 1 summarises the performance of homogeneous AA_L, AA_H and AA_D markets. We see that P_{max} has virtually no effect on efficiency, but has a large effect on Smith's α and profit dispersion. There is no significant difference between the efficiencies or α values of homogeneous AA_D and AA_H markets. We believe the reason AA_D did not outperform AA_H on these metrics is due to the assignment distribution pattern. In all experiments, assignments are distributed in descending order, such that buy assignments with the highest limit

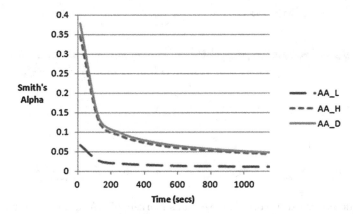

Fig. 6. Smith's α over time for each homogeneous AA market. AA$_L$ produces lower α than AA$_H$, demonstrating that lower values of P_{max} artificially encourage equilibration. AA$_D$ performs similarly to AA$_H$, but does not rely on the market dependent P_{max} value and hence is more robust.

Table 1. Performance of AA with varying values of P_{max}. While efficiency varies little between the three settings, AA$_L$ produces significantly lower Smith's α and profit dispersion, verifying that the spurious variable P_{max} affects market dynamics.

Strategy	Efficiency	Alpha	Profit dispersion
AA$_L$	0.999372	0.0114	97.3
AA$_H$	0.999365	0.0436	204.4
AA$_D$	0.999323	0.0469	253.4

prices are always allocated first. Therefore, initial values of P_{max} for AA$_D$ agents are higher than they would be otherwise.

Having shown that AA agents are sensitive to the system value P_{max}, we propose that AA agents should be modified to dynamically adapt their own *internal* value of P_{max}. For the remainder of this paper, unless stated otherwise, we use the dynamic AA$_D$ version of AA.

The Effect of *maxSpread* on AA. In OpEx version 1 [18], AA agents had a fixed parameter value $maxSpread = 15\%$. These agents were used in [7,12]. Here, we test the effect of this parameter by comparing homogeneous and heterogeneous markets containing two AA versions: AA$_D$ with no *maxSpread* condition; and AA$_D^{MS}$ with $maxSpread = 15\%$.

Figure 7 displays the time series of trade prices from one example run of a homogeneous AA$_D^{MS}$ market (left) and homogeneous AA$_D$ market (right). As we would expect, AA$_D^{MS}$ markets have greater price volatility and less equilibration to P_0, with AA$_D^{MS}$ happy to "jump" a spread of 15%. Conversely, AA$_D$ agents will post quotes closer to equilibrium and wait to be "hit". Table 2

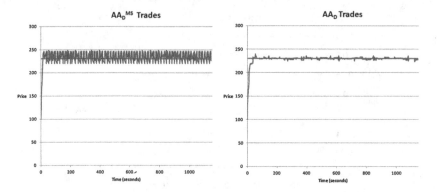

Fig. 7. Trade prices executed in homogeneous markets of AA agents with maxSpread rule (left) and no maxSpread rule (right). Left: AA_D^{MS} agents ($maxSpread = 15\%$) produce volatile trading dynamics, with execution prices rapidly fluctuating above and below equilibrium price $P_0 = 230$, within a region approximately bounded by $P_0 \pm 7.5\%$. Right: AA_D agents ($maxSpread = 0\%$) produce much more stable dynamics, with executions clustered closely around P_0. Since AA_D^{MS} agents are happy to accept prices away from equilibrium (within the maxSpread limit), maxSpread markets (left) are more *liquid* (produce more trade executions) than non-maxSpread markets (right).

Table 2. Mean results summary (5 runs) of *fast* homogeneous markets, allocating assignments every 3 s. ZIP_M performs significantly better than ZIP_S across all measures. AA_D outperforms AA_D^{MS}, and significantly dominates overall.

Agent	Trials	Efficiency	Smith's α	Profit disp.	Total shouts	Total trades
ZIP_S	5	0.974	0.0664	678.6	4245	582
ZIP_M	5	0.995	0.0529	308.6	7479	594
AA_D^{MS}	5	0.988	0.0658	530.5	4036	639
AA_D	5	0.999	0.0469	253.4	4104	577

summarises mean results (5 runs) across all homogeneous markets. Comparing AA_D^{MS} with AA_D, we see that the "spread jumping" behaviour of AA_D^{MS} results in lower efficiency, higher α (less equilibration) and greater profit dispersion. AA_D^{MS} markets also execute roughly 10% more trades than AA_D, producing the most *liquid* markets of all strategies tested. However, it should be noted that although AA_D^{MS} made more trades, they were not more profitable. In heterogeneous markets containing 2 agent types (with 3 agents of each type on each side), AA_D gained significantly higher efficiency than AA_D^{MS} (RRO, $p \leq 0.004$).

4.2 ZIP Modifications

Single vs. Multiple Profit Margins. We tested multi-profit margin, ZIP_M, and single-profit margin, ZIP_S, in a series of homogeneous markets. Table 2 summarises mean results (5 runs). ZIP_M is significantly more efficient than ZIP_S

in *fast* continuous replenishment markets, with 3 s between assignments (RRO, $p \leq 0.004$). However, this superiority diminishes as the market slows. With 6 s between assignments, ZIP_M still has significantly greater efficiency (RRO, $0.004 \leq p \leq 0.008$), but with 12 and 24 s between assignments, ZIP_M are no longer more efficient. This suggests that holding a vector of simultaneously adjustable profit margins is more effective in markets where a quick response is necessary.

Overall, AA_D is the dominant strategy of the four tested (see Table 2), with significantly higher allocative efficiency and significantly lower Smith's α than both ZIP_M and ZIP_S across all market speeds (RRO, $p < 0.048$). This confirms the dominance of AA over ZIP reported in the literature (for the full set of detailed results, see [22]).

4.3 Market Shocks

Thus far, we have assessed the performance of agents in *static* markets with a fixed theoretical equilibrium, P_0. Here, we test the performance of agents in *dynamic* markets that experience a market "shock", such that P_0 changes value mid-way though an experiment. For brevity, we only present results for shocks where the market equilibrium, P_0, increases. However, the reader should note that shocks where P_0 decreases are equally likely and lead to symmetrically similar results (see Fig. 8). As such, where buyers benefit from a shock in one direction, sellers will equally benefit from a shock in the other. When a market shock occurs, new assignments entering the market are perturbed by the same value as the shock. For example, if a market shock moves P_0 from 230 to 300, all new assignment allocations are given an increased limit price 70 units higher than they were before the shock. Real-world financial markets are inherently dynamic, experiencing continual supply and demand fluctuations. By exploring dynamic markets we aim to better understand the dynamics of agent traders in real-world markets.

When a market shock occurs, assignments that have already been allocated into the market are *not* recalled. Thus, the *actual* market equilibrium P_0' does not immediately move to the new theoretical market equilibrium P_0. Rather, P_0' asymptotically tends toward P_0, only reaching P_0 when all assignments allocated *before* the market shock have executed. We use this model of assignment *persistency* since we assume agents are acting as sales traders—assigned by a client to buy or sell on their behalf. Figure 8 illustrates example markets containing, from left to right, ZIP_S, ZIP_M and AA_D agents. In each case, we see transaction prices gradually tend toward the new equilibrium after a market shock. These results are different to those seen in discrete *trading day* experiments presented in the literature, where markets tend to re-equilibrate much quicker. However, we believe the setup we use here to be a more accurate model of real markets.

Table 3 summarises the mean profits of traders across 5 experiments with *positive* market shocks; i.e., shocks in which P_0 *increases*. Results for *negative* market shocks are symmetrically similar. For brevity, we do not present results for negative shocks, since all conclusions drawn are the same as those for positive

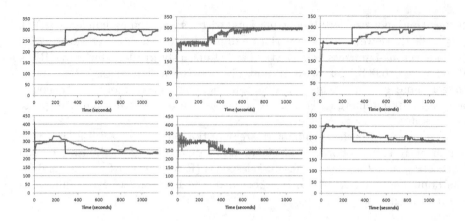

Fig. 8. Illustrative example of a market shock. Top row: a *positive* shock from $P_0^t = 230$ to $P_0^{t+1} = 300$. Bottom row: a *negative* shock from $P_0^t = 300$ to $P_0^{t+1} = 230$. Markets containing only ZIP$_M$ agents (centre) re-equilibrate after a market shock more quickly than ZIP$_S$ (left) and AA$_D$ (right). Market dynamics are symmetrically similar for positive (top) and negative (bottom) shocks.

Table 3. Mean profit in *positively* shocked homogeneous markets.

	Average profit per trade		
Strategy	Buyers	Sellers	% difference
ZIP$_S$	97.08	71.65	35.50 %
ZIP$_M$	90.62	72.50	24.99 %
AA$_D$	98.28	69.46	41.49 %

shocks. We see that, in all cases, positive shocks benefit buyers (similarly, negative shocks benefit sellers). This is because, for the period that P_0' is below P_0, buyers have the opportunity to trade at a "cheap" price. In Fig. 8, top row, the area between the new equilibrium line (in red) and the transaction time-series (in blue) is additional profit that buyers are making and that sellers miss out on (similarly, for negative shocks, bottom row, this is additional profit for sellers). We can quantify this by the percentage difference in the average profit per trade of buyers and sellers (Table 3). We see that ZIP$_M$ markets have significantly lower profit spread (RRO, $0.071 < p < 0.089$), indicating quicker re-equilibration after market shock. There is no significant difference in profit spread between ZIP$_S$ and AA$_D$ markets. We believe shocked homogeneous markets containing ZIP$_M$ agents are able to re-equilibrate more quickly due to ZIP$_M$ agents' ability to update multiple orders each time they "wake". Thus, if we ran further experiments using AA$_D$ agents with multiple profit margins, we would similarly expect a decrease in re-equilibration time.

However, while both AA and ZIP agents are able to re-equilibrate *after* market shocks, neither algorithm is specifically designed to *anticipate* price movements following a shock. In the following section, we explore the effects of adding such a novel mechanism.

4.4 Assignment-Adaptive Agents

If an agent is capable of analysing their own assignments to see if there is an inherent rise (or fall) in value, then it may be possible to infer that a market shock has occurred, thus enabling the agent to anticipate a rise (fall) in transaction prices. By adjusting profit margins accordingly, the agent may be able to secure greater profit. Here, we introduce a preliminary method for agents to adapt their profit margins using information contained in their own assignment orders. We call these agents *Assignment Adaptive* (ASAD). This is exploratory work and is not intended to be a definitive solution. Rather, we are more interested in the dynamics of markets that contain such agents. For all experiments, we use ZIP_M agents, previously shown to most quickly re-equilibrate after market shocks. Once again, we present results for positive market shocks only. However, results for negative shocks are symmetrically similar and the same conclusions can be drawn for shocks in both directions.

ASAD agents store assignment limit prices in a rolling memory window containing the last 20 prices, ordered oldest to youngest. Agents only begin acting on these prices once the window is filled (i.e., once an agent has received and stored 20 assignment prices). ASAD agents then calculate the gradient of change in assignment prices using Ordinary Least Squares (OLS) regression [21], such that gradient, ∇, is:

$$\nabla = \frac{\sum x_i y_i - \bar{y} \sum x_i}{\sum x_i^2 - \bar{x} \sum x_i},$$

(8)

where x_i is the index position of assignment limit price y_i in the assignment price window. Figure 9 provides a visual example of how this gradient calculation can help to detect a change in prices. This gradient value, ∇, is then transformed using a simple logarithm function, in order to return a value greater than 1 for positive gradients and a value less than 1 for negative gradients:

$$\phi = \begin{cases} -\ln(1 - \nabla) & \text{if } \nabla < 0 \\ \ln(\nabla + 1) & \text{otherwise.} \end{cases}$$

(9)

We call this value the *shock indicator*, ϕ. Values of $\phi > 1$ indicate prices in the market may increase; values of $\phi < -1$ indicate prices in the market may fall.

ASAD agents use ϕ to alter profit margin according to the following two rules:

```
if (seller & phi > 1) increase profit margin,
if (buyer & phi < -1) increase profit margin.
```

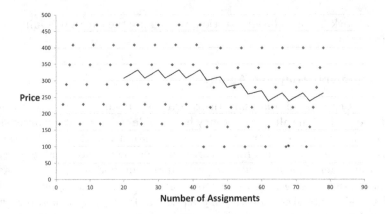

Fig. 9. Illustrative example of an agent's assignment sequence, subject to a *negative* market shock after assignment 42. Blue dots plot the limit price of each assignment. The black line plots a moving average over 20 assignments (the ASAD agent memory window). Ordinary Least Squares (OLS) regression is used to calculate the gradient of change in assignment prices (i.e., the gradient of the moving average), which between assignments 43 and 61 is significantly negative, indicating a negative market shock (Color figure online).

While $\phi > 1$ for sellers (or $\phi < -1$ for buyers), agent calculated quotes are increased, or *inflated*, by 20 %. To prevent ASAD agents from returning to market clearing price (P_0') too early after a shock is detected, the cumulative value of ϕ is used to "wind-down" ASAD price inflation from 20 % to 0 % over time. This decline in percentage over time is proportional to the size of the cumulative value of ϕ, reduced (increased) by 0.5 every time the ASAD agent can update its orders (subject to no current shock occurring), until cumulative ϕ, and therefore percentage, equals zero.

Results from one homogeneous market containing ASAD agents is shown in Fig. 10. We see that immediately following a positive market shock prices begin to rise. Prices then overshoot the new equilibrium value, before returning to near-equilibrium value. This suggests that ASAD agents are sensitive to market shocks, but require tuning. In homogeneous markets with all ASAD agents, sellers benefit from a positive market shock, being able to either match or beat buyers' average profit. This is in stark contrast to ZIP_M markets, where sellers consistently lose out by a margin of $\approx 25\%$. Further, very little profit is lost in the market itself, suggesting that assignment adaptation can equalise profit between buyers and sellers during a market shock.

However, when testing ASAD (adapted ZIP_M) agents in positive shock markets containing naïve ZIP_M agents, results were somewhat surprising:

- In heterogeneous markets containing six ASAD and six ZIP_M agents, ASAD sellers performed significantly worse than ZIP_M sellers. Surprisingly, ZIP_M sellers also outperformed all buyers.

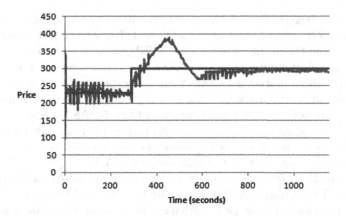

Fig. 10. Example of a *positive* market shock in a homogeneous ASAD market. The market quickly reacts to the shock, but initially overshoots the new equilibrium.

- In heterogeneous markets containing eleven ZIP_M agents and only one ASAD seller, once again the profits of every ZIP_M seller was increased, while the ASAD agent significantly under-performed.
- The profit spread between buyers and sellers of homogeneous markets containing twelve ZIP_M agents was significantly higher than in markets containing at least one ASAD agent; although in every case the ASAD agent(s) suffered.

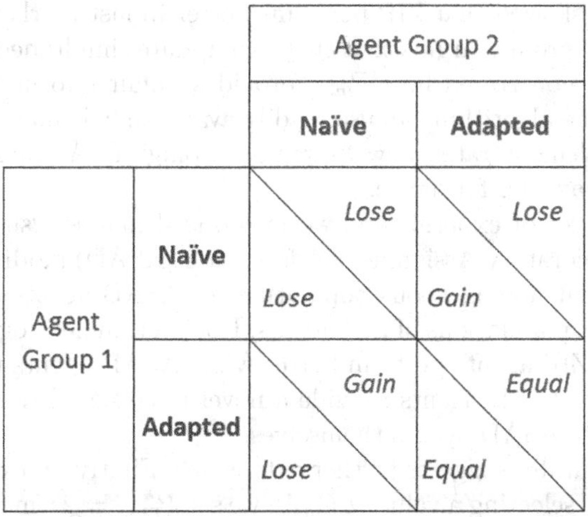

		Agent Group 2	
		Naïve	**Adapted**
Agent Group 1	**Naïve**	Lose / Lose	Lose / Gain
	Adapted	Gain / Lose	Equal / Equal

Fig. 11. Normal form matrix of results between competing ASAD (adapted) and non-ASAD (naïve) agents. Homogeneous markets of adapted (ASAD) agents perform better than homogeneous markets of naïve (ZIP_M) agents. However, in heterogeneous markets, naïve (ZIP_M) agents gain while adapted (ASAD) agents lose.

These findings suggest that ASAD agents generate a new price signal to which price sensitive ZIP_M agents can react and benefit. However, ASAD agents themselves suffer from the resulting behaviour of ZIP_M agents. If we consider longer-term market evolution, a population of ASAD agents can be easily invaded by ZIP_M. If the entire market is ASAD then everyone benefits, but if any non-ASAD agent enters the market, it parasitically benefits from the behaviour of ASAD and will flourish, eventually exterminating the ASAD agents from the marketplace. We summarise these outcomes in Fig. 11. Although these results may appear counter-intuitive, such dynamics are not unusual in co-adaptive systems of competing populations (for example, see [1,3,4]).

Potentially, these findings could be due to the simple ASAD strategy implemented here. For example, ASAD agents are not designed to consider the rate of change of prices in the market. Perhaps a more suitable approach would be to implement an adaptive learning rule, such as the Widrow-Hoff delta rule [28], which is the basis of the adaptation mechanism in ZIP [8] and AA [26]. We reserve this extension for future work.

5   Conclusion

We have used the Exchange Portal (ExPo) platform to perform a series of agent-based computational economics experiments between populations of financial trading agents, using continuous replenishment of order assignments.

In the first set of experiments, we exposed several idiosyncrasies and ambiguities in AA and ZIP, two of the standard "reference" algorithms from the literature. First, we showed that ZIP performs better in fast markets when agents contain a vector of profit margins that they can update simultaneously. Then, for AA agents, we demonstrated how P_{max} provides unfair information about the market and how the algorithm can use readily available information to overcome this. Finally, we demonstrated how "spread jumping" in AA negatively affects market dynamics and performance.

In the second set of experiments, we introduced market "shocks" and presented a novel exploratory Assignment Adaptation (ASAD) modification to ZIP. Results showed that homogeneous populations of ASAD agents perform better than homogeneous populations of ZIP agents. However, in heterogeneous ASAD-ZIP populations, ZIP agents perform better while ASAD agents perform worse. This suggests that ASAD agents provide a novel price signal that benefits ZIP, to the detriment of ASAD agents themselves.

This work naturally suggests further extensions. Firstly, to expose the benefits of dynamically selecting a value of P_{max}, we set $P_{max} = 2 \times \max(limitPrice)$. The multiplier value, 2, was arbitrarily selected and should be optimised for performance. Secondly, it is likely that the introduction of an adaptive learning algorithm (similar to that used by ZIP) could improve the performance of ASAD. Thirdly, unlike ZIP agents, AA agents have never been adapted to contain a vector of profit margins that they can update simultaneously (i.e., an AA_M). We reserve these avenues of research for further work.

Perhaps more interestingly, we also reserve more general open questions for future exploration. Firstly, in the work presented here all market shocks are exogenous. It would be very interesting to see how results are affected when shocks are endogenous to the market. However, to answer this, it is first necessary to have agents acting as "proprietary" ("prop") traders—buying and selling on their own behalf for profit—rather than "sales" traders (trading on behalf of a client). This is a more difficult challenge, but one that is pertinent if we are to further our understanding of the global financial markets. Secondly, since real financial markets include human traders and "robot" automated trading agent systems, we hope to explore the dynamic interactions between these groups by introducing human participants into our experiments. ExPo has been specifically designed to enable human participation; and further, since ExPo participants (whether human, or robot) connect to the exchange using HTTP messaging across a network, ExPo allows geographically dis-located human participants to sign in via a web browser and then leave or return at will. Theoretically, this enables us to run experiments with large numbers of participants, over long time periods of days, weeks, or even months. As far as we are aware, this has never been done before and has the potential to provide valuable insight into real world financial markets.

Acknowledgments. The authors would like to thank Tomas Grażys for significant development of the ExPo platform. John Cartlidge is supported by EPSRC grant, number EP/H042644/1; primary financial support for Dave Cliff's research comes from EPSRC grant, number EP/F001096/1.

References

1. Cartlidge, J., Ait-Boudaoud, D.: Autonomous virulence adaptation improves coevolutionary optimisation. IEEE Trans. Evol. Comput. **15**(2), 215–229 (2011)
2. Cartlidge, J.: Trading experiments using financial agents in a simulated cloud computing commodity market. In: Duval, B., van den Herik, J., Loiseau, S., Filipe, J. (eds.) 6th International Conference on Agents and Artificial Intelligent, Agents (ICAART-2014), vol. 2, pp. 311–317. SciTePress, March 2014
3. Cartlidge, J., Bullock, S.: Caring versus sharing: how to maintain engagement and diversity in coevolving populations. In: Banzhaf, W., Ziegler, J., Christaller, T., Dittrich, P., Kim, J.T. (eds.) ECAL 2003. LNCS (LNAI), vol. 2801, pp. 299–308. Springer, Heidelberg (2003)
4. Cartlidge, J., Bullock, S.: Unpicking tartan CIAO plots: understanding irregular coevolutionary cycling. Adapt. Behav. **12**(2), 69–92 (2004)
5. Cartlidge, J., Cliff, D.: Exploring the "robot phase transition" in experimental human-algorithmic markets. The Future of Computer Trading in Financial Markets-Foresight Driver Review-DR25, Crown Copyright, Oct 2012. http://bitly.com/SvqohP
6. Cartlidge, J., Cliff, D.: Evidencing the "robot phase transition" in experimental human-algorithmic markets. In: Filipe, J., Fred, A. (eds.) 5th International Conference on Agents and Artificial Intelligent, Agents (ICAART-2013), vol. 1, pp. 345–352. SciTePress, Feb 2013

7. Cartlidge, J., Szostek, C., De Luca, M., Cliff, D.: Too fast too furious: faster financial-market trading agents can give less efficient markets. In: Filipe, J., Fred, A. (eds.) 4th International Conference on Agents and Artificial Intelligent, Agents
   • (ICAART-2012), vol. 2, pp. 126–135. SciTePress, Feb 2012
8. Cliff, D.: Minimal-intelligence agents for bargaining behaviors in market-based environments. Technical report, HPL-97-91, Hewlett-Packard Labs, Aug 1997. http://bit.ly/18uC9vM
9. Das, R., Hanson, J., Kephart, J., Tesauro, G.: Agent-human interactions in the continuous double auction. In: Nebel, B. (ed.) 17th International Joint Conference on Artificial Intelligent (IJCAI-01), pp. 1169–1176. Morgan Kaufmann, Aug 2001
10. De Luca, M., Cliff, D.: Agent-human interactions in the continuous double auction, redux: using the OpEx lab-in-a-box to explore ZIP and GDX. In: Filipe, J., Fred, A. (eds.) 3rd International Conference on Agents and Artificial Intelligent (ICAART-2011), pp. 351–358. SciTePress, Jan 2011
11. De Luca, M., Cliff, D.: Human-agent auction interactions: adaptive-aggressive agents dominate. In: Walsh, T. (ed.) 22nd International Joint Conference on Artificial Intelligent (IJCAI-11), pp. 178–185. AAAI Press, Jul 2011
12. De Luca, M., Szostek, C., Cartlidge, J., Cliff, D.: Studies of interactions between human traders and algorithmic trading systems. The Future of Computer Trading in Financial Markets-Foresight Driver Review-DR13, Crown Copyright, Sep 2011. http://bitly.com/RoifIu
13. ExPo: The Exchange Portal, Mar 2012. http://sourceforge.net/projects/exchangeportal/
14. Feltovich, N.: Nonparametric tests of differences in medians: comparison of the wilcoxon-mann-whitney and robust rank-order tests. Exp. Econ. **6**, 273–297 (2003)
15. Feltovich, N.: Critical values for the robust rank-order test. Commun. Stat. Simul. Comput. **34**(3), 525–547 (2005)
16. Gjerstad, S., Dickhaut, J.: Price formation in double auctions. Games Econ. Behav. **22**(1), 1–29 (1998)
17. Gode, D., Sunder, S.: Allocative efficiency of markets with zero-intelligence traders: markets as a partial substitute for individual rationality. J. Polit. Econ. **101**(1), 119–137 (1993)
18. OpEx: Open Exchange software, Mar 2012. https://sourceforge.net/projects/open-exchange/
19. Preist, C., van Tol, M.: Adaptive agents in a persistent shout double auction. In: 1st International Conference on Information and Computation Economies, pp. 11–18. ACM Press (1998)
20. Smith, V.: An experimental study of comparative market behavior. J. Polit. Econ. **70**, 111–137 (1962)
21. Stock, J.H., Watson, M.M.: Introduction to Econometrics, Chap. 4, 3rd edn. Pearson, Upper Saddle River (2012)
22. Stotter, S.: Improving the strategies of algorithmic traders and investigating further realism in their market environment. Master's thesis, Department of Computer Science: University of Bristol, UK, July 2012
23. Stotter, S., Cartlidge, J., Cliff, D.: Exploring assignment-adaptive (ASAD) trading agents in financial market experiments. In: Filipe, J., Fred, A.L.N. (eds.) 5th International Conference on Agents and Artificial Intelligent, Agents (ICAART-2013), vol. 1, pp. 77–88. SciTePress, Feb 2013
24. Tesauro, G., Das, R.: High-performance bidding agents for the continuous double auction. In: ACM Conference on Electronic Commerce, pp. 206–209. ACM Press (2001)

25. van Montfort, G.P.R., Bruten, J., Rothkrantz, L.: Arbitrageurs in segmented markets. Technical report, HPL-97-120, Hewlett-Packard Labs, Oct 1997. http://www.hpl.hp.com/techreports/97/HPL-97-120.pdf

26. Vytelingum, P.: The structure and behaviour of the continuous double auction. Ph.D. thesis, School of Electronics and Computer Science, University of Southampton, UK (2006)

27. Vytelingum, P., Dash, R.K., David, E., Jennings, N.R.: A risk-based bidding strategy for continuous double auctions. In: López de Mánataras, R., Saitta, L. (eds.) 16th European Conference on Artificial Intelligence (ECAI-2004), pp. 79–83. IOS Press (2004)

28. Widrow, B., Hoff, Jr., M.E.: Adaptive switching circuits. In: Institute of Radio Engineers, Western Electron, Show and Convention (IRE WESCON), Convention Record, Part 4, pp. 96–104, Aug 1960

An Overview of the Interrelation Among Agent Systems, Learning Models and Formal Languages

Leonor Becerra-Bonache[1] and M. Dolores Jiménez-López[2]([✉])

[1] Laboratoire Hubert Curien, Université Jean Monnet,
Rue du Professeur Benoit Lauras 18, 42000 Saint Etienne, France
`leonor.becerra@univ-st-etienne.fr`
[2] Research Group on Mathematical Linguistics, Universitat Rovira i Virgili,
Av. Catalunya 35, 43002 Tarragona, Spain
`mariadolores.jimenez@urv.cat`

Abstract. Considering the important role of interdiciplinarity in current research, this article provides an overview of the interchange of methods among three different areas: *agent technologies*, *learning models* and *formal languages*. The ability to learn is one of the most fundamental attributes of the intelligent behaviour. Therefore, any progress in the theory and computer modelling of learning processes is of great significance to fields concerning with understanding intelligence, and this includes, of course, artificial intelligence and intelligent agent technology. Agent technologies can offer good solutions and alternative frameworks to classic models in the area of computing languages and this can benefit formal models of learning. Formal language theory –considered as the stem of theoretical computer science– provides mathematical tools for the description of linguistic phenomena. This theory is central to grammatical inference, a subfield of machine learning. The interest of the interrelation among these disciplines is based on the idea that the collaboration among researchers in these areas can clearly improve their respective fields. Our goal here is to present the state-of-the art of the relationship among these three areas and to emphasize the importance of this interdisciplinary research.

1 Introduction

Nowadays, although disciplines are highly specialized, research areas are getting more and more interdisciplinary. Researchers realize that in order to solve problems in their respective areas, it is necessary to cross traditional academic boundaries. There is a great need to connect and integrate disciplines, methods and technologies in order to improve our knowledge. Subjects must be attacked from various angles and across disciplines. Interdisciplinarity should be an essential trait of research and, of course, the three areas considered in this paper are not an exception. This is why in this article we focus not on single fields but on the common space delimited by those three areas: agent technologies, learning

© Springer-Verlag Berlin Heidelberg 2014
N.T. Nguyen (Ed.): TCCI XVII 2014, LNCS 8790, pp. 46–65, 2014.
DOI: 10.1007/978-3-662-44994-3_3

models, and formal language theory (see Fig. 1). The main goal here is to show how interdisciplinarity among people working in such disciplines can provide new models that may improve the current scientific results in artificial intelligence technologies.

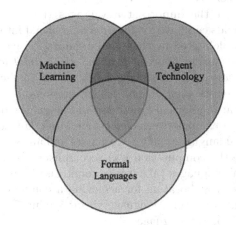

Fig. 1. Intersection among *machine learning, agent technology* and *formal language theory.*

Understanding human learning well enough to reproduce aspects of that learning capability in a computer system is a worthy scientific goal that have been considered by the research on *machine learning,* a field of artificial intelligence that aims to develop techniques that allow computers to learn. As Nilsson says, "a machine learns whenever it changes its structure, program or data (based on its inputs or in response to external information) in such a manner that its expected future performance improves" [35]. Machine learning techniques have been successfully applied to different domains, such as bio-informatics (e.g., gene finding), natural language processing (e.g., machine translation), speech and image recognition, robotics, etc.

Agent technology is one of the most important areas of research and development that have emerged in information technology in the 1990s. It can be defined as a *distributed artificial intelligence* approach to implement autonomous entities driven by beliefs, goals, capabilities, plans and agency properties. Roughly speaking, an agent is a computer system that is capable of flexible autonomous action in dynamic, unpredictable, multi-agent environments. The metaphor of autonomous problem solving entities cooperating and coordinating to achieve their objectives is a natural way of conceptualizing many problems. In fact, the multi-agent system literature spans a wide range of fields including robotics, mathematics, linguistics, psychology, and sociology, as well as computer science.

Formal languages originated from mathematics and linguistics as a theory that provides mathematical tools for the description of linguistic phenomena. The main goal of formal language theory is the syntactic finite specification of infinite languages. The theory was born in the middle of the 20th century as a tool for modelling and investigating the syntax of natural languages. However, very soon it developed as a new research field, separated from linguistics, with specific problems, techniques and results and, since then, it has had an important role in the field of computer science, in fact it is considered as the stem of theoretical computer science.

Taking into account the important advantages that collaboration among researchers of these fields can have for the area of artificial intelligence, we focus on the common space delimited by them and organize the paper as follows.

In Sect. 2 the relationship between *learning* and *formal languages* is taken into account. The theory of formal language is central to the field of machine learning, since there exists even an area called *grammatical inference* dealing with the process of learning formal grammars and languages from a set of data.

In Sect. 3, the relationship between *agents* and *formal languages* is considered. While in classic formal language theory, grammars and automata modelled computing devices where the computation was accomplished by one central agent, new models in formal languages take into account distributed computing. The idea of several devices collaborating for achieving a common goal was formalized in many subfields of formal language theory giving rise to the so-called *agent-based models* of formal languages.

In Sect. 4, we consider the relationship between *learning* and *agents*. The intersection of multi-agent systems and machine learning techniques have given rise to two different research areas [21]: (1) *learning in multi-agent systems* where machine learning solutions are applied to support agent technology and (2) *agent-based machine learning techniques* where agent technology is used in the field of machine learning with the interest on applying agent-based solutions to learning.

Finally, Sect. 5 concludes the paper by suggesting potential and promising directions of future research on the intersection among learning, agents and formal languages.

2   Learning and Formal Languages

The intersection between machine learning and formal languages constitutes a well-established research area known as *grammatical inference*. As A. Clark says, "grammatical inference is the study of machine learning of formal languages" [8]. This new area was born in the 1960s and since then has attracted the attention of researchers working on different fields, including machine learning, formal languages, computational linguistics, information theory, pattern recognition, and many others.

E.M. Gold [17] originated the study of grammatical inference and gave the initial theoretical foundations of this field. Motivated by the problem of children's language acquisition, E.M. Gold aimed "to construct a precise model for the intuitive notion able to speak a language in order to be able to investigate theoretically how it can be achieved artificially" [17]. After Gold's work, there has been developed a considerable amount of research to establish a grammatical inference theory, to find efficient methods for inferring formal grammars, and to apply these methods to practical domains, such as bioinformatics or natural language processing.

As H. Fernau and C. de la Higuera pointed out [16], there is a number of good reasons for formal language specialists to be interested in the field of grammatical inference, among others:

- Grammatical inference deals with formalisms describing formal languages, such us formal grammars, automata, etc.
- Grammatical inference uses formal language methodologies for constructing learning algorithms and for reasoning about them.
- Grammatical inference tries to give mathematical descriptions of the classes of languages that can be learned by a concrete learning algorithm.

Most of grammatical inference research has been focused on learning *regular* and *context-free* languages. Although these are the basic classes of the Chomsky hierarchy, it has been proved that even to learn these classes is already too hard under certain learning paradigms. Next, we review the main formal models proposed in this field and some of the main learnability results obtained.

2.1   Learning Paradigms

Broadly speaking, in a grammatical inference problem, we have a *teacher* that provides data to the learner (or learning algorithm), and a *learner* that must identify the underlying language from this data. Depending on the kind of data given to the learner, how this data is provided to it and the criteria used to say that a learner has successfully acquired the language, we can distinguish three main learning paradigms:

- Identification in the limit, proposed by Gold [17].
- Query learning, proposed by Angluin [1].
- Probably Approximately Correct learning (PAC), proposed by Valiant [48].

Imagine an adult and a child that is learning his native language. The adult uses his grammar, G, to construct sentences of his language, L. The child receives sentences and, after some time, he is able to use grammar G to construct sentences of L. From a mathematical point of view, the child is described by a learning algorithm, which takes a list of sentences as input and generates a language as output. Based on these ideas, Gold introduced a new formal model known as *identification in the limit* [17], with the ultimate goal of explaining the process of children's language acquisition. In this model, examples of the unknown language are presented to the learner, and the learner has to produce a hypothesis of this language. Its hypothesis is updated after receiving each example; if the new examples received are not consistent with the current hypothesis, it changes its hypothesis. However, at some point, always, the learner will found the correct hypothesis and will not change from it. Therefore, according to Gold's model, the learner identifies the target language in the *limit* if after a finite number of examples, the learner makes a correct hypothesis and does not change it from there on.

There are two traditional settings within Gold's model: (a) learning from text, where only examples of the target language are given to the learner (i.e., only *positive data*); (b) learning from informant, where examples that belong and do not belong to the target language are provided to the learner (i.e., *positive and negative* information).

It is desirable that learning can be achieved from only positive data, since in the most part of applications the available data is positive. However, one of Gold's main results is that *superfinite classes* of languages (i.e., classes of languages that contains all finite languages and at least one infinite language) *are not identifiable in the limit* from *positive data* [17]. This implies that even the class of regular languages is not identifiable in the limit from positive data. The intuitive idea is that, if the target language is a finite language contained in an infinite language, and the learner infers that the target language is the infinite language, it will not have any evidence to refute its hypothesis and it will never converge to the correct language. Due to these results, learning from only positive data is considered a hard task. However, learnability results have been obtained by studying subclasses of the languages to be learned, providing additional information to the learner, etc. For more details, see [14].

In Gold's model, the learner *passively* receives examples of the language. Angluin proposed a new learning model known as *query learning model* (or active learning), where the learner is allowed to *interact* with the teacher, by making questions about the strings of the language [1]. There are different kinds of queries, but the standard combination to be used are: (a) *membership queries*: the learner asks if a concrete string belongs to the target language and the teacher answers "yes" or "no"; (b) *equivalence queries*: the learner asks if its hypothesis is correct and the teacher answers "yes" if it is correct or otherwise gives a counterexample. According to Angluin's model, the learner has successfully learnt the target language if it returns the correct hypothesis after asking a finite number of queries.

The learnability of DFA (Deterministic Finite Automata) has been successfully studied in the context of query learning. One of the most important results in this framework was given by D. Angluin [1]. She proved that DFA can be identified in polynomial time using membership and equivalence queries. Later, there were developed more efficient versions of the same algorithm trying to increase the parallelism level, to reduce the number of EQs, etc. (see [3,18,41]). Moreover, some new type of queries have been proposed to learn DFA, such as corrections queries, that has led to some interesting results [5]. Angluin and Kharitonov [2] showed that the problem of identifying the class of context-free languages from membership and equivalence queries is computationally as hard as the cryptographic problems.

In order to obtain some positive learnability results for classes of languages more powerful than regular, researchers have used different techniques: to investigate subclasses of context-free languages, to give structural information to the learner, to reduce the problem to the learning of regular languages, etc. For more details, see [14].

In Gold's and Angluin's model, exact learning is required. However, this has always been considered a hard task to achieve. Based on these ideas, Valiant introduced the *PAC model*: a distribution-independent model of learning from random examples [48]. According to this model, there exist an unknown distribution over the examples, and the learner receives examples sampled under this distribution. The learner is required to learn under any distribution, but exact learning is not required (since one may be unlucky during the sampling process). A successful learning algorithm is one that with high probability finds a grammar whose error is small.

In the PAC learning model, the requirement that the learning algorithm must learn under any distribution is too hard and has led to very few positive results. Even for the case of DFA, most results are negative. For a review of some positive results in this model, see [14].

3   Agents and Formal Languages

Multi-agent systems offer strong models for representing complex and dynamic real-world environments. The formal apparatus of agent technology provides a powerful and useful set of structures and processes for designing and building complex applications. Multi-agent systems promote the interaction and cooperation of autonomous agents to deal with complex tasks. Taking into account that computing languages is a complex task, formal language theory [42] has taken advantage of the idea of formalizing architectures where a hard task is distributed among several task-specific agents that collaborate in the solution of the problem: in this case, the generation/recognition of language.

The first generation of formal grammars, based in rewriting, formalized classical computing models. The idea of several devices collaborating for achieving a common goal has given rise to a new generation of formal languages that form an agent-based subfield of the theory. *Colonies, grammar systems* and *eco-grammar systems* are examples of this new generation of formal languages. All these new types of formalisms have been proposed as grammatical models of agent systems. The main advantage of those agent-based models is that they increase the generative power of the system thanks to interaction, distribution and cooperation.

A third generation of formal language theory has started with the introduction of biological ideas in the field. In the last decades, natural computing has become the most extended framework where new models in formal language theory have been developed. DNA computing [39] is an example of those models. During the last years, systems biology and cellular biology have achieved an important development. These advances have provided new models for computer science. One of them is cellular computing, a model that emphasizes the concept of microbiological populations as well as the equilibrium of the devices and the relationships between the elements. P systems [38] can be considered an example of this emerging paradigm. On the other hand, natural computing has evolved from the first numeric models –like neural networks– to symbolic models –as cellular computing– which are closer to multi-agent systems. *Networks of evolutionary processors* (NEPs) [7] are inspired in both, bio cellular models and basic structures for parallel and distributed symbolic processing. The main reason for adopting such theoretical perspectives is the need to reach a more realistic human-designed computing, both understanding the processes the nature carries out and taking advantage of the natural mechanisms that science is discovering.

3.1   Colonies

Colonies as well-formalized language generating devices have been proposed in [24], and developed during the nineties in several directions in many papers [4, 12, 23, 25, 26, 30, 31, 37, 45, 46].

Colonies can be thought of as grammatical models of multi-agent systems motivated by Brooks' subsumption architectures [6]. They describe language classes in terms of behaviour of collections of very simple, purely reactive, situated agents with emergent behaviour.

A colony consists of a finite number of simple agents which generate finite languages and operate on a shared string of symbols –the *environment*– without any explicitly predefined strategy of cooperation. Each component has its own reactive behaviour which consists in: (1) sensing some aspects of the *context* and (2) performing elementary tasks on it in order to achieve some local changes.

Formally, a colony is defined as follows.

Definition 1. *A colony C is a 3-tuple: $C = (R, V, T)$, where $R = \{R_i | 1 \leq i \leq n\}$ is a finite set of regular grammars $R_i = (N_i, T_i, P_i, S_i)$ producing finite languages $L(R_i) = F_i$ for each i. R_i will be referred to as a component of C; $V = \bigcup_{i=1}^{n}(T_i \cup N_i)$ is the alphabet of the colony; $T \subseteq V$ is the terminal alphabet of the colony.*

Components $R_i \in R$ ($1 \leq i \leq n$) of a colony C are regular grammars generating finite languages and operating on a shared string of symbols –the *environment*– without any explicitly predefined strategy of cooperation of the components.

An *environment* of a colony is formed by strings of symbols from V. Strings are modified only by sequential activities of components of a colony. Because of the lack of any predefined strategy of cooperation between components, each component may participate in the rewriting of the current string whenever its start symbol is present in the current string. Conflicts are solved non-deterministically, as it is usual in classical theory of formal grammars. The activity of components in a colony is performed by string transformation on a common tape. Elementary changes of strings are determined by a basic derivation step:

Definition 2. *For $x, y \in V^*$ we define $x \Longrightarrow y$ iff $x = x_1 S_i x_2$, $y = x_1 z x_2$, where $z \in F_i$ for some $i, 1 \leq i \leq n$.*

The behaviour of a colony is defined as the set of all strings which can be generated by the colony from a given starting string. A terminal symbol of one component can occur as a non-terminal symbol of another one, so that the possibility of cooperation of components of the colony allows to generate substantially more than finite languages. The global behaviour of the whole colony emerges from the strictly individual behaviours of components.

Definition 3. *The language determined by a colony C starting with the word $w_0 \in V^*$ is given by: $L(C, w_0) = \{v | w_0 \Longrightarrow^* v, v \in T^*\}$.*

A colony is outlined in Fig. 2.

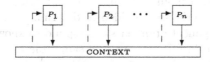

Fig. 2. A colony.

Colonies offer a formal framework for the emergence of complex behaviours by using purely reactive simple components. The main advantage of colonies is their generative power, the class of languages describable by colonies that make use of strictly regular components is beyond the set describable in terms of individual regular grammars.

3.2 Grammar Systems

Grammar system theory is a consolidated and active branch in the field of formal languages that provides syntactic models for describing multi-agent systems at the symbolic level, using tools from formal grammars and languages. The attempt of the 'parents' of the theory was "to demonstrate a particular possibility of studying complex systems in a purely syntactic level" [10] or, what is the same, to propose a grammatical framework for multi-agent systems.

A grammar system is a set of grammars working together, according to a specified protocol, to generate a language. Note that while in classical formal language theory *one* grammar (or automaton) works individually to generate (or recognize) *one* language, here we have *several* grammars working together in order to produce *one* language.

The theory was launched in 1988 [9], when Cooperating Distributed Grammar Systems (CDGS) were proposed as a syntactic model of the blackboard architecture of problem solving. A CDGS consists of a finite set of generative grammars with a common sentential form (axiom) that cooperate in the derivation of a common language. Component grammars generate the string in turns (thus, sequentially), under some cooperation protocol. At each moment in time, one grammar (and just one) is active, this is, rewrites the common string, while the rest of grammars of the CDGS are inactive. Conditions under which a component can start/stop its activity on common sentential form are specified in the cooperation protocol. Terminal strings generated in this way form the language of the system.

An analogy can be drawn between CDGS and the blackboard model of problem solving described in [34] as consisting of three major components: (1) *Knowledge sources*. The knowledge needed to solve the problem is partitioned into knowledge sources, which are kept separate and independent; (2) *Blackboard data structure*. Problem solving state data are kept in a global database, the *blackboard*. Knowledge sources produce changes in the blackboard that lead incrementally to a solution to the problem. Communication and interaction among knowledge sources take place solely through the blackboard; (3) *Control*. Knowledge sources respond opportunistically to changes in the blackboard. There is a set of control modules that monitor changes in the blackboard and decide what actions to take next. Criteria are provided to determine when to terminate the process. In CDGS, component grammars correspond to knowledge sources. The common sentential form in CDGS plays the same role as the blackboard data structure. And finally, the protocol of cooperation in CDGS encodes control on the work of knowledge sources. The rewriting of a non-terminal symbol can be interpreted as a developmental step on the information contained in the current state of the blackboard. And, finally, a solution to the problem corresponds to a terminal word.

One year later, in 1989, Parallel Communicating Grammar Systems (PCGS) were introduced as a grammatical model of parallelism [40]. A PCGS consists of several grammars with their respective sentential forms. In each time unit, each component uses a rule, which rewrites the associated sentential form. Cooperation among agents takes place thanks to the so-called *query symbols* that allow communication among components.

If CDGS were considered a grammatical model of the blackboard system in problem solving, PCGS can be thought of as a formal representation of the *classroom model*. Let us take the blackboard model and make the following modifications: (1) Allow each knowledge source to have its own 'notebook' containing the description of a particular subproblem of a given problem; (2) Allow each knowledge source to operate only on its own 'notebook' and let exist one distinguished agent which operates on the 'blackboard' and has the description of the problem; (3) and finally, allow agents to communicate by request the content of their own 'notebook'. These modifications on the blackboard model lead to the 'classroom model' of problem solving where the classroom leader (the master) works on the blackboard while pupils have particular problems to solve in their notebooks. Master and pupils can communicate and the global problem is solved through such cooperation on the blackboard. An easy analogy can be established between PCGS and the classroom model: pupils correspond to grammars which make up the system, and their notebooks correspond to the sentential forms. The set of rules of grammars encodes the knowledge of pupils. The distinguished agent corresponds to the 'master'. Rewriting a nonterminal symbol is interpreted as a developmental step of the information contained in the notebooks. A partial solution, obtained by a pupil corresponds to a terminal word generated in one grammar, while solution of the problem is associated to a word in the language generated by the 'master.'

The sequential CDGS and the parallel PCGS are the two main types of grammar systems. However, since 1988, the theory has developed into several directions, motivated by several scientific areas. Besides distributed and decentralized artificial intelligence, artificial life, molecular computing, robotics, natural language processing, ecology, sociology, etc. have suggested some modifications of the basic models, and have given rise to the appearance of different variants and subfields of the theory. For more information on those new types see [10,13].

3.3   Eco-Grammar Systems

Eco-grammar systems have been introduced in [11] and provide a syntactical framework for eco-systems, this is, for communities of evolving agents and their interrelated environment. An eco-grammar system is defined as a multi-agent system where different components, apart from interacting among themselves, interact with a special component called 'environment'. Within an eco-grammar system we can distinguish two types of components *environment* and *agents*. Both are represented at any moment by a string of symbols that identifies the current state of the component. These strings change according to sets of evolution rules. Interaction among agents and environment is carried out through agents' actions performed on the environmental state by the application of some productions from the set of action rules of agents.

An eco-grammar system can be thought of as a generalization of CDGS and PCGS. If we superpose a CDGS and a PCGS, we obtain a system consisting of grammars that contain individual strings (like in PCGS) and a common string (like in CDGS). If we call this common string *environment* and we mix the functioning of CDGS and PCGS, letting each component to work on its own string and on the environmental string, something similar to an ecosystem is obtained. If we add one more grammar, expressing evolution rules of the environment, and we make evolution of agents depend on the environmental state, the thing we obtain is an eco-grammar system.

The concept of eco-grammar system is based on six postulates formulated according to properties of artificial life [27]:

1. An ecosystem consists of an *environment* and a *set of agents*.
2. In an ecosystem there is a *universal clock* which marks time units, the same for all the agents and for the environment, according to which agents and environment evolution is considered.
3. Both *environment* and agents have characteristic *evolution rules* which are in fact L systems [22,28], hence are applied in a parallel manner to all the symbols describing agents and environment; such a (rewriting) step is done in each time unit.
4. *Evolution rules of environment* are *independent* of agents and on the state of the environment itself. Evolution rules of agents *depend on* the state of the environment.

5. Agents act on the environment according to *action rules*, which are pure rewriting rules used sequentially. In each time unit, each agent uses one action rule which is chosen from a set depending on the current state of the agent.
6. *Action has priority over evolution* of the environment. At a given time unit exactly the symbols which are not affected by action are rewritten by evolution rules.

Main features of eco-grammar systems are captured in Fig. 3.

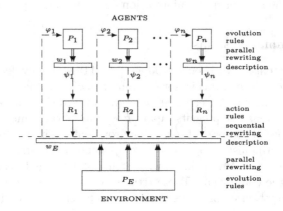

Fig. 3. An eco-grammar system.

Definition 4. *An Eco-Grammar System (EG-system) is an $n + 1$-tuple: $\Sigma = (E, A_1, \ldots, A_n)$, where:*

- *$E = (V_E, P_E)$, V_E is a finite alphabet; P_E is a finite set of $0L$ rules over V_E.*
- *$A_i = (V_i, P_i, R_i, \varphi_i, \psi_i)$ for i, $1 \leq i \leq n$, where: V_i is a finite alphabet; P_i is a finite set of $0L$ rules over V_i; R_i is a finite set of rewriting rules of the form $x \rightarrow y$ with $x \in V_E^+$, $y \in V_E^*$;*
- *$\varphi_i : V_E^* \longrightarrow 2^{P_i}$;*
- *$\psi_i : V_i^+ \longrightarrow 2^{R_i}$.*

Definition 5. *A state of an Eco-Grammar System $\Sigma = (E, A_1, \ldots, A_n)$ is an $(n+1)$-tuple: $\sigma = (w_E, w_1, w_2, \ldots, w_n)$, where $w_E \in V_E^*$ and $w_i \in V_i^*$, $1 \leq i \leq n$; w_E is the state of the environment, and w_i is the state of i-th agent, $1 \leq i \leq n$.*

Definition 6. *Let $\sigma = (w_E, w_1, w_2, \ldots, w_n)$ be a state of EG-system $\Sigma = (E, A_1, \ldots, A_n)$. Agent A_i is said to be active in state σ if the set of its current action rules, this is $\psi_i(w_i)$, is nonempty. By an action of an active agent A_i in state σ we mean an application of an action rule r, $r \in \psi_i(w_i)$, to the environmental state w_E. A simultaneous action of agents $A_{i_1}, \ldots, A_{i_r}$, $\{i_1, \ldots, i_r\} \in \{1, \ldots, n\}$ being active in state σ, onto the environment is a parallel derivation step $w_E \implies w'_E$ such that $w_E = x_1 u_1 x_2 u_2 \ldots u_r x_{r+1}$, and $w'_E = x_1 v_1 x_2 v_2 \ldots v_r x_{r+1}$, where $u_j \rightarrow v_j \in \psi_{i_j}(w_{i_j})$, $1 \leq j \leq r$, and $x_i \in V_E^*$, $1 \leq i \leq r+1$.*

Definition 7. *Let $\sigma = (w_E, w_1, w_2, \ldots, w_n)$ be a state of EG-system $\Sigma = (E, A_1, \ldots, A_n)$. We say that w_i' is a current evolution of agent A_i in state w_i, if w_i' can be derived from w_i by productions of $\varphi_i(w_E)$, in 0L-manner, $1 \leq i \leq n$. For two states w_E and w_E' of the environment we say that w_E' is an evolution of w_E if w_E' can be derived from w_E by productions of P_E in 0L-manner. A change of a state of an Eco-Grammar System means an evolution of the state of every agent and an evolution of the environment at each place except some distinguished ones where currently active agents perform simultaneously an action.*

Definition 8. *Let $\sigma = (w_E, w_1, w_2, \ldots, w_n)$ and $\sigma' = (w_E', w_1', w_2', \ldots, w_n')$ be two states of EG-system $\Sigma = (E, A_1, \ldots, A_n)$. We say that σ changes into σ', written as: $\sigma \Longrightarrow_\Sigma \sigma'$, iff the following conditions hold: (i) w_E' arises from w_E by an evolution affected by all the active agents in state σ: $w_E = z_1 x_1 z_2 x_2 \ldots z_m x_m z_{m+1}$ and $w_E' = z_1' y_1 z_2' y_2 \ldots z_m' y_m z_{m+1}'$ such that: $z_1 x_1 z_2 x_2 \ldots x_m z_{m+1} \Longrightarrow z_1 y_1 z_2 y_2 \ldots y_m z_{m+1}$ is a simultaneous action of all the agents $A_{i_1}, \ldots, A_{i_m}$, $\{i_1, \ldots, i_m\} \subseteq \{1, \ldots, n\}$, that are active in state σ and, $z_1' z_2' \ldots z_{m+1}'$ is an evolution of $z_1 z_2; \ldots z_{m+1}$; (ii) w_i' is an evolution of A_i in state w_i, $1 \leq i \leq n$.*

3.4 NEPs-Networks of Evolutionary Processors

Networks of Evolutionary Processors (NEPs) are new computing mechanisms directly inspired in the behaviour of cell populations. NEPs, introduced in [7,29], can be defined as systems consisting of several devices whose communication is regulated by an underlying graph. Such devices, which are an abstract formalization of cells, are described by a set of words (DNA) evolving by mutations, according to some predefined rules. Their outcome travels to the other nodes if they accept it after passing a filtering process. At the end of the process, only the cells with correct strings will survive.

The cellular basis of NEPs relate them with P systems, especially with tissue P systems [32,33]. In tissue P systems, cells form a multitude of different associations performing various functions. NEPs could be linked to systems biology as well, because the model aims to develop a holistic theory where the behaviour of each agent can influence the environment and the other agents. From the computational point of view, NEPs are related to the Connection Machine [19] and the Logic Flow paradigm [15]. Another important theoretical relationship of NEPs is the theory of grammar and eco-grammar systems [10,11] which share with NEPs the idea of several devices working together and exchanging results.

With all this background and theoretical connections, it is easy to understand how NEPs can be described as agential bio-inspired context-sensitive systems. Many disciplines are needed of these types of models that are able to support a biological framework in a collaborative environment. The conjunction of these features allows applying the system to a number of areas, beyond generation and recognition in formal language theory.

Definition 9. *A Network of Evolutionary Processors of size n is a construct:* $\Gamma = (V, N_1, N_2, \ldots, N_n, G)$, *where:*

– V is an alphabet and for each $1 \leq i \leq n$,
– $N_i = (M_i, A_i, PI_i, PO_i)$ is the i-th evolutionary node processor of the network. The components of every processor are (we denote by e the empty word): M_i is a finite set of evolution rules of one of the following forms only (i) $a \rightarrow b, a, b \in V$ (substitution rules), (ii) $a \rightarrow e, a \in V$ (deletion rules), (iii) $e \rightarrow a, a \in V$ (insertion rules); A_i is a finite set of strings over V. The set A_i is the set of initial strings in the i-th node; PI_i and PO_i are subsets of V^* representing the input and the output filter, respectively. These filters are defined by the membership condition, namely a string $w \in V^*$ can pass the input filter (the output filter) if $w \in PI_i(w \in PO_i)$.
– $G = (\{N_1, N_2, \ldots, N_n\}, E)$ is an undirected graph called the underlying graph of the network. The edges of G, that is the elements of E, are given in the form of sets of two nodes. The complete graph with n vertices is denoted by K_n.

Definition 10. *Configuration of a NEP is an n-tuple $C = (L_1, L_2, \ldots, L_n)$, with $L_i \subseteq V^*$ for all $1 \leq i \leq n$. It represents the sets of strings which are present in all the nodes at a given moment.*

A given configuration of a NEP can change either by an evolutionary step or by a communicating step. When changing by an evolutionary step, each component L_i of the configuration is changed in accordance with the evolutionary rules associated with the node i. The change in the configuration by an evolutionary step is written as $C_1 \Rightarrow C_2$. When changing by a communication step, each node processor N_i sends all copies of the strings it has which are able to pass its output filter to all the node processors connected to N_i and receives all copies of the strings sent by any node processor connected with N_i, if they can pass its input filter. The change in the configuration by a communication step is written as $C_1 \vdash C_2$.

A scheme of the basic architecture of NEPs is shown in Fig. 4.

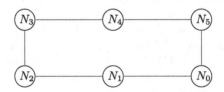

Fig. 4. Basic architecture of a NEP.

4   Learning and Agents

The intersection of agent technology and machine learning constitutes a research area whose importance is nowadays broadly acknowledged in artificial intelligence: *learning in multi-agent systems*. This new area has emerged as a topic of research in the late 1980s and since then has attracted increasing attention in both the multi-agent systems community and the machine learning area. However, until the late 80s, multi-agent learning had been widely ignored by both researchers in distributed artificial intelligence and in machine learning. This situation was due to two facts: (1) work in distributed artificial intelligence mainly concentrated on developing multi-agent systems whose organization and functioning were fixed and, (2) research in machine learning mainly concentrated on learning techniques and methods for single-agent settings [51].

Nowadays, it is commonly agreed by distributed artificial intelligence and machine learning communities that multi-agent learning –this is, learning that requires the interaction among several intelligent agents [20]-deserves particular attention. Two important reasons for the interest in studying learning in multi-agent systems have been stressed [49]:

1. The need for learning techniques and methods in the area of multi-agent systems in order to equip multi-agent systems with learning abilities to allow agents to automatically improve their behaviour.
2. The need in the area of machine learning of considering not only single-agent learning but also multi-agent learning in order to improve the understanding of the learning processes in natural multi-agent systems (like human groups or societies).

The area of multi-agent learning shows how developments in the fields of machine learning and agent technologies have become complementary. In this intersection, researchers from both fields have opportunities to profit from solutions proposed by each other. In fact we can distinguish two directions in this intersection [21]:

1. *Learning in Multi-Agent Systems* (MAS), this is, using machine learning techniques in agent technology.
2. *Agent-Based Machine Learning*, this is, using agent technology in the field of machine learning.

4.1   Learning in Multi-agent Systems

Learning is increasingly being seen as a key ability of agents and, therefore, several agent-based frameworks that utilize machine learning for intelligent decision support have been reported. Theoretical developments in the field of learning agents focus mostly on methodologies and requirements for constructing multi-agent systems with learning capabilities.

Many terms can be found in the literature that refer to learning in multi-agent systems [43]: *mutual learning, cooperative learning, collaborative learning, co-learning, team learning, social learning, shared learning, pluralistic learning*, and *organizational learning* are just some examples.

In the area of multi-agent learning –the application of machine learning to problems involving multiple agents [36]–, two principal forms of learning can be distinguished [43,49]:

1. *Centralized or isolated learning* where the learning process is executed by one single agent and does not require any interaction with other agents.
2. *Decentralized, distributed, collective or interactive learning* where several agents are engaged in the same learning process and the learning is done by the agents as a group.

There are three main methods/approaches to learning in multi-agent systems which are distinguished by taking into account the kind of feedback provided to the learner [36,49]:

1. *Supervised learning*, where the correct output is provided. This means that the environment or an agent providing feedback acts as a "teacher".
2. *Reinforcement learning*, where an assessment of the learner's output is provided. This means that the environment or an agent providing feedback acts as a "critic".
3. *Unsupervised learning*, where no explicit feedback is provided at all. This means that the environment or an agent providing feedback acts as an "observer".

A third classification can be obtained by taking into account the learning strategies used by agents [43]. The main difference between the types of learning included in this classification is the amount of learning effort required:

1. *Rote learning* consists of the direct implantation of knowledge and skills.
2. *Learning form instruction and by advice taking.* This type of learning transforms new information (instruction or advice) into an internal representation and integrates it with prior knowledge.
3. *Learning from examples and practice* consists of the extraction and refinement of knowledge from positive and negative examples or from practical experience.
4. *Learning by analogy* is as solution-preserving transformation of knowledge from a solved problem to a similar unsolved problem.
5. *Learning by discovery* consists of gathering new knowledge by observations, experiments, testing hypotheses or theories on the basis of the observational and experimental results.

Space limitation prevents us of going deeper in the above models. For more information the reader can see [36,43,44,47,49–51]. Our goal in this section has been just to stress the fact that several dimensions of multi-agent interaction can be subject to learning –when to interact, with whom to interact, how to interact, and what exactly the content of the interaction should be [20]–, and machine learning can be seen as a primer supplier of learning capabilities for agent and multi-agent systems.

4.2   Agent-Based Machine Learning

In the intersection between multi-agent systems and machine learning we find the so-called *agent-based machine learning techniques* where agent technology is applied to solve machine learning problems. According to Jedrzejowicz [21], there are several ways in which the research of machine learning can profit from the application of agent technology:

- First of all, there are machine learning techniques where parallelization can speed-up learning, therefore, in these cases using a set of agents may increase the efficiency of learning.
- Secondly, there are machine learning techniques that rely on the collective computational intelligence paradigm, where a synergetic effect is expected from combining efforts of various agents.
- Thirdly, in the so-called distributed machine learning problems, a set of agents working in distributed sites can be used to produce some local level solutions independently and in parallel.

Taking into account those advantages, several models have been proposed that apply agent-based solutions to machine learning problems:

- Models of collective or collaborative learning.
- Learning classifier systems that use agents representing set of rules as a solution to machine learning problem.
- Ensemble techniques.
- Distributed learning models.

According to [21], agent technology has brought to machine learning several capabilities including parallel computation, scalability and interoperability. In general, agent based solutions can be used to develop more flexible machine learning tools. For the state of the art of agent-based machine learning see [21].

5   Conclusions

According to [49], the interest in multi-agent systems is founded on the insight that many real-world problems are best modelled using a set of agents instead of a single agent. Multi-agent modelling makes possible to cope with natural constraints like the limitation of the processing power of a single agent and to profit from inherent properties of distributed systems like robustness, fault tolerance, parallelism and scalability. These properties have facilitated the application of multi-agent technology to many types of systems that help humans to perform several tasks.

Machine learning is one of the core fields of artificial intelligence, since artificial intelligence has been defined as "the science and engineering of making intelligent machines" and the ability to learn is one of the most fundamental attributes of intelligent behaviour. It is usually agreed that a system capable of learning deserves to be called intelligent; and conversely, a system being considered as intelligent is, among other things, usually expected to be able to learn.

Formalization has a long tradition in science, besides traditional fields such as physics or chemistry, other scientific areas such as medicine, cognitive and social sciences and linguistics have shown a tendency towards formalization. The use of formal methods has led to numerous results that would have been difficult to be obtained without such formalization. Formal language theory provides good tools to formalize different problems. This flexibility and abstraction has been proven by the application of formal languages to the fields of linguistics, economic modelling, developmental biology, cryptography, sociology, etc.

From what we have said, it follows that multi-agent systems, machine learning and formal language theory provide flexible and useful tools that can be used in different research areas due to their versatility. All three areas have revealed to be very useful for dealing with complex systems. MAS provide principles for the construction of complex systems and mechanisms for coordination. Formal language theory offers mathematical tools to formalize complex systems. And machine learning techniques help to deal with the complexity of complex systems by endowing agents with the ability of improving their behaviour. We have seen in this paper that some intersection between those areas has been already performed: *agents with learning, agents with formal languages* and *formal languages with learning.*

Future research should help to further integrate the three fields considered in this paper in order to obtain what in [20] is seen as a must: a *formal theory of multi-agent learning.*

Another important and challenging working direction is the application of this formal theory of multi-agent learning to a real world domain as is the area of processing natural language. The interaction between researchers in those three topics can provide good techniques and methods for improving our knowledge about how languages are processed. The advances in the area of natural language processing may have important consequences in the area of artificial intelligence since they can help the design of technologies in which computers will be integrated into the everyday environment, rendering accessible a multitude of services and applications through easy-to-use human interfaces.

Acknowledgements. The work of Leonor Becerra-Bonache has been supported by Pascal 2 Network of Excellence. The work of M. Dolores Jiménez-López has been supported by the Spanish Ministry of Science and Innovation under the Coordinated Research Project TIN2011-28260-C03-00 and the Research Project TIN2011-28260-C03-02.

References

1. Angluin, D.: Learning regular sets from queries and counterexamples. Inf. Comput. **75**, 87–106 (1987)
2. Angluin, D., Kharitonov, M.: When won't membership queries help? In: STOC'91: 24th Annual ACM Symposium on Theory of Computing, pp. 444–453. ACM Press, New York (1991)
3. Balcázar, J.L., Díaz, J., Gavaldà, R., Watanabe, O.: Algorithms for learning finite automata from queries: a unified view. In: Du, D.Z., Ko, K.I. (eds.) Advances in Algorithms, Languages, and Complexity, pp. 73–91. Kluwer Academic Publishers, Dordrech (1997)

4. Baník, I.: Colonies with position. Comput. Artif. Intell. **15**, 141–154 (1996)
5. Becerra-Bonache, L., Dediu, A.-H., Tîrnăucă, C.: Learning DFA from Correction and equivalence queries. In: Sakakibara, Y., Kobayashi, S., Sato, K., Nishino, T., Tomita, E. (eds.) ICGI 2006. LNCS (LNAI), vol. 4201, pp. 281–292. Springer, Heidelberg (2006)
6. Brooks, R.A.: Elephants don't play chess. Robot. Auton. Syst. **6**, 3–15 (1990)
7. Castellanos, J., Martín-Vide, C., Mitrana, V., Sempere, J.M.: Networks of evolutionary processors. Acta Informatica **39**, 517–529 (2003)
8. Clark, A.: Grammatical inference and first language acquisition. In: Workshop on Psychocomputational Models of Human Language Acquisition, Geneva, pp. 25–32 (2004)
9. Csuhaj-Varjú, E., Dassow, J.: On cooperating/distributed grammar systems. J. Inf. Process. Cybern. (EIK) **26**, 49–63 (1990)
10. Csuhaj-Varjú, E., Dassow, J., Kelemen, J., Păun, G.: Grammar Systems: A Grammatical Approach to Distribution and Cooperation. Gordon and Breach, London (1994)
11. Csuhaj-Varjú, E., Kelemen, J., Kelemenová, A., Păun, G.: Eco-grammar systems: a grammatical framework for life-like interactions. Artif. Life **3**(1), 1–28 (1996)
12. Dassow, J., Kelemen, J., Păun, G.: On parallelism in colonies. Cybern. Syst. **14**, 37–49 (1993)
13. Dassow, J., Păun, G., Rozenberg, G.: Grammar systems. In: Rozenberg, G., Salomaa, A. (eds.) Handbook of Formal Languages, vol. 2, pp. 155–213. Springer, Berlin (1997)
14. de la Higuera, C.: Grammatical Inference: Learning Automata and Grammars. Cambridge University Press, Cambridge (2010)
15. Errico, L., Jesshope, C.: Towards a new architecture for symbolic processing. In: Plander, I. (ed.) Artificial Intelligence and Information-Control Systems of Robots'94, pp. 31–40. World Science, Singapore (1994)
16. Fernau, H., de la Higuera, C.: Grammar induction: an invitation to formal language theorists. Grammars **7**, 45–55 (2004)
17. Gold, E.M.: Language identification in the limit. Inf. Control **10**, 447–474 (1967)
18. Hellerstein, L., Pillaipakkamnatt, K., Raghavan, V., Wilkins, D.: How many queries are needed to learn? In: 27th Annual ACM Symposium on the Theory of Computing, pp. 190–199. ACM Press (1995)
19. Hillis, W.D.: The Connection Machine. MIT Press, Cambridge (1985)
20. Huhns, M., Weiss, G.: Guest editorial. Mach. Learn. **33**, 123–128 (1998)
21. Jędrzejowicz, P.: Machine learning and agents. In: O'Shea, J., Nguyen, N.T., Crockett, K., Howlett, R.J., Jain, L.C. (eds.) KES-AMSTA 2011. LNCS, vol. 6682, pp. 2–15. Springer, Heidelberg (2011)
22. Kari, L., Rozenberg, G., Salomaa, A.: L Systems. In: Rozenberg, G., Salomaa, A. (eds.) Handbook of Formal Languages, vol. 1, pp. 253–328. Springer, Berlin (1997)
23. Kelemen, J.: Colonies - a theory of reactive agents. In: Kelemenová, A. (ed.) Proceedings on the MFCS'98 Satellite Workshop on Grammar Systems, pp. 7–38. Silesian University, Opava (1998)
24. Kelemen, J., Kelemenová, A.: A grammar-theoretic treatment of multiagent systems. Cybern. Syst. **23**, 621–633 (1992)
25. Kelemenová, A.: Timing in colonies. In: Păun, G., Salomaa, A. (eds.) Grammatical Models of Multi-agent Systems. Gordon and Breach, London (1999)
26. Kelemenová, A., Csuhaj-Varjú, E.: Languages of colonies. Theoret. Comput. Sci. **134**, 119–130 (1994)

27. Langton, C.: Artificial life. In: Life, A. (ed.) Artificial Life, pp. 1–47. Addison-Wesley, Redwood City (1989)

28. Lindenmayer, A.: Mathematical models for cellular interaction in development, I and II. J. Theor. Biol. **18**, 280–315 (1968)

29. Martín-Vide, C., Mitrana, V., Pérez-Jiménez, M., Sancho-Caparrini, F.: Hybrid networks of evolutionary processors. In: Cantú-Paz, E., Foster, J.A., Deb, K., Davis, L., Roy, R., O'Reilly, U.-M., Beyer, H.-G., Kendall, G., Wilson, S.W., Harman, M., Wegener, J., Dasgupta, D., Potter, M.A., Schultz, A., Dowsland, K.A., Jonoska, N., Miller, J., Standish, R.K. (eds.) GECCO 2003. LNCS, vol. 2723, pp. 401–412. Springer, Heidelberg (2003)

30. Martín-Vide, C., Păun, G.: PM-colonies. Comput. Artif. Intell. **17**, 553–582 (1998)

31. Martín-Vide, C., Păun, G.: New topics in colonies theory. Grammars **1**, 209–223 (1999)

32. Martín-Vide, C., Păun, G., Pazos, J., Rodríguez-Patón, A.: Tissue P systems. Theoret. Comput. Sci. **296**(2), 295–326 (2002)

33. Martín-Vide, C., Pazos, J., Păun, G., Rodríguez-Patón, A.: A new class of symbolic abstract neural nets: tissue P systems. In: Ibarra, O.H., Zhang, L. (eds.) COCOON 2002. LNCS, vol. 2387, pp. 290–299. Springer, Heidelberg (2002)

34. Nii, H.P.: Blackboard systems. In: Barr, A., Cohen, P.R., Feigenbaum, E.A. (eds.) The Handbook of Artificial Intelligence, vol. IV, pp. 3–82. Addison-Wesley, Stanford (1989)

35. Nilsson, N.J.: Introduction to Machine Learning. An Early Draft of a Proposed Textbook (1998). http://robotics.stanford.edu/people/nilsson/mlbook.html

36. Panait, L., Luke, S.: Cooperative multi-agent learning: the state-of-the-art. Auton. Agent. Multi-Agent Syst. **11**(3), 387–434 (2005)

37. Păun, G.: On the generative power of colonies. Kybernetika **31**, 83–97 (1995)

38. Păun, G.: Computing with membranes. J. Comput. Syst. Sci. **61**(1), 108–143 (2000)

39. Păun, G., Rozenberg, G., Salomaa, A.: DNA Computing: New Computing Paradigms. Springer, Berlin (1998)

40. Păun, G., Sântean, L.: Parallel communicating grammar systems: the regular case. Ann. Univ. Bucharest **38**, 55–63 (1989)

41. Rivest, R.L., Schapire, R.E.: Inference of finite automata using homing sequences. Inf. Comput. **103**(2), 299–347 (1993)

42. Rozenberg, G., Salomaa, A. (eds.): Handbook of Formal Languages. Springer, Berlin (1997)

43. Sen, S., Weiss, G.: Learning in multiagent systems. In: Weiss, G. (ed.) Multiagent Systems, pp. 259–298. MIT Press, Cambridge (1999)

44. Shoham, Y., Powers, R., Grenage, T.: If multi-agent learning is the answer, what is the question? Artif. Intell. **171**(7), 365–377 (2007)

45. Sosík, P.: Parallel accepting colonies and neural networks. In: Păun, G., Salomaa, A. (eds.) Grammatical Models of Multi-agent Systems. Gordon and Breach, London (1999)

46. Sosík, P., Štýbnar, L.: Grammatical inference of colonies. In: Păun, G., Salomaa, A. (eds.) New Trends in Formal Languages. LNCS, vol. 1218. Springer, Heidelberg (1997)

47. Stone, P., Veloso, M.: Multiagent systems: a survey from a machine learning perspective. Auton. Robot. **8**, 345–383 (2000)

48. Valiant, L.G.: A theory of the learnable. Commun. ACM **27**, 1134–1142 (1984)

49. Weiss, G.: Learning to coordinate actions in multi-agent systems. In: Proceedings of the 13th International Conference on Artificial Intelligence, pp. 311–316 (1993)

50. Weiss, G.: A multiagent perspective of parallel and distributed machine learning. In: Proceedings of the 2nd International Conference on Autonomous Agents, pp. 226–230 (1998)
51. Weiss, G., Dillenbourg, P.: What is "Multi" in multi-agent learning? In: Dillenbourg, P. (ed.) Collaborative Learning: Cognitive and Computational Approaches (Chapter 4). Pergamon Press, Oxford (1998)

An Agent-Based Approach for Accident Analysis in Safety Critical Domains: A Case Study on a Runway Incursion Incident

Tibor Bosse and Nataliya M. Mogles[(✉)]

Agent Systems Research Group, Vrije Universiteit Amsterdam,
de Boelelaan 1081, 1081 HV Amsterdam, The Netherlands
{tbosse,nm.mogles}@few.vu.nl

Abstract. This paper introduces an agent-based approach to analyze the dynamics of accidents and incidents in aviation. The approach makes use of a number of elements, including formalization of a real world scenario, agent-based simulation of variations of the scenario, and formal verification of dynamic properties against the (empirical and simulated) scenarios. The scenario formalization part enables incident reconstruction and formal analysis of it. The simulation part enables the analyst to explore various hypothetical scenarios under different circumstances, with an emphasis on error related to human factors. The formal verification part enables the analyst to identify scenarios involving potential hazards, and to relate those hazards (via so-called interlevel relations) to inadequate behavior on the level of individual agents. The approach is illustrated by means of a case study on a runway incursion incident, and a number of advantages with respect to the current state-of-the-art are discussed.

Keywords: Aviation · Incidents · Agent-based simulation · Verification · Interlevel relations

1 Introduction

Within aviation, analyzing the exact causes of accidents and incidents is a nontrivial task. Even if detailed flight data from the 'black box' are available, it is usually still difficult to come up with a clear analysis, for the simple reason that the causes of incidents cannot be attributed to a single point of failure of one individual entity. Instead, most incidents in aviation are found to be caused by a complex interplay of processes at various levels of the socio-technical system, involving pilots, air traffic controllers, technical systems, and their interaction. For example the famous accident in 2009 of Air France Flight 447 is still under investigation and seems to have been the consequence of a rare combination of factors. On May 31, 2009, this flight disappeared

---

Parts of this article appeared in the Proceedings of the Twenty-Fifth International Conference on Industrial, Engineering and Other Applications of Applied Intelligent Systems (IEA/AIE'12) and in the Proceedings of the Fifth International Conference on Agents and Artificial Intelligence (ICAART'13).

© Springer-Verlag Berlin Heidelberg 2014
N.T. Nguyen (Ed.): TCCI XVII 2014, LNCS 8790, pp. 66–88, 2014.
DOI: 10.1007/978-3-662-44994-3_4

somewhere over the Atlantic Ocean, during a route from Rio de Janeiro to Paris. The crash was the deadliest accident in the history of Air France, killing all 228 people on board. This accident seems to have been the consequence of a rare combination of factors, like inconsistent airspeed sensor readings, the disengagement of the autopilot, and the pilot pulling the nose of the plane back despite stall warnings.[1]

For the analysis of accidents and incidents in aviation, roughly two streams can be distinguished in the literature, namely *accident analysis* and *risk analysis*. Whilst the former has the goal to determine the cause of an accident that actually took place, the latter aims to assess the likelihood of the occurrence of future accidents. Hence, although both streams have similar purposes, a main difference is that accident analysis attempts to identify one specific combination of hazardous factors, whereas risk analysis basically explores a whole range of such factors, and the associated risks. Nevertheless, most of the existing approaches are used for both streams.

Traditionally, accident and incident analyses are done via fault and event trees, graphical representations of Boolean logic relations between success and failure types of events. However, although widely used, there is an increasing awareness that fault and event trees have serious limitations, especially when it comes to analysing dynamic systems with time-dependent interactions (see [6] for a more extensive argumentation). More recently, alternative approaches have been developed, such as FRAM [7] and STAMP [11]. While these approaches have proved successful in various case studies, they still have some drawbacks. In particular, FRAM lacks a formal semantics, which makes a computational analysis of complex non-linear processes impossible. STAMP does have a formal basis, but takes an aggregated, organisational perspective (based on system dynamics), which hinders an analysis at the level of individual agents (such as pilots and air traffic controllers), and their underlying mental processes.

As an alternative, the current paper presents an approach for analysis of aviation incidents that takes a multi-agent perspective, and is based on formal methods. The approach is an extension of the approach introduced in the work of Bosse and Mogles [4], which was in turn inspired by Blom, Bakker, Blanker, Daams, Everdij and Klompstra [1]. Whereas this approach mainly focuses on the analysis of existing accidents (also called *accident analysis* or *retrospective analysis*), the current paper also addresses analysis of potential future accidents (called *risk analysis* or *prospective analysis*). This is done by means of a multi-agent simulation framework that addresses both the behaviour of individual agents (operators, pilots) as well as their mutual communication, and interaction with technical systems. By manipulating various parameters in the model, different scenarios can be explored. Moreover, by means of automated checks of dynamic properties, these scenarios can be assessed with respect to their likelihood of the occurrence of accidents. The approach is illustrated by a case study on a runway incursion incident at a large European airport in 1995.

The remainder of this paper is structured as follows. In Sect. 2, the modelling approach used in the paper is presented. In Sect. 3, the scenario used within the case study is described. Section 4 introduces the agent-based model to simulate this (and similar)

---

[1] http://en.wikipedia.org/wiki/Air_France_Flight_447

scenarios, and Sect. 5 presents the simulation results. Section 6 addresses formal analysis of the model and its results, and Sect. 7 concludes the paper with a discussion.

2 Modeling Approach

In this section, first an overview of the modeling paradigm underlying the proposed methodology is given. After that, the modeling language and the methodology used for accident analysis are introduced.

2.1 Agent-Based Modeling

Agent-oriented approaches have been widely used for modeling complex socio-technical systems [8]. The essence of agent-based modeling is the agent-oriented world view that implies that the world consists of active, purposeful agents that interact to achieve their objectives. There is still much debate, however, about what exactly constitutes an agent or agenthood. The majority of researchers agree on the following definition of an agent proposed in [15]: 'An agent is an encapsulated (computer) system that is situated in some environment and that is capable of flexible, autonomous action in that environment in order to meet its design objectives'. The agent-based approach for modeling is characterized by flexibility of outcomes and the strong possibility of system's emergent behavior that cannot be predicted from behavior of its individual components, or agents. The class of agent models that has beliefs (what the agent knows about the world and other agents), desires (what the agent wants or which goals he has) and intentions (what the agent intends to do) have been used in a wide variety of applications including air traffic control, process control and transportation [8]. Such a Belief-Desire-Intention (BDI) paradigm [13] is powerful for the representation of cognitive states of agents and will be adopted in the current work in order to model internal cognitive states of human agents that may be crucial for understanding of human performance in critical domains and in air traffic in particular. Instead, entities with less autonomy (like aircraft and runways) will not be modeled using the BDI approach; these entities will simply be represented as static objects that are part of the environment with which the agents interact.

2.2 Temporal Trace Language

To model the different aspects of aviation operations from an agent perspective, an expressive modeling language is needed. On the one hand, qualitative aspects have to be addressed, such as observations, beliefs, and actions of human operators. On the other hand, quantitative aspects have to be addressed, such as the locations and speeds of aircraft. Another requirement of the chosen modeling language is its suitability to express both the basic mechanisms of aviation operations (for the purpose of simulation), as well as more global properties of these operations (for the purpose of logical analysis and verification). For example, basic mechanisms of aviation operations involve decision functions for individual agents (e.g., an operator may decide to give runway clearance, and a pilot to abort a take-off procedure in case of an emergency). Instead, examples of global properties address the overall safety of an operation, such as "no collisions take place".

The predicate-logical Temporal Trace Language (TTL) introduced in the work of Bosse, Jonker, van der Meij, Sharpanskykh and Treur [2] fulfils all of these desiderata. It integrates qualitative, logical aspects and quantitative, numerical aspects. This integration allows the modeler to exploit both logical and numerical methods for analysis and simulation. Moreover it can be used to express dynamic properties at different levels of aggregation, which makes it well suited both for simulation and logical analysis.

The TTL language is based on the assumption that dynamics can be described as an evolution of states over time. The notion of state as used here is characterised on the basis of an ontology defining a set of physical and/or mental (state) properties that do or do not hold at a certain point in time. These properties are often called *state properties* to distinguish them from dynamic properties that relate different states over time. A specific state is characterised by dividing the set of state properties into those that hold, and those that do not hold in the state. Examples of state properties are 'aircraft A moves with speed S', or 'Air Traffic Controller C provides runway clearance to aircraft A'. Real value assignments to variables are also considered as possible state property descriptions.

To formalise state properties, ontologies are specified in a (many-sorted) first order logical format: an *ontology* is specified as a finite set of sorts, constants within these sorts, and relations and functions over these sorts (sometimes also called signatures). The examples mentioned above then can be formalised by n-ary predicates (or proposition symbols), such as, moves_with_velocity(A, S) or communicate_from_to(C, A, runway_clearance). Such predicates are called *state ground atoms* (or *atomic state properties*). For a given ontology Ont, the propositional language signature consisting of all ground atoms based on Ont is denoted by APROP(Ont). One step further, the *state properties* based on ontology Ont are formalised by the propositions that can be made (using conjunction, negation, disjunction, implication) from the ground atoms. Thus, an example of a formalised state property is moves_with_velocity(A, S) & communicate_from_to(C, A, runway_clearance). Moreover, a *state* S is an indication of which atomic state properties are true and which are false, i.e., a mapping S: APROP (Ont) $\rightarrow$ {true, false}. The set of all possible states for ontology Ont is denoted by STATES(Ont).

To describe dynamic properties of complex processes such as in aviation, explicit reference is made to *time* and to *traces*. A fixed time frame T is assumed which is linearly ordered. Depending on the application, it may be dense (e.g., the real numbers) or discrete (e.g., the set of integers or natural numbers or a finite initial segment of the natural numbers). Dynamic properties can be formulated that relate a state at one point in time to a state at another point in time. A simple example is the following (informally stated) dynamic property about the absence of collisions:

For all traces γ,
there is no time point t
on which a collision takes place.

A *trace* γ over an ontology Ont and time frame T is a mapping γ : T → STATES (Ont), i.e., a sequence of states $γ_t$ (t ∈ T) in STATES(Ont). The temporal trace language TTL is built on atoms referring to, e.g., traces, time and state properties. For example, 'in trace γ at time t property p holds' is formalised by state(γ, t) |= p. Here |= is a predicate symbol in the language, usually used in infix notation, which is comparable to the Holds-predicate in situation calculus. *Dynamic properties* are expressed by temporal statements built using the usual first-order logical connectives (such as ¬, ∧, ∨, ⇒) and quantification (∀ and ∃; for example, over traces, time and state properties). For example, the informally stated dynamic property introduced above is formally expressed as follows:

∀γ:TRACES ¬∃t:TIME
state(γ, t) |= collision

In addition, language abstractions by introducing new predicates as abbreviations for complex expressions are supported.

To be able to perform (pseudo-)experiments, only part of the expressivity of TTL is needed. To this end, the executable LEADSTO language described in [3] has been defined as a sublanguage of TTL, with the specific purpose to develop simulation models in a declarative manner. In LEADSTO, direct temporal dependencies between two state properties in successive states are modelled by *executable dynamic properties*. The LEADSTO format is defined as follows. Let α and β be state properties as defined above. Then, $α \rightsquigarrow_{e, f, g, h} β$ means:

> *If state property α holds for a certain time interval with duration g,*
> *then after some delay between e and f*
> *state property β will hold for a certain time interval with duration h.*

Based on TTL and LEADSTO, two dedicated pieces of software have recently been developed. First, the LEADSTO Simulation Environment [3] takes a specification of executable dynamic properties as input, and uses this to generate simulation traces. Second, to automatically analyse the resulting simulation traces, the TTL Checker tool [2] has been developed. This tool takes as input a formula expressed in TTL and a set of traces, and verifies automatically whether the formula holds for the traces.

2.3   Accident/Incident Analysis Methodology

Based on the agent-based modelling paradigm and TTL, the current paper proposes the following 7-step methodology for formal analysis of aviation incidents:

(1) *Development of formal ontology*: to develop the state ontology Ont introduced above, all relevant sorts, constants, functions and predicates have to be specified for the domain under investigation, enabling the modeller to describe the relevant aspects of the world (e.g., pilots, controllers, aircraft, actions, communications, mental states, and so on). This step is addressed in Sect. 4.1 of the current paper.

(2) *Formalisation of real world scenarios in terms of traces*: for each scenario, express the different events using the formal ontology developed in step 1), and allocate a time stamp to them. This step is described in Sect. 4.2.

(3) *Specification of local executable dynamic properties* of agents involved in the ATM system of the scenario under consideration: identify the relevant executable dynamic properties and express them in LEADSTO. This step is applied in Sect. 4.3.

(4) Perform *dynamic simulations* of the scenario: identify parameters and/or initial settings that might be crucial for occurring of an incident or an accident, manipulate the parameters and observe the behavior of the agents and the emergent behavior of the whole system. This step enables the analyst to observe a variety of alternative developments of the scenario (simulation traces) under investigation. Section 5 is devoted to this methodological step.

(5) *Specification of non-local dynamic properties at different levels*: identify non-local dynamic properties that are relevant for the domain, and express them in TTL. Section 6.1 is dedicated to this step.

(6) *Specification of interlevel relations between dynamic properties*: the dynamic properties identified in step (3) and (5) may be classified according to different levels of aggregation of the aviation domain. For instance, some properties may apply to the air traffic organisation as a whole (e.g., 'no incident will occur'), whereas others apply to the level of individual agents (e.g., 'agent A will only communicate correct information'). In this step, logical relationships between dynamic properties at different levels are established, to ensure that conjunctions of properties at one level imply properties at higher levels. This step is addressed in Sect. 6.2.

(7) *Verification of properties against (real life and simulated) traces*: using the TTL Checking Tool mentioned above, dynamic properties at different levels are checked automatically against the traces generated in step 2) and 4), allowing the analyst to find out what exactly went wrong in the scenarios under investigation. This step is described in Sect. 6.3.

Note that this approach is in principle not restricted to the domain of aviation. In fact, it is completely domain-independent, as long as it is applied to systems that consists of multiple interacting agents, and of which it is possible to obtain empirical data in the form of scenario descriptions. Nevertheless, the main purpose of the current paper is to study the applicability of this approach to the domain of aviation. Hence, in the remainder of the paper, the 7 steps are illustrated by means of the runway incursion case study.

3   Case Study

One of the possible approaches in analyzing the behavior of complex systems in aviation is by identification and formal analysis of case studies. This type of analysis allows researchers to acquire possible underlying information about incidents or almost-incidents within the air traffic domain. Our interest was mainly focused on incidents where a small mistake of one or multiple actors could have led to severe consequences at the level of the whole system, but was corrected by another actor and thus the possible accident was prevented. This focus on incidents was motivated by the fact that the numerous descriptions of air traffic accidents that could be found in the published literature are one-sided, as these cases cover just a small top of the iceberg of all risky situations occurring daily in air traffic interactions. However, it is not so easy to get access to these incidents, as they are mostly company confidential and not available for broad publications, or they are not officially reported at all. To obtain such a case study, it was decided to perform a semi-structured interview with an available expert, a two years retired pilot of a European civil aviation company.

The following subsections provide the overview of an interview that was performed with the available expert and the description of the extracted incident that has been selected for the formal analysis.

3.1 Interview

The interview with a retired pilot of a civil aviation company took place on May 12, 2011 and lasted approximately 1 hour and 15 minutes. It was a semi-structured interview with a predefined set of questions concerning the incidents that the pilot or any of his colleagues had experienced during his flight career. In the beginning of the interview it was clearly announced to the interviewee that we were interested in the cases within air traffic where a small local mistake could have led to severe global consequences, but was corrected before an actual accident would occur. The interviewee was asked to recall such incidents. This question contained the following subquestions:

1. Who was involved in the incident?
2. What was the cause of the problem?[2]
3. How was the problem solved?
4. What were the consequences?
5. Was the situation familiar to you from trainings or procedures?

During the interview a case study was identified that describes an incident where, due to the mistake of a pilot of one taxiing aircraft, two aircraft were taking off almost simultaneously from crossing runways. After the correct intervention of the air traffic controllers from the ATC Tower, and adequate decision making, coordination and action of the pilots of one of the aircraft, a collision was prevented. This incident is described (in an anonymised manner) in the following section.

3.2 Runway Incursion Incident Description

The runway incursion incident took place during the departure of an Airbus A310 of a civil aviation company from one large airport in Europe. A summary of the scenario is provided below. A schematic overview of the situation is provided in Fig. 1.

---

[2] Possible causes that might be relevant include failure of technical systems, miscommunication, fatigue, high or low workload (restricted Situation Awareness or decreased vigilance), strong positive or negative emotions, power influences, (dis)trust in colleagues or computer systems, little experience, negligence of the existing procedures, organisational management etc.

The Airbus was preparing for the departure: the pilot-in-command was sitting on the left and the co-pilot on the right seat in the cockpit and they were ready to start taxiing. They were supposed to taxi to runway 03 in the north-east direction. The Airbus received permission to taxi and started taxiing to its runway. Approximately at the same time, a military Hercules aircraft that was ready for the departure as well received permission to taxi in the north-west direction from its parking gate. The Hercules was supposed to take off from runway 36 that crossed with runway 03 that was designated for the Airbus. Both aircraft were taxiing to their runways. During the taxiing, the Airbus received its flight route from the air traffic controllers. Some time later, when the Airbus was near the runway designated for taking off, it switched from the taxiing radio frequency to the frequency of the Tower and received permission to line up on the assigned runway. The Hercules was still at the taxiing radio frequency and also received permission to line up, while at the same time the Airbus received permission to take off at the radio frequency of the Tower. However, due to unknown reasons,[3] the Hercules pilot interpreted his permission for lining up as permission for taking off and started taking off on runway 36. As a result of this mistake of the pilot of the Hercules, two aircraft were taking off simultaneously on crossing runways, and none of the crews were aware of that. The air traffic controllers in the Tower observed the conflicting situation and communicated a 'STOP' signal to the pilot-in-command of the Airbus, while the Airbus was still on the ground (but at high speed). The pilot had to make a quick decision about the termination of the take-off as there is a point in this process that one cannot safely do this anymore. After having analysed the situation, the pilot-in-command of the Airbus gave a command to the co-pilot (who controlled the aircraft) to abort the take-off and start braking on the runway. During braking, the crew of the Airbus saw the Hercules flying close in the air above their own aircraft at a distance of about 5 m. A serious collision was prevented.

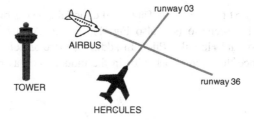

Fig. 1. Schematic overview of the case study.

---

[3] This misinterpretation might be explained by the fact that the pilot of the Hercules got used to the routine procedure of taxiing from the same military parking place at this airport and perhaps also of taking off from the same runway. And in many past cases, the line up procedure was often immediately followed by taking off, as permissions for lining up and taking off were sometimes given simultaneously.

4 Agent-Based Model

The following subsections describe, respectively, the formal ontology for the case study, a formalized trace of the case study based on this ontology, and a set of executable dynamic properties (or rules) that can be used to simulate the scenario (and variations of it).

4.1 Formal Ontology

As the first step towards the formalization of the incident identified during the interview, formal domain ontology was developed in TTL. In Tables 1 and 2, an overview of the ontology elements is shown, including the relevant sorts and subsorts relations, elements (constants) of sorts, and logical predicates over sorts.

Table 1. Domain ontology: sorts and elements.

SORT	ELEMENTS
AGENT	{tower sub-sorts: PILOT, AIRCRAFT}
PILOT	{airbus_pilot, hercules_pilot}
AIRCRAFT	{hercules, airbus}
ROADWAY	sub-sorts: RUNWAY, TAXIWAY, STARTINGPOINT, CROSSINGPOINT
RUNWAY	{runway_03, runway_36}
TAXIWAY	{taxiway_1, taxiway_2}
STARTINGPOINT	{startingpoint_1, startingpoint_2}
CROSSINGPOINT	{crossing_point(runway_03), crossing_point(runway_36)}
ACTION	{start_taxiing, start_line_up, start_take_off, take_off_from, stop_take_off}
VELOCITY	{low, high, very_high}

As shown in the first three rows of Table 1, the model consists of five active agents that play a role in the scenario (see also Fig. 1): Tower, Airbus Aircraft, Hercules Aircraft, Airbus Pilot and Hercules Pilot. In addition, there are elements of the environment that influence the agents' behavior in the model, such as runways, taxiways and other locations.

4.2 Formal Trace

The informal scenario described in Sect. 3 was formalized using the ontology presented in the previous subsection. A time point was assigned to each event of the case study under consideration.

The time points in the trace indicate the relative timing of the events. The trace was visualized in the LEADSTO software environment [3], as shown in Fig. 2. The states that hold in the world are represented on the vertical axis and the time line on the horizontal axis. The dark lines on the right indicate time intervals within which the given states are true.

Table 2. Domain ontology: logical predicates.

PREDICATE	DESCRIPTION
Communication	
communicate_from_to(A:Agent, B: Agent, C:Action, R:Roadway)	agent A communicates permission for action C on roadway R to agent B
incoming_communication(A: Agent, C:Action, R:Roadway)	agent A receives permission for action C on roadway R
Internal states of agents	
observation(A:Agent, I:Info_El)	agent A observes information element I from the world
belief(A:Agent, I:Info_El)	agent A believes that information element I is true in the world
expectation(A:Agent, C:Action)	agent A has expectation for action C
Actions of agents	
move_from_to(R1: Roadway, R2: Roadway)	action of moving from roadway R1 to roadway R2
performed(A:Agent, C:Action)	agent A performs action C
set_velocity(A:Aircraft, V:Velocity)	aircraft A acquires velocity V
take_off_from(R:Runway)	take-off is performed from runway R
stop_take_off(R:Runway)	take-off from runway R is aborted
Positions of agents	
is_at_position(A:Agent, R:Roadway)	agent A is on roadway R
is_adjacent_to(R1:Roadway, R2:Roadway)	roadway R1 is adjacent to roadway R2
crossing_ways(R1:Roadway, R2:Roadway	roadways R1 and R2 cross
is_half_way(A:Agent,R:Roadway))	agent A is half way on roadway R
in_air(A:Aircraft)	aircraft A is in air
Other information elements used within predicates	
is_available(R:Roadway)	roadway R is available
is_pilot_of(A:Agent, B:Aircraft)	agent A is a pilot of aircraft B
has_role(A:Agent)	an agent has role A
start_taxiing	start taxiing
start_line_up	permission to line up
start_take_off	permission to take off
velocity(A:Aircraft, V:Velocity)	aircraft A has velocity V
has_priority_over(A:Aircraft, B:Aircraft)	aircraft A has priority over aircraft B
not_in_conflict(A1:Agent, A2: Agent)	agent A1 is not in conflict with agent A2
similarity(A1:Action, A2:Action)	action A1 is similar to action A2
velocity(A:Aircraft, V:Velocity)	aircraft A has velocity V
collision(A:Aircraft, B:Aircraft)	aircraft A collides with Aircraft B

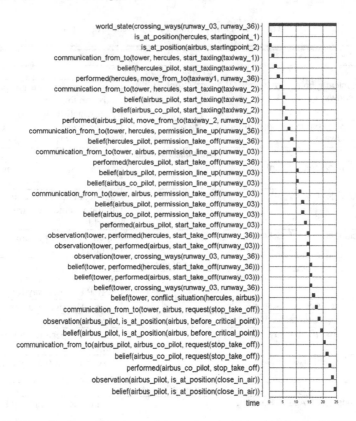

Fig. 2. Formalised empirical trace of the runway incursion incident in LEADSTO.

4.3 Executable Dynamic Properties

This subsection presents an agent-based simulation model of the runway incursion scenario, which consists of a number of executable dynamic properties (EPs) in LEADSTO. This model can be used both to reproduce the trace as shown in the previous subsection, but also (by slightly changing initial parameter settings) to generate a variety of alternative traces. The executable properties can be subdivided into four different categories, namely properties related to (1) belief formation, (2) communicative action generation, (3) physical action generation, and (4) transfer.

Below some examples of properties in formal LEADSTO notation per category are given (for simplicity, the time parameters have been left out). Note that most properties are applied to all agents. Only some of the properties (e.g., EP2, EP6 and EP16) are specific to a particular agent role (e.g., Tower or Pilot).

4.3.1 Belief Formation

Belief formation properties specify how agents create beliefs about the world on the basis of the observations or communications they receive. For instance, EP1 states that, if an agent observes no other agents at a certain roadway, it concludes that this roadway is available.

Belief formation properties may also represent erroneous behavior, e.g. related to cognitive biases such as the ATC expectation bias,[4] which is related to the well known confirmation bias [12]. For example, EP5 states that, if an agent receives an instruction I1, while it has a strong expectation to receive a similar, but slightly different instruction I2, it will believe that it actually did receive I2. This property can be used to model the fact that the Hercules pilot interpreted his permission for lining up as permission for taking off.

EP1 - Belief formation on roadway availability
observation(A:Agent, not_at_position(B:Agent, R:Roadway))
→ belief(A:Agent, is_available(R:Roadway))

EP5 - Communication misinterpretation
incoming_communication(A:Agent, I1:Action, R:Roadway)
& belief(A:Agent, similarity(I1: Action, I2: Action))
& I1 ≠ I2
& expectation(A:Agent, I2:Action)
→ belief(A:Agent, I2:Action, R:Roadway)

4.3.2   Communicative Action Generation

These properties specify how agents derive actions to communicate to other agents, based on the beliefs they possess. For instance, EP2 determines when the Tower agent communicates a permission to start taxiing to the different aircraft, whereas EP16 when the Tower communicates a request to abort take-off.

EP2 - Tower: Taxiing request communication
belief(A:Agent, is_at_position(B:Aircraft, S: Startingpoint))
& belief(A:Agent, is_adjacent_to(T:Taxiway, S: Startingpoint))
& belief(A:Agent, is_available(T:Taxiway))
& belief(A:Agent, has_role(tower))
→ communicate_from_to(A:Agent, B:Aircraft, start_taxiing(T:Taxiway))

EP16 - Tower: Take-off abort request communication
belief(tower, is_half_way(A:Aircraft, R1: Runway))
& belief(tower, is_half_way(B:Aircraft, R2: Roadway))
& belief(tower, crossing_ways(R1:Runway, R2:Roadway))
& belief(tower, velocity(B:Aircraft, high))
& not collision(A:Aircraft, B:Aircraft)
& B ≠ A
→ communicate_from_to(tower, B:Aircraft, stop_take_off, R1:Runway)

4.3.3   Physical Action Generation

In addition to communicative actions, agents may also derive physical actions. An example of this is represented by property EP6, which determines that pilot agents may start taxiing when they believe this is appropriate.

EP6 - Pilot: Taxiing initiation
belief(P:Pilot, start_taxiing(T:Taxiway)
& is_a _pilot_of(P:Pilot, A:Aircraft)
& belief(P:Pilot, is_available(T:Taxiway))
& is_at_position(A:Aircraft, S:Startingpoint)
& belief(P:Pilot, is_adjacent_to(T:Taxiway, S:Startingpoint))
→ performed(P:Pilot, move_from_to(S:Startingpoint, T:Taxiway))
& performed(P:Pilot, set_velocity(A:Aircraft, low))

---

[4] http://www.skybrary.aero/index.php/ATC_Expectation_Bias

4.3.4   Transfer

Finally, transfer properties represent correct transfer of information. For instance, EP3 states that information that is communicated from agent A to agent B is also received as such by agent B (of by the pilot of agent B, if agent B is an aircraft).

EP3 - Communication Transfer
communicate_from_to(A:Agent, B:Agent, I:Action, R:Roadway)
& is_pilot_of(P:Pilot, B:Aircraft)
→ incoming_communication(P:Pilot, I:Action, R:Roadway)

To enhance readability, only a number of the executable properties per category have been listed. However, the full specification (using the notation of the LEADSTO simulation tool) can be found at http://www.cs.vu.nl/~tbosse/aviation.

5   Simulation Results

This section describes simulation results of the case study across three different scenarios. The first scenario represents the real situation as described in Sect. 3, and the other two scenarios simulate two hypothetical situations that would occur when the perceptions and the actions of the agents involved would slightly differ from the real case. These hypothetical situations were created by making small changes in some of the relevant parameters.

In the simulation traces depicted in Figs. 3, 4, 5, again a time line is represented on the horizontal axis and the states that hold in the world are represented on the vertical axis. For the sake of transparency, the atoms that represent *observations* and *beliefs* of the agents are not depicted in the traces.

5.1   Scenario 1: Intervention of Tower

The simulation trace of scenario 1 is shown in Fig. 3. This scenario simulates the real events of the case study. It represents the situation that the pilot of the Hercules aircraft misinterprets the information that is communicated to him by controllers in the Tower because of an incorrect expectation (see atom expectation(hercules_pilot, start_take_off) at the top of the trace that is true during the whole simulation), and consequently initiates take-off without take-off clearance (see atom performed(hercules_pilot, take_off_from (run-way_36)) that is true from time point 15–21).

There is no atom that states that take-off clearance from the Tower is communicated to the Hercules. At the same time, the clearance for take-off is given to the Airbus aircraft that almost simultaneously initiates take-off from the crossing runway at time point 20; see atom performed(airbus_pilot, take_off_from(runway_03)). Luckily, the Tower observes the conflict situation (this atom is not depicted in the trace) and communicates a "STOP" signal to the Airbus at time point 24. As a result, the pilot of the Airbus aborts the take-off at time point 27 and a severe collision is prevented by this action. As can be seen this scenario is almost identical (with the exception of some minor differences in terminology and timing) to the empirical trace shown in Fig. 2.

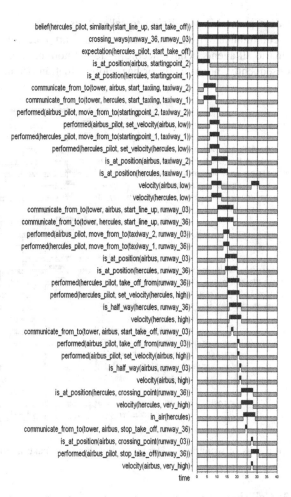

Fig. 3. Simulation results of scenario 1 - intervention of tower prevents severe collision.

Hence, it is an example of a case when a hazardous situation created by the wrong decision and action of one agent can be corrected by appropriate intervention of other agents.

5.2 Scenario 2: Nominal Behaviour

The simulation trace of scenario 2 is shown in Fig. 4. This trace represents an ideal scenario where all agents behave properly. In the initial settings of this hypothetical scenario the pilot of the Hercules has no erroneous expectation about the take-off clearance as in scenario 1. As a result, he performs line-up correctly and does not initiate any take-off, as shown in Fig. 4. After both aircraft have performed line-up on their runways at time point 14, permission to take off is communicated only to the Airbus (see atom communicate_from_to(tower, air-bus, start_take_off, runway_03))). Hence, in this scenario all agents behave according to the nominal prescriptions of the agent system. Consequently, no collision or hazardous situation occurs.

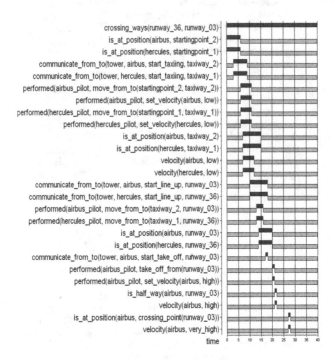

Fig. 4. Simulation results of scenario 2 - Hercules pilot does not make interpretation error.

5.3   Scenario 3: Collision

The simulation of scenario 3 is shown in Fig. 5. This scenario represents a situation when the pilot of the Hercules aircraft has erroneous expectations about the take-off clearance and initiates take-off while he should not (like in scenario 1). However, in this case the controllers in the Tower observe the conflict situation rather late, and therefore they do not have the time to interfere. As a result, both aircraft collide; see atom collision(hercules, airbus) at the end of the trace.

In this scenario the time parameters of the rule that generates the action to take off have been modified in such a way that this action is performed more quickly. This has important consequences for the opportunity of the Tower to interfere and prevent the collision. As can be seen in Fig. 5, the short duration of the take-off procedure leads to severe consequences as both aircraft perform take-off almost simultaneously on crossing runways.

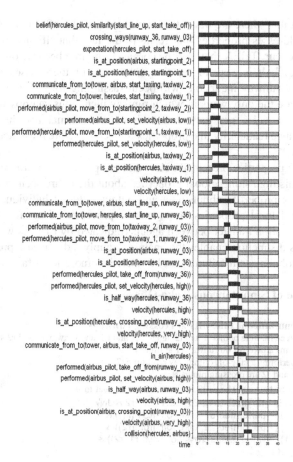

Fig. 5. Simulation results of scenario 3 - interpretation error by Hercules results in severe collision.

6 Formal Analysis

This section addresses formal analysis of the simulated traces. Section 6.1 addresses specification of (global) dynamic properties, Sect. 6.2 address specification of interlevel relations between dynamic properties at different aggregation levels, and Sect. 6.3 discusses some results of verification of properties against empirical and simulated traces.

6.1 Global Dynamic Properties

Various dynamic properties for the aviation domain have been formalized in TTL, a number of which are introduced below. All of these properties are related in some way to the occurrence of collisions. More specifically, Sect. 6.1.1 addresses properties that relate to the fact that 'there are never two simultaneous take-offs at crossing runways'. Section 6.1.2 addresses properties that relate to the fact that 'IF any of such simultaneous take-offs occur, THEN they will be corrected on time because one of the aircraft aborts its take-off'. It is easy to see that either one of these cases is sufficient to guarantee that no runway incursions will occur (assuming for simplicity that simultaneous take-offs are the only ways in which runway incursions can possibly occur). All properties in Sect. 6.1.1 are presented both in semi-formal and in formal (TTL) notation; to enhance readability, the properties in Sect. 6.1.2 are presented only in semi-formal notation.

Note that the properties presented below address processes at different aggregation levels, thereby distinguishing global properties about the entire scenario (indicated by GP), intermediate properties about input and output states of individual agents (indicated by IP), and local properties about mental processes of agents or about information/communication transfer between agents (indicated by LP). As will be explained in Sect. 6.3, this distinction enables the analyst to apply a diagnostic process in which the causes of global system failures can be related to more local fault and errors.

6.1.1   Absence of Simultaneous Take-Offs

GP1 - No simultaneous take-offs at crossing runways
There are no trace m, time points t1 and t2, agents a1 and a2, and runway r1 and r2 such that
agent a1 performs a take-off on runway r1 at time t1
and agent a2 performs a take-off on runway r2 at time t2
and runway r1 and r2 are crossing runways
and the difference between t1 and t2 is smaller than or equal to d[5].

$\neg$ [∃m:TRACE ∃t1,t2:TIME ∃a1,a2:AGENT ∃r1,r2:RUNWAY
   state(m, t1) |= performed(a1, take_off_from(r1)) &
   state(m, t2) |= performed(a2, take_off_from(r2)) &
   state(m, t1) |= world_state(crossing_ways(r1, r2)) &
   | t1 - t2 | ≤ d]

IP1 - No simultaneous permissions to take off at crossing runways
There are no trace m, time points t1 and t2, agents a1 and a2, and runway r1 and r2 such that
the tower gives agent a1 permission for take-off on runway r1 at time t1
the tower gives agent a2 permission for take-off on runway r2 at time t2
and runway r1 and r2 are crossing runways
and the difference between t1 and t2 is smaller than or equal to d.

$\neg$ [∃m:TRACE ∃t1,t2:TIME ∃a1,a2:AGENT ∃r1,r2:RUNWAY
   state(m, t1) |= communicate_from_to(tower, a1, start_take_off(r1)) &
   state(m, t2) |= communicate_from_to(tower, a2, start_take_off(r2)) &
   state(m, t1) |= world_state(crossing_ways(r1, r2)) &
   | t1 - t2 | ≤ d]

---

[5] Many of the properties given in this section contain some parameters d and e. These should be seen as constants, of which the value can be filled in by the modeller.

IP2 - Each take-off is preceded by a corresponding permission
For all traces m, time points t1, agents a, and runways r
if agent a performs a take-off on runway r at time t
then there was a time point t2 with t1-d ≤ t2 ≤ t1 on which
the tower gave agent a permission for take-off on runway r.

∀m:TRACE ∀t:TIME ∀a:AGENT ∀r:RUNWAY
state(m, t1) |= performed(a, take_off_from(r)) ⇒
[∃t2:TIME state(m, t2) |= communicate_from_to(tower, a, start_take_off(r)) &
t1-d ≤ t2 ≤ t1]

LP1 - Each take-off is preceded by a corresponding belief
For all traces m, time points t1, agents a, and runways r
if agent a performs a take-off on runway r at time t
then there was a time point t2 with t1-d ≤ t2 ≤ t1 on which
agent a believed that it had permission for take-off on runway r.

∀m:TRACE ∀t:TIME ∀a:AGENT ∀r:RUNWAY
state(m, t1) |= performed(a, take_off_from(r)) ⇒
[∃t2:TIME state(m, t2) |= belief(a, start_take_off(r)) &
t1-d ≤ t2 ≤ t1]

LP2 - Each belief about permissions is preceded by a corresponding communication
For all traces m, time points t1, agents a, and runways r
if agent a believes that it has permission for take-off on runway r at time t
then there was a time point t2 with t1-d ≤ t2 ≤ t1 on which
the tower gave agent a permission for take-off on runway r.

∀m:TRACE ∀t:TIME ∀a:AGENT ∀r:RUNWAY
state(m, t1) |= belief(a, start_take_off(r)) ⇒
[∃t2:TIME state(m, t2) |= communicate_from_to(tower, a, start_take_off(r)) &
t1-d ≤ t2 ≤ t1]

6.1.2   Correction of Simultaneous Take-Offs

GP2 - All simultaneous take-offs are corrected on time
For all traces m, time points t1 and t2, agents a1 and a2, and runways r1 and r2,
if agent a1 performs a take-off on runway r1 at time t1
and agent a2 performs a take-off on runway r2 at time t2
and runway r1 and r2 are crossing runways
and the difference between t1 and t2 is smaller than or equal to d
then there is a time point t3 with t1 ≤ t3 ≤ t1+e and t2 ≤ t3 ≤ t2+e on which either agent a1 or agent a2
aborts take-off.

IP3 – For all simultaneous take-offs that are observed an abort request is communicated
For all traces m, time points t1 and t2, agents a1 and a2, and runways r1 and r2,
if at time t1 the tower observes that agent a1 performs a take-off on runway r1
and at time t2 the tower observes that agent a2 performs a take-off on runway r2
and runway r1 and r2 are crossing runways
and the difference between t1 and t2 is smaller than or equal to d
then there is a time point t3 with t1 ≤ t3 ≤ t1+e and t2 ≤ t3 ≤ t2+e on which the tower communicates either
to agent a1 or to agent a2 a request to abort take-off.

IP4 - All received abort requests are followed
For all traces m, time points t1, agents a1 and a2, and runways r1,
if at time t1 agent a1 receives from agent a2 a request to abort take-off from runway r1
then there is a time point t2 with t1 ≤ t2 ≤ t1+d on which agent a1 indeed aborts take-off from r1.

LP3 - All simultaneous take-offs are observed
For all traces m, time points t1 and t2, agents a1 and a2, and runways r1 and r2,
if agent a1 performs a take-off on runway r1 at time t1
and agent a2 performs a take-off on runway r2 at time t2
and runway r1 and r2 are crossing runways
and the difference between t1 and t2 is smaller than or equal to d
then there are two time points t3 and t4 with t1 ≤ t3 ≤ t1+e and t2 ≤ t4 ≤ t2+e on which the tower observes both take-offs.

LP4 - All communicated abort requests are received
For all traces m, time points t1, agents a1 and a2, and runways r1,
if at time t1 agent a1 communicates to agent a2 a request to abort take-off from runway r1
then there is a time point t2 with t1 ≤ t2 ≤ t1+d on which this request is received from a1 by 2.

LP5 - All observed take-offs are converted into corresponding beliefs
For all traces m, time points t1, agents a1, and runways r1,
if at time t1 the tower observes that agent a1 performs a take-off on runway r1
then there is a time point t2 with t1 ≤ t2 ≤ t1+d on which the tower believes that agent a1 performs a take-off on runway r1.

LP6 – For all beliefs on simultaneous take-offs an abort request is communicated
For all traces m, time points t1 and t2, agents a1 and a2, and runways r1 and r2,
if at time t1 the tower believes that agent a1 performs a take-off on runway r1
and at time t2 the tower believes that agent a2 performs a take-off on runway r2
and runway r1 and r2 are crossing runways
and the difference between t1 and t2 is smaller than or equal to d
then there is a time point t3 with t1 ≤ t3 ≤ t1+e and t2 ≤ t3 ≤ t2+e on which the tower communicates either to agent a1 or to agent a2 a request to abort take-off.

LP7 - All received requests are converted into corresponding beliefs
For all traces m, time points t1, agents a1 and a2, and runways r1,
if at time t1 agent a1 receives from agent a2 a request to abort take-off from runway r1
then there is a time point t2 with t1 ≤ t2 ≤ t1+d on which agent a1 believes that it should abort take-off from r1.

LP8 - All believed requests are followed
For all traces m, time points t1, agents a1, and runways r1,
if at time t1 agent a1 believes that it should abort take-off from runway r1
then there is a time point t2 with t1 ≤ t2 ≤ t1+d on which agent a1 indeed aborts take-off from r1.

6.2   Interlevel Relations

A number of logical relationships have been identified between properties at different aggregation levels. An overview of all identified logical relationships relevant for GP1 is depicted as an AND-tree in Fig. 6.

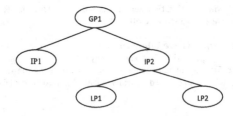

Fig. 6. AND-tree of interlevel relations between dynamic properties related to GP1.

The relationships depicted in this figure should be interpreted as semantic entailment relationships. For example, the relationship at the highest level expresses that the implication IP1 & IP2 => GP1 holds, whereas the relationship at the lower level expresses that LP1 & LP2 => IP2 holds. A sketch of the proof for the first implication is as follows (for simplicity reasons abstracting from time constrains):

> Suppose that IP1 and IP2 hold. Then, according to IP1, no two permissions to take off at crossing runways will be communicated simultaneously. Moreover, since take-offs are only performed immediately after a corresponding permission has been communicated (as guaranteed by IP2), no simultaneous take-offs are performed at crossing runways. This confirms GP1.

Such logical relationships between dynamic properties can be very useful in the analysis of (both simulated as well as empirical) scenarios, especially when used in combination with the TTL Checker Tool mentioned earlier. For example, for the empirical trace 1, checking GP1 pointed out that this property was not satisfied. As a result, by a refutation process (following the tree in Fig. 6 top-down) it could be concluded that either IP1 or IP2 failed (or a combination of them). When, after further checking, IP2 was found to be the cause of the failure, the analysis could proceed by focusing on LP1 and LP2. Eventually, LP1 was found satisfied, whereas LP2 failed. Thus, (part of) the source of the incident could be reduced to failure of LP2, i.e., there was an agent (namely the pilot of the Hercules) that believed to have the permission to take off, whilst this was not communicated by the tower. A discussion with our domain expert confirmed that this was indeed the case. One level deeper, such local properties can even be related to executable properties. For instance, the failure of LP2 can be explained because the Hercules pilot applied property EP5. A full connection of local properties to executable properties is beyond the scope of this paper, but a detailed discussion can be found in [10].

Similar to Fig. 6, an AND-tree representing all identified logical relationships relevant for GP2 is shown in Fig. 7.

Note that the example scenario provided here is mainly meant as an illustration of the approach. In addition to this relatively simple case, similar trees of interlevel relations are being constructed that involve more properties at multiple levels. For such more complex cases, the diagnostic process is economic in the sense that, when a certain property holds, the entire subtree under this property does not have to be examined.

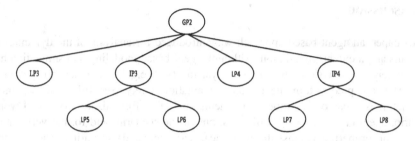

Fig. 7. AND-tree of interlevel relations between dynamic properties related to GP2.

6.3   Checking Results

Using the TTL Checker, all dynamic properties introduced in Sect. 6.1 have been checked against the three simulation traces discussed in Sect. 5 as well as the empirical trace discussed in Sect. 4.2. The results of these checks are shown in Table 3 (where 'X' denotes 'satisfied'). As can be seen from the table, scenario 2 is indeed a nominal case in which all expected properties hold. In contrast, in scenario 1, two simultaneous take-offs at crossing runways occur (since GP1 fails), which can eventually be related to an incorrectly derived belief of permission for take-off (failure of LP2). However, since the situation is corrected on time (GP2 succeeds), no collision occurs in this scenario. In scenario 3, GP1 also fails, but in addition GP2 fails, which can be related partly to failure of LP3 (the simultaneous take-offs are observed, but too late) and to failure of LP6 (once the tower believes that there are simultaneous take-offs, it is too late to communicate an abort request). As a result, the collision is not prevented. As can be seen, the same system properties failed for the empirical trace as for scenario 1, which makes sense because these scenarios are identical.

Table 3. Checking dynamic properties against (simulated and empirical) traces.

Property	Scenario 1	Scenario 2	Scenario 3	Empirical
GP1	–	X	–	–
IP1	X	X	X	X
IP2	–	X	–	–
LP1	X	X	X	X
LP2	–	X	–	–
GP2	X	X	–	X
IP3	X	X	–	X
IP4	X	X	X	X
LP3	X	X	+/–	X
LP4	X	X	X	X
LP5	X	X	X	X
LP6	X	X	–	X
LP7	X	X	X	X
LP8	X	X	X	X

7   Discussion

In this paper, an agent-based approach was introduced for analysis of the dynamics of accidents and incidents in aviation. Although agent-based modeling and simulation has been widely applied to study complex systems (see, e.g. [8]), it has not yet been commonly accepted within the domain of aviation safety (see [6]). The presented approach makes use of a number of elements, including formalization of a real world scenario, agent-based simulation of variations of the scenario, and formal verification of dynamic properties against the (empirical and simulated) scenarios. The scenario formalization part enables incident reconstruction and formal analysis of it. The simulation part enables the analyst to explore various hypothetical scenarios under different circumstances, with an emphasis on error related to human factors. The formal verification part enables the analyst to identify scenarios involving potential hazards, and to relate those hazards (via interlevel relations) to inadequate behavior on the level of individual agents. The approach was illustrated by means of a case study on a runway incursion incident.

To obtain information about this incident, an interview with a domain expert was conducted. In the current paper, this interview was used as the only source of information to construct the formal ontology and the traces. Nevertheless, for more complex case studies it may be interesting to consider more extensive knowledge elicitation techniques, involving a larger number of experts. Some example case studies in which such techniques were applied in the aviation domain are reported in [5] and [9].

The approach introduced in the current paper in principle addressed both *retrospective* and *prospective* analysis of scenarios. In particular, the possibility to check properties against formalized empirical traces is an adequate way to analyze past scenarios. This has been illustrated by the analysis of the empirical trace shown in Sect. 4.2, which was a formalization of a real world scenario. In contrast, the possibility to run simulations and to check properties against the simulated traces enables analysts to study future scenarios as well. This has been illustrated by the analysis of the simulation traces in Sect. 5, most of which addressed hypothetical future scenarios. Nevertheless, one should keep in mind that the scope of the prospective analysis is restricted to those elements that are part of the formal ontology.

For a more quantitative type of agent-based dynamic risk analysis, often Monte Carlo methods are applied; see e.g. the work of Blom et al. [1] or Stroeve, Blom and Bakker [14]. These methods are very useful for quantitative collision risk estimations, but one of their disadvantages is lack of transparency due to the complex stochastic relations between the elements of the agent-based models that are used. In contrast, the approach presented in this paper is highly transparent; it provides a visible trace of risk related events that can be analyzed manually or automatically with the help of special tools. Moreover, the roles of the agents involved in risk creation and reduction (as well as their underlying cognitive processes, like the influence of biased reasoning) are clear from the trace, while in dynamic quantitative risk models used for Monte Carlo simulations this is usually not the case. The complexity of Monte Carlo methods makes it also difficult for the non-specialist to understand the implications of actions and thus makes a public debate of issues a problem. However, a disadvantage of the method proposed in this paper is that it cannot provide a precise risk estimation as is provided by Monte Carlo methods. In follow-up research, we therefore intend to explore the possibilities to combine our approach with elements from Monte Carlo methods.

Another promising direction for future work would be to automate more steps in the analysis method. For example, the ontology developed in step 1 of the methodology could make use of standard templates for common agent-based concepts, such that it does not have to be designed by hand for any new domain. Similarly, templates for dynamic properties could be developed, as well as computer-supported techniques to automate parts of step 4 (e.g., systematically generating large numbers of simulation runs) and step 7 (e.g., systematically checking multiple properties against large sets of traces).

As mentioned earlier, agent-based modeling and simulation has been widely applied outside the aviation domain, and the state-of-the-art in this area is extensive. A comparison with other (agent-based) dynamic modeling approaches is therefore outside the scope of this article; for this purpose, the interested reader is referred to [2, 3].

Acknowledgements. This work was performed under the auspices of the SESAR WP-E research network ComplexWorld. It is co-financed by Eurocontrol on behalf of the SESAR Joint Undertaking. The authors are grateful to the retired airline pilot who participated in the interview for his useful input on the case study, and to Jan Treur for a number of fruitful discussions.

References

1. Blom, H.A.P., Bakker, G.J., Blanker, P.J.G., Daams, J., Everdij, M.H.C., Klompstra, M.B.: Accident risk assessment for advanced air traffic management. In: Donohue, G.L., Zellweger, A.G. (eds.) Air Transport Systems Engineering, pp. 463–480. AIAA, Washington, D.C. (2001)
2. Bosse, T., Jonker, C.M., van der Meij, L., Sharpanskykh, A., Treur, J.: Specification and verification of dynamics in agent models. Int. J. Coop. Inf. Syst. **18**(1), 167–193 (2009)
3. Bosse, T., Jonker, C.M., van der Meij, L., Treur, J.: A language and environment for analysis of dynamics by simulation. Int. J. Artif. Intell. Tools **16**(3), 435–464 (2007)
4. Bosse, T., Mogles, N.M.: Formal analysis of aviation incidents. In: Jiang, H., Ding, W., Ali, M., Wu, X. (eds.) IEA/AIE 2012. LNCS, vol. 7345, pp. 371–380. Springer, Heidelberg (2012)
5. Bosse, T., Treur, J., Mogles, N.M., Stroeve, S.H., Blom, H.A.P., Sharpanskykh, A.: Model constructs validation. SESAR Joint Undertaking. Technical report E.02.10-MAREA-D3.1 (2013)
6. Everdij, M.H.C.: Review of techniques to support the EATMP safety assessment methodology. Report for EEC Safety Methods Survey Project, volume I and II (2004)
7. Hollnagel, E.: Barriers and Accident Prevention. Ashgate, Aldershot (2004)
8. Jennings, N.R.: On agent-based software engineering. Artif. Intell. **117**, 277–296 (2000)
9. de Jong, H.H., Blom, H.A.P., Stroeve, S.H.: How to identify unimaginable hazards? In: 25th International System Safety Conference (ISSC 2007), Baltimore, USA (2007)
10. Jonker, C., Treur, J.: Compositional verification of multi-agent systems: a formal analysis of pro-activeness and reactiveness. Int. J. Coop. Inf. Syst. **11**, 51–92 (2002)
11. Leveson, N.: A new accident model for engineering safer systems. Saf. Sci. **42**, 237–270 (2004)
12. Nickerson, R.S.: Confirmation bias: a ubiquitous phenomenon in many guises. Rev. Gen. Psychol. **2**(2), 175–220 (1998)
13. Rao, A.S., Georgeff, M.P.: BDI-agents: from theory to practice. In: Lesser, V. (ed.) Proceedings of the International Conference on Multiagent Systems, pp. 312–319 (1995)
14. Stroeve, S.H., Blom, H.A.P., Bakker, G.J.: Systemic accident risk assessment in air traffic by Monte Carlo simulation. Saf. Sci. **47**, 238–449 (2009)
15. Wooldridge, M.: Agent-based software engineering. IEE Proc. Softw. Eng. **144**(1), 26–37 (1997)

Inference of Markov Chain Models by Using k-Testable Language: Application on Aging People

Catherine Combes[1]([⊠]) and Jean Azema[2]

[1] University of Lyon, Hubert CURIEN Laboratory,
UMR CNRS 5516, University of Jean Monnet, 18 rue Benoît Lauras,
42023 Saint-Etienne Cedex 2, France
combes@univ-st-etienne.fr
[2] University of Jean Monnet, 23 avenue du Docteur Paul Michelon,
42023 Saint-Etienne Cedex 2, France
azema@univ-st-etienne.fr

Abstract. We investigate the contribution of unsupervised learning and regular grammatical inference to respectively identify profiles of elderly people and their development over time in order to evaluate care needs (human, financial and physical resources). Grammatical Inference (also known as automata induction, grammar induction and automatic language acquisition) allows grammar and language learning from data. Machine learning by using grammar has a variety of applications: pattern recognition, adaptive intelligent agents, diagnosis, biology, systems modelling, prediction, natural language acquisition, data mining... The proposed approach is based on regular grammar. An adaptation of k-Testable Languages in the Strict Sense Inference algorithm is proposed in order to infer a probabilistic automaton from which a Markovian model which has a discrete (finite or countable) state-space has been deduced. In simulating the corresponding Markov chain model, it is possible to obtain information on population ageing. We have verified if our observed system conforms to a unique long term state vector, called the stationary distribution and the steady-state.

Keywords: Grammar inference · k-Testable language in strict sense · Probabilistic deterministic finite automata · Timed-transition systems · Evolution of elderly people disability

1 Introduction

Demographic shifts in the population and the fact that people are living longer have created an awareness that the health care system is and will be increasingly difficult to control, organize and finance especially where the ageing population are concerned. The senior citizen population is increasing along with the diversity of their health backgrounds and medico-social needs which cannot be provided easily because of health aspects, social conventions and lifestyles that are intertwined with the ageing process. Long-term care is a variety of services that includes medical and non-medical

© Springer-Verlag Berlin Heidelberg 2014
N.T. Nguyen (Ed.): TCCI XVII 2014, LNCS 8790, pp. 89–106, 2014.
DOI: 10.1007/978-3-662-44994-3_5

care to people who have a chronic illness or disability. This illness or disability could include a problem with memory loss, confusion, or disorientation. This is called cognitive impairment and can result from conditions such as Alzheimer's disease [15]. Care needs often progress as age or as chronic illness or as disability progresses. Long-term care helps meet health or personal needs. Most long-term care is to assist people with support services such as activities of daily living like dressing, bathing, and using the toilet. Approximately 70 % of individuals over the age of 65 will require at least some type of long-term care services during their lifetime. Over 40 % will need care in a nursing home for some period of time. Nursing homes provide long-term care to people who need more extensive care, particularly those whose needs include nursing care or 24-hour supervision in addition to their personal care needs. We focus our interest on nursing homes.

This presentation is split up into eight sections. After an introduction describing the scope of the study, the study context is presented in Sect. 2. The characteristics of the collected data are described in Sect. 3. The profiles of residents obtained by using cluster analysis are presented in Sect. 4. A brief review of previous works is presented in Sect. 5. Section 6 deals with the techniques used (regular probabilistic grammar inference) to model the automaton symbolizing the changing profiles and their development over time. Starting from this automaton, a Markov model is deduced. Thereby, it is possible to verify if our system is achieving a steady state. Section 7 presents the results obtained concerning the four medical nursing homes (called Bernadette, Soleil, Les Myosotis, Val Dorlay situated in France) and dementia. We conclude with some future works.

2 Study Context

This project is being carried out in close collaboration with a French mutual benefit organization called "Mutualité Française de la Loire" which manages several nursing homes.

To fully explore the opportunities for our approach, we propose a modelling environment. This allows one to manage the resources, to elaborate medico-social resource planning and to simulate them in order to evaluate the performance of each of them (Fig. 1).

The Decisional Information System is crucial in the methodological framework. The objective is to design an environment for decision aid-tools dedicated to health-care and social services professionals for strategic and tactical decisions such that:

− Which activity should be developed, and at what cost?
− Whether or not to open additional facilities - and if so which ones?
− etc.

The aim is to provide a certain standard of care to dependent old people in nursing homes, through the sharing of resources (staff, finance and equipment) thanks to all the key indicators (via the managers' choices).

The methodological framework is described in Fig. 2.

So, in order to do this, we have to identify different senior citizen profiles as well as the length of stay according to these profiles and to study their development over time. The collected data comes from administrative data, previous medical history, etc.

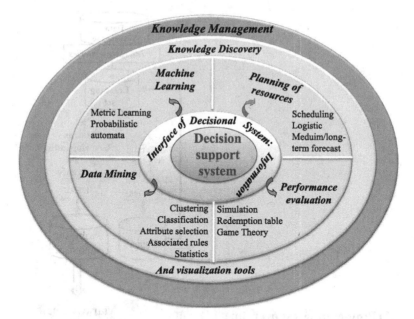

Fig. 1. Modelling environment

We evaluate the workload in function of the profile of each elderly person in the nursing home. Based on nursing home pricing (for accommodation and care in function of the degree of dependence...), we can verify that:

- the budget will not be exceeded,
- we have enough staff to carry out the workload.

Simulations are used to forecast population ageing. So we can identify the workload in the short-term, medium-term and long-term and estimate the resources needed. From the potential elderly people needs, we can also evaluate which profiles should be accepted to ensure that both quality and safety criteria are respected from a workload and financial point of view.

In this article, we will present the study of the progression over time of elderly people autonomy-disability. The steps of the project consist in:

1. The specification of elderly people profiles by using unsupervised learning approach [9],
2. The study of the development of these profiles over time by using a probabilistic graph of transitions between the clusters inferred by k-TSSI (k-Testable Languages in the Strict Sense Inference) algorithm. The objective is to deduce Markov process which has a discrete (finite or countable) state-space.
3. Discrete-time Markov chain simulation is used to forecast population ageing. It allows to identify the elderly people care needs and the workload in short-term, medium-term and long-term and to predict the future costs. An application is presented in [8].

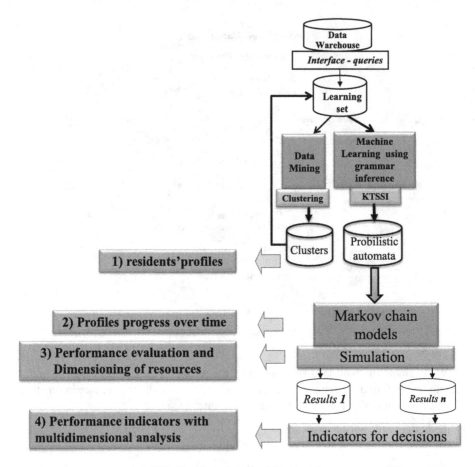

Fig. 2. Methodological framework

3   Data Collected

The quantitative data arises from the databases and the corresponding information system deals with the evaluation of autonomy/disability of elderly people. Dependence evaluation in France is carried out using a specific national grid called AGGIR: Autonomy-Gerontology-Group-Iso-Resources. The quantitative data concerns 628 residents and more than 2,200 observations of independence evaluations. The evaluations are made by the resident doctor in collaboration with the medical staff. An item can be evaluated using the four adverbs (see Fig. 3):

- Spontaneously corresponding to the letter S,
- Entirely corresponding to the letter E,
- Correctly corresponding to the letter C,
- Usually corresponding to the letter U.

The codification is the following. If all four adverbs are marked, the code is *C*. If less than four adverbs are checked (three or two or one), the code is **B**. If no adverb is checked, the code is *A*.

The proposed algorithm uses numerical data. So, the corresponding values are:

– 0 for code *A* meaning the person can do it alone,
– 1 for code *B* meaning the person can partially do it,
– 2 for code *C* meaning the person cannot do it alone.

The first step is to analyze the degree of autonomy-disability in order to identify clusters.

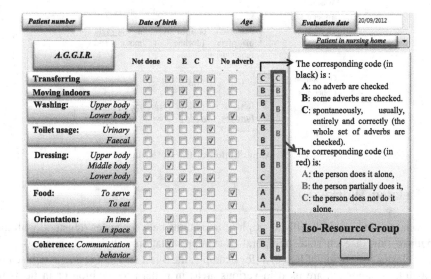

Fig. 3. A.G.G.I.R. grid

4   Identification of Residents' Profiles

The aim is to find feature-patterns related to the autonomy-disability level of elderly people living in nursing homes. These levels correspond to profiles based on the people's ability to perform activities of daily living like being able to wash, dress and move. To achieve this aim, an unsupervised learning approach is proposed [9]. It is based on principal component analysis technique to direct the determination of the clusters with self-organizing partitions. Cluster analysis is made on the 8 variables: Transferring to or from bed or chair, Moving indoors, Washing, Toilet, Dressing, Food, Orientation, Coherence. The cluster analysis identifies two kinds of patterns (see Fig. 4):

– The decline in executive functions regarding to motor and functional abilities called apraxia disorders,
– The cognitive impairment and neuropsychological deficits.

By combining clustering with a machine learning process, we could be able to predict the development of physical autonomy loss or mental autonomy loss in elderly people over time. To reach this objective, we use machine learning approach based on grammar inference in order to infer a probabilistic automaton. In the article, we only present the patients' profiles evolution regarding to upper body functional disorders (cognitive impairment).

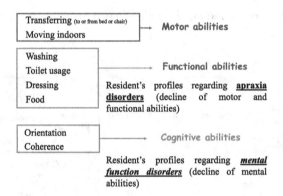

Fig. 4. Contribution of the clustering

5   Related Works

We want to obtain a probabilistic graph of transitions between states (clusters) with the length-of-stay in each state (temporal state representations). It is also interesting to study cluster succession of length k (for example, the 3 last states of resident's clusters). Probabilistic automata are used in various areas in pattern recognition or in fields to which pattern recognition is linked. Different concept learning algorithms have been developed for different types of concepts.

We are interested by the class of regular grammars that are the simplest class of formal grammars in the Chomsky hierarchy and it consists in the identification of the corresponding learning of deterministic finite automata (DFA).

The learning of DFA, also called regular inference is based on acceptance of regular languages which allow to model the behaviour of systems. The aim consists in constructing a DFA from information about the set of words it accepts. There are many algorithms for learning DFAs, the most well-known being the algorithm due to Dana Angluin [4, 5]. There are many approaches for regular inference [6, 7, 11, 16, 17, 19]. For more information, the book [14] presents an overview on learning automata and grammar inference.

A finite automaton with transition probabilities represents a distribution over the set of all strings defined over a finite alphabet. The articles [18, 24] present a survey and a study of the relations and properties of probabilistic finite-automata and tree. The article [10] clarifies the links between probabilistic automata and Hidden Markov Models (HMM). In a first part of this work, the authors present:

- the probabilities distributions generated by these models,
- the necessary and sufficient conditions for an automaton to define a probabilistic language.

The authors show that one the one hand, probabilistic deterministic finite automata (PDFA) form a proper subclass of probabilistic non-deterministic automata (PNFA) and the other hand, PNFA and HMM are equivalent.

However, there are almost no extensions of these algorithms to the setting of timed systems. A variant of a DFA including the notion of time is called Timed Automaton (TA). These models are based on the fact that each symbol of a word occurs at a certain point in time. TA can see that an automaton that generates strings with event-time value pairs called timed strings. Very few works exist in the domain [1–3, 13, 20, 21]. Timed automata correspond to finite state models where explicit notion of time is taken into account and is represented by timed events. Time can be modelled in different ways, e.g. discrete or continuous. The more recent works [22, 23] propose an algorithm for learning simple timed automata, known as Deterministic Real-Time Automata (DRTA) where the transitions of real-time automata can have a temporal constraint on the time of occurrence of the current symbol relative to the previous symbol. The main drawback of such approaches is that it can result in an exponential blow-up of both the input data and the resulting size of the model and the obtained models are quite difficult to interpret.

The main objective of the study is the ability to analyze an identified model in identifying automaton models from observations. We want to take an established method to learn a DFA and apply it to our timed sequences. Our problem could be modelled as a timed-state transition graph, a probabilistic deterministic finite automaton (PDFA) taking into account timed-event. We also have a set of positive timed-strings (or time-stamped event sequences).

From a set of labelled (positive only) time stamped event sequences, the problem to solve is to find the automaton model that most likely produce the data. We do not want to learn (identify) a DRTA such that [22], with time constraints because we do not exactly have the same problematic of real-time system. We only have timed-strings from which we propose to automatically deduce a Markov chain model.

The k-TSSI (k-Testable Languages in the Strict Sense Inference) algorithm [11, 12] could be useful, convenient and suitable for two reasons: the simplicity of implementation and the possibility to take into account memory effects (macro-states). The inductive inference of the class of k-testable languages in the strict sense (k-TLSS) has been studied and adapted to local languages, N-grams and tree languages. A k-TLSS is essentially defined by a finite set of substrings of length k that are permitted to appear in the strings of then language. Given a size k of memory, the objective is to find an automaton for the language. This subclass of language called k-testable language has the property that the next character is only dependent on the previous $k-1$ characters. In our case, it is interesting to be able to identify the substrings (memory) of length k.

But, our goal is to infer a timed-system model and an automaton inferred by the k-TSSI algorithm does not take into account the timed strings.

The problem is also that it is difficult to take into account a set of substrings of length $k(k > 1)$ and the algorithm is not generalized to probabilistic timed-automata. In this section we propose a model in order to take into account the concept of time in the automaton inferred by the k-TSSI algorithm (i.e. the duration of time a resident spends in a particular cluster) taking into account timed-transition system. In the next section, we present the implementation of the model.

6   Development of Patients' Profiles: Model Implementation

We present an algorithm for inferring a model of a timed transition system based on the K-Testable Language in Strict Sense (K-TLSS).

The method consists of:

1. Learning a Deterministic Finite Automata (DFA) of timed-transition systems by using an extension of k-TSSI algorithm.
2. Transforming this DFA into a probabilistic DFA.
3. Converting this probabilistic DFA in a Markov chain model.

6.1   Preliminaries

The aim of grammatical inference is to learn models of languages from sample sentences in these languages. A sentence can be any structured composition of primitive elements or symbols, though the most common type of composition is concatenation. So we infer grammar and the corresponding representation is an automaton.

A finite automaton is a 5-tuple $A = (\mathbf{Q}, \Sigma, \delta, \mathbf{q_0}, \mathbf{F})$ with:

- Σ: a finite input alphabet of symbols,
- $\mathbf{Q}$: a finite set of states with $\mathbf{q_0}$ as start state,
- $\mathbf{F}$: a set of final states $(\mathbf{F} \subseteq \mathbf{Q})$,
- δ: a transition function of $\mathbf{Q} \times \Sigma \to \mathbf{Q}$. So that $q' = \delta(q, \sigma)$ returns a state for current state q and input symbol σ from Σ. Each transition is noted by 3-tuple (q, σ, q').

If for all $q \in \mathbf{Q}$ and for all $\sigma \in \Sigma$, $\delta(q, \sigma)$ corresponds to a unique state of $\mathbf{Q}$, then the automaton is said to be a Deterministic Finite Automaton (DFA). Grammatical inference refers to the process of learning rules from a set of labelled examples. It belongs to a class of inductive inference problems [4] in which the target domain is a formal language (a set of strings generated from some alphabet Σ) and the hypothesis space is a family of grammars. It is also often referred to as automata induction, grammar induction, or automatic language acquisition. The inference process aims at finding a minimum automaton (the canonical automaton) that is compatible with the examples. In regular grammar inference, we have a finite alphabet Σ and a regular language $L \subseteq \Sigma^*$ where:

- Σ^*: the set of all finite length strings generated from Σ,
- L: a sub-set of Σ^* corresponding to the words recognized from the automaton A.

Given a set of examples that are in the language (L_+) and a (possibly empty) set of examples not in the language (L_-), the task is to infer a deterministic finite automaton A that accepts the examples in L_+ and rejects the examples in L_-.

6.2 Automata Induction

The k-TSSI algorithm [11] allows us to infer k-Testable Languages in the Strict Sense. The inductive inference of the class of k-Testable Languages in the Strict Sense is defined by a finite set of substrings of length k that are allowed to appear in the strings of the language. Given a positive sample $I_+ \in L$ of strings of an unknown language, a deterministic finite-state automaton that recognizes the smallest k-TLSS containing I_+ is obtained. An automaton inferred by the k-TSSI algorithm is by its construction, non-ambiguous. Moreover, our choice is justified by the fact that k-testable ($k > 1$) can take into account a memory effect (i.e. N-gram). Indeed, we observed during data analysis that the change in evolution of the autonomy/disability state depends on the previous resident's states and their diseases (especially for chronic and disabling diseases such as osteoarticular degenerative diseases, anxio-depressive disorder, behavioural disorders...). To illustrate our approach and for the sake of simplicity, we will present in this article, the results obtained with 1-TSSL (the next state depends only on the previous states) in order to explain how we turn the timed transitions into sequences (time-series). We choose to divide up the length-of-stay in each cluster (for example, one discrete step $T = 30$ days).

Consequently, the corresponding automaton is a 6-tuple ($Q, \Sigma, \delta, q_0, F, d$) where d corresponds to the length-of-stay in the clusters. At each cluster, we assign a symbol $\sigma \in \Sigma$. Each symbol is represented by a pair (σ_i, d_i), where d_i is the delay on the symbol σ_i which corresponds to an application d: $\Sigma \rightarrow N$ with $d(\sigma_i) = d_i$.

In the following sections, we explain the implementation of the model through an example (on only six residents: 7, 12, 17, 14, 8, 44 corresponding to an excerpt of the collected data).

Setting Up the Alphabet. The assessment of elderly people's autonomy/disability allows us to classify residents into five levels of mental dependence situation (5 to 1 in decreasing order of severity). Figure 5 presents the data collected from the database.

The resident assessment is made on different dates. For example, resident number 7 was evaluated at level 3 (mental disorder) on the 06/24/2002. For all the assessments concerning resident number 7, we can deduce the sequence: *3321111*. But this sequence does not express the amount of time the person spends in each state (level of mental disorder). In this model, each symbol of a word occurs at a certain point in time.

From such observations, we only obtain positive data I_+, and now we have to describe how we can obtain timed strings. The following paragraph present the basic notions explaining how we take into account timed-transitions between clusters.

Preliminary Mapping of the Set of Strings. The objective is to obtain a stochastic state transition graph taking into account the length-of-stay in each state. So we have to associate for each occurrence of a symbol (event) in order to model time value. In practice, we use the evaluation date.

The **first step** consists in the definition of the alphabet (the set Σ). The set Σ is based on an alphabet of 6 symbols - {*a, b, c, d, e, f*} which correspond to:

- *a* length-of-stay in cluster number 1 during a given period T (example: 30 days) meaning $d(a) = T$,
- *b* length-of-stay in cluster number 2 during a given period,
- etc. (until the symbol *e* for cluster number 5).

Problem:
How can we analyze the resident's level-score of mental autonomy-disability and identify the development over time?

Objective:
To obtain stochastic state transition graph taking into account the lengh-of-stay in each state (5 to 1).

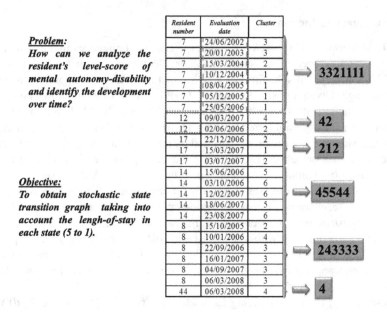

Resident number	Evaluation date	Cluster
7	24/06/2002	3
7	20/01/2003	3
7	15/03/2004	2
7	10/12/2004	1
7	08/04/2005	1
7	05/12/2005	1
7	25/05/2006	1
12	09/03/2007	4
12	02/06/2006	2
17	22/12/2006	2
17	15/03/2007	1
17	03/07/2007	2
14	15/06/2006	5
14	03/10/2006	6
14	12/02/2007	6
14	18/06/2007	5
14	23/08/2007	6
8	15/10/2005	2
8	10/01/2006	4
8	22/09/2006	3
8	16/01/2007	3
8	04/09/2007	3
8	06/03/2008	3
44	06/03/2008	4

3321111

42

212

45544

243333

4

Fig. 5. Data and sequencing

The symbol *f* models the fact that a resident can leave the nursing home or corresponds to the last resident assessment during the last 30 days before the data extraction. It is only used when we want to deduce the Markov model. Consequently, in the following example, the symbol *f* does not exist in Fig. 6.

The **second step** concerns the identification of the words which corresponds to the translation of the initial sequence in order to take into account length of time spent in each cluster. Resident number **7** stayed in cluster number **3** from **06/24/2002 to 03/15/2004** (date at which the resident was evaluated and changed to cluster number 2). Thus resident number **7** stayed in cluster number **3** for about **22 periods** of **30 days**. The symbol modeling cluster number **3** for 30 days is **c**, consequently the initial sequence "**33**" becomes "*cccccccccccccccccccccc*". The resident stayed in cluster number **2** for **9 periods**…

And the corresponding word is:

cccccccccccccccccccccccbbbbbbbbbaaaaaaaaaaaaaaaaaaa

So we obtain the set $I_+ \subseteq \Sigma^*$. I_+ corresponds to the learning set from which the automaton is inferred. The initial set of sequences (Fig. 5)

{*3321111, 42, 212, 56656, 243333, 4*}

becomes:

$I_+ = \{$*cccccccccccccccccccccccbbbbbbbbbaaaaaaaaaaaaaaaaaaa, ddb, bbbbbaaaab, ddddeeeeeeeeddee, bbbddddddddccccccccccccccccc, dd*$\}$

From the set I_+ by using k-TSSI algorithm (to simplify, we present the case corresponding to $k = 1$), we obtain the automaton described in Fig. 6. The algorithm [12]

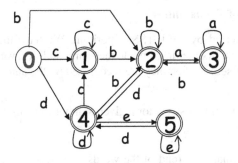

Fig. 6. The automaton inferred by the algorithm k-TSSI with $q_0 = 0$

consists in building the sets $\mathbf{Q}$, $\mathbf{\Sigma}$, $\mathbf{\delta}$, $\mathbf{q_0}$, $\mathbf{F}$ by observation of the corresponding events in the training strings. From these sets, a finite-state automaton that recognizes the associated language is straightforwardly built.

Let I_+ be a positive sample of the regular language L.
Input
$\quad\quad k$ *// substrings of length k*
$\quad\quad I_+ = \{x_1,\ldots,x_{|I_+|}\}$ *//collected sample*
$\quad\quad D=\{(\sigma,\mathrm{d}(\sigma))$ with $\sigma \in \Sigma\}$
Output $A_k = (Q, \Sigma, \delta, q_0, F, \mathrm{d})$ *//the obtained automaton*
Begin
$\quad Q \leftarrow q_0$ *// initial state*
$\quad \Sigma \leftarrow \varnothing, \delta \leftarrow \varnothing, F \leftarrow \varnothing$
$\quad q_0 \leftarrow \lambda$ *// λ corresponds to an empty string*
For $i=1$ **until** $|I_+|$ *// for all words x_i in I_+*
$\quad\quad q' \leftarrow q_0$
$\quad\quad$ **For** $j=1$ **until** $|x_i|$ *//For all symbol x_{ij} of the word $x_i \in I_+$*
$\quad\quad\quad \Sigma \leftarrow \Sigma \cup \{x_{ij}\}$ *// to add a symbol x_{ij} to the alphabet*
$\quad\quad\quad y \leftarrow q' x_{ij}$ *// to build the substrings of length $\leq k$ regarding the*
$\quad\quad\quad\quad\quad\quad\quad\quad\quad\quad\quad\quad$ *word x_i*
$\quad\quad\quad$ **If** $|y| > k$ **then**
$\quad\quad\quad y \leftarrow y_{2\ldots}, y_{|y|}$ *// the length of the substring must be equal to k.*
$\quad\quad\quad\quad\quad\quad\quad\quad\quad\quad$ *// =>Shift of one symbol*
$\quad\quad\quad$ **EndIf**
$\quad\quad\quad q \leftarrow y$ *//the state representing the substring*
$\quad\quad\quad Q \leftarrow Q \cup \{q\}$ *//to add this state*
$\quad\quad\quad \delta \leftarrow \delta \cup \{(q',x_{ij},q)\}$ *//to add the transition*
$\quad\quad\quad$ **If** $j = |x_i|$ **Then**   *// at the end of the word*
$\quad\quad\quad\quad F \leftarrow F \cup \{q\}$ *// the state is final*
$\quad\quad\quad$ **EndIf**
$\quad\quad\quad q' \leftarrow q$ *// progression on the state in order to process the next*
$\quad\quad\quad\quad\quad\quad\quad\quad\quad\quad\quad\quad$ *symbol*
$\quad\quad$ **EndFor**
$\quad$ **EndFor**
$\quad$ **Return** A_k
End k-TSSI

6.3 Computation of Probabilities

The automaton is inferred by the k-TSSI algorithm. We have to associate transition probabilities with states. In order to compute these probabilities, we use the learning set I_+. From the words of set I_+, when they are recognized by the automaton inferred by k-TSSI, we count:

– The transition between two states for a given symbol (transition from the state q by the symbol σ): $cp_{\delta(q,\sigma)}$,
– each transition in a state q: cp_q,
– if a state q is the final state (end of the words): cp_{q_final}.

For the algorithm, we use the three epochs-counts in order to estimate the probabilities. The algorithm computing the probabilities from a learning set is the following.

```
Input   I+ = {x1,...,x |I+| }     //collected sample
        Ak = (Q, Σ, δ,q0,F,d) //the inferred
                              automaton
Output  PAk = { p*(q,xij), pq_final} //the obtained probabilities
Begin
For i=1 until |I+|    //for all words xi in I+
    q ← q0
    For j=1 until |xi|    //for all symbol xij of the word xi ∈ I+
        q' ← δ( q,xij)       //the corresponding transition
        cpq ++               //epoch-count in passing state
        cp*(q,xij) ++        //epoch-count in passing transition
        q ← q'
    EndFor
    cpq_final++          //epoch-count concerning the final states
    cpq ++
EndFor
For all q ∈ Q
    pq_final= cpq_final / cpq  //Computation of final-state probabilities
EndFor
For all δ( q,σ) ∈ δ
    p*(q,σ) = cp*(q,σ)/ cpq        //Computation of transition probabilities
EndFor
Return PAk
```

From the automaton (Fig. 6) and the set I_+, we count:

- cp_q: The number of times the state q was used while generating the set of words of I_+.
- $cp_{\delta(q,\sigma)}$: The number of times the transition $\delta_{(q,\sigma)}$ was used while generating the set of words of I_+.
- cp_{q_final}: The number of times that a state q is final (state gets at end of the words).

The obtained results from the sample presented in Fig. 5 are:

➤ $cp_q = (6_{(0)}, 39_{(1)}, 19_{(2)}, 22_{(3)}, 17_{(4)}, 10_{(5)})$,

➤ $cp_{q\_final} = (0_{(0)}, 1_{(1)}, 2_{(2)}, 1_{(3)}, 1_{(4)}, 1_{(5)})$,

➤ $cp_{\delta(q,\sigma)} = (2_{\delta(0,b)}, 1_{\delta(0,c)}, 3_{\delta(0,d)}, 0_{\delta(0,e)}, 1_{\delta(1,b)}, 37_{\delta(1,c)}, 2_{\delta(2,a)}, 14_{\delta(2,b)},$
   $1_{\delta(2,d)}, 20_{\delta(3,a)}, 1_{\delta(3,b)}, 1_{\delta(4,b)}, 1_{\delta(4,c)}, 12_{\delta(4,d)}, 2_{\delta(4,e)}, 1_{\delta(5,d)}, \cdot^{8}_{\delta(5,e)})$.

And afterwards, we deduce *the probabilities:*

➤ P_{q_final} $= {}^{c}p_{q\_final} / {}^{c}p_q$

            $= (0/6_{(0)}, 1/39_{(1)}, 2/19_{(2)}, 1/22_{(3)}, 1/17_{(4)}, 1/10_{(5)})$,

➤ $p_{\sigma(q,\sigma)}$ $= cp_{\sigma(q,\sigma)} / cp_q$

            $= (2/6_{\delta(0,b)}, 1/6_{\delta(0,c)}, 3/6_{\delta(0,d)}, 1/39_{\delta(1,b)}, 37/39_{\delta(1,c)}, 2/19_{\delta(2,a)},$
              $14/19_{\delta(2,b)}, \quad 1/19_{\delta(2,d)}, \quad 20/22_{\delta(3,a)}, \quad 1/22_{\delta(3,b)}, 1/17_{\delta(4,b)},$
              $1/17_{\delta(4,c)}, 12/17_{\delta(4,d)}, 2/17_{\delta(4,e)}, 1/10_{\delta(5,d)}, 8/10_{\delta(5,e)})$.

So we obtain the probabilistic deterministic automaton where the time series are taken into account. The advantage of using 1-TSSL (k-TSSI algorithm with $k = 1$) lies in the fact that one state corresponds to one symbol. We have added a new symbol f and a final state q_6 in order to facilitate the translation of the probabilistic automaton into a Markov process. For all q states where $p_{q\_final} > 0$, we add a transition $\delta(q, g) = q_6$, $p_{\delta(q,g)} = p_{q\_final}$ and $p_{q\_final} \leftarrow 0$. We note that $p_{q6\_final} = 1$.

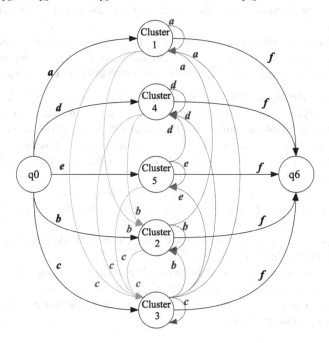

Fig. 7. The automaton inferred by the algorithm k-TSSL (Soleil nursing home: residents suffering from dementia).

Table 1. The corresponding probability matrix of transitions between states (Fig. 7).

To ⇨ From ⇩	Cluster 5	Cluster4	Cluster3	Cluster2	Cluster1	q_6
q_0	0.5072	0.0580	0.3333	0.0290	0.0725	
Cluster5	0.9738	0.0005	0.0009	0	0	0.0248
Cluster4	0.0629	0.9021	0.0210	0	0	0.0140
Cluster3	0.0229	0.0134	0.9408	0.0019	0.0019	0.0191
Cluster2	0	0.0299	0.0299	0.8955	0	0.0448
Cluster1	0	0	0.0122	0.0488	0.9268	0.0122

From patients' file living in Soleil nursing home and suffering from Alzheimer disease, the probability matrix of transitions between states and the corresponding automaton are respectively presented in Table 1 and in Fig. 7.

6.4   Markov Model

The final state q_6 does not only represent the resident state when they left the system but also the last resident assessment (resident present in the system at the date of database extraction).

In order to obtain the Markov chain model, we have to compute the probabilities:

- Pe_i: Input probabilities (i.e. the initial resident assessments) in each $cluster_i$ ($i = 1..5$),
- Psi: Output probabilities (i.e. the last resident assessments when residents leave the system) in being $cluster_i$ ($i = 1..5$) after $d(cluster_i) = 30$ days (corresponding to the equidistant discrete time described in the automaton definition in the paragraph 5.2).

We have also to modify the probabilities of staying in $cluster_i$ ($i = 1..5$), regarding if the patient is staying in the nursing home at the at the date of database extraction (these evaluations are taken into account in the transition with the symbol f to q6 in Table 1). We add the number of evaluations in the corresponding $cluster_i$. It is the reason that the probability to be in cluster1, (initially is 0.9738 in Table 1) becomes 0.9902 in the Markov matrix.

When a resident leaves the system, he is immediately replaced by a new resident. Consequently, two other probabilities are taken into account PE and PS. The Markov matrix is presented in Table 2.

We verify if the system reaches a steady state. Out of definition, an eigenvector x is associated to eigenvalue l if: $A * x = l * x$.

(A corresponding to the probabilities matrix presented in Table 2*)*

If an eigenvector of x is associated to a unique eigenvalue 1, such a vector is called a **steady state vector**. *If we identify only one eigenvalue 1, then the distribution is said to be irreducible and aperiodic.*

The eigenvector associated with the eigenvalue 1 has been computed. We have one eigenvalue 1 and the corresponding eigenvector x is the following:

$$0.00692\ 0.01263\ 0.01966\ 0.12108\ 0.03768\ 0.79510\ 0.00693.$$

The interpretation of this eigenvector is that the system (ratio of the resident profiles without 0.69 % of resident turnover of input/output in the nursing home) evolves towards a state where the percentages of population are:

- 1.28 % are in *cluster1*,
- 1.99 % are in *cluster2*,
- 12.28 % are in *cluster3*,
- 3.82 % are in *cluster4*,
- 80.63 % are in *cluster5*.

Table 2. The Markov matrix obtained from the collected data - Soleil Nursing home: patient suffering from dementia.

	Pe_i	Cluster1	Cluster2	Cluster3	Cluster4	Cluster5	PSS
PEE	0	0	0	0	0	0	1
Cluster1	0.0725	0.9390	0	0.0019	0	0	0
Cluster2	0.0290	0.0488	0.9403	0.0019	0	0	0
Cluster3	0.3333	0.0122	0.0299	0.9580	0.0210	0.0009	0
Cluster4	0.0580	0	0.0299	0.0134	0.9161	0.0005	0
Cluster5	0.5072	0	0	0.0229	0.0629	0.9902	0
Psi	0	0	0	0.0019	0	0.0084	0

7 Experiments

The experiment deals with the evolution of a patient's loss of cognitive autonomy over time. Table 3 presents the steady state vectors from different samples which correspond to a stable condition that does not change over time or in which change in one direction is continually balanced by change in another. We see that the decline is more significant for elderly people with dementia than non-demented elderly people.

Now, we simulate the evolution over time by using transition matrix used to model the Markov chain concerning each population. The results concerning the patients' profile progress in 2 years are presented in Tables 4 and 5.

Table 3. Steady state: population staying in medical nursing homes.

	4 Nursing Homes	Patient Without Dementia Disease	Patient Suffering from Dementia
Cluster5	3.57%	35.98%	0.32%
Cluster4	13.42%	27.00%	1.93%
Cluster3	27.80%	15.96%	5.21%
Cluster2	11.54%	5.65%	6.84%
Cluster1	43.66%	15.40%	85.69%

Table 4. Evolution of patients' profiles in 2 years (patients without dementia)

No Dementia	Cluster5	Cluster4	Cluster3	Cluster2	Cluster1	Exit
Cluster5	50.9%	16.0%	5.8%	1.6%	2.4%	23.3%
Cluster4	3.8%	56.0%	10.6%	3.4%	4.1%	22.2%
Cluster3	4.3%	4.0%	25.2%	9.1%	13.8%	43.6%
Cluster2	0.8%	0.9%	11.4%	29.4%	29.6%	27.9%
Cluster1	0.1%	0.6%	0.7%	1.3%	33.1%	64.2%

Table 5. Evolution of patients' profiles in 2 years (patients suffering from dementia)

Dementia	Cluster5	Cluster4	Cluster3	Cluster2	Cluster1	Exit
Cluster5	9.7%	20.6%	27.1%	12.7%	19.4%	10.5%
Cluster4	0.5%	20.2%	32.4%	14.7%	20.0%	12.2%
Cluster3	0.6%	1.5%	21.8%	17.7%	34.1%	24.3%
Cluster2	0.1%	0.1%	1.9%	11.9%	31.7%	54.3%
Cluster1	0.2%	0.1%	1.5%	15.5%	64.8%	17.9%

If the patient does not suffer from dementia disease, if he is initially in cluster5, in 2 years, the probabilities that the patient will be staying in:

– *Cluster5* is 50.9 %,
– *Cluster4* is 16 %,
– *Cluster3* is 5.8 %…
– and leaves the system with a probability near to 23 %.

If the patient suffers of *dementia*, the probabilities that the patient which will be staying in:

– *Cluster5* is 9.7 %,
– *Cluster4* is 20.6 %,
– *Cluster3* is 27.1 %,…
– and leaves the system with a probability near to 10 %.

8   Conclusion

A real case application of grammatical inference to identify the progression of a resident's autonomy-disability over time has been presented. From profiles identified by using clustering approach [9], we propose preliminary results of an investigation where regular grammars are used for modeling the evolution of ageing over time. The finite automaton is inferred by using the k-TSSI algorithm and afterward modified in order to obtain a probabilistic graph of transitions between states (clusters) with the length-of-stay in each state. From this graph, we automatically deduce the corresponding Markov chain model. For the sake of simplicity, we only present in the article, the case where $k = 1$. It is evident that in this case, we can use a bi-gram. But we have also studied the evolution with $k = 2..n$. So, the approach allows identifying a sub-sequence of n items from sequences.

In future work, we will extend and validate the different models to other class of diseases. Approximately 1–1.5 % of the French population suffer from dementia and the causes of dementia are neurological disorders such as Alzheimer's disease (which causes 50 %–70 % of all dementia), blood flow-related (vascular) disorders such as multi-infarct diseases, inherited disorders such as Huntington's disease, and infections such as HIV [15]. In fact, we would like to simulate the patient's progress in order to forecast and to analyze the need for long, medium and short-term care. This allows us to evaluate human, financial and physical resources in the future.

Acknowledgements. The authors would like to acknowledge Mr. F. Navarro (Chairman of the Board of "Mutualité Française" Rhône-Alpes - France), as well as all the staff who had the kind enough to entrust us this project, data to validate our models and who answered our numerous questions. The authors are very grateful to the reviewers for their comments which were both useful and helpful.

References

1. Alur, R., Courcoubetis, C., Dill, D.: Model-checking for real-time systems. In: Proceedings of the Fifth IEEE Symposium on Logic in Computer Science, pp. 414–425 (1990)
2. Alur, R., Courcoubetis, C., Dill, D.: Model-checking for probabilistic real-time systems. In: Albert, J.L., Monien, B., Artalejo, M.R. (eds.) Automata, Languages and Programming. LNCS, vol. 510, pp. 115–126. Springer, Heidelberg (1991)
3. Alur, R., Dill, D.: A theory of timed automata. Theoret. Comput. Sci. **126**, 183–235 (1994)
4. Angluin, D., Smith, C.H.: Inductive inference: theory and methods. ACM Comput. Surv. **15** (3), 237–269 (1983)
5. Angluin, D.: Learning regular sets from queries and counterexamples. Inf. Comput. **75**, 87–106 (1987)
6. Balczar, J.L., Daz, J., Gavald, R.: Algorithms for learning finite automata from queries: a unified view. In: Du, D.-Z., Ko, K.-I. (eds.) Advances in Algorithms, Languages, and Complexity, pp. 53–72. Kluwer Academic Publishers, Dordrecht (1997)
7. Bugalho, M., Oliveira, A.: Inference of regular languages using state merging algorithms with search. Pattern Recogn. **38**(9), 1457–1467 (2005)
8. Combes, C., Azéma, J., Dussauchoy, A.: Coupling Markov model – optimization: an application in medico-social care. In: 7e International Conference MOSIM'08, Paris, France, 31 March–2 April, pp. 1310–1319 (2008)
9. Combes, C., Azéma, J.: Clustering using principal component analysis applied to autonomy-disability of elderly people. Decis. Support Syst. **55**, 578–586 (2013). http://dx.doi.org/10.1016/j.dss2012.10.016
10. Dupont, P., Denis, F., Esposito, Y.: Links between probabilistic automata and hidden Markov models: probability distributions, learning models and induction algorithms. Patterns Recogn. **38**(9), 1349–1371 (2005)
11. Garcia, P., Vidal, E.: Inference of k-testable languages in the strict sense and applications to syntactic pattern recognition. IEEE Trans. Pattern Anal. Mach. Intell. **12**(9), 920–925 (1990)
12. Garcia, P., Vidal, E., Oncina, J.: Learning locally testable language in strict sense. In: Proceedings of the Workshop on Algorithmic Learning Theory, by Japanese Society for Artificial Intelligence (1990). http://users.dsic.upv.es/grupos/tlcc/papers/fullpapers/GVO90.pdf

13. Grinchtein, O., Jonsson, B., Leucker, M.: Inference of timed transition systems. Proc. Int. Workshop Verification Infinite State Syst. Electron. Notes Theoret. Comput. Sci. **138**(3), 87–99 (2005)
14. de la Higuera, C.: Grammatical Inference: Learning Automata and Grammars. Cambridge University Press, New York (2010). ISBN 978-0-521-7636-5
15. Khachaturian, Z.S.: A chapter in the development of Alzheimer's disease research: a case study of public policies on the development and funding of research programs. Alzheimer's Dement. J. Alzheimer's Assoc. **3**(3), 243–258 (2007)
16. Parekh, R., Honavar, V.: Learning DFA from simple examples. Mach. Learn. **44**(1/2), 9–35 (2001)
17. Parekh, R., Nichitiu, C.M., Honavar, V.: A polynomial time incremental algorithm for learning DFA. In: Proceeding of International Colloquium on Grammatical Inference: Algorithms and Applications, pp. 37–49 (1998)
18. Rico-Juan, J.R., Calera-Rubio, J., Carrasco, R.C.: Probabilistic k-testable tree languages. In: Oliveira, A.L. (ed.) ICGI 2000. LNCS (LNAI), vol. 1891, pp. 221–228. Springer, Heidelberg (2000)
19. Rivest, R.L., Schapire, R.E.: Inference of finite automata using homing sequences. Inf. Comput. **103**, 299–347 (1993)
20. Verwer, S., de Weerdt M., Witteveen, C.: An algorithm for learning real-time automata. In: Adriaans, P., van Someren, M., Katrenko, S. (eds.) Proceedings of the 18th Benelearn (2007)
21. Verwer, S., de Weerdt, M., Witteveen, C.: One-clock deterministic timed automata are efficiently identifiable in the limit. In: Dediu, A.H., Ionescu, A.M., Martín-Vide, C. (eds.) LATA 2009. LNCS, vol. 5457, pp. 740–751. Springer, Heidelberg (2009)
22. Verwer, S., de Weerdt, M., Witteveen, C.: a likelihood-ratio test for identifying probabilistic deterministic real-time automata from positive data. In: Sempere, J.M., García, P. (eds.) ICGI 2010. LNCS, vol. 6339, pp. 203–216. Springer, Heidelberg (2010)
23. Verwer, S., de Weerdt, M., Witteveen, C.: The efficiency of identifying timed automata and the power of clocks. Inf. Comput. **209**(3), 606–625 (2011)
24. Vidal, E., Thollard, F., de la Higuera, C., Casacuberta, F., Carrasco, R.C.: Probabilistic finite-states machine. IEEE Trans. Patterns Anal. Mach Intell. **27**(7), 1013–1039 (2005)

Finite Automata with Translucent Letters Applied in Natural and Formal Language Theory

Benedek Nagy[1,2]([✉]) and László Kovács[3]

[1] Faculty of Informatics, University of Debrecen, PO Box 12, Debrecen, Hungary
nbenedek@inf.unideb.hu
[2] Department of Mathematics, Faculty of Arts and Sciences,
Eastern Mediterranean University, Mersin-10, Famagusta, North Cyprus, Turkey
[3] Department of Information Technology, University of Miskolc,
Miskolc-Egyetemváros, Hungary
kovacs@iit.uni-miskolc.hu

Abstract. An important direction of computational and formal linguistics is to find good (mathematical and computational) models to describe linguistic phenomena. These models can also help to understand language acquisition, thinking and other mental activities. In this paper we consider finite automata with translucent letters. These models do not read their input strictly from left to right as traditional finite automata, but for each internal state of such a device, certain letters are translucent, that is, in this state the automaton cannot see them. We solve the parsing problem of these automata, both in the deterministic and in the nondeterministic cases. By introducing the permutation operator the class of regular languages is extended. It is shown that this extended class inside the class of languages that can be accepted by nondeterministic finite automata with translucent letters. Some interesting examples from the formal language theory and from a segment of the Hungarian language are shown presenting the applicability of finite automata with translucent letters both in formal and natural languages.

Keywords: Finite automata · Mildly context-sensitive languages · Natural languages · Formal linguistics · Free-order languages · Computational linguistics · Formal models

1 Introduction

Finite automata are fundamental computing devices for accepting languages. Their deterministic versions (DFA) and their nondeterministic versions (NFA) both accept exactly the regular languages, and they are applied in many areas like compiler construction, text editors, computational linguistics, etc. For regular languages the membership problem is decidable by a real-time (i.e., linear) computation. However, the expressiveness of regular languages is quite limited, and thus, these automata are too weak for several further applications. It is a

© Springer-Verlag Berlin Heidelberg 2014
N.T. Nguyen (Ed.): TCCI XVII 2014, LNCS 8790, pp. 107–127, 2014.
DOI: 10.1007/978-3-662-44994-3_6

well-known fact of the Chomsky hierarchy that all regular languages are context-free. Pushdown automata accept exactly the class of context-free languages. Their deterministic counterpart has less expressive power, they define the class of deterministic context-free languages. However, the world is not context-free, as it is stated, for instance, in [4], where seven circumstances are described where context-free grammars are not enough. Some of these circumstances are the logical laws of the predicate logic, some aspects of the programming languages and the natural languages. Accordingly, much more powerful models of automata have been introduced and studied like, e.g., linear-bounded automata, and Turing machines. This larger expressive power comes at a price that certain algorithmic questions like the membership problem or the emptiness problem become more complex or even undecidable. Hence, when dealing with applications, for example in natural language processing or concurrency control, it is important to find models of automata that reconcile two contrasting goals: they have sufficient expressiveness and, at the same time, a moderate degree of complexity. We note here that there are unconventional computing models that can also be used to model some phenomena of natural languages (see [1], for example).

An interesting question concerning applications of formal languages is whether the sentences of natural languages (NL) can be modeled with a class of the Chomsky hierarchy or not. There are many different views and approaches in the literature regarding the position of natural languages in this hierarchy. It is folklore that finite languages are regular, and hence the simplest model for NL uses regular form approach based on the idea that the set of all sentences of humans are finite (sentences have a limited length). There are also different approaches which use context-free grammars [8] while others like Matthews [13] consider NL even more complex than the recursively enumerable languages. Since we do not understand all features of the human brain, one may believe that human brain can do more effective 'computations' than the computers/Turing machines can do.

The first finite state model for NL was developed in 1955 by Hockett [9]. Later, in 1969, Reich [21] has argued that NLs are not self-embedding to any arbitrary degree. Another argument for regularity is given by among others Sullivan [22]: an individual neuron in the brain can be modeled with a finite automaton and the brain contains only finite number of neurons thus the resulting structure also corresponds to a finite automaton. The number of states of the resulting non-deterministic finite automaton is approximated with 10^{10^9}. Thus the only way to prove that NL are more complex than regular grammars is to exhibit some infinite sequences of grammatical sentences [12]. Chomsky [2] himself argues that English and other NLs are not regular languages. The most famous example for non-regular behaviour is the following pattern [23]:

A white male $(whom\ a\ white\ male)^n\ (hired)^n$ hired another white male.

Also in the case, when the argumentation is accepted that the given structure can't be realized in infinite depth, it is clear that the corresponding base regular grammar/finite automata for finite depth may have a very large complexity. Thus, from a practical point of view it is worth to find more compact grammars that can describe the special behaviour of the different natural languages.

There are also very strong arguments that NLs are not context-free (but more complex). In the area of formal languages in conjunction with computational linguistics and natural language processing the formulation of the notion of "mildly context-sensitive languages" [11,14] has been appeared and used. These classes are proper subclasses of the class of context-sensitive languages and proper superclasses of the class of context-free languages. They contain some typical examples of non-context-free languages that show important features of natural languages, e.g., $\{a^n b^n c^n | n \geq 0\}$, $\{ww | w \in \{a,b\}^*\}$ and $\{a^n b^m c^n d^m | m,n \geq 0\}$. At the same time mildly context-sensitive languages share many of the nice properties with the context-free languages. For example, they have semi-linear Parikh images and their parsing complexity is polynomially bounded.

In this paper, the permutation operation is introduced and used for languages allowing any order of the terminals below this operation, e.g., $(abc)^!$ is equivalent to $(bac)^!$ and both of them denote the set $\{abc, acb, bac, bca, cab, cba\}$.

An interesting extension of the class of finite automata that vastly increases its expressive power, the so-called finite automaton (or finite-state acceptor) with translucent letters (*NFAwtl* for short) was introduced in [19]. The idea of this new model comes from the research of cooperative distributed systems of stateless deterministic restarting automata with window size 1 [18,20]. An NFAwtl does not read its input strictly from left to right as the traditional finite automaton does, but for each of its internal states, certain letters are translucent, that is, in this state the NFAwtl cannot see them. Accordingly, it may read (and erase) a letter from the middle or the end of the given input. They accept certain non-regular and even some non-context-free languages, but all languages accepted by NFAwtls have semi-linear Parikh images [20]. These issues are important for the linguistic applications point of view. In contrast to the classical finite-state acceptors, the deterministic variants of the NFAwtls, the so-called *DFAwtls*, are less expressive than the nondeterministic ones [18]. In this paper, as a continuation of the work started in [19], we consider the parsing (membership or word problem, i.e., to decide whether an arbitrary input word is accepted or not by a given automaton, and in affirmative case how the word is accepted) of these automata by showing a nondeterminsitic/deterministic almost linear-time algorithm that decides if a given word is accepted or not by an NFAwtl/DFAwtl, respectively. We introduce the permutation operation for languages and we show that the set of regular operations (concatenation, union, Kleene-star) extended with the permutation operation defines a class of languages that is strictly between the class of regular languages and the class of languages accepted by NFAwtl. Some linguistical examples are also shown to demonstrate the efficiency of DFAwtls.

This paper is structured as follows. In Sect. 2 we recall the definition of the finite automata with translucent letters and we also present an example. In Sect. 3 the parsing problem is considered with some further examples, while in Sect. 4 we consider the extension of regular languages by permutations. Further, in Sect. 5 we show examples for the usage of finite automata with translucent letters modeling some phenomena of the Hungarian language. In our investigation, the Hungarian language was selected because it differs from English in the following important aspects:

- it is an agglutinative language (in Hungarian most grammatical information is given through suffixes: cases, conjugation, etc.),
- it has no dominant word order (as we will see, in Hungarian, several kinds of order of the words within a sentence can be considered emphasizing slightly different special meanings),
- reduced use of postpositions (since suffixes are often equivalent to English prepositions, there are only few postpositions in Hungarian).

In Sect. 6 we summarize our work and give some open problems for future work.

2   Preliminaries and Basic Definitions

In this section we fix our notation and recall the definition and some basic facts about the finite automata with translucent letters.

The class REG of regular languages contains all the languages that are described by regular expressions. Let Σ be a finite alphabet. Then each $a \in \Sigma$ is a regular expression and describes the singleton language $\{a\}$. The signs ε and $\emptyset$ are also regular expressions and describe the languages $\{\varepsilon\}$ and $\{\}$, respectively. If r_1 and r_2 are regular expressions describing the languages L_1 and L_2, then $(r_1 \cdot r_2)$, $(r_1 + r_2)$ and r_1^* are also regular expressions, and they are describing the languages $L_1 \cdot L_2$, $L_1 \cup L_2$ and L_1^*, respectively. (Note here that the sign of the concatenation, the sign '·', is usually eliminated and some of the brackets can be removed, e.g., by the associative property of union, and by precedence relation defined on these operations, see, e.g., [24] for details.)

A *nondeterministic finite automaton* (NFA) is described by a tuple $A = (Q, \Sigma, I, F, \delta)$, where Q is a finite set of internal states, Σ is a finite alphabet of input letters, $I \subseteq Q$ is the set of initial states, $F \subseteq Q$ is the set of final states, and $\delta : Q \times \Sigma \to 2^Q$ is a transition relation. If $|I| = 1$ and $|\delta(q, a)| \leq 1$ holds for all $q \in Q$ and all $a \in \Sigma$, then A is a *deterministic finite automaton* (DFA).

An NFA A works as follows. It is given an input string $w \in \Sigma^*$, and A starts its computation/run in a state q_0 that is chosen nondeterministically from the set I of all initial states. This configuration is encoded as $q_0 w$. Now it reads the first letter of w, say a, thereby deleting this letter, and it changes its internal state to a state q_1 that is chosen nondeterministically from the set $\delta(q_0, a)$. Should $\delta(q_0, a)$ be empty, then A gets stuck (in this run), otherwise, it continues its run by reading letters until w has been consumed completely. We say that A accepts w with a run if A is in a final state $q_f \in F$ after reading w completely at the end of this run. By $L(A)$ we denote the set of all strings $w \in \Sigma^*$ for which A has an accepting computation in the sense described above.

It is well-known that the class $\mathcal{L}$(NFA) of languages $L(A)$ that are accepted by NFAs coincides with the class REG of regular languages, and that DFAs accept exactly the same languages.

Now we recall a recently developed variant of the nondeterministic finite automata that does not process its input strictly from left to right [19].

Definition 1. *A* finite-state acceptor with translucent letters *(NFAwtl) is defined as a 7-tuple* $A = (Q, \Sigma, \$, \tau, I, F, \delta)$, *where Q is a finite set of internal states, Σ is a finite alphabet of input letters, $\$ \notin \Sigma$ is a special symbol that is used as an endmarker, $\tau : Q \rightarrow 2^{\Sigma}$ is a translucency mapping, $I \subseteq Q$ is a set of initial states, $F \subseteq Q$ is a set of final states, and $\delta : Q \times \Sigma \rightarrow 2^{Q}$ is a transition relation that satisfies the following condition: $\forall q \in Q \, \forall a \in \tau(q) : \delta(q, a) = \emptyset$. For each state $q \in Q$, the letters from the set $\tau(q)$ are translucent for q. A is called* deterministic, *abbreviated as DFAwtl, if $|I| = 1$ and if $|\delta(q, a)| \leq 1$ for all $q \in Q$ and all $a \in \Sigma$.*

A configuration of an NFAwtl is written in the form $qw\$$, where $q \in Q$ is the current state and w is the tape content (without the endmarker). The NFAwtl $A = (Q, \Sigma, \$, \tau, I, F, \delta)$ works as follows. For an input word $w \in \Sigma^*$, it starts in a nondeterministically chosen initial state $q \in I$ with the word $w \cdot \$$ on its input tape, i.e., with configuration $qw\$$. A single step computation of A is as follows. Assume that $w = a_1 a_2 \cdots a_n$ for some $n \geq 1$ and $a_1, \ldots, a_n \in \Sigma$. Then A looks for the first occurrence from the left of a letter that is not translucent for the current state q, that is, if $w = uav$ such that $u \in (\tau(q))^*$ and $a \notin \tau(q)$, then A nondeterministically chooses a state $q' \in \delta(q, a)$, erases the letter a from the tape thus producing the tape contents $uv \cdot \$$, and its internal state is set to q'. Formally, we write the single-step computation relation in the form $quav\$ \vdash_A q'uv\$$. In state q' the automaton considers the tape $uv\$$ and continues the process by another single step computation looking for the first visible letter of uv at state q'. In case $\delta(q, a) = \emptyset$, A halts without accepting. Finally, if $w \in (\tau(q))^*$, then A reaches the \$-symbol and the computation halts. In this case A accepts if q is a final state; otherwise, it does not accept. Observe that this definition also applies to configurations of the form $q \cdot \$$, that is, $q \cdot \varepsilon \cdot \$ \vdash_A$ Accept holds if and only if q is a final state. A word $w \in \Sigma^*$ is *accepted by* A if there exists an initial state $q_0 \in I$ and a computation $q_0 w \cdot \$ \vdash_A^*$ Accept, where $\vdash_A^*$ denotes the reflexive transitive closure of the single-step computation relation $\vdash_A$. Now $L(A) = \{\, w \in \Sigma^* \mid w$ is accepted by $A \,\}$ is the *language accepted by* A.

Observe that for each state $q \in Q$, the letters from the set $\tau(q)$ are translucent for q, that is, in state q the automaton A does not see these letters.

The classical *nondeterministic finite automata* (NFA) is obtained from the NFAwtl by removing the endmarker \$ and by ignoring the translucency relation τ, and the *deterministic finite-state acceptor* (DFA) is obtained from the DFAwtl in the same way. Thus, the NFA (DFA) can be interpreted as a special type of NFAwtl (DFAwtl). Accordingly, all regular languages are accepted by DFAwtl. Moreover, DFAwtls are much more expressive than standard DFAs as shown by the following example.

Example 1. Let $A = (Q, \Sigma, \$, \tau, I, F, \delta)$, where $Q = \{q_0, q_1, q_2\}$, $I = \{q_0\} = F$, $\Sigma = \{a, b, c, d\}$, and the functions τ and δ are defined as follows:

$$\tau(q_0) = \emptyset, \qquad \delta(q_0, a) = \{q_1\},$$
$$\delta(q_0, b) = \{q_2\},$$
$$\tau(q_1) = \{a, b\}, \quad \delta(q_1, c) = \{q_0\},$$
$$\tau(q_2) = \{b\}, \qquad \delta(q_2, d) = \{q_0\},$$

and $\delta(q, x) = \emptyset$ for all other pairs $(q, x) \in Q \times \Sigma$. Observe that A is in fact a DFAwtl.

Let us consider some example input words. Given the word $w = aacc$ as input, A executes the following computation:

$$q_0 aacc \cdot \$ \vdash_A q_1 acc \cdot \$ \vdash_A q_0 ac \cdot \$ \vdash_A q_1 c \cdot \$$$
$$\vdash_A q_0 \varepsilon \cdot \$ \quad \vdash_A \text{Accept},$$

as q_0 is a final state, A accepts the input $aacc$.

Given the word $w = aabcc$ as input, A executes the following computation:

$$q_0 aabcc \cdot \$ \vdash_A q_1 abcc \cdot \$ \vdash_A q_0 abc \cdot \$ \vdash_A q_1 bc \cdot \$$$
$$\vdash_A q_0 b \cdot \$ \quad \vdash_A q_2 \varepsilon \cdot \$,$$

and, since $q_2 \notin F$, this input word is not accepted.

One can prove that $L(A)$ consists only words with $|w|_a = |w|_c$ and $|w|_b = |w|_d$, moreover $L(A) \cap (a^* \cdot b^* \cdot c^* \cdot d^*) = \{a^n b^m c^n d^m \mid n, m \geq 0\}$ and thus this language is not context-free.

Observe that automaton A accepts the language $L'(A) = (ac)^*(bd)^* \subsetneq L(A)$ by its computations without effectively using the translucency mapping, i.e., when every transition erases the first letter of the remaining input.

We have seen that already DFAwtls accept non-context-free languages.

An NFAwtl $A = (Q, \Sigma, \$, \tau, I, F, \delta)$ is described more intuitively by a graph, similar to the graph representation of standard NFAs [24]. A state $q \in Q$ is represented by a node (circle on figures) labelled with a pair q, T, where $T = \tau(q) \subset \Sigma$ shows the set of translucent letters at the given state. Moreover the node of an initial state p is marked by a special incoming edge without a label, and the node of a final state p is marked by double-lined circle. For each state $q \in Q$ and each letter $a \in \Sigma \setminus \tau(q)$, if $\delta(q, a) = \{q_1, \ldots, q_s\}$, then there is a directed edge labelled by a from the node corresponding to state q to the node corresponding to state q_i for each $i = 1, \ldots, s$. The graph representation of the DFAwtl A of Example 1 is given in Fig. 1.

According to the definition, an NFAwtl may accept a word without processing it completely. This, however, is only a convenience that makes for simple instructions, since for every NFAwtl A one can effectively construct an NFAwtl B such that $L(B) = L(A)$, but for each word $w \in L(B)$, each accepting computation of B on input w consists of $|w|$ many reading steps plus a final step that accepts the empty word (i.e., the input is totally processed). Nevertheless it is an open problem whether the same fact holds for DFAwtls in general. If A is an NFAwtl on Σ that is accepting only totally processed input, then by

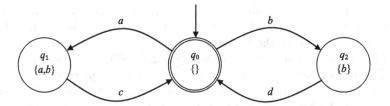

Fig. 1. A graphical representation of the DFAwtl A of Example 1.

removing the translucency relation from A, we obtain a standard NFA A' that accepts a letter equivalent language of the original language $L(A)$, moreover $L(A) \supseteq L(A')$.

3   The Parsing Problem

In this section we address the membership problem (it is also known as the word problem and as the acceptance problem), i.e., how we can decide if a given word is accepted by an NFAwtl/DFAwtl.

One may feel that in every step of our automaton the input should be processed from the beginning by searching an occurrence of the letter indicated by the transition; and in this way the time complexity of the membership problem looks quadratic. In the next part of this section we show a representation method which gives lower complexity for the membership problem.

Let us start this section with a kind of description of our automata, i.e., how it could work. Our aim is to reach easily the next occurrence of a given letter. To do so, first, let us divide the tape into as many parts as the cardinality of the alphabet (about a similar way as a one-tape Turing machine can simulate a multi-tape Turing machine [10]). See Fig. 2 as well. In each division exactly one of the letters is used: there is a bijection from Σ to the parts of the tape.

Fig. 2. Divided tape model of NFAwtl.

Then in each state those parts of the tape are not used that are assigned to translucent letters. With this picture in mind, one can construct the 'linked-list' data structure of the tape content in a linear number of steps (by the length of the input). The notation w_n is used for the n-th letter of the word w. The linked-list structure contains the array $STORE$ with dimension $|w|$ and $|\Sigma|$ pointers. A pointer $HEAD_a$ shows the first occurrence of letter a in w. In that position in the array there is a value that shows the second occurrence of letter a in w, etc.

At the last occurrence of a there is a special marker that shows that there is no further occurrences of the letter a. The formal algorithm is shown in Fig. 3. Starting from the end of the word we easily find the last occurrence of every type of letters of the word, we mark these places of $STORE$ by special markers ($NULL$). Further preprocessing the input, we put every place to $STORE$ the value that indicates the next occurrence of the given letter. Finally, the pointers $HEAD_j$ show the first occurrences of the letters.

```
Input: the alphabet Σ and the input word w.
Output: linked lists for every element a ∈ Σ:
    stored in a |w|-long string STORE and HEADs of the lists.
  Initialization: For every a ∈ Σ let HEADₐ = NULL.
    For i = |w| downto 1 step −1 do
        Let STOREᵢ = HEAD_{wᵢ}
        Let HEAD_{wᵢ} = i
    EndFor.
```

Fig. 3. Preprocessing **algorithm** to obtain linked list representation of the input word.

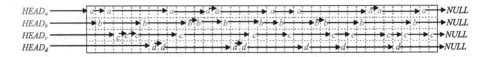

Fig. 4. Linked list model of NFAwtl with preprocessed input.

Then the constructed data structure is used in computation as a representation of the input word (see Fig. 4). Let us see, how this structure can be used in processing the input. By the constructed data structure one can easily access the first occurrence of any letters a of any word w by the pointer $HEAD_a$. When a machine should read a letter a then one needs a constant number (at most $|\Sigma| - 1$) of comparisons: if $HEAD_a > HEAD_b$ for any non-translucent letters b occurring in the unprocessed part of the input (here the value $NULL$ is considered as ∞, i.e., larger than any value of $n \in \mathbb{N}$), then the machine gets stuck, else a is read by the machine: it is done by erasing the current head of the list representing a's: let $HEAD_a = STORE_{HEAD_a}$. When a list is empty, then all the occurrences of the given letter have been processed. If all the non translucent letters have empty lists in a final state, then the NFAwtl accepts the input by this computation. When all lists are empty, i.e., $HEAD_a = NULL$ for every input letter a, then the input is fully processed. Remember that for NFAwtl one can construct an equivalent NFAwtl that erases all the input letters before acceptance in accepting runs [19].

3.1   Complexity of Parsing

The preprocessing part goes in a linear number of steps, where a step (i.e., to store a value) has time complexity at most $\log(n)$ where n is the length of the input, and so, the maximal number that will be stored is n. (We assume a non-unary coding of the values.)

In this way a DFAwtl processes the input of length n in $n \log(n)$ time: the preprocessing and processing together executed by a linear number of simple operations (comparisons and assignment statements). Their number is bounded by $(|\Sigma| + 2|w|) + (|\Sigma| - 1)|w|)$.

Each comparison and assignment statement (or storing a value) needs at most $\log(n)$ time.

Therefore the membership problem for DFAwtl is almost as simple as for DFA, this family of languages has this very pleasant and effective property.

For NFAwtl the membership problem using our representation is $n \log(n)$ with a nondeterministic version of our algorithm, i.e., the problem is solvable in $n \log(n)$ time nondeterministically.

3.2 Examples from Formal Languages

In this subsection we present some additional examples (both for DFAwtl languages and for our parsing algorithm). The next example is one of the most typical and important (deterministic) context-free languages.

Example 2. The Dyck language is accepted by the DFAwtl shown in Fig. 5. The input *abaababb* is represented by $HEAD_a = 1$, $HEAD_b = 2$, $STORE = 35467\infty 8\infty$ (where ∞ represents the value $NULL$ as discussed before). The run of the machine on this input is as follows:

State q_0, $HEAD_a = 1$ ($HEAD_a < HEAD_b$) is changing to $STORE_{HEAD_a} = STORE_1 = 3$; the next state is q_1.

State q_1, $HEAD_b = 2$ is changing to $STORE_{HEAD_b} = STORE_2 = 5$; the next state is q_0.

State q_0, $HEAD_a = 3$ ($HEAD_a < HEAD_b$) is changing to $STORE_{HEAD_a} = STORE_3 = 4$; the next state is q_1.

State q_1, $HEAD_b = 5$ is changing to $STORE_{HEAD_b} = STORE_5 = 7$; the next state is q_0.

State q_0, $HEAD_a = 4$ ($HEAD_a < HEAD_b$) is changing to $STORE_{HEAD_a} = STORE_4 = 6$; the next state is q_1.

State q_1, $HEAD_b = 7$ is changing to $STORE_{HEAD_b} = STORE_7 = 8$; the next state is q_0.

State q_0, $HEAD_a = 6$ ($HEAD_a < HEAD_b$) is changing to $STORE_{HEAD_a} = STORE_6 = \infty$; the next state is q_1.

State q_1, $HEAD_b = 8$ is changing to $STORE_{HEAD_b} = STORE_8 = \infty$; the next state is q_0.

The input is empty (both $HEAD_a$ and $HEAD_b$ are $NULL$ and q_0 is a final state, the input is accepted.

The input *abbabaab* is represented by $HEAD_a = 1$, $HEAD_b = 2$, $STORE = 435687\infty\infty\infty$. The run of the machine on this input is as follows:

State q_0, $HEAD_a = 1$ ($HEAD_a < HEAD_b$) is changing to $STORE_{HEAD_a} = STORE_1 = 4$; the next state is q_1.

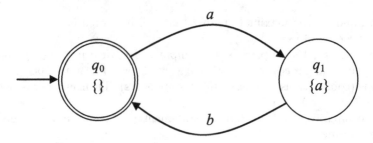

Fig. 5. The DFAwtl of Example 2.

State q_1, $HEAD_b = 2$ is changing to $STORE_{HEAD_b} = STORE_2 = 3$; the next state is q_0. The first two letters of the input are already processed.

State q_0, $HEAD_a = 4$, $HEAD_b = 3$, therefore $HEAD_a > HEAD_b$ this transition cannot be executed. The machine gets stuck. This input is not accepted, *abbabaab* is not in the Dyck language.

In the previous example the language $(ab)^*$ is accepted if the first letter is erased in every transition.

Further, we present two non-context-free languages that are closely related to basic mildly context-sensitive languages.

Example 3. Let $A = (Q, \Sigma, \$, \tau, I, F, \delta)$, where $Q = \{q_0, q_1, q_2\}$, $I = \{q_0\} = F$, $\Sigma = \{a, b, c\}$, and the functions τ and δ are defined as follows:

$$\tau(q_0) = \{\}, \quad \delta(q_0, a) = \{q_1\},$$
$$\tau(q_1) = \{a\}, \quad \delta(q_1, b) = \{q_2\},$$
$$\tau(q_2) = \{a, b\}, \quad \delta(q_2, c) = \{q_0\},$$

and $\delta(q, x) = \emptyset$ for all other pairs $(q, x) \in Q \times \Sigma$. The language $\{w \in \{a, b, c\}^* \mid |w|_a = |w|_b = |w|_c$ and for all $u, v \in \{a, b, c\}^*$ such that $w = uv : |u|_a \geq |u|_b$ and $|u|_b \geq |u|_c\}$ is accepted by this DFAwtl. Its graphical representation is shown in Fig. 6.

An example run on input *abaabccbc* is:

Representation of the input: $HEAD_a = 1$, $HEAD_b = 2$, $HEAD_c = 6$, $STORE = 354\infty879\infty\infty$.

Starting from the initial state q_0 an a is read. This step can be done, since $HEAD_a < HEAD_b$ $(1 < 2)$ and $HEAD_a < HEAD_c$ $(1 < 6)$. In this step $HEAD_a$ is changing from 1 to $STORE_1 = 3$.

Then in state q_1 a b is read. It can be done, since $HEAD_b < HEAD_c$ $(2 < 6)$. In this step $HEAD_b$ is increasing from 2 to $STORE_2 = 5$.

In state q_2 a c is read by changing $HEAD_c$ from 6 to $STORE_6 = 7$. Since both a and b are translucent in state q_2, there were no condition on this step.

Now the system is in q_0 and an a is read. It is allowed, since $HEAD_a < HEAD_b$ $(3 < 5)$ and $HEAD_a < HEAD_c$ $(3 < 7)$, and thus $HEAD_a$ is changed to $STORE_3 = 4$.

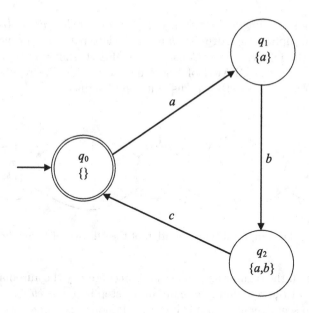

Fig. 6. The DFAwtl of Example 3.

In state q_1: $HEAD_b < HEAD_c$ (5 < 7) and so, a b is read: $HEAD_b$ is increased to $STORE_5 = 8$.

In state q_2 $HEAD_c$ is changed to $STORE_7 = 9$.

In state q_0 an a is read ($HEAD_a < HEAD_b$ (4 < 8) and $HEAD_a < HEAD_c$ (4 < 9)) and thus, $HEAD_a$ is increased to $STORE_4 = \infty$.

In state q_1 ($HEAD_b < HEAD_c$ (8 < 9)), therefore $HEAD_b$ is increased to $STORE_8 = \infty$.

In state q_2 $HEAD_c$ is changed to $STORE_9 = \infty$ and the system is arrived to q_0.

Since all lists are empty (all $HEAD$s are $NULL$) the input is fully processed and the system is in its final state, the input is accepted.

Note that in this example without using translucency (deleting the first letter of the remaining input at each transition), the language $L' = (abc)^*$ is accepted. This regular language is a special subset of the language accepted by the automaton of the example.

The language accepted by the previous automaton intersected by the regular language $a^*b^*c^*$ gives the language $a^nb^nc^n$. The language $\{a^nb^mc^nd^m\}$ can be recognized in a similar way: it can be obtained as an intersection of the DFAwtl language presented in Example 1 and the regular language $a^*b^*c^*d^*$. These languages are belonging to mildly context-sensitive language families and they are important from linguistic point of view. The next language is closely connected to the copy language that is also belonging to mildly context-sensitive language families.

Example 4. The disjoint copy language $\{ww' | w \in \{a, b\}^*, w' \in \{a', b'\}, w' = h(w)$, where the alphabetic morphism h maps the letters to their primed versions$\}$ is accepted in the following way. Consider the DFAwtl shown in Fig. 7. The language accepted by the DFAwtl of Fig. 7 intersected by the regular language $(a + b)^*(a' + b')^*$ gives exactly the disjoint copy language.

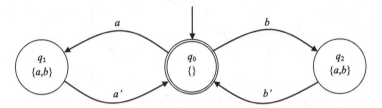

Fig. 7. The graphical representation of the DFAwtl of Example 4.

In Example 4, the regular language that is accepted by the automaton erasing the first letter of the remaining input in every step is $(aa' + bb')^*$.

As we have seen, versions of all the three 'famous', i.e., linguistically important non context-free mildly context-sensitive languages can easily be described based on DFAwtl languages. Actually, the technique to use the intersection with the regular language is a standard technique for language classes that are not closed under intersection with regular languages [16]. Moreover it does not cause any difficulties in membership problems, for example, since to check whether the given word is in the given regular class can be done in a deterministic real-time (i.e., linear) algorithm.

4   Extending Regular Languages with Permutations

In this section we formally define a permutation operation on languages and extend the family of regular languages. We also show that NFAwtls can accept all the languages that belong to this extended class.

In theory of formal grammars, the word-order freedom usually means a certain level of robustness against permutations of sentential forms [15]. To simplify the formulae with permutation elements, a permutation symbol is introduced as follows. Let $s = s_1 s_2 \ldots s_m$, where every $s_i \in \Sigma$ ($i \in \{1, \ldots, m\}$). Then define

$$s^{!} = \{s_{p_1} s_{p_2} \ldots s_{p_m} \mid p_i \in \{1, \ldots, m\}, \forall i \neq j : p_i \neq p_j\}.$$

The permutation operator yields the set of all possible permutations of the elements of the sequence s. Considering the length of the sequence $|s| = m$, the number of permutations is finite (at most $m!$, it is actually $m!$ if every two letters of s are distinct), but grows faster with m than the exponential function. Based on the finiteness of this set, it can be described with an NFA or DFA. Considering the cost value of the corresponding automaton, a storage and a parse execution cost (the space and time complexities) can be investigated.

The storage cost is equal to the size of the required data structure representing the automaton. A compact solution can be achieved with the application of a prefix tree (trie) [3]. The trie structure is an index tree, where the first level corresponds to the first symbol of the key sequence, and the i-th level is assigned to the i-th symbol of the sequence. The common prefix parts of the different keys are stored in the same node of the tree, thus a significant space reduction can be achieved with this structure. Having $|s| = 3$, the finite automata for $s^!$ can be given with tree-structure graph as it is shown in Fig. 8 (the levels of the tree can be seen vertically). By further minimizing these structures, one can easily prove the following. Let a word w over an n-letter alphabet $\Sigma = \{a_1, \ldots, a_n\}$ be given with Parikh vector $(m_1, m_2, \ldots, m_n)$ (i.e., w contains the letter a_i m_i times for each $1 \le i \le n$). Let $m = |w|$. Then the number of states of the minimal deterministic automaton accepting the language $w^!$ is $(m_1 + 1)(m_2 + 1) \ldots (m_n + 1)$ by counting how many of the letters have already read. (It seems that this language cannot be accepted by less number of states even with NFAs.) The number of states can be approximated by $O(|w|^{|\Sigma|}) = O(m^n)$. Also the number of edges (transitions) of these automata, and thus, their storage cost, can be approximated by $O(|\Sigma| \cdot |w|^{|\Sigma|}) = O(n \cdot m^n)$. These values may be too high for real applications due to the length of the possible sentences and the large size of the alphabet. In the case of DFAwtl, m nodes are sufficient, but the management of the corresponding sets of translucent symbols requires additional space. However at each state only those letters could be translucent for which there is no transition defined. The storage of a translucent letter for a state cannot require more space than an edge. Thus the storage cost (based on edge complexity) can be estimated with $O(nm)$. (The measure of edge complexity is recently investigated for not complete finite automata, see, e.g., [7]. In case of a DFAwtl (NFAwtl) that uses non-empty translucency relation, there must be transitions that are not defined, due to the translucent letters of the given states.) This kind of structure enables a much more efficient implementation for large alphabets too.

Regarding the execution costs (i.e. runtime), the two variants have very similar characteristics, as we have seen in Subsect. 3.1. Thus, the significantly reduced storage cost of DFAs will result a slightly increased execution cost for DFAwtls.

In the previous part we used the permutation operation to reduce the descriptional complexity of regular languages. In the next part we extend the notion to go beyond regular, i.e., to present non-regular languages using permutation.

The permutation operator can be extended for languages: let $L \subseteq \Sigma^*$, then let $L^! = \bigcup_{s \in L} s^!$. Actually $L^!$ gives the commutative closure of L.

For example, taking $L = \{a^n b^n \mid n \in \mathbb{N}\}$ we have $L^! = \{\varepsilon, ab, ba, aabb, abab,$ $abba, baab, baba, bbaa, \ldots\} = \{w \in \{a, b\}^* \mid |w|_a = |w|_b\}$.

The language $L^!$ is letter-equivalent to L (their Parikh images are the same).

It is known that none of the classes of regular, linear and context-free languages are closed under commutative closure, however, the commutative closure of regular and linear and context-free languages coincide, and this class is the class of commutative semi-linear languages.

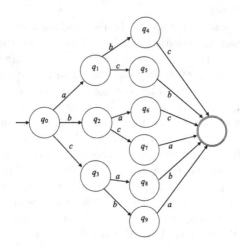

Fig. 8. The tree form of a DFA accepting all the permutations of a word

Let us define the *regular expressions with permutations*. Let Σ be a finite alphabet. Then each $a \in \Sigma$, ε and $\emptyset$ are regular expressions with permutations. If r_1 and r_2 are regular expressions with permutations describing the languages L_1 and L_2, then $(r_1 \cdot r_2)$, $(r_1 + r_2)$, r_1^* and $r_1^!$ are also regular expressions with permutations, where the latter expression describes the language $L_1^!$. (We can use the permutation operation with the same precedence as the Kleene-star operation to reduce the number of used brackets.) Observe that for a given alphabet Σ, $(\Sigma^*)^! = \Sigma^*$.

It is clear that the regular expressions with permutations describes all regular languages and they also describes some non-context-free languages, e.g., $(abc)^{*!} = \{w \in \{a, b, c\}^* \mid |w|_a = |w|_b, |w|_b = |w|_c\}$.

Now we show that the class of NFAwtl languages are closed under the operations used in this section. Let us consider two NFAwtls

$$A_1 = (Q_1, \Sigma, \$, \tau_1, I_1, F_1, \delta_1) \text{ and } A_2 = (Q_2, \Sigma, \$, \tau_2, I_2, F_2, \delta_2)$$

with $Q_1 \cap Q_2 = \emptyset$ such that they accept only completely processed input words. Let $A = (Q_1 \cup Q_2, \Sigma, \$, \tau, I_1 \cup I_2, F_1 \cup F_2, \delta)$ where $\tau(q) = \begin{cases} \tau_1(q) & \text{if } q \in Q_1, \\ \tau_2(q) & \text{if } q \in Q_2; \end{cases}$ and $\delta(q) = \begin{cases} \delta_1(q) & \text{if } q \in Q_1, \\ \delta_2(q) & \text{if } q \in Q_2 \end{cases}$. It is clear by the construction that A accepts exactly the union $L(A) = L(A_1) \cup L(A_2)$ of the languages accepted by A_1 and A_2. Now let us construct the automaton $A' = (Q_1, \Sigma, \$, \tau', I_1, F_1, \delta_1)$, where $\tau'(q) = \{a \in \Sigma \mid$ there is no defined transition on q with letter $a\}$. By this construction, one can prove that A' accepts the commutative closure $L(A_1)^!$ of the language accepted by A_1.

In [19,20] it is constructively proved that the class of NFAwtl languages are closed under the regular operations. Actually the proof of closure under concatenation is very long and technical, the construction is based on a nondeterministic guess whether the last occurrence of a letter is being read and erased in a transition. Based on that construction, closure under Kleene-star was also proved.

Therefore the class of NFAwtl languages are closed under the regular operations and also under commutative closure. Based on these constructive proofs one can construct NFAwtl for any regular expressions with permutations.

Unfortunately, the class of DFAwtl languages is not closed under union, concatenation, Kleene-star, and taking the commutative closure [18]. Therefore they cannot be used in such a wide area as NFAwtls. Despite of this fact we believe that DFAwtls can be used to model several phenomena in linguistics, as we use them in the next section.

We close this section by a hierarchy result showing that our automata model has larger expressive power than regular expressions with permutations.

Proposition 1. *The DFAwtl language of Example 2 cannot be described by regular expressions with permutations.*

Instead of the full formal proof we give the idea of the proof. The Dyck language L is not regular and thus, for each of its regular sublanguages L' ($L' \subset L$, L' regular) there are infinitely many words of L that are not contained in L'. To go beyond regular the permutation operation must be used for an expression describing an infinite language. To describe an infinite language Kleene-star must be used. Since the number of a's and b's are the same in each word of L, under a Kleene-star the number of a's and b's must be the same, i.e., we have a subexpression $(s_1 o_1 s^* o_2 s_2)^!$, where s, s_1, s_2 are expressions, o_1, o_2 are the operations concatenation and/or union such that each word of s has the same number of a's and b's. However, in this case, the number of a's and b's of s^* can be arbitrarily large, and thus, the permutation operation allows to have arbitrarily many b's preceding the large number of a's in the subexpression $(s_1 o_1 s^* o_2 s_2)^!$. In this way some words can be obtained that are outside of L.

Based on Proposition 1 we can claim that the class of languages accepted by NFAwtls is a strict superset of the class of languages defined by regular expressions with permutations.

5   Applications in a Natural Language: Modeling Some Structures of Hungarian Language

In the previous section we gave some examples how NFAwtls/DFAwtls can be used to model languages that are not context-free and closely connected to the main mildly context-sensitive languages. In this section we make a further step: we use NFAwtls to present some features of a natural language, namely, of the Hungarian language.

In our investigation, the Hungarian language was selected which differs from English in many aspects. As we already mentioned, the Hungarian language is an agglutinative language, it has no dominant word order, and there is a reduced use of postpositions. We note here that, among other languages, Finnish and

Table 1. Hungarian words used in Example 5.

person	én *I*	te *you*	ő *she/he*	Jani *Johnny*	Mari *Mary*
thing	a könyv	az újság	a kenyér	a keksz	a sajt
	the book	*the newspaper*	*the bread*	*the biscuit*	*the cheese*
object	a könyvet	az újságot	a kenyeret	a kekszet	a sajtot

Table 2. Hungarian verbs used in Example 5.

	(I)	*(you)*	*(she/he/it)*		*(I)*	*(you)*	*(she/he/it)*
definite	eszem	eszed	eszi		olvasom	olvasod	olvassa
	eat	*eat*	*eats*		*read*	*read*	*reads*
indefinite	eszek	eszel	eszik		olvasok	olvasol	olvas
situation	fekszem	fekszel	fekszik		vagyok	vagy	van
	lay	*lay*	*lays*	be	*am*	*are*	*is*

Japanese allow also various word orders in sentences. However, in this paper, we consider only some segments of the Hungarian language.

Our next example is modeling the two types of conjugation of the Hungarian language. The Hungarian language is a free order language therefore our new model can effectively be used. In our example we consider a very small segment of the language focusing on the phenomenon.

Example 5. We present the used 'alphabet', i.e., the Hungarian words in Tables 1 and 2. Conjugation of verbs can be seen in Table 2.

One of the most widely investigated distinguishing features of languages is the ordering of subject (S), object (O) and verb (V) within a sentence. Theoretically there are seven different ways and each way is represented by a set of living languages. According to the statistical analysis [6], the dominating sequence is the SOV order with about 565 languages, the smallest group is the cluster with 4 languages for OSV order. An example of OSV order can be found in the Nadeb language, where the sentence 'the child sees the jaguar' is given with

awad (jaguar) kalapéé (child) hapúh (to see).

Note that in Hungarian it also makes sense to use OSV order: Jaguárt a gyerek lát. or A jaguárt a gyerek látja (a gyerek = the child, lát = (can) see) However, in Hungarian this sentence may have an additional meaning, it underlines the child, i.e., not the adult (or anybody else), but the child sees the jaguar.

In a significant number of languages, no single dominant order can be found. These languages use a relatively free word order. According to some recent approaches [5] the SOV order has a marginal role in the categorization of the languages as in more languages some of these components can be eliminated from the sentences, the corresponding clause will be pronominal or it is expressed by some verbal affixes. It is argued that a more useful typology is the one based on two more basic features, whether the language is OV or VO and whether it is SV or VS.

Correct sentences in Hungarian can be formed in the following way: a person or a thing and a situation verb can be paired in any order (respecting the person of the conjugation), e.g., "Én fekszem.", "Vagyok én.", "Fekszel te.", "Te vagy.", "Ő fekszik.", "Fekszik Jani.", "Mari van.", "Az újság van.", "A könyv fekszik."

A person and a verb in indefinite form can also be paired in any order (respecting the person of the conjugation), e.g., "Én eszek.", "Olvasok én.", "Te eszel.", "Olvas ő.", "Mari eszik.", "Eszik Jani."

A person, a verb in definite form and an object can also be grouped to form a sentence in any order (respecting the person of the conjugation), e.g., "Én eszem a kenyeret.", "A kenyeret te eszed.", "Eszi Mari a kenyeret.", "Én az újságot olvasom.", "Te a könyvet olvasod.", "A kekszet eszi Jani.", "Én eszem kenyeret.", "Olvassa ő a könyvet."

We wish to parse similar sentences and we plan to use some automata with translucent letters. The appropriate automaton may look first for the subject (having everything else translucent), and then depending on the object the automaton looks for the verb (with everything else translucent). If a definite version of a verb is used with a person, then the automaton checks the existence of the object also.

From the theoretical point of view, the main interest in modeling natural language grammars focuses on the sentences with unlimited length. Regarding the set of sublanguages belonging to the class accepted by NFAwtl the following condition should be met [19]: any language accepted by an NFAwtl should contain a regular sublanguage being letter equivalent with the language itself. Allowing an unbounded length, this regular sublanguage must have the following structure

$$S_1 S_2^* S_3$$

where S_1, S_2, S_3 are regular expressions that describes finite languages (and therefore sentences of finite length) in the simplest case. Thus the pattern accepted by the NFAwtl is letter equivalent with this regular pattern. In the simplest cases, this part is equal to

- the repetition of a fixed subsequence or
- the repetition of any permutations of elements of the subsequence or
- the permutation of equal numbers of elements from each different symbols in the subsequence.

Considering the first case, the pattern includes the repetition of the same element:
$$S_1 w^* S_3.$$

A sample sentence can be given as

Péter szereti Annát, Évát, Katit, Marit,... (Peter likes Ann, Eve, Kate, Mary,...)

This kind of pattern can be described with a simple regular grammar, thus no translucent symbols are needed. Thus, the power of $NFAwtl$ can be demonstrated at such pattern where the ordering of the elements can be arbitrary. The next sentence demonstrates this kind of pattern:

Anna egy könyvet olvas arról, hogy egy könyvet olvas Zoli arról, hogy olvas Mari egy könyvet arról, hogy Tibor olvas egy könyvet arról,... (Anna is reading a book about that Zoli is reading a book about that Mari is reading a book about that Tibor is reading a book about that ..)

In this example, the order of some words within the repeating subsentence can be arbitrary, as the semantic role is encoded in Hungarian language with case-making (inflection) of the words. The word "könyvet" is the accusative form of the stem "könyv" (book). Thus all of the following sentences can be used:

- hogy Anna könyvet olvas
- hogy könyvet olvas Anna
- hogy Anna olvas könyvet
- hogy olvas Anna könyvet
- hogy olvas könyvet Anna
- hogy könyvet Anna olvas.

The pattern of the corresponding subsentence can be given with

$$(x(yzv)^! w)^* \ .$$

In general, the form of the sublanguage is

$$(S_1 S_2^! S_3)^* \ .$$

The pattern $(x(yzv)^! w)^*$ can be validated with the $NFAwtl$ given in Fig. 9.

In natural languages, the semantic role can be represented at the syntax level by different ways. The two most usual encoding methods are the inflection

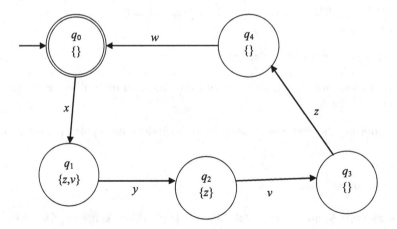

Fig. 9. The graphical representation of the DFAwtl for $(x(yzv)^! w)^*$.

and the relative position of the words. In Hungarian language, where free orders can be accepted, the different permutations usually convey different marginally semantic contents like emphases or the opinion of the sender. For example, taking the sentence

Mari sokat olvas (Mary reads a lot)

the following permutations can be constructed:

- Mari sokat olvas (correct, natural)
- Mari olvas sokat (rare use, special situation)
- olvas Mari sokat (special situation)
- olvas sokat Mari (special situation)
- sokat Mari olvas (very special situation, sounds strange)
- sokat olvas Mari (correct, natural).

The complexity of natural languages can be well demonstrated with the phenomena that acceptance of a permutation depends on the semantic of the situation. In the next example a similar sentence is used:

Mari olvas egy könyvet (Mary reads a book)

The related permutations are

- Mari olvas egy könyvet (correct)
- Mari egy könyvet olvas (correct)
- olvas egy könyvet Mari (correct)
- olvas Mari egy könyvet (correct)
- egy könyvet Mari olvas (special situation, may sound strange)
- egy könyvet olvas Mari (correct).

There are some cases also in Hungarian where the order of the words has a key role in correct interpretation of the sentence. Let us take the following example:

Péter segítette Jóskát (acc) Tomit (acc) kifesteni (Peter helped John to paint Tom).

The sentence

Péter segítette Tomit (acc) Jóskát (acc) kifesteni (Peter helped Tom to paint John).

means on the other hand a very different situation.

6   Conclusions

In this paper, the theory of finite automata with translucent letters is further developed with several applications related to (computational) linguistics. A language class is defined by extending the regular languages with a permutation operation. We showed that this extended class can be accepted by nondeterministic automata with translucent letters. A large group of natural languages has no single dominant word order, several permutations of the symbols are grammatical. The traditional finite automata represent every possible orders explicitly resulting in a huge/complex structure. The presented finite automata with translucent letters can be used for a more compact modeling of free word order in natural languages. The NFAwtl provides a more expressive and precise description of the grammar than the base (regular) finite automaton. The next step of the investigation is to cover also the non-regular and non-context-free elements of natural languages, since DFAwtls and NFAwtls are good candidates to handle some of these features...

Other main result is that we provide an almost linear time algorithm for the membership problem. The considered algorithm is non-deterministic in case of NFAwtls and deterministic in case of DFAwtls. Thus, it remains open to give an efficient deterministic algorithm for NFAwtl languages, if possible.

For technical reasons we have used an endmarker at the end of the input. It allows to check if every important parts of the sentence are already read, i.e., the main structure of the sentence is checked; since some other optional parts may be left on the tape, the process is finished by seeing the endmarker (having the remained optional parts translucent). It is an open problem whether each language accepted by DFAwtl can be accepted by a DFAwtl such a way that all the input letters (including the optional parts) of each accepted input word are erased during the computation.

Acknowledgements. The comments of the reviewers are gratefully acknowledged. The publication was supported by the TÁMOP-4.2.2/C-11/1/KONV-2012-0001 project. The project has been supported by the European Union, co-financed by the European Social Fund. This paper is an extended version of the paper [17], presented at ICAART 2013, Barcelona.

References

1. Enguix, G.B., Nagy, B.: Modeling syntactic complexity with P systems: a preview. In: Ibarra, O.H., Kari, L., Kopecki, S. (eds.) UCNC 2014. LNCS, vol. 8553, pp. 54–66. Springer, Heidelberg (2014)
2. Chomsky, N.: Syntatic Structures. Mouton & Co, The Hague (1957)
3. Clément, J., Flajolet, P., Vallée, B.: Dynamical sources in information theory: a general analysis of trie structures. Algorithmica **29**(1), 307–369 (2001)
4. Dassow, J., Păun, G.: Regulated Rewriting in Formal Language Theory. Springer, Berlin (1989)
5. Dryer, M.S.: On the six-way word order typology. Stud. Lang. **21**, 69–103 (1997)

6. Dryer, M.S., Haspelmath, M. (eds.): The World Atlas of Language Structures. Max Planck Digital Library, Munich (2011)
7. Gao, Y., Salomaa, K., Yu, S.: Transition complexity of incomplete DFAs. Fundamenta Informaticae **110**, 143–158 (2011)
8. Gazdar, G.: Natural languages and context-free languages. Linguist. Philos. **4**, 469–473 (1982)
9. Hockett, C.: A Manual of Phonology. Waverly Press, Baltimore (1955)
10. Hopcroft, J.E., Ullman, J.D.: Formal Languages and Their Relation to Automata. Addison-Wesley Longman Publishing Co., Boston (1969)
11. Joshi, A.K.: Mildly Context-Sensitive Grammars. http://www.kornai.com/MatLing/mcsfin.pdf (2010)
12. Kornai, A.: Natural languages and the Chomsky hierarchy. In: Proceedings of EACL'85, pp. 1–7 (1985)
13. Matthews, R.J.: Are the grammatical sentences of a language a recursive set. Synthese **40**, 209–224 (1979)
14. Mery, B., Amblard, M., Durand, I., Retoré, C.: A case study of the convergence of mildly context-sensitive formalisms for natural language syntax: from minimalist grammars to multiple context-free grammars. INRA Rapport de recherche p. nr 6042 (2006)
15. Mráz, F., Otto, F., Plátek, N.: Degrees of free word-order and freely rewriting restarting automata. Techical report 5/05, Kassel University (2005)
16. Nagy, B.: Linguistic power of permutation languages by regular help. In: BelEnguix, G., Jiménez López, M.D. (eds.) Bio-Inspired Models for Natural and Formal Languages, pp. 135–152. Cambridge Scholars (2011)
17. Nagy, B., Kovács, L.: Linguistic applications of finite automata with translucent letters. In: ICAART 2013: 5th International Conference on Agents and Artificial Intelligence, vol. 1, pp. 461–469 (2013)
18. Nagy, B., Otto, F.: On globally deterministic CD-systems of stateless R-automata with window size one. Int. J. Comput. Math. **90**, 1254–1277 (2013)
19. Nagy, B., Otto, F.: Finite-state acceptors with translucent letters. In: BILC 2011– 1st International Workshop on AI Methods for Interdisciplinary Research in Language and Biology, ICAART 2011–3rd International Conference on Agents and Artificial Intelligence, pp. 3–13 (2011)
20. Nagy, B., Otto, F.: On CD-systems of stateless deterministic R-automata with window size one. J. Comput. Syst. Sci. **78**(3), 780–806 (2012)
21. Reich, P.A.: The finiteness of natural languages. Language **45**, 831–843 (1969)
22. Sullivan, W.J.: Syntax and linguistic semantics in stratificational theory. Current approaches to syntax, pp. 301–327 (1980)
23. Wintner, S.: Formal language theory for natural language processing. In: Proceedings of ACL'02, pp. 71–76 (2002)
24. Yu, S.: Regular languages (Chaper 2). In: Rozenberg, G., Salomaa, A. (eds.) Handbook of Formal Languages, vol. 1, pp. 41–110. Springer, Berlin (1997)

Distributed Evacuation Route Planning
Using Mobile Agents

Alejandro Avilés[1]([✉]), Munehiro Takimoto[2], and Yasushi Kambayashi[3]

[1] University of Granada, Granada, Spain
aam00028@red.ujaen.es
[2] Department of Information Sciences, Tokyo University of Science, Tokyo, Japan
mune@is.noda.tus.ac.jp
[3] Department of Computer and Information Engineering,
Nippon Institute of Technology, Saitama, Japan
yasushi@nit.ac.jp

Abstract. This paper proposes a distributed multi-agent framework for discovering and optimizing evacuation routes on demand. Our framework assumes mobile ad hoc networks (MANETs) composed of smartphones with geo-location capabilities. On the network, heterogeneous mobile agents cooperatively insert knowledge about crowd in our mass evacuation framework. They are relying exclusively on crowd sourcing; therefore our framework is layout independent and adaptable for any situation. The mobile agents take advantage of ant colony optimization (ACO) in order to collect such knowledge. Once users reach safe areas, they distribute agents to inform the directions of the locations of the safe areas. On the other hand, evacuating users distribute agents to search safe areas, based on guidance given by the agents from the safe areas. Once each searching agent reaches the safe area, it traces its path backwardly collecting geographical information of intermediate nodes for composing an evacuation route. During the backward travel, agents lay down pheromone as they migrate back based on the ACO algorithm, strengthening quasi-optimal physical routes, and hence guiding succeeding agents. A characteristic of pheromone in this family of algorithms is that it lessens during run-time, keeping the information about successful escape routes current, as is essential in an evacuation scenario. We have implemented a simulator based on our framework in order to show the effectiveness of our technique. We discuss the behaviors of our system with various settings on the simulator for real world implementation in the near future.

1 Introduction

In cases of emergency, people in a building, facility or even whole cities might need to be evacuated. Known routes, however, found to be congested or compromised can lead crowds to panic when there is a lack of information for an alternate route to reach a safe area. Therefore, it is desirable to have an infrastructure-less, adaptable, real-time framework to assist evacuees to find

© Springer-Verlag Berlin Heidelberg 2014
N.T. Nguyen (Ed.): TCCI XVII 2014, LNCS 8790, pp. 128–144, 2014.
DOI: 10.1007/978-3-662-44994-3_7

routes on demand. Such a system would not need any previous specific preparation of roads or buildings with monitoring and communication equipment in order to increase the survival rate.

We apply swarm intelligence-based routing mechanisms that are well known to be useful in virtual environments as shown in [4,10,11]. Adapting them, crowd flow guidance in the real world through handheld devices such as smartphones is possible.

Nowadays, smartphones are increasingly relevant in daily life among a very wide range of users. This remarkable growth results from some features such as portability, which traditional computers lack. This feature as well as relatively small size can be applied to solve old problems in new ways. In particular, there are two key features for the implementation of our framework: (1) The smartphones wireless connectivity, which allows the deployment of a swarm intelligent system, and (2) built-in Global Positioning System (GPS) reception that provides location information.

The combination of these technologies on a single portable device along with swarm mechanisms assists to identify not only the main successful evacuation routes but also alternative ones. In addition, it also makes it possible to take into account the congestion in the routes. Moreover, found routes can reflect unpredictable human behavior that could have been overseen by safety policies [16].

We propose a distributed multi-agent framework for discovering optimized evacuation routes on demand. We call this framework Evacuation Routing Using Ant Colony Optimization over Mobile Ad hoc Networks (ERAM). This framework has evolved from AntHocNet [6–8], a framework for routing in Mobile Ad hoc Networks (MANETs) and the algorithm for resource discovery in P2P networks presented in [13,14]. Both approaches use Ant Colony Optimization (ACO) providing indirect communication between agents in order to achieve self-organized optimization.

ACO is a biologically inspired framework based on ant foraging behaviors, as proposed in [2,9]. Ant agents laying pheromone down reinforce paths that are more likely to lead towards fruitful nodes. This way, pheromone level indicates the goodness of a node regarding the goal. Thanks to the ant agents constantly modifying the pheromone level the system becomes quasi-optimized during runtime. This indirect method is called *stigmergy*.

The structure of the balance of this paper is as follows. In the second section, we describe an evacuation scenario in which ERAM performs the guidance for the users. The third section describes the ERAM framework. ERAM consists of several static and mobile agents. The static agents interact with users and store routing information, and the mobile agents effectively work together with *stigmergy* to find optimal evacuation routes. The fourth section demonstrates the usefulness of the framework with the results of numerical experiments on a simulator we built. Finally, the fifth section discusses conclusion and future work.

2   Scenario

ERAM presents a novel hybrid solution for physical environment routing using networked resources, a field that has not been previously investigated, in contrast with other swarm intelligence-based routing frameworks such as the ones proposed in [13,20]. Whereas the latter focus basically on data packet routing over networks, ERAM aims to discover physical resources over physical layouts instead of virtual ones. ERAM, however, uses networks as a means to locate those resources, and thus previous researches on ACO routing provide it a robust background.

2.1   Scenario Description

As derived from the previous section, in an evacuation scenario resources correspond to physical safe areas. Such information may be actively input by users on their smartphones when safe a area is reached. Each user holding a smartphone is referred to as node. Paths discovered with ERAM take into account physical locations. GPS is used to provide geographic information that will be collected on ERAM as described later. This information is also used to evaluate the congestion of crowd flows and to optimize them.

In order to perform resource discovery and routing, both active and passive sources of information are important. Users provide active input when they reach safe areas and smartphones provide passive input by constantly storing GPS tracks.

Finally, optimal routing discovery both in network and in physical environments is achieved by indirect communication through migrations of mobile agents over nodes of a MANET applying the ACO algorithm described in the next section.

In order to make the scenario mentioned above technically feasible, we assume that each node has the following functionalities:

– Built-in Wi-Fi connectivity to construct the MANET with other smartphones.
– Ability to use an existing, strong GPS signal.

2.2   Scenario Difficulties

A real implementation of ERAM framework, however, reveals some difficulties mainly related with the reliability of the information.

The first problem is simply that of relying on human knowledge in a stressful situation to obtain routes. To deal with this, the framework assumes that, at least, a few people are able to reach a safe area, i.e. shelter, out of the building, etc. and mark it on their smartphone. Then, by the unsupervised usage of the pheromone, those nodes closer to these areas will be more likely to lead people to a secure area.

The second problem is to identify safe areas accurately. It is possible that inaccurate or even false indications of a safe area could be made by users. A possible solution is to weight safe flags by their concentration in a given area. This is based on the fact that the majority of people will not lie. In this manner, the more safe flags that are close to a node, the more likely that node is to attract mobile agents, and thus, to produce correct evacuation routes avoiding those leading to fake or mistaken safe areas. Another way to enforce reliability is a distributed trust protocol, as proposed in [15], which makes it almost impossible to deceive the system. This set of issues is not further addressed in this paper.

Additionally, GPS signal is probably the most troublesome aspect of the framework. It is hardly available indoors and obstacles like trees or buildings outdoors can easily hinder precision. In order to obtain precise GPS samples, there are some widespread solutions currently available. One of them is the usage of differential GPS, which relies on static devices with known position such as cell-phone antennas. Another one is using external sensors or measurement of Wi-Fi signal to estimate absolute position like the one proposed in [19]. This solution implies relying on infrastructure or preloaded information, which might be eventually necessary in order to improve this framework. There are also more innovative approaches such as [1], which propose a taxonomic GPS that would provide precise and ubiquitous positioning.

3   ERAM Framework

In this section, ERAM framework is described in detail. It first covers the agents that are involved in the consecution of the goal, conditions of the algorithm to guarantee the negotiability of the evacuation route, and the formal definition of the pheromone calculation.

3.1   Agents

Due to the similarities of ERAM's scenario with the one proposed in [13], the solutions are also similar. In particular, its concept of a set of collaborative static and mobile agents for discovery of resources in P2P networks has also been adapted to ERAM. This concept is necessary to deal with the complexity and uncertainty to be managed by a hybrid network-physical scenario.

Figure 1 depicts the different kinds of agents participating in the framework. The following descriptions are brief explanation of their tasks.

1. Information Agent (IA): IA is a static agent residing on each node. It is in charge of perceiving physical context as well as storing knowledge about its hosting node. It also acts as an interface with the user, receiving input and providing directions to follow.
2. Node management Agent (NA): NA is a static agent also residing on each node. It is in charge of storing knowledge of the network context, namely storing information about other nodes.
3. Goal Agent (GA): GA is a mobile agent that floods the network with information about the safe area recently reached. An IA on a safe node creates GA.

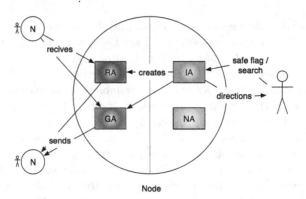

Fig. 1. ERAM participators. Nodes host mobile agents (RAs and GAs), and static agents (IA and NA). Users communicate with IA. IA creates RAs and GAs. Mobile agents migrate towards other nodes.

4. Routing Agent (RA): RA is a mobile agent that tries to find safe nodes in order to obtain evacuation routes. IA on a node in search of evacuation routes, which is called swarm node, creates RA.

The interactions between them can be illustrated as shown in Fig. 2. We describe the details of each agent below.

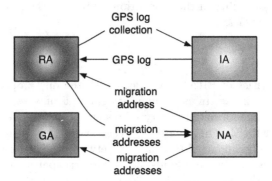

Fig. 2. Interactions between agents. Here, IA provides the node GPS log and receives GPS log collections for calculations; NA provides IP address to mobile agents, and both RAs and GAs update pheromone value on the NA.

Information Agent (IA). Each node hosts an IA that updates the GPS log by taking position samples periodically. On top of that, whenever two nodes establish Wi-Fi connection, their IAs start initiate a session in order to constantly exchange GPS logs. This method is similar as shown in SLS [12], but storing the whole GPS log instead of a single position. Collected GPS logs and all received information from such exchange is then stored in the NA of each node. We describe NA in the next section.

User can interact with the IA by activating the safe flag or by activating the evacuation search. These two modes are mutually exclusive.

- Safe flagged: When a user reaches a safe area, he or she hoists the safe flag in his or her smartphone. Once the safe flag is activated, the IA starts creating GAs periodically in order to flood the network with information about the safe area position.
- Searching evacuation: When a user is in need of evacuation route, he or she sets his or her smartphone in search mode. In this process, the IA produces RAs constantly, making them migrate to search negotiable paths towards safe areas. Once one RA returns from a safe flagged node storing GPS logs of intermediate nodes, the IA composes an evacuation route from them. If the estimated time of the new evacuation route is better, the current one is replaced by it. Finally, the route is provided to the user in a form of directions to be followed.

As pointed in [17,18], routes composed of pairs of positions should be smoothed to reduce unnecessary loops.

Node Management Agent (NA). In addition to an IA, every node hosts an NA. The NA keeps information about neighbor nodes such as IP address, GPS log and other data used for pheromone calculation. Each entry is created when the IA successfully initiates sessions with neighboring nodes, which are updated as mobile agents arrive and add new information.

As shown by Table 1, an NA encodes the basic knowledge in its matrix to cover the following fields.

Table 1. Knowledge encoded within an NA

IP:port	GPS log	Jumps	SAV	GA ID
9.163.251.45:50000	(3,4), ...	4	0.8	2435
92.71.112.26:50001	(0,1), ...	1	0.1	8431
...	...	...	...	...

- Jumps: the number of hops from a safe flagged node. It is updated by GAs.
- Speed Ahead Value (SAV): this encodes congestion level and it is modified by RAs. It is covered later in detail.
- GA ID: the unique identification of the GA that last updated the entry. This is used for stopping GAs from migrating endlessly.

When mobile agents need to migrate, they request the NA to provide them the IP addresses of the nodes to which they migrate next.

Goal Agent (GA). A safe flagged node's IA creates GAs in order to dissem-
inate the information in the network about the safe area. The GA, therefore,
requests the NA information of all the connected nodes, and clones itself on
each of them. As the GA migrates through the network, it counts the number of
hops it has performed. When it steps to a new node, this information is provided
to the NA of that node in order to update the Jumps entry of the neighboring
nodes. This information is used for subsequent pheromone calculation.

The terminating condition of a GA's migration is as follows. When it is
created, every GA has a unique identification. Thus, if it steps into a node with
the same GA ID as it has it means that node has been previously visited by one
of the other clones of the GA, and therefore the GA is killed. GA's life span is
graphically explained in Fig. 3.

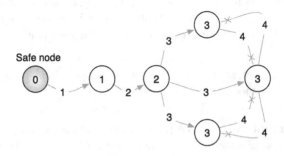

Fig. 3. Migration activity of a GA through a simple ad hoc network. Numbers represent
Jumps value. Arrows with an X at the end mean the GA is killed.

Routing Agent (RA). A routing agent is an agent created by an IA on a node
that searches for safe areas. The RA migrates while it satisfies the condition
where a GPS log on a new node to which it is migrating has some intersections
with the GPS log of the current node as shown in Fig. 4. It means that there
are some intersections between GPS logs such as a chain, and this is possible
because the NA of the hosting node stores the GPS log of nodes surrounding
that node.

This condition enables ERAM to identify the shortest known route to a safe
area for the node following paths derived from GPS logs.

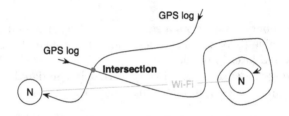

Fig. 4. Condition for RA to perform a migration

In order to optimize this evacuation route, the RA will choose nodes with higher pheromone value at present. As ACO states, this is merely probabilistic as explained in [5]; therefore, this allows stochastic exploration of routes.

If a situation in which a sequence of connecting nodes meets the mentioned condition and it reaches a safe flagged node, the RA becomes a backward RA immediately. The backward RA follows the same path as the forward RA but in the opposite direction.

There may be some situations in which the forward RA arrives at a node using an evacuation route already created. In this case the RA will copy the evacuation route and become a backward RA.

On its way back, the RA collects the GPS logs of the nodes while laying pheromone down in the NAs on the nodes. This pheromone, represented by Speed Ahead Value (SAV), reflects the congestion present along the path. When the RA reaches the original node where it was created, the GPS logs are provided to the IA. Once this happens the evacuation route is established.

3.2   Route Construction

The route composed from GPS logs is expected to be an evacuation route because a chain of intersecting GPS logs ends in a safe flagged node, which is in a safe area.

This is the expected result of the algorithm used to compose the evacuation route, when intersecting GPS logs have been received. The composed route avoids loops and unnecessary paths by deleting those parts that do not lead towards a safe flagged node.

As depicted in Fig. 5, sometimes the GPS logs may be not exactly intersecting but should be considered for having physical reachability. In such a case, fuzzy approaches provide flexibility for dealing with uncertainty as well as with constraints that accept some degree of error.

In our system, instead of binary functions returning whether some intersections exist or not, a radial basis function is used to loosen intersection constraints.

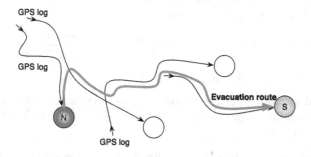

Fig. 5. When GPS logs are not exactly intersecting but proximity can be used for calculating the evacuation route.

Notice here that such a radial basis function needs a predefined threshold of distance to be regarded as an intersection between GPS tracks.

3.3   ACO Algorithm

The following equation determines the pheromone level of a node.

$$pheromone(n) = \frac{speed_n}{jumps_n} * SAV_n \tag{1}$$

$speed_n$ is the average speed of node n, using the GPS track stored in its IA. The length of the time window of the GPS track affects the sensibility of this parameter. This implies that the shorter the length of the window becomes, the fewer samples for calculating the parameter we get. That results in a highly responsive value, causing the last few seconds of the movement to be reflected more precisely.

$jumps_n$ reflects how many migrations are needed to reach the closest safe flagged node. Due to the agents wireless capabilities this is a heuristically determined parameter as it positively estimates how far the node is from a safe area. This is because even if agents can migrate through obstacles such as walls, human beings will not be able to pass through.

SAV_n stands for Speed Ahead Value. It serves the purpose of estimating congestion ahead. For SAV, having a lower value means that nodes ahead are moving more slowly, therefore the probability of congestion is higher and RAs will be less likely to follow these nodes while seeking a safe flagged node.

Like pheromone as described in [13], our framework does not implement a pheromone decay system through evaporation. Instead, because RAs are constantly migrating through the network, this value is frequently updated and serves as the pheromone decay mechanism.

SAV of any safe node is 1. SAV of a non-safe given node n starts at 1 and it is recalculated based on: its SAV previous value and both the SAV and average speed from the node straight ahead. The RA carries that information. In this way, knowledge about congestion is propagated backward through the network while updating each node through iterations.

The formal calculation is as follows.

$$SAV(n) = w_1 SAV_n + w_2 SAV_{n-1} + w_3 \frac{speed_{n-1}}{speedNorm} \tag{2}$$

$$Where\ 0 < SAV \leq 1, and\ w_1 + w_2 + w_3 = 1$$

w_1, w_2 and w_3 are predefined weights that determine how SAV will be modified through iterations. Fine-tuning these three constants is the key to obtaining a self-optimizing routing system.

- w_1: represents how slowly SAV is modified through iterations. The higher the weight is, the slower SAV will be affected. Having values near to 1 means that it will hardly change, and near to 0 means that will be overridden every iteration.

- w_2: represents how much overall congestion ahead from node n influences its SAV calculation. Having values near to 1 means that initial SAV will be carried all the way back.
- w_3: represents how much the speed of the node straight ahead influences on the node SAV. Having values near to 1 means that SAV only represents congestion of the node straight ahead.

In addition, the variable *speedNorm* is a normalizer of the speed that keeps the value between 0 and 1.

In summary, the pheromone level of a node is directly proportional to the average speed of movement. The pheromone level is inversely proportional to the number of migrations to the closest safe area. Thus, the pheromone level is reduced by distance from a safe area and congestion.

4 Results

In order to demonstrate the effectiveness of our framework, we have built a simulator and have conducted numerical experiments. The results addressed in this section were acquired using the simulation environment that provides graphical representation of the framework and statistical results for further analysis. We call this simulation environment ERAMsim.

First, we give a brief explanation of the simulator; second, we describe the simulation settings; and last, we discuss the simulation results.

4.1 Simulator Overview

ERAMsim is a software program developed for running basic simulations of the ERAM framework. Providing both simplified physical and network environment simulations, it implements the ACO algorithm as well as the behavior of individuals trying to reach a safe area in a floor plan. Figure 6 shows a screenshot of the simulation environment.

It can be perceived that white ground represents the interior of a building whereas green grounds are safe areas outside the building and black lines are walls. Consequently, the basic unit for space is the pixel, and the time is discrete.

The simulator takes account of physical constraints such as maximum density of people or the impossibility of them to pass through others, producing bottlenecks in doors. It also assumes that there are some nodes that already know where to go, referred as to informed nodes, and others using ERAM exclusively, swarm nodes. As soon as any of them reaches a safe area it becomes a safe node, starting to produce GAs, and then walking away from the building.

4.2 Simulation Settings

Table 2 shows the default values of the main parameters used for running the simulator.

Fig. 6. Simulation screenshot with 300 nodes (10 % swarm). Blue nodes are informed nodes, pink nodes swarm nodes, and red nodes swarm nodes with evacuation route. Green grounds represent safe area, white ground floor within the building, and black impassable walls. It also shows Wi-Fi connections between nodes, GAs and RAs, and GPS logs in red trajectories (Color figure online).

Table 2. Default parameter values

Parameter	Value	Parameter	Value
Total nodes	200	w_1	0.1
Swarm nodes	10 % nodes	w_2	0.5
GPS log length	100 samples	w_3	0.4
Wi-Fi range	70 pixels	GA cooldown	50 rounds
ACO randomness	10 %	RA cooldown	5 rounds

These parameters are clarified as follows:

- "Total nodes" determines how many individuals-smartphone are participating in the evacuation. 200 nodes provide a density of 4.71 %.
- "Swarm nodes" configures the percentage of the total nodes using ERAM to find their way.

- "GPS log length" refers to the maximum amount of GPS samples that are stored within a NA with a frequency of 0.25 samples/round.
- "Wi-Fi range" determines the range, in pixels, of the Wi-Fi signal of the smartphones.
- "ACO random" determines the chance of a RA to migrate randomly instead of following the best pheromone value.
- "w_{1-3}" are the weights for SAV calculation.
- "GA/RA" cooldown values are the number of rounds that takes for a node to produce the next mobile agent.

We use discrete time, a floor plan with 800 px × 600 px, and nodes represented by circumferences of 6 px radius moving at a maximum speed of 2 px/round. Approximating these values to meters, nodes are 70 cm diameter circumferences. From the circumference diameter it can be derived that a pixel is 5.83 cm and it can move up to 1.16 m/s in a 46.7 m × 35 m physical environment.

Finally, default values have been chosen for the purpose of keeping the performance metric low, which enables the behavior of the framework to be easily analyzed through modifying them.

4.3 Simulation Results

The results focus on the success rate of finding a safe evacuation route rather than on overall route optimization. This is due to the fact that, for measuring the improvement comparison between virtual evacuations, time using ERAM and real evacuation time is required. In order to obtain the real one, sophisticated human behavior simulation is needed.

In these results, the performance is measured as the success rate of finding an evacuation route in terms of variables previously defined. Assuming that all swarm nodes that successfully reach a safe area are caused by the usage of ERAM, success rate of the route discovery algorithm can be formally described as follows.

$$success\,rate = \frac{swarm\,nodes\,saved}{total\,swarm\,nodes} \tag{3}$$

Because of the probabilistic nature of the simulator, in order to get reasonable results, each sample reflects the average of five simulations using the same parameter values.

GPS Log Length. When configuring a real implementation of ERAM, one of the main parameters is the GPS log length. Every node needs to exchange this information constantly with connected nodes in order to reflect lag-free geographic information. This data exchange is critical for the framework but it is also the most bandwidth consuming, and thus, it is crucial to size it optimally.

As can be seen in Fig. 7, the longer the length of the GPS log, the higher the success rate of route discovery. This is caused by the fact that it is then more

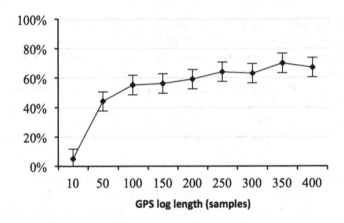

Fig. 7. Success rate depending on GPS log length

probable to find intersections between GPS logs and consequently for the system to allow more agent migrations. By easing agent migration, route discovery of swam nodes increases and so does the success rate.

Nevertheless, this metric is mainly bounded by two facts, both responsible for the plateau at around 70 % success rate in Fig. 7. The first one is related to a physical constraint and is impossible to avoid. It is that regardless the GPS log length there might be nodes located where others have never come, making any GPS intersection nonexistent. The second one has to do with technical limitations and is interesting as can be handled more easily. The problem is that although there may be GPS intersections, if the Wi-Fi signal is much shorter than the GPS log, nodes cannot be aware of it, and therefore migrations will not take place.

Wi-Fi Signal. Studying how Wi-Fi signal influences the success rate is interesting, because it not only determines the bounding the GPS log length, but also eventually provides minimum technical requirements for the ERAM framework to work properly.

Figure 8 shows an improvement in success rate similar to the one exposed for the GPS log length. Again, by increasing the Wi-Fi signal more nodes will be connected in the MANET, and this way, more GPS log intersections will be found by agents.

On the other hand, the GPS log length also bounds the improvement of Wi-Fi signal. Regardless of the range of the signal connecting nodes, technically allowing agents to migrate, when GPS logs are not long enough, intersections will hardly occur and then the migration condition will not be satisfied.

With this simulation configuration, having a Wi-Fi signal 1.5 times longer than the GPS log length produces a success rate of 93 %.

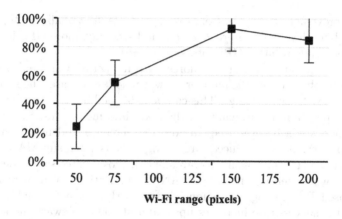

Fig. 8. Success rate depending on Wi-Fi range

Density and Swarm Nodes. Finally, we discuss the effectiveness of using ERAM depending on the density of people in the evacuation and how the framework performs when only a few of them know the way to a safe zone.

Note that swarm nodes in this simulation walk towards safe zones only when they have obtained an evacuation route through ERAM. Hence, measurements do not concern about 0 % or 100 % swarm nodes scenarios. Having no swarm nodes would mean there is nothing to measure, and having all swarm nodes would mean no human knowledge about safe areas and therefore success rate will be very close to zero.

As shown in Fig. 9, as density grows the overall success rate increases, demonstrating that ERAM presents superior performance for mass evacuations. Given the map that the simulation uses, 100 nodes mean a density of 2.36 %, and 500 nodes 11.78 %.

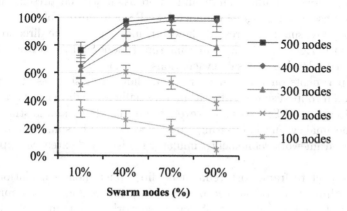

Fig. 9. Success rate depending on density and percentage of swarm nodes

This improvement is derived from two main facts: first of all, the topology of the MANET mesh is more interconnected; and secondly, more GPS logs stored in the system leads to more GPS intersections.

Another dimension that Fig. 9 explores is the impact of swarm nodes percentage. As can be observed, as the number of swarm nodes increases the success rate decreases in low-density settings. This can be explained because the more swarm nodes participating in the evacuation, the fewer informed nodes, and thus, only a few safe nodes will be produced. In addition, having low densities makes the MANET connectivity too reduced, producing some isolated sub-MANETs with fewer chances to transmit agents towards one of those scarce safe nodes.

However when density increases MANET connectivity also increases, and thus increased RAs laying pheromone down, so that even for highly isolated MANETs, the success rate increases up to almost 100 % of swarm nodes. Thus, almost all the swarm nodes eventually reach safe areas even when only a few nodes know the way to the safe area.

These results indicate that encouraging the active usage of ERAM (swarm nodes) for evacuations in scenarios such as public buildings, sport events, or cities will provide good results.

It should be clear that this metric is extremely pessimistic due to the simplistic human behavior simulated. As in a real situation a swarm node can become an informed one by asking other people, following signs or by visual contact with the safe area.

5   Conclusions and Further Works

ERAM represents a novel usage of ACO for hybrid environments. Routing people by the passive and active usage of the smartphone opens a new horizon of study. This project provides not only the first formal definition of the framework but also a software tool to test it.

A great amount of uncertainty and imprecision will be present in a real scenario because of the usage of commercial GPS, and unsuitable conditions for geo-location. The simulation results, however, indicate that the direction of our investigation is right. It is now clear that smartphone and ACO are a suitable combination to develop new safe evacuations systems.

Our experiments on the simulator so far show promising results regarding the evacuation route discovery algorithm, especially for high-density evacuation. This first iteration of ERAM is, however, the initial stage, and is still far from achieving optimal evacuation routing. Further works can be summarized in three main topics: framework refinement, simulator realism, and extensive experimentation.

With respect to framework refinement, first, pheromone calculation of the ACO algorithm needs to find the proper values for weights. One approach to solve this is to apply some sort of neural network to dynamically adapt the weights to different contexts, i.e. pedestrian or car evacuations. In addition, this would make the framework even more flexible. It is also of interest to incorporate into the framework solutions for scenario difficulties as described in Sect. 2.

ERAMsim needs further works in order to demonstrate the feasibility of the framework in different scenarios under much more complex environments. For doing so, it will be necessary to adopt more realistic simulation approaches. On the one hand, a realistic network simulation would allow measuring the congestion that agents interactions produce as well as obtaining the actual time it takes to find an evacuation route. On the other hand, utilizing physical environment simulations as shown in [3,17,18] would allow to measure how optimizing routing improves survival rate.

The simulator, although it must be improved, is good enough to show a current state and to explore the limits of this framework by retrieving results beyond the ones shown in this paper.

In conclusion, regarding the feasibility of a future real implementation, we believe that we have enough technological components to implement ERAM. The usage of smartphones is already widespread. We are trying to implement an ad hoc network solely using smartphones. Upon completion of such network, it will be possible to have a mobile agent system without explicit network infrastructures. It is also possible to have alternative location systems other than GPS. For example, it should be relatively easy to construct infrastructure using RFID rather than GPS that provides the precision needed to provide dynamic routing in controlled environments such as museums for providing new features besides evacuation routing.

Acknowledgments. Kimiko Gosney has provided useful comments. The authors appreciate them.

References

1. Bejuri, W.M., Mohamad, M.M., Sapri, M.: Ubiquitous positioning: a taxonomy for location determination on mobile navigation system. Int. J. Signal Image Process. **2**(1), 24–34 (2011)
2. Colorni, A., Dorigo, M., Maniezzo, V.: Distributed optimization by ant colonies. In: Proceedings of the 1st European Conference on Artificial Life, Cambridge, pp. 132–142 (1992)
3. Bonomi, A., Manenti, L., Manzoni, S., Vizzari, G.: MAKKSim: dealing with pedestrian groups in MAS-based crowd simulation. CEUR Workshop Proc. (WOA) **741**, 166–170 (2011)
4. De Rango, F., Socievole, A.: Meta-heuristics techniques and swarm intelligence in mobile ad hoc networks. In: Mobile Ad-Hoc Networks: Applications (2011)
5. Ducatelle, F., Di Caro, G.A., Gambardella, L.M.: An analysis of the different components of the AntHocNet routing algorithm. In: Dorigo, M., Gambardella, L.M., Birattari, M., Martinoli, A., Poli, R., Stützle, T. (eds.) ANTS 2006. LNCS, vol. 4150, pp. 37–48. Springer, Heidelberg (2006)
6. Di Caro, G., Ducatelle, F., Gambardella, L.: AntHocNet: an adaptive nature-inspired algorithm for routing in mobile ad hoc networks. Eur. Trans. Telecommun. **16**, 443–455 (2005)

7. Di Caro, G.A., Ducatelle, F., Gambardella, L.M.: AntHocNet: an ant-based hybrid routing algorithm for mobile ad hoc networks. In: Yao, X., Burke, E.K., Lozano, J.A., Smith, J., Merelo-Guervós, J.J., Bullinaria, J.A., Rowe, J.E., Tiňo, P., Kabán, A., Schwefel, H.-P. (eds.) PPSN 2004. LNCS, vol. 3242, pp. 461–470. Springer, Heidelberg (2004)

8. Di Caro, G., Ducatelle, F., Gambardella, L.: Using ant agents to combine reactive and proactive strategies for routing in mobile ad hoc networks. Int. J. Comput. Intell. Appl. (IJCIA) **5**(2), 169–184 (2005)

9. Dorigo, M., Gambardella, L.: Ant colony system: a cooperative learning approach to the traveling salesman problem. IEEE Trans. Evol. Comput. **1**, 53–66 (1997)

10. Ducatelle, F.: Adaptive routing in ad hoc wireless multi-hop networks. Ph.D. thesis, Universit della Svizzera Italiana, Istituto Dalle Molle di Studi sull'Intelligenza Artificiale, Lugano (2007)

11. Ducatelle, F., Di Caro, G., Gambardella, L.: Principles and applications of swarm intelligence for adaptive routing in telecommunications networks. Swarm Intell. **4**(3), 173–198 (2010)

12. Gajurel, S., Heiferling, M.: A distributed location service for MANET using swarm intelligence. In: Proceedings on the IEEE Mobile WiMAX Symposium, pp. 220–225 (2009)

13. Kambayashi, Y., Harada, Y.: A resource discovery method based on multi-agents in P2P systems. In: Nguyen, N.T., Grzech, A., Howlett, R.J., Jain, L.C. (eds.) KES-AMSTA 2007. LNCS (LNAI), vol. 4496, pp. 364–374. Springer, Heidelberg (2007)

14. Kambayashi, Y., Harada, Y.: Integrating ant colony optimization in a mobile-agent based resource discovery algorithm. In: Proceedings of the IADIS International Conference on Intelligent Systems and Agents, pp. 149–158 (2009)

15. Nakamoto, S.: Bitcoin: A Peer-to-Peer Electronic Cash System. From Bitcoin (2008). http://bitcoin.org/bitcoin.pdf

16. Proulx, G.: Occupant behaviour and evacuation. In: Proceedings of the 9th International Fire Protection Symposium, pp. 25–26 (2001)

17. Rodriguez, S., Amato, N.: Behavior-based evacuation planning. In: Proceedings of the IEEE International Conference on Robotics and Automation (ICRA), Anchorage, pp. 350–355 (2010)

18. Rodriguez, S., Amato, N.: Utilizing roadmaps in evacuation planning. In: Proceeding of the Computer Animation and Social Agents, pp. 67–73 (2011)

19. Woodman, O., Harle, R.: Pedestrian localization for indoor environments. In: Proceedings of the 10th International Conference on Ubiquitous Computing. ACM, New York, pp. 114–123 (2008)

20. Ziane, S., Melouk, A.: A swarm intelligent multi-path routing for multimedia traffic over mobile ad hoc networks. In: Proceedings of the Q2SWinet, New York, pp. 55–62 (2005)

Situation Theory, Situated Information, and Situated Agents

Roussanka Loukanova$^{(\boxtimes)}$

Independent Research, Uppsala, Sweden
rloukanova@gmail.com

Abstract. Situation Theory is mathematical modelling of concepts such as information, information units, situations, states, events, context, agents, and agent perspectives. We introduce major type-theoretical objects of Situation Theory, which model situated, partial, and parametric information. The system of situated objects is defined by mutual recursion. The main contribution to Situation Theory in this article is the distinction between situated propositions, as contents of statements and intentions, and situated factuality of the verified propositions. We use this distinction to define complex, propositional types. Another contribution is that we define complex, restricted parameters by using propositional types. The article demonstrates potential applications of the introduced complex, situation-theoretical objects. Among the many applications of Situation Theory are developments of intelligent language processing and user-computer interfaces, by integrations of human and computer languages. We focus on modelling major objects that have potentials in such applications, e.g., contexts, situated agents, and usage of names to designate objects depending on agents and information available to agents.

Keywords: Situation theory · Information · Situation semantics · Parameters · Partiality · Situations · Types · Restricted parameters · Context · Agents

1   Introduction

1.1   Background

In 80's, Barwise [2] and Barwise and Perry [5] introduced Situation Theory with the ideas that partiality, factual content, and situatedness are crucial features of the meaning concepts that involve mental states, including attitudes. Situation Theory developed as a theory of the inherent relational and situational nature of information, in general, not only of linguistic meanings, by diverging from the traditional possible-world theories of semantics with type-theoretic settings, in particular from Montague's IL (see [27]). Detailed discussions and motivations

---

I am grateful to anonymous readers for valuable inspirations and suggestions.

© Springer-Verlag Berlin Heidelberg 2014
N.T. Nguyen (Ed.): TCCI XVII 2014, LNCS 8790, pp. 145–170, 2014.
DOI: 10.1007/978-3-662-44994-3_8

of the situation-theoretic objects, such as situation types similar to the ones introduced in this article, are given in [5]. A more formal introduction, in the lines of our work here, is given in [17]. For an informal introduction to Situation Theory and Situation Semantics, with examples and intuitions, see [9]. One of the most distinguished applications of Situation Theory has been Situation Semantics for computational analysis of human language. Head-driven Phrase Structure Grammar (HPSG) (see [22,23]) is one of the first practical grammar frameworks, based on formal syntax of human language by using typed, linguistic feature-value structures, which was introduced by the ideas of Situation Theory for information distribution. HPSG came with ambitions to use Situation Semantics for including semantic representations in syntactic analyses. Current HPSG systems have been successfully realizing such semantic representations with a specialized language, Minimal Recursion Semantics (MRS), for handling scope ambiguities (see [8,15]). Situation Semantics has inspired other work in linguistics, e.g., it was used for semantic analysis of questions (see [10]) and for semantics of tense and aspect, in settings of logic programing, from cognitive perspective (e.g., see [28]).

1.2   Mathematics of Situation Theory

Situation Theory presented in this article is a mathematical structure consisting of primitive and complex objects defined recursively. It includes primitive and complex types that classify the system of all objects. The domain of situation-theoretical objects can be a proper class, instead of a set, depending on the needs of applications.

Situation Theory includes propositions as complex objects, which are abstract, mathematical objects, e.g., representing information asserting that some objects a is of certain type T. While some of these abstract propositions can serve in semantic representations of syntactic expressions such as sentences, the situation-theoretical propositions are not syntactic expressions per se. One of our contributions in this article is that we introduce Situation Theory that distinguishes between propositions as asserting informational units and information about verified propositions. E.g., a proposition $(a : T)$ carry asserting information that some objects a is of certain type T, while the factual information that a is of the type T is $a : T$. We also define complex, propositional types that are abstractions over propositions.

Another contribution is that we define complex, restricted parameters by using types, including propositional types. In this aspect, the parameters in this article are different from the parameters presented in [5] that are restricted with event-types, which we include as complex relations. In particular, a parameter that is restricted by a type, as a model of an underspecified object constrained to be of certain kind, can be instantiated only with objects that are of the restriction type. Such situation-theoretical parameters are especially useful for modelling context and resource situations that provide objects satisfying the information in the restricted parameters. Situation Theory with similar parametric objects has been used for semantics of attitude expressions and quantifier ambiguities (e.g., see [11–13]).

From model-theoretic point, similarly to many fields of mathematics, the meta-theory of Situation Theory is set theory. This means that it has a complex, hierarchical system of abstract objects, which are set-theoretic constructs (see [5]). Furthermore, the more powerful versions of Situation Theory are distinguished by representing circular pieces information, which are non-well-founded. The typical examples of such circularity involves situations that carry information about mutual belief and common knowledge shared by different agents. Such information units can be represented in Situation Theory by objects that do not conform with the classic axiom of foundation supporting cumulative hierarchy of sets. To accommodate such non-well-founded circularity, as discussed in [3], Situation Theory uses hypersets that are based on a version of Aczel's non-well-founded set theory (see [1]). Aczel's non-well-founded set theory replaces the foundation axiom, FA, of the standard axiom system ZFC of axiomatic set theory, with an axiom of anti-foundation, AFA, which was motivated by modelling non-well-founded situations in theory of processes. Applications of Situation Theory, for which non-well-founded objects and sets are not needed, use versions of Situation Theory based on standard ZFC set theory. A modern approach to the phenomena of circularity, in various applications, including in semantics of human languages and programming, is presented in [4].

A set-theoretic modelling of Situation Theory as an axiomatic system, which insures identification of the situation-theoretic objects as set constructions is presented in [26]. The situation-theoretic objects introduced in our paper allow variants of such axiomatic systems for modelling partial, underspecified, and parametric information, by adding restricted parameters introduced here. Of particular interest are applications to logic programming and in areas that require relational structures with partially defined and parametric objects.

1.3   Related Lines of Work: Interdisciplinary Technologies

Recent years have been characterised with technological advancements across sciences and industries, by involving hardware and software engineering. Well established, classical theories and methodologies may be fully sufficient as the foundations of some of these new technologies. But the most challenging technological advances occur concurrently with new developments of their scientific foundations, including new methodologies, and new approaches to mathematical models of the domains, for which the technologies are used and applied. From this perspective, a new interdisciplinary areas are emerging, which conjoin theoretical developments in sub-areas that are often considered to be disjoint and developed separately, but are getting co-involved in the context of new technologies. In particular, the primary sub-areas that are forming foundations of new technology advances involve (1) mathematics of the concepts of computations, e.g., mathematics of algorithms and programs (2) classic and new approaches to computational models of various domains of applications (3) hardware and software engineering (4) computational approaches in life sciences.

A representative of new interdisciplinary areas has been emerging as *Domain Science and Engineering* (DSaE) (e.g., see [7]). On its side, our article represents ongoing research on development of Situation Theory, as a computational theory of information, which contributes to domain science, by modelling domains and domain dependent entities, parts, materials, relations, situations, states, events, etc. Situation Theory is information type-theory of domains of objects, materials, their properties, and relations between them, i.e., a typed model-theory of domains. We view DSaE approach as a realisation, in its domain science, of versions of Situation Theory specialised for applications in computer software engineering. The versions of Situation Theory vary depending on areas of applications. In its current stage, DSaE encompasses series of versions of Situation Theory that are software implementable. We consider that a new line of research is in due in DSaE, on inclusion of models of states, events, actions, processes, relations, and Situation Theory is a theory of such modelling, with versions depending on areas of applications.

1.4   The Main Goals of the Article

Situation Theory as a model of information with complex relations between compound objects, partiality, underspecification, and restricted parameters. Situation Theory is a powerful mathematical model of information, with expressiveness that is broad and ranges across many contemporary applications. Computerized information systems call for reliable, faithful representation of information. This requires theory of information, which does not distort information, especially when it is partial, or underspecified, and can be dynamically specified. Partiality can appear in various ways. For example, some objects have components that are partially defined functions or relations. Some of these partial functions and relations may or may not be extended over some of the objects that are not in their domains, regardless of circumstances. In other cases, information is underspecified by missing pieces of information and components, which can be added by dynamic updates or depending on the context of usage. Parametric information is a very important kind of information, e.g., where information structure is available, but various components participate as parameters, which can be either totally unrestricted (which is rarely the case), or vary within a broader type of objects, or are restricted to vary within a narrow domain subject by various compound conditions. Naturally, such conditions are expressed by propositional constraints. Situation Theory is an information theory that targets namely such goals: representation of information, which is relational and partial. It handles partially defined objects, which comprise parametric and otherwise underspecified information. Typically, such parametric objects are restricted to satisfy constraints and their specific instantiations vary depending on context.

Applications that need models of contexts, situated agents, resource situations. The use of computational semantics of human language, which is still an open initiative, can be resourceful and ranging across many applications, alongside the area of human language processing that includes semantic representations. Many of the contemporary systems in new technologies and information processing integrate human language processing, which can be more functional when integrated with related semantic information. Computational semantics has to meet various adequateness criteria (see [14]). A primary criterion is representation of partiality, underspecification, and context-dependency of semantic information. Typically, semantic information is essentially dependent on features such as contexts, described situations, agents, and agents' perspectives. We demonstrate application of Situation Theory to modelling such information structures, which include situations and objects that naturally occur in situations and participate in relations to other situated objects. Situations can vary across these relations and objects. Information that is presented in the situation-theoretical objects, including in situations, is partial and parametric. Parameters can be subject to restrictions consisting of partial information.

In the first part of this article, we concentrate on mathematics of its objects and concepts. In Sects. 2–5, we introduce Situation Theory as a type based information theory. It takes some set-theoretic objects as its primitive, basic objects and uses them in construction of more complex situation-theoretic objects, including situated types. We give examples from human language. They provide a clear grasp of the abstract mathematical objects, which can be used in other areas of application. In Sect. 6, we give a brief motivation of situation-theoretical objects as biologically realistic.

In the second part of the article, we demonstrate the potentials of Situation Theory for applications related to human language processing. E.g., we demonstrate that phenomena such as linguistic contexts and agents, which are traditionally considered as pragmatic and external to computational models, are subject to precise mathematical modelling in Situation Theory. This provides the foundation of integrating such objects in computational systems. In Sect. 7, we focus on modelling contexts and situated agents. In Sect. 8, we give situational models of objects designated by names and other definite descriptions, which depend on information available to agents and agents' references in contexts. This section provides a strong motivation of restricted parameters.

2 Situation Theory — Typed Information Theory

In this section, we introduce situation theoretical notions and objects that are fundamental for fine-grained modelling of information and information components. Situation Theory takes some set-theoretic objects as its basic objects. These basic objects then are used in the recursive construction of more complex situation theoretic objects. Informally, the basic informational pieces, called *infons*, are composite objects carrying information about relations and objects filling the arguments of the relations, at certain time and space locations. Infons can be basic or complex, by recursively defined system of objects. Infons are the ground, informational content of basic and complex informational objects, the informational content of situated propositions (introduced in Sect. 3), and other objects that carry information about situations. Infons are facts when supported by actual situations, e.g., in real or virtual worlds, theoretical models, or computerized models.

Primitive Individuals. A collection (typically, a set) $\mathcal{A}_{IND}$ is designated as the set of primitive *individuals* of the Situation Theory:

$$\mathcal{A}_{IND} = \{a, b, c, \ldots\} \tag{1}$$

The objects in $\mathcal{A}_{IND}$ are set-theoretic objects, but they are considered as primitives, not as complex situation-theoretic constructions. In various versions of Situation Theory, designated for specific applications, some of the individuals in $\mathcal{A}_{IND}$ may be parts of other individuals in $\mathcal{A}_{IND}$, and as such can be in respective *part-of* relations.

Space-Time Locations. Simplified versions of Situation Theory use a collection (typically, a set) $\mathcal{A}_{LOC}$ of space-time points and regions units:

$$\mathcal{A}_{LOC} = \{l, l_0, l_1, \ldots\} \tag{2}$$

The collection $\mathcal{A}_{LOC}$ is endorsed with relations of time precedence $\prec$, time overlapping $\circ$, space overlapping $\circ$, and inclusion $\subseteq_t$, $\subseteq_s$, $\subseteq$, between locations. In some versions of Situation Theory, the space-tile locations can be given by complex objects. E.g., a simple option (equivalent to the above) is that space-time locations are pairs of two components, one for space locations, and one for time points or periods.

Primitive Relations. Significantly, Situation Theory has a collection (typically, a set) $\mathcal{A}_{REL}$ of abstract, primitive objects that are relations:

$$\mathcal{A}_{REL} = \{r_0, r_1, \ldots\} \tag{3}$$

The elements of $\mathcal{A}_{REL}$ are abstract representatives of real or virtual relations. For example, if Situation Theory is used to model real world situations, these are abstract representatives of properties of objects and relations between objects. E.g., humans (as well as other living species) are attuned to distinguish properties of and relations between objects, perceptually in the reality, or cognitively, i.e., conceptually. We normally can recognise the property of an object to be a book, while the specifics of that property may be context dependent, a hardback book, a paperback, or e-book.

Note 1. In set theory, set-theoretic relations are defined as sets of tuples of set-theoretic elements that are being in those relations. On the contrary, the primitive relations of Situation Theory, i.e., the objects in $\mathcal{A}_{REL}$, are conceived as primitive entities: they are not sets of tuples of individuals being in those relations. E.g., to model this, the primitive relations in $\mathcal{A}_{REL}$, as well as the other primitive objects in Situation Theory, such as individuals and types, can be taken as urelements of the modelling set theory.

We maintain the notion of *extension*, by introducing more complex situation-theoretic objects: for a given relation $r \in \mathcal{A}_{REL}$ and a situation s, the extension of r in s is the set of all tuples of objects that are in the relation r in s. For example, we can distinguish when a primitive relation of reading holds between two objects: a reader and an object that is read.

The set $\mathcal{A}_{REL}$ depends on the actual application of Situation Theory[1]. For example,

$$\mathcal{A}_{REL} = \{\, man, woman, dog, run, smile, like, \dots \,\} \qquad (4)$$

Primitive Types. A collection (typically, a relatively small set) of objects, which are called *primitive* or *basic* types:

$$B_{TYPE} = \{\, IND, LOC, REL, POL, ARG, \qquad (5a)$$

$$INFON, SIT, PROP, PAR, TYPE, \models \,\} \qquad (5b)$$

where the listed basic types are used in the following way: IND is the type for individuals; LOC: for space-time locations; REL for relations, primitive and complex (see (3) and Definition 10); $TYPE$: for primitive and complex types (see (5a)–(5b) and Definition 9); PAR: for basic and complex parameters (see (19a)–(19e) and Definition 12); POL: for two polarity objects, e.g., presented by the natural numbers 0 and 1; ARG: for abstract argument roles, basic and complex (see Definitions 1, 2, 9, 10); $INFON$: for situation-theoretical objects that are basic or complex information units (see Definition 4); $PROP$: for abstract objects that are propositions (see Definition 7); SIT: for situations (see Definitions 6, 5); $\models$ is a designated type called "supports".

We assume that Situation Theory has a set of basic $\mathcal{B}\mathcal{A}_{ARG}$ argument roles, which are associated with primitive relations and properties, by respecting the following Definition (1).

Definition 1 (Assignment of basic argument roles). *A set of argument roles is assigned to each of the primitive relations and each of the primitive types, by a function Args having domain and range such that $Dom(Args) = \mathcal{A}_{REL} \cup B_{TYPE}$ and $Range(Args) \subseteq \mathcal{A}_{ARG}$, where $\mathcal{A}_{ARG}$ is the set of basic and complex (see Definition 2, 9, 10) argument roles, for a given set of basic roles $\mathcal{B}\mathcal{A}_{ARG} \subset \mathcal{A}_{ARG}$.*

For example, we can associate relations, such as *smile, read, give*, respectively denoted by the lexemes smile, read, give, etc., with arguments roles:[2].

$$Args(smile) = \{smiler\} \qquad (6a)$$

$$Args(read) = \{reader, read\text{-}ed\} \qquad (6b)$$

$$Args(give) = \{giver, receiver, given\} \qquad (6c)$$

Another option is to use a common set of shared primitive objects for argument roles: $\mathcal{B}\mathcal{A}_{ARG} = \{arg_1, \dots, arg_n\}$, for a specific, sufficiently large natural number $n \geq 0$. Depending on applications of Situation Theory, the set $\mathcal{B}\mathcal{A}_{ARG}$ of the

---

[1] The set-theoretical meta-theory of Situation theory, including representation of $\mathcal{A}_{REL}$, is not the subject of this article.

[2] In what follows, we shall follow a practice of naming the argument role of the object that is read, by the "misspelled" notations *read-ed* and *readed*.

available, basic argument roles can be chosen to be infinite. We can use as many argument roles as needed, e.g.:

$$Args(smile) = \{arg_1\} \tag{7a}$$

$$Args(read) = \{arg_1, arg_2\} \tag{7b}$$

$$Args(give) = \{arg_1, arg_2, arg_3\} \tag{7c}$$

$$Args(\gamma) = \{arg_1, \ldots, arg_n\}, \text{for any relation } \gamma \text{ with } n\text{-arguments} \tag{7d}$$

Note that there is no implicit order over the argument roles in (7a)–(7d), where the indexing with numbers has the sole purpose of distinguishing the argument roles. Which role is for what in a relation depends on the actual modelling[3] of the relations and their arguments in the abstract theoretic constructions. For example, one can fix that: in (7b), arg_1 is for the *reader* and arg_2 — for what is *readed*; and in (7c), arg_1 is for the *giver*, arg_2 — for the *recipient*, and arg_3 — for the object *given*. After such setting, it has to be used consistently throughout in the constructions and in the modeled situations.

$$Args(read) = \{reader, readed\} \tag{8a}$$

$$Args(give) = \{giver, recipient, given\} \tag{8b}$$

Each relation that has a single argument role is called a *unary relation*, or more commonly a *property*.

Typically, properties of objects, like the property of smiling, and relations between objects, like the relation of reading, pertain in space-time locations. An optional choice is to consider such properties and relations as having a specialized argument role for a location:

$$Args(read) = \{reader, readed, Loc\} \tag{9a}$$

$$Args(give) = \{giver, recipient, given, Loc\} \tag{9b}$$

Another option is to take space-time locations as a special component of the basic informational units, which we shall introduce shortly. Our choice is based on our vision for future developments and applications of Situation Theory, by inclusion of complex spice-time models. For example by using time models integrated with three dimensional space models, objects, such as individuals, that are components of informational pieces can occupy specific space locations at various times. Informational pieces with relations, properties, and actions involving objects as components typically pertain to space-time locations.

Similarly to relations, each type is associated with a set of argument roles. If a type T has a single argument role, we call it a *unary type*, or a *property type*. In particular, *IND*, *LOC*, *POL*, *PAR*, *TYPE*, are unary types, each with one argument role, that can be declared as filled only by elements of the corresponding sets:

---

[3] Another option, "intermediate" between the above two, is to accept a relatively small set of common, abstract roles, which are similar to those used by traditional grammarians, and reintroduced in linguistics by the so-called Θ-theory of the Government and Binding Theory (GBT).

$$IND: \xi, \text{ for each } \xi \in \mathcal{A}_{IND} \cup \mathcal{P}_{IND} \tag{10a}$$

$$LOC: \xi, \text{ for each } \xi \in \mathcal{A}_{LOC} \cup \mathcal{P}_{LOC} \tag{10b}$$

$$REL: \xi, \text{ for each } \xi \in \mathcal{A}_{REL} \cup \mathcal{P}_{REL} \tag{10c}$$

$$\text{and for each complex relation } \xi \text{ (introduced later)}$$

$$POL: \xi, \text{ for each } \xi \in \{0,1\} \cup \mathcal{P}_{POL} \tag{10d}$$

$$PAR: \xi, \text{ for each } \xi \in \mathcal{P}_{IND} \cup \mathcal{P}_{LOC} \cup \mathcal{P}_{REL} \cup \mathcal{P}_{POL} \cup \mathcal{P}_{SIT} \tag{10e}$$

$$\text{and for each complex parameter } \xi \text{ (introduced later)}$$

$$TYPE: \xi, \text{ for each } \xi \in B_{TYPE} \tag{10f}$$

$$\text{and for each complex type } \xi \text{ (introduced later)}$$

Argument Roles and Appropriateness Constraints. The argument roles of both relations and types can be associated with types as constraints for their appropriate filling.

Definition 2 (Argument roles with appropriateness constraints). *A set of argument roles is assigned to each of the primitive relations, and to each of the primitive types, by a function Args, with its domain and range of values such that*

$$Dom(Args) = (\mathcal{A}_{REL} \cup B_{TYPE}), \tag{11a}$$

$$Range(Args) \subseteq (\mathcal{A}_{ARG} \times TYPE) \tag{11b}$$

so that for every n-ary primitive relation and every n-ary type γ, i.e., for every $\gamma \in \mathcal{A}_{REL} \cup B_{TYPE}$, which has n arguments:

$$Args(\gamma) = \{\langle arg_{i_1}, T_{i_1}\rangle, \ldots, \langle arg_{i_n}, T_{i_n}\rangle\}, \tag{12}$$

where $arg_{i_1}, \ldots, arg_{i_n} \in \mathcal{A}_{ARG}$ and $T_1, \ldots, T_n$ are sets of types (basic or complex).

The objects $arg_{i_1}, \ldots, arg_{i_n}$ are called the argument roles *(or argument slots, or simply arguments) of γ. The sets of types $T_1, \ldots, T_n$ are specific for the argument roles γ and are called the* basic appropriateness constraints *of the argument roles of γ.*

Notation 1. *Often, we shall use the notation* (13)*:*

$$Args(\gamma) = \{T_{i_1} : arg_{i_1}, \ldots, T_{i_n} : arg_{i_n}\} \tag{13}$$

The most basic appropriateness constraints can be expressed by associating argument roles with primitive types, $T_{i_1}, \ldots, T_{i_n} \in B_{TYPE}$. For example:

$$Args(give) = \{ IND : giver, \tag{14a}$$

$$IND : receiver, \ IND : given \} \tag{14b}$$

For any relation or type (which can be primitive or complex), the objects that fill its argument roles are restricted to satisfy the constraints associated with the roles.

Definition 3 (Argument filling). *For any given relation* $\gamma \in \mathcal{R}_{REL}$ *and for any given type* $\gamma \in \mathcal{T}_{type}$ *associated with the set of argument roles* $Args(\gamma) = \{T_{i_1} : arg_{i_1}, \ldots, T_{i_n} : arg_{i_n}\}$, *an argument filling for* γ *is any total function* θ *with* $Dom(\gamma) = \{arg_{i_1}, \ldots, arg_{i_n}\}$, *which is set-theoretically defined by a set of ordered pairs* $\theta = \{\langle arg_{i_1}, \xi_1\rangle \ldots, \langle arg_{i_n}, \xi_n\rangle\}$, *so that its values,* $\theta(arg_{i_1}) = \xi_1$, *...,* $\theta(arg_{i_n}) = \xi_n$, *satisfy the appropriateness constraints of the argument roles of* γ: $T_{i_1} : \xi_1, \ldots, T_{i_n} : \xi_n$.

Infons, State of Affairs (soas), Situations. Next, we shall give a mutually recursive definition of several sets of situational objects:

- the set $\mathcal{I}_{INF}$, the elements of which are called infons, and are basic or complex information units;
- the set $\mathcal{R}_{REL}$ of all primitive and complex relations (complex relations are defined later): $\mathcal{A}_{REL} \subset \mathcal{R}_{REL}$;
- the set $\mathcal{T}_{TYPE}$ of all primitive and complex types: $\mathcal{B}_{TYPE} \subset \mathcal{T}_{TYPE}$;
- the collection $\mathcal{S}_{SIT}$ of situations.

The basic informational units are identified by a unique relation, an assignment of its argument roles and a corresponding negative or positive polarity.

Definition 4 (Infons). *The set* $\mathcal{I}_{INF}$ *of all infons:*

1. *Basic infon is every tuple* $\langle \gamma, \theta, \tau, i\rangle$, *where* $\gamma \in \mathcal{R}_{REL}$ *is a relation (primitive or complex),* $LOC : \tau$ *is a space-time location, (i.e.,* $\tau \in \mathcal{A}_{LOC}$), $POL : i$ *is polarity (i.e.,* $i \in \{0,1\}$), *and* θ *is an argument filling for* γ, *i.e.:*

$$\theta = \{\langle arg_{i_1}, \xi_1\rangle, \ldots, \langle arg_{i_n}, \xi_n\rangle\} \tag{15}$$

for some situation-theoretical objects $\xi_1, \ldots, \xi_n$ *satisfying the appropriateness constraints of* γ.
2. *Let* $\mathcal{BI}_{INF}$ *be the set of all basic infons.* $\mathcal{BI}_{INF} \subset \mathcal{I}_{INF}$.
3. *For representation of conjunctive and disjunctive information,* complex infons *are formed by operators (i.e., primitive relations, for which locations are irrelevant) for conjunction and disjunction:*
For any infons $\sigma_1, \sigma_2 \in \mathcal{I}_{INF}$,

$$\langle \wedge, arg_1 : \sigma_1, arg_2 : \sigma_2\rangle \in \mathcal{I}_{INF} \tag{16a}$$

$$\langle \vee, arg_1 : \sigma_1, arg_2 : \sigma_2\rangle \in \mathcal{I}_{INF} \tag{16b}$$

Other complex infons are constructed from various situation theoretic objects, which we can add later.

Notation 2. *Often, in this article, we shall use a traditional linear notation of basic infons:*

$$\ll \gamma, arg_{i_1} : \xi_1, \ldots, arg_{i_n} : \xi_n, LOC : \tau; i \gg \tag{17a}$$

$$\ll \gamma, \xi_1, \ldots, \xi_n, \tau; i \gg \tag{17b}$$

$$\sigma_1 \wedge \sigma_2 \in \mathcal{I}_{INF}, \quad \sigma_1 \vee \sigma_2 \in \mathcal{I}_{INF} \tag{17c}$$

Note 2. The notation (17a) does not assume any innate order over the argument roles of γ. On the other hand, in case that γ has more than one argument roles, the notation (17b), e.g. as in (18b), (18d), makes sense only by having some agreement about a notational order over the argument roles of γ and their assignments, which does not imply that this is a 'natural order' of the argument roles of the relevant relation or type.

Example 1.

$$\ll book, arg : b, Loc : l; 1 \gg \tag{18a}$$
$$\ll book, b, l; 1 \gg \tag{18b}$$
$$\ll read, reader : a, readed : b, l; 1 \gg \tag{18c}$$
$$\ll read, a, b, l; 1 \gg \tag{18d}$$

Definition 5 (States of affairs, events, situations). *We define the following complex situational objects:*

1. State of affairs (soa) *is any set of infons that have the same location component.*
2. An event (course of event, coa) *is any set of infons.*
3. A situation *is any set of infons.*

Basic Parameters. For each of the basic types IND, LOC, REL, POL, SIT, Situation Theory that has a collection (a set) of *basic (primitive) parameters*:

$$\mathcal{P}_{IND} = \{\dot{a}, \dot{b}, \dot{c}, \ldots\}, \tag{19a}$$
$$\mathcal{P}_{REL} = \{\dot{r}_0, \dot{r}_1, \ldots\}, \tag{19b}$$
$$\mathcal{P}_{LOC} = \{\dot{l}_0, \dot{l}_1, \ldots\}, \tag{19c}$$
$$\mathcal{P}_{POL} = \{\dot{i}_0, \dot{i}_1, \ldots\}, \tag{19d}$$
$$\mathcal{P}_{SIT} = \{\dot{s}_0, \dot{s}_1, \ldots\}. \tag{19e}$$

Basic parameters are also called *indeterminates.* here we follow the original Situation Theory, by denoting specific basic parameters by dots. Often, we shall use "meta-variables" for basic parameters and the type shall be either explicitly stated or understood, e.g., typically, x is any parameter of type IND.

Definition 6 (Parametric states of affairs, events, situations). *Infons, states of affairs, and situations, in which some of the argument roles, including the space-time location and polarity components, are filled by parameters, are called, respectively,* parametric infons, parametric soas, *and* parametric situations.

Example 2

$$\ll read, reader : \dot{a}, readed : \dot{b}, \dot{l}; 1 \gg \tag{20a}$$
$$\ll read, reader : a, readed : \dot{b}, \dot{l}; 1 \gg \tag{20b}$$
$$\ll read, a, b, l; \dot{i} \gg \tag{20c}$$

3 Situated Propositions and Constraints

The version of Situation Theory that we introduce in this article is general, especially with respect to the nature of many of the primitive objects, and has capacities for covering a broad spectrum of applications. We use a specialized primitive type $PROP \in B_{TYPE}$, with two argument roles: a type $\mathbb{T} \in \mathcal{T}_{TYPE}$, and an appropriate argument filling θ for $\mathbb{T}$. We shall use the type $PROP$ for constructing abstract objects (set-theoretic tuples) to model the abstract notion of a proposition, which states that the objects given by θ are of the type $\mathbb{T}$, in the following way:

Definition 7 (Propositions). Proposition *is any tuple* $\langle PROP, \mathbb{T}, \theta \rangle$, *where* $\mathbb{T} \in \mathcal{T}_{TYPE}$ *is a type that is associated with a set of argument roles*

$$Args(\mathbb{T}) = \{T_{i_1} : arg_{i_1}, \ldots, T_{i_n} : arg_{i_n}\} \tag{21}$$

and θ *is an argument filling for* $\mathbb{T}$, *i.e.:*

$$\theta = \{\langle arg_{i_1}, \xi_1 \rangle, \ldots, \langle arg_{i_n}, \xi_n \rangle\} \tag{22}$$

for objects $\xi_1, \ldots, \xi_n$, *such that* θ *satisfies the appropriateness constraints of* $\mathbb{T}$:

$$T_{i_1} : \xi_1, \ldots, T_{i_n} : \xi_n. \tag{23}$$

Notation 3. *We use the notation* $(\mathbb{T}, \theta)$ *for* $\langle PROP, \mathbb{T}, \theta \rangle$.

When a proposition $\langle PROP, \mathbb{T}, \theta \rangle$ is true, we say that the objects $\xi_1, \ldots, \xi_n$ are of type $\mathbb{T}$ with respect to the argument role filling θ, and we write $\mathbb{T} : \theta$, or, in case it is clear which roles are filled by which objects, $\mathbb{T} : \xi_1, \ldots, \xi_n$. I.e., propositions are the result of filling up the argument roles of a type with appropriate objects. We shall use a special kind of propositions defined by Definition 8, based on the primitive type $\models$. The type $\models$, pronounced "support", has two argument roles, one that can be filled by any object that is of the type SIT of situations, and the other can be filled by any object that is of the type INF of informs. I.e.:

$$Args(\models) = \{\, \langle arg_{sit}, SIT \rangle, \langle arg_{infon}, INF \rangle \,\} \tag{24a}$$

$$\equiv \{\, SIT : arg_{sit}, INF : arg_{infon} \,\} \tag{24b}$$

Definition 8 (Situated propositions). Situated proposition *is a situation-theoretical object*

$$\langle PROP, \models, s, \sigma \rangle \tag{25}$$

where $s \in \mathcal{P}_{SIT}$ *and* $\sigma \in \mathcal{I}_{INF}$.

Notation 4. *We use the notation* $(s \models \sigma)$ *and say "the proposition that* σ *holds in the situation* s*" or "the proposition that the situation* s *supports the infon* σ*".*

Example 3.

$$(s \models \ll book, arg : b, Loc : l; 1 \gg \wedge \tag{26a}$$

$$\ll read, reader : x, readed : b, Loc : l; 1 \gg) \tag{26b}$$

4   Complex Types and Relations

Situation Theory uses an abstraction operator, which recalls the λ-abstraction in functional λ-calculi, but, in Situation Theory, the abstraction operator is different. It is purely semantic, i.e., informational abstraction (not for a syntactic construction of a λ-expression in a language), and defines abstract, complex types and relations, some of which can be encoded by functions, but some of them can not. In this version of Situation Theory, we introduce the abstraction operator as producing complex types, with abstract argument roles.

Definition 9 (Complex types and appropriateness constraints). *Let Θ be a given proposition, and $\{\xi_1, \ldots, \xi_n\}$ be a set of parameters that occur in Θ. Let, for each $i \in \{1, \ldots, n\}$, T_i be the union of all the appropriateness constraints of all the argument roles that occur in Θ, and which ξ_i fills up[4].*

Then the object $\lambda\{\xi_1, \ldots, \xi_n\}\Theta \in \mathcal{T}_{TYPE}$, i.e., $\lambda\{\xi_1, \ldots, \xi_n\}\Theta$ is a complex type, *with abstract argument roles denoted by $[\xi_1], \ldots, [\xi_n]$ and corresponding* appropriateness constraints *associated in the following way:*

$$Args(\lambda\{\xi_1, \ldots, \xi_n\}\Theta) = \{T_1 : [\xi_1], \ldots, T_n : [\xi_n]\} \tag{27a}$$

The type $\lambda\{\xi_1, \ldots, \xi_n\}\Theta$, where Θ is a proposition, is alternatively denoted by

$$[\xi_1, \ldots, \xi_n \mid \Theta] \tag{28a}$$
$$[T_1 : \xi_1, \ldots, T_n : \xi_n \mid \Theta]. \tag{28b}$$

Sometimes, we shall use a mixture of λ and bracketed notation, for discriminating between the types of the abstracted away parameters.

Example 4. The situation-theoretical object (29a) is the type of situations and locations where the specific individual a walks; (29b) is the type of individuals that walk in a specific situation s and a specific location l; (30a)–(30b) is the type of individuals that read a specific book b, in a specific situation s and a specific location l; (31a)–(31b) is the type of situations, locations and individuals, where the individual reads a specific book b:

$$\lambda\dot{s}, \dot{l}\,(\dot{s} \models \ll walk, walker : a, Loc : \dot{l}; 1 \gg) \tag{29a}$$
$$\lambda x\,(s \models \ll walk, walker : x, Loc : l; 1 \gg) \tag{29b}$$

$$\lambda x\,(s \models \ll read, reader : x, readed : b, Loc : l; 1 \gg \wedge \tag{30a}$$
$$\ll book, arg : b, Loc : l; 1 \gg) \tag{30b}$$

$$\lambda\dot{s}, \dot{l}, x\,(\dot{s} \models \ll read, reader : x, readed : b, Loc : \dot{l}; 1 \gg \wedge \tag{31a}$$
$$\ll book, arg : b, Loc : \dot{l}; 1 \gg) \tag{31b}$$

---

[4] Note that ξ_i may fill more than one argument role in Θ.

Notation 5. *For given object α and a set of appropriateness constraints T, we write $T : \alpha$ iff α satisfies all the constraints in T.*

Property 1. Let Θ be a given proposition and $\{\xi_1, \ldots, \xi_n\}$ be a set of parameters that occur in Θ. Let, for each $i \in \{1, \ldots, n\}$, T_i be the union of all the appropriateness constraints of all the argument roles that occur in Θ and ξ_i fills up. Given that $\alpha_1, \ldots, \alpha_n$ are objects that satisfy appropriateness constraints $T_1 : \alpha_1, \ldots, T_n : \alpha_n$, we have:

1. by Definition 9, $\lambda\{\xi_1, \ldots, \xi_n\}\Theta \in \mathcal{T}_{TYPE}$ is a complex type with argument roles such that

$$Args(\lambda\{\xi_1, \ldots, \xi_n\}\Theta) = \{T_1 : [\xi_1], \ldots, T_n : [\xi_n]\} \tag{32a}$$

2. Let θ be the total function that is set-theoretically defined by the set of ordered pairs $\theta = \{\langle [\xi_1], \alpha_1 \rangle \ldots, \langle [\xi_n], \alpha_n \rangle\}$,
   (a) by Definition 3, θ is an argument filling for the type $\lambda\{\xi_1, \ldots, \xi_n\}\Theta$.
   (b) by Definition 7: $(\lambda\{\xi_1, \ldots, \xi_n\}\Theta : \theta)$ is a proposition, i.e., the proposition that the objects from the argument the filling θ are of the complex type $\lambda\{\xi_1, \ldots, \xi_n\}\Theta$, i.e.:

$$\langle PROP, \lambda\{\xi_1, \ldots, \xi_n\}\Theta, \theta \rangle \equiv (\lambda\{\xi_1, \ldots, \xi_n\}\Theta : \theta) \tag{33}$$

Abstractions over individuals in propositions result in *complex types of individuals*. In general, for any given proposition Θ and a parameter ξ for an individual, i.e., $IND : \xi$, which occurs in Θ, the situation-theoretical object $\lambda\{\xi_1\}\Theta \in \mathcal{T}_{TYPE}$ is a complex type, that is the type of the individuals for which the proposition $\Theta(\xi_1)$ is true.

In order to complete the recursive definition of the complex objects in Situation Theory, next we define complex relations, while in this article we do not use them actively.

Definition 10 (Complex relations and appropriateness constraints). *Let $\rho \in \mathcal{R}_{REL}$ be a given relation, and $\{\xi_1, \ldots, \xi_n\}$ be a set of parameters that occur in ρ. Let, for each $i \in \{1, \ldots, n\}$, T_i be the union of all the appropriateness constraints of all the argument roles that occur in ρ, and which ξ_i fills up[5].*

Then the object $\lambda\{\xi_1, \ldots, \xi_n\}\rho \in \mathcal{R}_{REL}$, i.e., $\lambda\{\xi_1, \ldots, \xi_n\}\rho$ is a complex relation, with abstract argument roles denoted by $[\xi_1], \ldots, [\xi_n]$, and corresponding appropriateness constraints associated in the following way:

$$Args(\lambda\{\xi_1, \ldots, \xi_n\}\rho) = \{T_1 : [\xi_1], \ldots, T_n : [\xi_n]\} \tag{34a}$$

The relation $\lambda\{\xi_1, \ldots, \xi_n\}\rho$, is alternatively denoted by

$$[\xi_1, \ldots, \xi_n \mid \rho] \tag{35a}$$

$$[T_1 : \xi_1, \ldots, T_n : \xi_n \mid \rho]. \tag{35b}$$

---

[5] Note that ξ_i may fill more than one argument role in ρ.

5 Complex Parameters with Restrictions

Any basic parameter x of type τ (i.e., $\tau : x$) can be properly assigned only to a situation theoretic object of type τ. Complex restricted parameters can be properly assigned only to objects that satisfy the constraints associated with the restricted parameters. Associating basic parameters with types has constraining effect. Thus, parameter assignments of both basic and restricted parameters are constrained.

Definition 11 (Consistent types). *For any finite set T of types:*

1. *T is consistent iff there is at least one situation theoretic object that is of each of the types in T.*
2. *A type τ is compatible with T iff the set $\{\tau\} \cup T$ is consistent.*

Definition 12 (Parameters). *Basic (19a)–(19e) and restricted parameters are parameters.*

Restricted Parameters.

1. *Let T be a finite (and consistent) set of types. If x is a fresh parameter of type τ, i.e., $\tau : x$, and τ is compatible with the set T of types, then $x^{\{\tau\}\cup T}$ is a parameter of type $\{\tau\} \cup T$. We say that $x^{\{\tau\}\cup T}$ is a parameter restricted by $\{\tau\} \cup T$.*
2. *Let ξ be a parameter and $\Theta(\xi)$ a proposition, such that ξ is a constituent of $\Theta(\xi)$ (i.e., ξ fills at least one argument role in $\Theta(\xi)$). Let T be the set of all types associated with all the argument roles in $\Theta(\xi)$ that are filled by ξ[6]. (I.e., $\lambda\xi\,\Theta(\xi)$ is a type and T is the set of the appropriateness constraints of its argument role.) If the set T of types is consistent, and x is a fresh parameter of type τ, i.e., $\tau : x$, such that τ is compatible with T, then $x^{\lambda\xi\,\Theta(\xi)}$ is also a parameter of type τ. We say that $x^{\lambda\xi\,\Theta(\xi)}$ is a parameter restricted by $\lambda\xi\,\Theta(\xi)$.*
With the alternative denotation of the complex type $[\xi \mid \Theta(\xi)]$, the restricted parameter $x^{\lambda\xi\,\Theta(\xi)}$ is denoted by $x^{[\xi\mid\Theta(\xi)]}$.

For any situation theoretic object $\gamma(x^r)$, in which the restricted parameter x^r is a constituent, we can "connect" some or all of the parameters in it to objects by a parameter assignment function.

A parameter assignment c is defined on x^T, where T is a set of consistent types, only if the proposition $(c(x^T) : \tau)$ is true for each type $\tau \in T$.

A parameter assignment c is defined on $x^{[\xi\mid\Theta(\xi)]}$ only if the proposition $(c(x^{[\xi\mid\Theta(\xi)]}) : [\xi \mid \Theta(\xi)])$ is true; i.e., only if there is a parameter assignment c' for $\Theta(\xi)$, such that $c'(\xi) = c(x^{[\xi\mid\Theta(\xi)]})$ and the proposition $c'(\Theta(\xi))$ is true.

Note that the restricted parameter $x^{[\xi\mid\Theta(\xi)]}$ is defined even if the proposition $\Theta(\xi)$ may not be true, but an object a can instantiate the parameter $x^{[\xi\mid\Theta(\xi)]}$ only if the proposition $(c(x^{[\xi\mid\Theta(\xi)]}) : [\xi \mid \Theta(\xi)])$ is true for $c(x^{[\xi\mid\Theta(\xi)]}) = a$, i.e., $c'(\Theta(\xi)]$ is true for some parameter assignment $c'(\xi) = a$. This has been our motivation for defining restricted parameters with types as restrictions, instead of with complex relations.

---

[6] Note that ξ may fill more than one argument role in $\Theta(\xi)$.

6   Biological Basis of Situation Theory

Restricted parameters represent generic patterns, "blueprints", that can be instantiated, i.e., realised, by specific objects that satisfy the corresponding restrictions and are of respective types. In nature, biological entities carry blueprints that are restricted according to shared features, e.g., of species. Parameter assignments represent specific realisations of the generic components in specific instances.

We take a stand that human cognitive abilities and faculties, that are universal for humans, are expressed by innate brain capacities for some fundamental operations:

- perception and recognition of entities, smells, sounds, etc., that are located in three-dimensional space, in time, and situated in environments
- perception and recognition of properties and relations, primitive and complex, "possessed" by entities, in space, time, and situated in environments
- human brain faculties associate properties and relations with abstract and specific objects, by argument roles and argument role assignments
- recognition of abstract patterns, i.e., of types and parametric objects
- pattern construction via primitive abstract types and abstraction over parametric objects
- pattern construction via restrictions over parameters
- pattern matching i.e., an entity $\mathcal{O}$ is of type τ, $\tau : x$.

Restricted parameters reflect innate human faculty for development and attainment of concepts of objects that have some properties and are in relations to other kinds of objects, not necessarily referring to specific objects in the reality. A youngster or an adult person can get an idea what an object with certain properties could be, without having seen any such objects, in reality or in other ways depicted. Such concepts are not necessarily expressed by or associated with language. Parameter assignments correspond to instantiations with particular objects and can represent references to particular objects, concrete and fully determined without parameters, or abstract, with parametric components.

7   Application of Situation Theory to Modelling Context Dependency

Human language is used in contexts, that can be spoken, written, pictural, virtual, in reasoning, "in the mind", or combining any of these ways of usage. Language can be used by speakers that know its abstract linguistic meanings and how the abstract linguistic meanings can be "connected", i.e., assigned to specific interpretations. Abstract linguistic meanings, taken out of any context of use, carry semantic information, which is partial, parametric and sometimes ambiguous. I.e., normally, abstract linguistic meanings, out of context, have structure with parametric constituents and abstractions over parameters. When used in specific contexts, the abstract linguistic meanings are assigned to specific interpretations, by the speakers and listeners. The interpretations in context can still be parametric and partial. Ambiguities are typically resolved by speakers' and listeners's who interpret depending on their perspectives.

Partiality of information about the objects designated by language parts is by introducing primitive and complex, i.e., restricted, parameters. The restriction r over a parameter x^r represents a constraint $r : a$ that is necessary for an object a to be associated with the parameter x^r in a larger piece of information $\gamma(x^r)$. The assignment of an object a to x^r in $\gamma(x^r)$ results in the instantiation $\gamma(a)$. The constraint r itself is not per-se a part of $\gamma(a)$, but is an additional, necessary-constraint information, satisfied by a, i.e., a is of type r, $r : a$. A speaker-agent uses the restriction r to designate the object a, by assigning it to x^r. The listener-agent identifies the object a filling the arguments in $\gamma(a)$, by the constraint $r : a$.

7.1 Linguistic Utterance Components

We follow a tradition of using the technical notion of an *utterance*, as a situation type representing minimal components of context, which are crucial for association of linguistic meanings with potentials for specific interpretations in specific contexts, i.e., in "utterances" of expressions, by speakers addressing listeners. In practice, the technical notion of an utterance can be realised for spoken, written, or combined language use. Depending on the areas of applications of Situation Theory, linguistic contexts can be extended. The context (discourse) components include, as a minimum, the following kinds of information:

1. *Pure linguistic information:* The expressions uttered are presented by a syntax-semantics interface structure, which determines its abstract linguistic meaning. The author of this article supports the view that the syntax-semantics interface in human language is innate faculty of brain physiology. Computational approaches to language processing would be more intelligent and adequate by taking such a perspective.
2. *Broad-linguistic information by utterance components:* Context contributes essential semantic information, which is not always explicitly present in the wording of expressions. The most prominent components of context are: the "speaker" agent that delivers the expression, for example by an utterance; the listener agent(s) that are addressed interpreters; the time and the space location of the utterance; the speaker's references that assign particular objects to language components; the knowledge and the intentions of the speaker and the listener that contribute to interpretations of abstract linguistic meanings, by assigning objects to parameters, and disambiguation. Such information can be presented by abstract utterance types, as parametric situation theoretic constructs.

3. *Extra-linguistic utterance information:* Various components of language use contribute semantic information, e.g., language specific word order and word inflection paradigms, punctuation, speech acts, intra-sentential punctuation, intonation, gesture and other means for expressing speaker's perspectives, stress, presenting "new" vs. "old" information.

7.2 Situated Linguistic Agents

Denotations of human language expressions in specific contexts may depend on reference acts. A *linguistic reference act* is an event consisting of at least the following components: a language expression, an object (real or abstract) referred to, which is called the referent of the expression, and an utterance situation (or a broader discourse). The *utterance situation* consists of subcomponents such as the *speaker*, the *speaker's reference act*, the *space-time location of the utterance*, and the *listener(s)*.

Definition 13. *1. The infon (36a) models the information that an individual x utters an expression α by addressing a listener y. We call any infon such as (36a) an* utterance infon. *By using Notation 2, this infon is represented as (36b).*

2. *The infon (36c) models the information that, an individual x refers to an object z by using an expression α. We call any infon such as (36c) a* reference infon. *By using Notation 2, this infon is represented as (36d).*

3. *A situation u that supports (i.e., has as an element) an utterance infon, as in (36e), is called an* utterance situation *(or briefly an* utterance*). In case that u supports exactly one utterance infon, the object x filling the argument role speaker of the relation tells is called the* speaker *in u; the object y filling the argument role listener is called the* listener(s) *in u. Note that, in general, y can be a set of individuals. i.e., listeners. We allow broader utterance situations with more than one utterance infons, speakers and listeners, which may have entirely different locations that may be related by overlapping or precedence.*

4. *When the expression α is an expression with which speakers can refer to objects[7], the utterance situation can support also a reference infon, as in (36f). In such a case, the respective reference infon $\ll referes\text{-}to, x, z, \alpha, l; 1 \gg$ is called a* speaker's reference act *in u.*

$$\ll tells, speaker : x, listener : y, uttered : \alpha, Loc : l; 1 \gg \tag{36a}$$
$$\ll tells, x, y, \alpha, l; 1 \gg \tag{36b}$$
$$\ll referes\text{-}to, speaker : x, referent : z, by : \alpha, Loc : l; 1 \gg \tag{36c}$$
$$\ll referes\text{-}to, x, z, \alpha, l; 1 \gg \tag{36d}$$
$$u \models \ll tells, x, y, \alpha, l; 1 \gg \tag{36e}$$
$$u \models \ll tells, x, y, \alpha, l; 1 \gg \wedge \ll referes\text{-}to, x, z, \alpha, l; 1 \gg \tag{36f}$$

---

[7] Such reference expressions include many noun phrases (NPs) in human languages, e.g., names, pronounce, and definite descriptions.

The object z in the reference act depends on the utterance u and its components. It can be a specific, fully identified object or a parameter that may be restricted, as in the examples that follow.

By using situation theoretical objects with restricted parameters, the utterance components can be modeled by situation-theoretical objects as follows (see also [11–13]).

The proposition expressing who is the speaker x, who is the listener y, what is the space-time location, and which is the expression α uttered in an utterance situation u, i.e., a minimum of context information is expressed by the situated proposition (37):

$$pu(u, l, x, y, \alpha) \equiv (u \models \ll tells, x, y, \alpha, l; 1 \gg) \tag{37}$$

Then, (38) is an abstract type of an utterance situation.

$$ru(l, x, y, \alpha) \equiv [u \mid pu(u, l, x, y, \alpha)] \tag{38}$$

The type (39) is the type of a speaker agent in an utterance situation u.

$$rsp(u, l, y, \alpha) \equiv [x \mid pu(u, l, x, y, \alpha)] \tag{39}$$

The type of an individual to be a listener agent in an utterance situation u is (40):

$$rlst(u, l, x, \alpha) \equiv [y \mid pu(u, l, x, y, \alpha)] \tag{40}$$

The type of an object to be the utterance (or discourse) space-time location is given by (41):

$$rdl(u, x, y, \alpha) \equiv [l \mid pu(u, l, x, y, \alpha)] \tag{41}$$

The type (42) is a type for the *referent agent*, i.e., of the objects to be referred to by an expression α in an utterance situation.

$$r_\alpha(u, l, x, y, s_{res}) = [z \mid q(u, l, x, y, z, \alpha)] \tag{42}$$

where $q(u, l, x, y, z, \alpha)$ is a proposition such as (43a) or (44a).

$$q(u, l, x, y, z, \alpha) \equiv \tag{43a}$$

$$(u^{ru(l,x,y,\alpha)} \models \tag{43b}$$

$$\ll referes\text{-}to, x^{rsp(u,l,y,\alpha)}, z, \alpha, l^{rdl(u,x,y,\alpha)}; 1 \gg) \tag{43c}$$

The proposition (43a), i.e., (43b)–(43c) asserts that the speaker x^{rsp} refers to z by using the expression α, in the location $l^{rdl(u,x,y,\alpha)}$. Here

– The situation parameter $u^{ru(l,x,y,\alpha)}$ is restricted by the type $ru(l, x, y, \alpha)$ of a situation being an utterance.
– The situation parameter s_{res} is for a resource situation, which in the case of (43b)–(43c) is $s_{res} \equiv u^{ru(l,x,y,\alpha)}$.

A more elaborate representation of the names can be expressed by the following version of the proposition $q(u, l, x, z, \alpha)$:

$$q'(u, l, x, y, z, \alpha, s_{res}) \equiv \tag{44a}$$

$$(u^{ru(l,x,y,\alpha)} \models \ll \textit{referes-to}, x^{rsp(u,l,y,\alpha)}, z, \alpha, l^{rdl(u,x,y,\alpha)}; 1 \gg \wedge \tag{44b}$$

$$\ll \textit{believes}, x^{rsp(u,l,y,\alpha)}, \tag{44c}$$

$$(s_{res} \models \ll \textit{named}, \alpha, z, l_{res}; 1 \gg), \tag{44d}$$

$$l^{rdl(u,x,y,\alpha)}; 1 \gg) \tag{44e}$$

The proposition (44a), i.e., (44b)–(44e), asserts that the speaker x^{rsp} refers to z by using the name α, by believing that z is named α. Alternatively, when the speaker knows that the referent z is named α, we can use the relation *knows* instead of *believes*. In what follows, all the above restrictions shall be written without explicitly specifying the parameter arguments.

8   Named Objects and Information Dependent on Names

In this section, we turn to examples of referential expressions, such as proper names and definite descriptions, for exposition of how Situation Theory can handle such semantic phenomena. Semantics of naming expressions gives essential contributions to semantics of larger, encompassing language constructions, e.g., such as sentences and upward to larger texts. However, it is important how those contributions are handled computationally, where is their proper placement in the semantic representations, all of which should also take into account the context and agent dependency of their semantics.

A distinctive semantic contribution of naming expressions provides means for *potential reference to objects*, by the language users, i.e., "speaker" and "listener" agents in context, e.g., by using sentences, and so forth, up to text discourse. Typically, by utterances of affirmative sentences, speakers describe some situations (not necessarily the same as the utterances) as holding facts (i.e., infons). The objects, which are the referents of name sub-expressions, participate as fillers of arguments roles of semantic relations, in the facts that are stated to hold in the described situations, by utterance situations.

It is important not to misplace the additional, auxiliary semantic contribution of the naming sub-expressions as direct components of the facts (i.e. of the infons) that are the informational content of the proposition stated by a sentence utterance, and not directly in the facts of the utterance itself.

E.g., by an utterance u of a sentence like "Maria is reading the book", a speaker may describe a situation s_1 as holding that a specific individual $z^{r_{\text{MARIA}}}$, referred to by the name "Maria", is involved in the activity of reading a specific book $w^{d_{\text{THE BOOK}}}$, referred to by the definite description "the book", in a location $l_1^{[l|lol^{rdl}]}$. This is expressed by the proposition (45):

$$(s_1 \models \ll \textit{read}, z^{r_{\text{MARIA}}}, w^{d_{\text{THE BOOK}}}, l_1^{[l|lol^{rdl}]}; 1 \gg) \tag{45}$$

The described situation s_1 may be part of or the same as the utterance u, i.e., $s_1 \subseteq u$. The possibility that s_1 is fully disjoint from u, i.e., $s_1 \cap u = \emptyset$, is left open. An utterance u of this sentence and the described situation s_1 are related via the speaker's references in the utterance. The speaker uses the name "Maria" and the definite description "the book" to identify correspondingly the participants $z^{r_{\text{MARIA}}}$ and $w^{d_{\text{THE BOOK}}}$ of the fact of reading in (45). By the inflection of the verb lexeme "read" (present-time continuous), the reading is located in a space-time location l_1, which is related to the space-time location of the utterance with overlapping via the restriction over it $l_1^{[l\,|\,l \circ l^{rdl}]}$. These pieces of information, including that the reader z is named "Maria" and that the object w is having the property of being a book (the unique one to which the speaker refers) are carried by the sentence, but they are auxiliary to the major propositional content expressed by the infon in (45). Such pieces of information should not be indiscriminately conjoined into the major propositional content. The restrictions over the parameters $z^{r_{\text{MARIA}}}$ and $w^{d_{\text{THE BOOK}}}$ "distribute" such information, which is linked to the facts in the utterance and the propositional content, i.e., to facts of the described situation.

In general, for a given naming expression α, its denotation[8] $\text{den}(\alpha) = z^{r_\alpha}$ is given by a restricted parameter, where r_α is like (42), i.e., $r_\alpha(u, l, x, y, s_{res}) = [z \mid q(u, l, x, y, z, \alpha)]$, which is dependent on the specific expression α and other context information expressed by the proposition $q(u, l, x, y, z, \alpha)$ as in (43a) or (44a). Depending on the expression α, context, and applications, r_α may have more or alternative constraints in it, e.g., by (44b)–(44e). Importantly, the object z^{r_α} is parametric and its instantiations are subject to the constraint r_α expressed by the semantics of a name α, e.g., as in (46a)–(46b), (47a), and a definite description α, e.g., as in (48a)–(48d).

Potentially, an utterance, the speaker's references in it, which are expressed by restricted parameters like z^{r_α}, and a broader context can provide a specific object referred to by an expression α, as an instantiation of the restricted parameter z^{r_α}. The instantiated object has to satisfy the restriction r_α. The restricted parameter z^{r_α} can get linked to a specific referent depending on the specific utterance context and the speaker agent. That specific referent, subjected to satisfaction of the constraint r_α, can fill up relation arguments in facts described by a larger expression, in which the name α occurs, e.g., as in (49). The restriction r_α, while a direct component of the restricted parameter z^{r_α} itself, provides "extra", i.e., "auxiliary", semantic information, which is linked to the direct semantic content of the larger expression.

Example 5.

$$r_{\text{MARIA}} \equiv [z \mid (u^{ru(l,x,y,\text{MARIA})} \models \tag{46a}$$

$$\ll \textit{referes-to}, x^{rsp}, z^{n_{\text{MARIA}}}, \text{MARIA}, l^{rdl}; 1 \gg)] \tag{46b}$$

---

[8] In order to keep the article into its major topic, we present the denotation function den without diverging to more theoretical technicalities, which are subjects to other ongoing and future work.

where the parameter z is recursively restricted by the type restriction n_{MARIA} in (47a), which expresses that the object z is named MARIA by x^{rsp} in a resource situation s_0:

$$n_{\text{MARIA}} \equiv [z \mid (s_0 \models \ll named, \text{MARIA}, x^{rsp}, z, l_0; 1 \gg) \tag{47a}$$

Example 6. The linguistic meaning of a noun phrase (NP) that is a definite description, e.g., "the book", can be expressed by $w^{d_{\text{THE BOOK}}}$, where $d_{\text{THE BOOK}}$ is the type (48a)–(48d), and s_2 and l_2 are parameters for a *resource situation* and its resource *location* for evaluation of the NP "the book". The resource situation s_2 and some of its component locations l_2 are provided by the references of the speaker agent, and while they might be the same as the utterance situation u and location, respectively, they might as well be "external" to the utterance situation and subjected to additional constraints over parameters.

$$d_{\text{THE BOOK}} \equiv [z \mid (s_2 \models \ll book, z, l_2; 1 \gg \wedge \tag{48a}$$
$$\ll unique, z, \tag{48b}$$
$$[z \mid (s_2 \models \ll book, z, l_2; 1 \gg)], \tag{48c}$$
$$l_2; 1 \gg)] \tag{48d}$$

Example 7. The abstract, linguistic meaning of a sentence like "Maria is reading the book" can be designated by the following situated propositional type:

$$\lambda s_0, s_1, s_2, l_0, l_1, l_2(s_1 \models \ll read, z^{r_{\text{MARIA}}}, w^{d_{\text{THE BOOK}}}, l_1^{[l \mid lol^{rdl}]}; 1 \gg) \tag{49}$$

where r_{MARIA} and $d_{\text{THE BOOK}}$ are, respectively, the constraints (46a)–(46b) and (48a)–(48d). The semantic λ-abstractions over the parameters $s_0, s_1, s_2, l_0, l_1, l_2$ represent the type of a relation between situations and locations, where s_0 and l_0 for the naming situation and location, s_1 and l_1 for the described situation of reading activity, s_2 and l_2 for the resource situation identifying the object that is the book.

Alternatively, the parameters for the described situation and location, any naming and resource situations and locations, in this example $s_0, s_1, s_2, l_0, l_1, l_2$, can be left as parameters that are free of λ-abstraction. In such a case, the abstract, linguistic meaning of a sentence like "Maria is reading the book" is an asserted parametric proposition, (50) for this specific sentence, where s_1 is the described situation:

$$(s_1 \models \ll read, z^{r_{\text{MARIA}}}, w^{d_{\text{THE BOOK}}}, l_1^{[l \mid lol^{rdl}]}; 1 \gg) \tag{50}$$

In both cases, (49) and (50), the proposition expressed by an utterance of the sentence is $(s_1 \models \ll read, z^{r_{\text{MARIA}}}, w^{d_{\text{THE BOOK}}}, l_1^{[l \mid lol^{rdl}]}; 1 \gg)$. The propositional information content is represented by the infon $\ll read, z^{r_{\text{MARIA}}}, w^{d_{\text{THE BOOK}}}, l_1^{[l \mid lol^{rdl}]}; 1 \gg$, where the restricted parameters $z^{r_{\text{MARIA}}}$, $w^{d_{\text{THE BOOK}}}$, $l_1^{[l \mid lol^{rdl}]}$ link the proposition with the additional information, which is carried by the sentence sub-expressions, about the objects denoted by the name "Maria" and the definite description "the book". The restrictions over the component parameters of the proposition carry information about any potential utterance u of the sentence and the utterance components, such as the speaker, the addressee, and the locations, via the situation-theoretic objects (37)–(41). These general parametric patterns for a potential utterance situation u, $(u \models \ll tells, x, y, \alpha, l; 1 \gg)$, and its components are instantiated for the specific expression α, i.e., the sentence $\alpha \equiv$ MARIA IS READING THE BOOK.

9 Conclusions and Future Work

Underspecification, partiality, and context dependency present major difficulties in related theoretical developments and adequate applications, including development of dedicated software systems, decision-problem models, and solutions involving models of states, events, actions, context, and other situations, where information can be partial and parametric. Situation Theory is a finely-grained, mathematical model of information, which respects the fundamentals of information in nature. We consider versions of Situation Semantics as its prominent applications for models of informational content for semantics of both natural and artificial languages. Various domain-dependent versions of Situation Semantics are proliferating in contemporary technologies and software systems. Mathematics of Situation Theory and its applications are open for developments depending on specific areas of applications in Computer Science and new technologies, such as Computational Semantics, Natural Language Processing, Artificial Intelligence, Cognitive Science, computational approaches to neuroscience, medical sciences, health care, ontology frameworks, etc.

Conclusions: Advances in Theory for Applications to New Technologies. This article is part of our broader work on theoretical development of Situation Theory for modelling complex information and development of computational syntax-semantics interfaces for natural languages. Mathematical models of the concepts of context and agents in context concern fundamentals of syntax-semantics interfaces in languages in general. Our specific goal is theoretical development of computational type-theory of information for language processing based on syntax-semantics interface. We target theory of information that is supported by the role of languages in nature, from the perspective of applications and software engineering in new technologies.

One of the primary applications of Situation Theory is to computational semantics of human languages, for modelling semantic domains and information that is designated by human language, including linguistic contexts and agents. Human language is notoriously ambiguous and context dependent. These phenomenal features present the core part of language productivity and efficiency, partly because they allow different agents, in different contexts, to express varying information, with familiar expressions. Moreover, language expressions, even when considered unambiguous, when out of context, carry partial and parametric information, which is not necessarily and fully instantiated in specific contexts when used by specific agents. In many cases, agents such as language users, speakers, listeners, and readers, appreciate parametric, partial and under-specified information expressed by language even in specific contexts. This presents needs of a theory that models partial, parametric and underspecified information, that also models the context-dependency of language and information. This means that such a theory of information has the capacities to model interrelated context components and language agents in context. Situation Theory has been under development for meeting such needs.

Future Work. Closely related line of research is development of new approach to the fundamentals of computation and the notion of intension. Moschovakis recursion (see [20, 21]) models the concepts of algorithm in a novel way that covers fundamental features of computation processes. In particular, the formal language and theory of Moschovakis acyclic recursion L_{ar}^λ (see [21]) introduces a novel approach to modelling the logical concepts of meaning, synonymy, and referential intension, by targeting adequateness of computational semantics of human language.

The formal system L_{ar}^λ has been used in work (see [16, 18]) on the theoretical aspects of computational syntax-semantics interface, by covering major syntactic constructions of human language, in Generalized Constraint-Based Lexicalized Grammar (CBLG). Further work is ongoing in the following directions:

- mathematical modelling of the domains of semantic structures of L_{ar}^λ. E.g., in this direction, we target versions of Situation Theory.
- developments of type-theory of recursion, in several directions for adequacy depending on applications (see [19]). Further work is necessary towards (1) type-theory of full recursion (2) type-theory of recursion with extended type systems, for example with dependent types (3) L_{ar}^λ includes states as contexts in all of its layers: a specialized type for states in its type system, variables for states in its syntax, and a specialized domain of states in its semantic structures. The concept of state, in the current stage of L_{ar}^λ, is rudimentary and in need of development. For this purpose, we envisage using a version of Situation Theory.

Another closely related work involves using versions of Situation Theory and type-theory of algorithms (i.e., Moschovakis recursion) in large-scale grammatical frameworks for human language. In particular, a highly expressive new grammatical framework (GF) (see [24, 25]) has been under developments for multi-lingual translations, by targeting universal, typed-directed syntax that covers major semantic features of human-language. We maintain the view that GF, as a new branch of CBLG, is open and highly prospective for further work on syntax-semantics interfaces, e.g., in the lines of the new ideas and approaches presented in this article.

New foundational developments, such as Situation Theory and Typed theory of Recursion, target more adequate, reliable and intelligent foundations of technological applications. In the same time, they are part of the ever advancing, scientific understanding of the fundamentals of information and computation.

References

1. Aczel, P.: Non-well-founded Sets. CSLI Lecture Notes, vol. 14. CSLI Publications, Stanford (1988)
2. Barwise, J.: Scenes and other situations. J. Philos. **78**, 369–397 (1981)
3. Barwise, J., Etchemendy, J.: The Liar: An Essay on Truth and Circularity. Oxford University Press, New York (1995)
4. Barwise, J., Moss, L.: Vicious Circles: On the Mathematics of Non-Wellfounded Phenomena. CSLI Publications, Stanford (1996)
5. Barwise, J., Perry, J.: Situations and Attitudes. MIT Press, Cambridge (1983). republished as [6]
6. Barwise, J., Perry, J.: Situations and Attitudes. The Hume Series. CSLI Publications, Stanford (1999)
7. Bjørner, D.: Domain science & engineering: a foundation for computation for humanity. In: Computation for Humanity: Information Technology to Advance Society, pp. 157–175 (2013)
8. Copestake, A., Flickinger, D., Pollard, C., Sag, I.: Minimal recursion semantics: an introduction. Res. Lang. Comput. **3**, 281–332 (2005)
9. Devlin, K.: Situation theory and situation semantics. In: Gabbay, D., Woods, J. (eds.) Handbook of the History of Logic, vol. 7, pp. 601–664. Elsevier, Amsterdam (2008)
10. Ginzburg, J., Sag, I.A.: Interrogative Investigations: The Form, Meaning, and Use of English Interrogatives. CSLI Publications, Stanford (2000)
11. Loukanova, R.: Russellian and strawsonian definite descriptions in situation semantics. In: Gelbukh, A. (ed.) CICLing 2001. LNCS, vol. 2004, pp. 69–79. Springer, Heidelberg (2001)
12. Loukanova, R.: Generalized quantification in situation semantics. In: Gelbukh, A. (ed.) CICLing 2002. LNCS, vol. 2276, pp. 46–57. Springer, Heidelberg (2002)
13. Loukanova, R.: Quantification and intensionality in situation semantics. In: Gelbukh, A. (ed.) CICLing 2002. LNCS, vol. 2276, pp. 32–45. Springer, Heidelberg (2002)
14. Loukanova, R.: Computational syntax-semantics interface. In: Bel-Enguix, G., Jiménez-López, M.D. (eds.) Language as a Complex System: Interdisciplinary Approaches, pp. 111–150. Cambridge Scholars Publishing, Cambridge (2010)
15. Loukanova, R.: From Montague's rules of quantification to minimal recursion semantics and the language of acyclic recursion. In: Bel-Enguix, G., Dahl, V., Jiménez-López, M.D. (eds.) Biology, Computation and Linguistics – New Interdisciplinary Paradigms, Frontiers in Artificial Intelligence and Applications, pp. 200–214. IOS Press, Amsterdam (2011)
16. Loukanova, R.: Semantics with the language of acyclic recursion in constraint-based grammar. In: Bel-Enguix, G., Jiménez-López, M.D. (eds.) Bio-Inspired Models for Natural and Formal Languages, pp. 103–134. Cambridge Scholars Publishing, Cambridge (2011)
17. Loukanova, R.: Situated propositions with constraints and restricted parameters. In: Blache, P., Christiansen, H., Dahl, V., Villadsen, J. (eds.) Proceedings of the 6th International Workshop on Constraints and Language Processing. Computer Science Research Reports, vol. 134, pp. 44–55, October 2011

18. Loukanova, R.: Syntax-semantics interface for lexical inflection with the language of acyclic recursion. In: Bel-Enguix, G., Dahl, V., Jiménez-López, M.D. (eds.) Biology, Computation and Linguistics - New Interdisciplinary Paradigms, Frontiers in Artificial Intelligence and Applications, vol. 228, pp. 215–236. IOS Press, Amsterdam (2011)

19. Loukanova, R.: Semantic information with type theory of acyclic recursion. In: Huang, R., Ghorbani, A.A., Pasi, G., Yamaguchi, T., Yen, N.Y., Jin, B. (eds.) AMT 2012. LNCS, vol. 7669, pp. 387–398. Springer, Heidelberg (2012)

20. Moschovakis, Y.N.: Sense and denotation as algorithm and value. In: Oikkonen, J., Vaananen, J. (eds.) Lecture Notes in Logic, vol. 2, pp. 210–249. Springer, Heidelberg (1994)

21. Moschovakis, Y.N.: A logical calculus of meaning and synonymy. Linguist. Philos. **29**, 27–89 (2006)

22. Pollard, C., Sag, I.A.: Information-Based Syntax and Semantics, Part I. CSLI Lecture Notes, vol. 13. CSLI Publications, Stanford (1987)

23. Pollard, C., Sag, I.A.: Head-driven Phrase Structure Grammar. University of Chicago Press, Chicago (1994)

24. Ranta, A.: Grammatical framework: a type-theoretical grammar formalism. J. Funct. Program. **14**(2), 145–189 (2004)

25. Ranta, A.: Grammatical Framework: Programming with Multilingual Grammars. CSLI Publications, Stanford (2011)

26. Seligman, J., Moss, L.S.: Situation Theory. In: van Benthem, J., ter Meulen, A. (eds.) Handbook of Logic and Language, pp. 239–307. Elsevier, Amsterdam (1996)

27. Thomason, R.H. (ed.): Formal Philosophy: Selected Papers of Richard Montague. Yale University Press, New Haven (1974)

28. Van Lambalgen, M., Hamm, F.: The Proper Treatment of Events. Explorations in Semantics. Wiley-Blackwell, Oxford (2004)

Conditional Preference Networks Support Multi-issue Negotiations with Mediator

Sujata Ghosh[1]([✉]), Thiri Haymar Kyaw[2], and Rineke Verbrugge[3]

[1] Indian Statistical Institute, SETS Campus, Chennai 600 113, India
sujata@isichennai.res.in
[2] University of Technology (Yatanarpon Cyber City),
Pyin Oo Lwin, Myanmar
thirihaymankyaw@gmail.com
[3] Department of Artificial Intelligence, University of Groningen,
Groningen, The Netherlands
rineke@ai.rug.nl

Abstract. Conflicts of interest occur in various aspects of our daily life and we often come to an understanding by negotiating our way through these conflicts. This paper presents a simple interactive negotiation approach to resolve certain conflicts that involve multiple issues. The focus is on mediation to facilitate a solution based on alternating offers over a finite-time bargaining game. The mediator explores the possibilities and proposes a jointly optimal negotiation text for all the players participating in the negotiation process, based on their conditional preference networks (CP-nets). Each individual player then makes a decision to accept or reject the proposal based on their utility CP-nets. If any player rejects, the mediator offers another negotiation text and the process goes on until an agreement is achieved or some time limit is reached. Two algorithms are developed with regard to the players as well as the mediator, and a daily-life situation is investigated based on them. A historically important negotiation event has also been investigated using this model.

1 Introduction

Negotiation occurs in several areas of real-world problems: personal cases such as marriage, divorce, and parenting; business cases such as pricing between seller and buyer and sharing a market between organizations; international crisis cases like the Cuba missile crisis, the North Korean crisis, and Copenhagen climate change control. Negotiation is a process for agents to communicate and compromise in order to reach beneficial agreements. In such situations, the agents have a common interest in cooperating, but have conflicting interests over exactly how to cooperate [9].

Bargaining is a simple form of a negotiation process. It is used to establish a price to trade a fixed and defined commodity between seller and buyer. One party usually attempts to gain advantage over another to obtain the best possible agreement. Splitting a pie between two players is a simple bargaining example.

© Springer-Verlag Berlin Heidelberg 2014
N.T. Nguyen (Ed.): TCCI XVII 2014, LNCS 8790, pp. 171–195, 2014.
DOI: 10.1007/978-3-662-44994-3_9

In such games with many periods of offers and counteroffers, strategies are not just actions, but rather ways for choosing actions based on the actions chosen by both agents in earlier periods [20].

In competitive bargaining, the process is viewed as a competition that is to be won or lost. Positional bargaining is a negotiation strategy that involves holding on to a fixed idea, or position, of what you want and arguing for it and it alone, regardless of any underlying interests. The classic example of positional bargaining is the haggling that takes place between proprietor and customer over the price of an item. The customer has a maximum amount she will pay and the proprietor will only sell something for a price above a certain minimum amount. Each side starts with an extreme position, which in this case is a monetary value, and proceeds from there to negotiate and make concessions. Eventually a compromise may be reached. A position is usually determined by the interests of a negotiating party, and reflected in a contract that it puts forward to its counterpart.

Integrative bargaining (also called "interest-based bargaining" or "win-win bargaining") is a negotiation strategy in which parties collaborate to find a "win-win" solution to accommodate their different interests. This strategy focuses on developing mutually beneficial agreements based on the interests of the disputants. Interests include the needs, desires, concerns, and fears important to each side [19]. Integrative bargaining usually produces more satisfactory outcomes for the players involved than does positional bargaining. Positional bargaining is based on fixed, opposing positions and tends to result in a compromise or no agreement at all. Our negotiation approach focuses on integrative bargaining for achieving a satisfactory agreement for all players.

Interest-based negotiation either can get the parties to an agreement point where they can bargain or even better, to a point where they do not need to bargain at all. Interest-based negotiation typically entails two or more issues to be negotiated. It involves an agreement process that better integrates the aims and goals of all the negotiating parties through creative and collaborative problem solving.

Mediation usually consists of a negotiation process that employs a mutually agreed upon third party to settle a dispute between negotiating parties in order to find a compatible agreement to resolve disputes [10]. In negotiation, the parties agree to work with each other to resolve a dispute. In mediation, the parties agree to work with a facilitator or mediator to resolve a conflict. In many cases, international negotiations aim to achieve an agreement on various issues between multiple parties. "Camp David" is an interesting example of a negotiation that happened between Egypt and Israel in 1978, resulting in a more or less successful agreement with the help of a mediator, the United States.

In this paper, we propose a simple mediated approach for multi-issue negotiation with incomplete information based on adjusting the players' preferences. In this approach, the mediator searches for a jointly optimal negotiation text for all players in their conditional preference networks (CP-nets), using a depth-first search based algorithm. The players use utility-based CP-nets to make a decision for agreement. The purpose of the paper is to achieve a *jointly optimal preference* for all players while each player has imperfect information about his opponents. Here, a jointly optimal preference refers to all players obtaining preferences of which the utilities are not less than the average utility of the preferences.

The rest of the paper is organized as follows. In Sect. 2, we briefly explain preliminaries about CP-nets, which are conditional preference networks for representing and reasoning with qualitative preferences. We also discuss utility CP-nets and mediation approaches using a single negotiation text in Sect. 2. In Sect. 3, we describe the proposed negotiation approach with algorithms and illustrations. We discuss other closely related approaches to negotiation based on CP-nets and compare our approach to them in Sect. 4. Finally, in Sect. 5, we conclude the paper and mention some future directions.

2 Preliminaries

We begin with background concepts of conditional preference networks (CP-nets), their induced preference graphs and the utility-based CP-nets in this section. We will also discuss a mediation approach using single negotiation text (SNT).

2.1 CP-nets and UCP-nets

Boutilier and colleagues introduced CP-nets as a graphical representation of conditional preference networks that can be used for specifying preference relations in a relatively compact, intuitive, and structured manner using conditional ceteris paribus (all other things being equal) preference statements [5,6]. CP-nets can be used to specify different types of preference relations, such as a preference ordering over potential decision outcomes or a likelihood ordering over possible states of the world.

CP-nets are similar to Bayesian networks [17]. Both utilize directed graphs; however, the aim of CP-nets in using the graph is to capture statements of qualitative conditional preferential independence. A CP-net over variables $V = X_1, ..., X_m$ is a directed graph G over $X_1, ..., X_m$ whose nodes are annotated with conditional preference tables $CPT(X_i)$ for each $X_i \in V$. Each conditional preference table $CPT(X_i)$ associates a total order $\succ_i^u$ with each instantiation u of X_i's parents $Pa(X_i) = U$ [5].

Let $V = X_1, ..., X_m$ be a demand set of m attributes; $X_i \in V$ ($i = 1$ to m). $D(X_i)$ is the domain of X_i and is represented as $D(X_i) = x_1, .., x_n$. There are $D(X_1) \times D(X_2) \times ... \times D(X_m)$ possible alternatives (outcomes), denoted by O. Elements of O are denoted by $o, o\prime, o\prime\prime$ etc. and represented by concatenating the values of the variables [13]. For example, if $V = \{A, B, C\}$, $D(A) = \{a_1, a_2, a_3\}$, $D(B) = \{b_1, b_2\}$ and $D(C) = \{c_1, c_2, c_3\}$, then the assignment $a_2 b_2 c_1$ assigns a_1 to variable A, b_2 to B and c_1 to C.

The preference information captured by an acyclic CP-net N can be viewed as a set of logical assertions about a user's preference ordering over complete assignments to variables in the network. These statements are generally not complete, that is, they do not determine a unique preference ordering. Those orderings consistent with N can be viewed as possible models of the user's preferences, and any preference assertion that holds in all such models can be viewed as a consequence of the CP-net [6].

The set of consequences $o \succ o\prime$ of an acyclic CP-net constitutes a partial order over outcomes: o is preferred to $o\prime$ in this ordering iff $N \models o \succ o\prime$. This partial order can be represented by an acyclic directed graph, referred to as the induced preference graph:

- The nodes of the induced preference graph correspond to the complete assignments to the variables of the network; and
- There is an edge from node $o\prime$ to node o if and only if the assignments at $o\prime$ and o differ only in the value of a single variable X, and given the values assigned by $o\prime$ and o to $Pa(X)$, the value assigned by o to X is preferred to the value assigned by $o\prime$ to X.

For example, consider the CP-net given in Fig. 1, whose variables are A, B and C. The preference statements on variable A mean that a_1 is strictly preferred to a_2. The preferences on variable B are conditioned on variable A: If a_1 is chosen, then b_1 is preferred to b_2 and if a_2 is chosen, then b_2 is preferred to b_1. The preferences of variable C are also conditioned on the variable B. The preference graph induced by the CP-net of Fig. 1 is shown in Fig. 2.

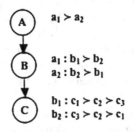

Fig. 1. CP-net, for Player 1.

The concept of Utility CP-net (UCP-net) was also introduced by Boutilier and colleagues. It extends the concept of CP-net by allowing quantification over nodes with conditional utility information. Semantically, Boutilier et al. treat the different factors $V = X_1, ..., X_m$ as *generalized additive independent* of one another for an underlying utility function u [4]; this means intuitively that the expected value of u is not affected by correlations between the variables, and implies that u can be decomposed as a sum of factors over each set of variables X_i [3]. For example, the CP-net in Fig. 1 can be extended with utility information by including a factor (f) for each variable in the network, specifically $f_1(A), f_2(A, B)$ and $f_3(B, C)$ as shown in Fig. 3. We calculate the total utility of preference strings as follows: $u(A, B, C) = f_1(A) + f_2(A, B) + f_3(B, C)$. Each of these factors is quantified by the *CPT* (conditional preference tables)

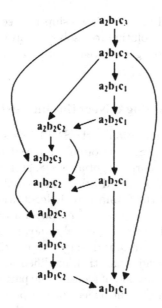

Fig. 2. Induced preference graph of the CP-net of Fig. 1, for Player 1.

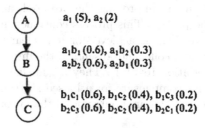

Fig. 3. UCP-net corresponding to the CP-net of Fig. 1, for Player 1.

in the network. For example, the utility of $a_1b_1c_1$ is as follows: $u(a_1, b_1, c_1) = f_1(a_1) + f_2(a_1, b_1) + f_3(b_1, c_1) = 5 + 0.6 + 0.6 = 6.2$ according to Fig. 3.

F. Rossi and colleagues presented an extension of the CP-net, called mCP-nets [21], to model the qualitative and conditional preferences of multiple agents. They allowed the individual agents to vote to obtain mCP-nets by combining several partial CP-nets. K.R. Apt and colleagues proposed an approach for analyzing strategic games that can be used to study CP-nets [1]. They introduced a generalization of strategic games in which each player has to his disposal a strict preference relation on his set of strategies, parameterized by a joint strategy of his opponents. They showed that optimal outcomes in CP-nets are Nash equilibria of strategic games with parameterized preferences. Z. Liu and colleagues also focused on the relationship between CP-nets and strategic games [15]. They proposed a solution to resolve the optimal outcomes of CP-nets by transforming a CP-net to a game tree and using a tree algorithm to find Nash equilibria.

2.2   Mediation Using a Single Negotiation Text (SNT)

The concept of a single negotiation text (SNT) was suggested as a mediation device by Roger Fisher [10]. SNT is often employed in international negotiations, especially with multi-party negotiations [8,11,19]. For example, the SNT approach was applied by the United States in mediating the Egyptian–Israeli conflict, which is known as the Camp David Negotiations [19]. During an SNT negotiation, a mediator first devises and proposes a deal (SNT-1) for the two protagonists to consider. The first proposal is not intended as the final agreement. It is meant to serve as an initial, single negotiating text: a version to be privately criticized by both sides and then modified in an iterative manner.

The SNT is utilized as a method of focusing the parties' attention on the same composite text [19]. The important aspect of the process is that it appears to be fair to both sides, and not divisive. Based upon the criticisms by the parties, voiced privately to the mediator only, the mediator prepares another proposal, which is not perfect, but which improves both parties' positions. Again, both parties provide suggestions on improving the proposal, and this new proposal is again criticized by the parties. This process continues until all the issues are settled and the final agreement is achieved or it is clear that no agreement is achievable. P. Korhonen and colleagues discussed the importance of the starting point of the single negotiation text [11]. They argue that, if the path taken in subsequent steps does not compensate for a biased starting point, the bias will have considerable impact on the final outcome of the negotiations.

3   The Proposed Approach to Negotiation

In real-world negotiations, negotiators need to achieve an agreement on multiple issues with multiple players. Sometimes, a mediator is included to facilitate the negotiation process. Some negotiations fail because the parties have too many conflicts and they cannot work with each other. Therefore, a mediator may be used if the parties prefer a third party who is neutral and does not represent any party's interests. Also in situations where the parties cannot meet to negotiate directly, a mediator may be needed.

Our approach is based on a natural way to negotiate in the real world. The proposed framework consists of two types of individuals: the mediator and the players. All players and the mediator specify the issues they need to negotiate before the negotiation process starts. Each player keeps his own private information and he does not know his opponents' private information. Each player reports his partial CP-nets to the mediator. They do not directly come to know their opponents' preferences at any stage. In addition, each player defines his own utility values for each attribute and calculates his total utility for all combinations of variables, as mentioned in Sect. 2.1. Each player creates his own UCP-net that is used for proposing a maximum preference and for deciding to accept or reject the proposal by the mediator. The mediator seeks to propose a single negotiation text that gains optimal joint outcomes for all players by comparing players' proposed preferences based on depth-first search [2,12,13].

3.1   Algorithms

We have developed two algorithms. Algorithm 1 (see p. 177) describes the way each of the players decides whether to accept a proposal by the mediator. Algorithm 2 (see p. 178) describes the way the mediator decides which single negotiation texts to propose, given the players' CP-nets and their answers to previous proposals.

Algorithm 1. Negotiation Decision by Player

1: Input :
2:     UCP-nets with total utility and ordering
3:     $Agreement \leftarrow 0$; $maxU \leftarrow$ maximum utility
4:     $threshold \leftarrow x$; Proposals $\leftarrow \emptyset$
5: **while** $Agreement \neq 1$ **and** $t \leqslant finalRound$ **do**
6:     Search S $(U(S) = maxU)$ in UCP-net   //search maximum preferred proposal
7:     Send (S) to Mediator
8:     currentProposal $\leftarrow$ Receive(Proposal by Mediator)
9:     Proposals $\leftarrow$ Proposals $\cup$ currentProposal
10:    **if** $(maxU - U(currentProposal)) \leqslant threshold$ **then**
11:        accept Proposal
12:        $Agreement \leftarrow 1$
13:    **else**
14:        reject Proposal
15:        Update $maxU$ //search and update the utility less than current maxU
16:        Send (S)
17:    **end if**
18: **end while**
19: **if** Receive(finalRound) **then**
20:    **while** $maxU > avgU$ **do**
21:        Update $maxU$ //search and update the utility less than current maxU
22:        Evaluate proposals
23:        **if** $\exists proposal : (maxU - U(proposal) \leqslant threshold)$ **then**
24:            accept proposal;
25:            $Agreement \leftarrow 1$
26:        **end if**
27:    **end while**
28: **end if**

Algorithm 2. Negotiation by Mediator

1: Input:
2:     *Player N*: $N = (1, 2, \ldots, n)$
3:     $CPN_1, CPN_2, \ldots, CPN_n$ //Players' CP-nets
4:     $S_1, S_2, \ldots, S_n$ //Players' proposals
5:     $maxP \leftarrow 0.9$; $avgP \leftarrow 0.5$ //maximum and average acceptable probability
6:     $Agreement \leftarrow 0$; $JointOptimal \leftarrow \emptyset$; $t \leftarrow 0$
7:     $threshold \leftarrow x$
8: **while** $Agreement \neq 1$ **and** $t \leqslant finalRound$ **do**
9:    **for** $i = 1$ **to** n **do**
10:       **for** $j = 1$ **to** n **do**
11:          Search acceptableProbability $(S_i, S_j : i \neq j)$
12:       **end for**
13:    **end for**
14:    Mark all S_i, S_j: acceptableProbability $< threshold$;
15:    **while** $maxP > avgP$ **do**
16:       **for** $i = 1$ **to** n **do**
17:          **for** $j = 1$ **to** n **do**
18:             **if** $\exists S_i : (\text{acceptableProbability}(S_i, S_j) = maxP ; i \neq j)$ **then**
19:                $JointOptimal \leftarrow S_i$
20:             **else**
21:                Search alternativeOptimal(S_i) //Other proposals with same maxP
22:                **if** $\exists S_l : (\text{acceptableProbability}(S_l, S_j) = maxP; l \neq j)$ **then**
23:                   $JointOptimal \leftarrow S_l$
24:                **else**
25:                   $maxP \leftarrow maxP - 0.1$
26:                **end if**
27:             **end if**
28:          **end for**
29:       **end for**
30:    **end while**
31:    Propose $JointOptimal$
32:    **if** $\forall$ Player $k \in N$ accept Proposal **then**
33:       $Agreement \leftarrow 1$
34:    **else if** Player k $(k \in N)$ rejects S_i **then**
35:       Ask new proposal to Player k
36:       Update S_i $(i = k)$
37:       $maxP \leftarrow 0.9$
38:       $t \leftarrow t + 1$
39:    **end if**
40: **end while**
41: **if** Agreement $= 0$ **and** $t = $ finalRound **then**
42:    Announce finalRound and Ask for evaluating all proposals to Players
43: **end if**

The initial input of Algorithm 1 is the utility CP-nets with the complete set of utility values and the resulting ordering (see e.g., Table 1). The initial assignments to the *Agreement* variable and the *Proposal* variable are zeros. The *Proposal* refers to a single negotiation text that combines preference variables according to the induced preference graph. The maximum utility of a player is assigned to the corresponding *maxU* variable. The threshold variable is defined to accept or reject the proposal. The threshold can change based on the nature of the negotiation problems. A player accepts the proposal if the difference between the *maxU* value and the utility value of the current proposal is less than or equal to the threshold. Otherwise, the player rejects the proposal and then he reduces and updates the *maxU* value. If the final round is reached, the player has to evaluate the previous rejected proposals. If the difference between the current *maxU* value and that corresponding to one of these proposals is less than the threshold, the player accepts this proposal. Finally, the *Agreement* variable is assigned to 1 and the player's negotiation process ends. Note that the final round is always specified, leading to the successful completion of this algorithm.

The inputs of the Algorithm 2 are N CP-nets of the N players and N proposals of the players. The algorithm omits the construction of the induced preference graphs from CP-nets. The proposal of the player is a maximum preferred string that gains the maximum utility (for instance, see Table 1). The variable *maxP* refers to the maximum acceptable probability and is assigned the value 0.9. The variable *avgP* refers to the average acceptable probability and is assigned the value 0.5. The term 'probability' is somewhat of a misnomer, because we use it to mention some value in $[0, 1]$ without any probabilistic meaning attached to it. Such values are assigned to the vertices of the induced preference graphs that are constructed from the players' CP-nets, where the ordering of the vertices is compatible to the natural ordering of the values assigned to them.

The initial assignments to the *Agreement* variable and the *JointOptimal* variable are zeros. The value of the variable t corresponds to the number of rounds in which the single negotiation text is proposed. The constant *finalRound* can take up values depending on the context of the negotiation problems. The negotiation process repeats until the *Agreement* variable becomes equal to 1 and the number of rounds is less than the value of *finalRound*. First, a value for the *acceptableProbability* variable is searched for each player compared with the other players' proposals. The idea of this *acceptableProbability* variable is as follows. Our starting point is the bottommost string of the induced preference graph corresponding to the concerned player and we assume that the string whose edge directly points to the bottommost string gets the acceptable probability 0.9. We define probability of a string on the graph by going backward from the bottommost or maximum preferred string. We count the intermediate edges from the bottommost string to the particular string by reducing the *acceptableProbability* value by 0.1 for each edge in between. This searching process continues until the *acceptableProbability* value reaches 0.5. Otherwise, the *acceptableProbability* variable is assigned the value zero.

Moreover, the mediator marks all *acceptableProbability* values less than the threshold value (line 14, Algorithm 2, see p. 178). If at least one the players rejects the proposal and the mediator has an alternative jointly optimal proposal in his previous marked list, the mediator can use the alternative as the next proposal. If there is no jointly optimal proposal among the players' proposals, the mediator tries to search for an alternative jointly optimal proposal (line 21, Algorithm 2, see p. 178) that has the same *acceptableProbability* value as the players' previous proposals. The mediator searches all strings that have one backward edge from the maximum preferred string (with *acceptableProbability* value 0.9) for all players. He then searches a common string of all players. If there is no common string, the mediator continues to search all possible strings with *acceptableProbability* value 0.8. This process continues until such a common string is found with the maximum possible *acceptableProbability* value.

The proposed algorithms can provide a negotiable agreement for multiple players via the mediator. The mediator does not have a bias among the players and he can search fairly optimal preferences for all players. Although most of the players may not gain their most preferred option, they accept an outcome of which the utility value is not less than the average utility value. Even if the players are not able to realize their maximum preferences, they receive reasonably acceptable outcomes, and in some cases that is all what is needed. In such contexts, the successfully negotiable situation becomes an optimal outcome.

We consider the time complexity of the two algorithms. The basic operation of Algorithm 1 (see p. 177) is searching maximum utility in the player's UCP-nets and comparing the difference with the threshold. Let the set of issues be denoted by $I = \{i_1, i_2, .., i_m\}$ and let the numbers of different preferences (that is, the number of possibilities or the cardinality of the domain) for each issue be $p_1, p_2, \ldots, p_m$, respectively. The total number of possible proposal strings is the combination of these $p_1, p_2, \ldots, p_m$ issues, and in the worst-case scenario, one needs to go through all these $p_1 * p_2 * \ldots * p_m$ possibilities, and thus a crude upper bound can be given by the $f \times p_1 * p_2 * \ldots * p_m$, where f is the value of *finalRound*. The computation time for constructing the induced graph grows linearly.

The basic operation in Algorithm 2 is searching the *acceptableProbability* values for all players. If n is the number of players, then the time needed for running this operation is bounded by $O(n^2)$. The basic operation runs in two loops, according to the number of rounds and the difference between the *maxP* value and the *avgP* value. Note that Algorithm 2 omits the construction of the induced preference graph from the players' CP-nets.

3.2 Case Study: Negotiation with Mediation

As an example case, let us consider three players and one mediator for three issues. In this framework, the players and mediator can be run on different computers. When starting the negotiation process, all players report their overall preference information about negotiation issues to the mediator. Then, the mediator creates induced preference graphs for all players based on their CP-nets.

Let N be the set of players: $N = \{1, 2, 3\}$. We consider the three variables A, B, C as three negotiation issues. The domains of the variables are $D(A) = a_1, a_2$; $D(B) = b_1, b_2$; and $D(C) = c_1, c_2, c_3$.

This can be seen as a simple real-world negotiation between different preferences of family members. Suppose that a family including father, mother and 20 years old son decided to buy a new house. They have different preferences for the three issues:

Type of house (A): house with small garden (a_1); condo apartment (a_2);
    Place near (B): market (b_1); park (b_2);
    Price range (C): high (c_1); medium (c_2); low (c_3).

For example, mother (Player 1) prefers to buy a house with a small garden, situated near a market. If the house is situated near a market, she prefers a high price to a medium or a low price. If it is situated near a park, she prefers a low price to a high price. Father (Player 2) prefers a place near a park to a place near a market. If the place is near a park, he prefers a condominium apartment and if it is near a market, he prefers a house with a small garden. He prefers a high price or a low price rather than a medium price. Their son (Player 3) prefers a house with a small garden to a condo apartment. He also prefers a place situated near a park to a place near a market. If it is a house near a market or an apartment near a park, he prefers a high price to a medium or a low price. Otherwise, he prefers a low price to a medium or a high price.

Let us suppose that the real estate agent acts as a mediator and that the family members do not want to share their preferences with one another. After proposing three negotiation texts by the mediator, all family members agree to buy a new house near a park with low price. We will illustrate the details of the negotiation process in Sect. 3.3.

3.3   Case Study: The Negotiation Process

Assume that the CP-net and the induced preference graph given in Figs. 1 and 2 have been proposed by Player 1. The CP-nets and their induced graphs of Player 2 are shown in Figs. 4 and 5, and those for Player 3 in Figs. 7 and 8. All players prepare UCP-nets with their private utility values as illustrated in Figs. 3, 6 and 9. Each player also calculates the total utility of strings in their UCP-nets, as shown in Table 1. They pick up one string with maximum utility outcomes in their UCP-nets and propose it to the mediator. In this example, Players 1, 2 and 3 propose a_1, b_1, c_1, a_2, b_2, c_1 and a_1, b_2, c_1 respectively. These are the bottommost strings of the induced graphs (see Figs. 2, 5 and 8).

We now proceed to show how the algorithms work for the case study. The mediator generates a single negotiation text that we call "the proposal", by searching jointly optimal gains of all players according to Algorithm 2 (see p. 178). After receiving the maximum preferred strings of all players, the mediator searches acceptable probability to the other players' strings (line 11, Algorithm 2, see p. 178).

Table 1. Utility table for Players 1, 2 and 3.

Strings	Player 1	Player 2	Player 3
$a_1b_1c_1$	6.2	3	7.2
$a_1b_1c_2$	6	2.7	7.4
$a_1b_1c_3$	5.8	2.9	7.6
$a_1b_2c_1$	5.5	5.8	8.6
$a_1b_2c_2$	5.7	5.5	8.4
$a_1b_2c_3$	5.9	5.7	8.2
$a_2b_1c_1$	2.9	2.7	4.6
$a_2b_1c_2$	2.7	2.4	4.4
$a_2b_1c_3$	2.5	2.6	4.2
$a_2b_2c_1$	2.8	6.1	4.2
$a_2b_2c_2$	3	5.8	4.4
$a_2b_2c_3$	3.2	6	4.6
Average	4.35	4.27	6.15

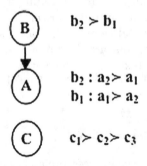

Fig. 4. CP-net for Player 2.

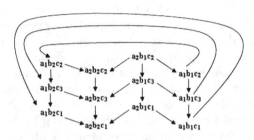

Fig. 5. Induced preference graph of the CP-Net of Fig. 4, for Player 2.

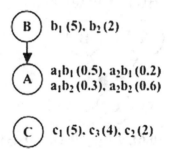

Fig. 6. UCP-net for Player 2.

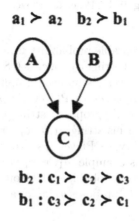

Fig. 7. CP-net for Player 3.

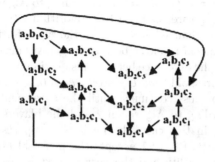

Fig. 8. Induced preference graph of the CP-Net of Fig. 7, for Player 3.

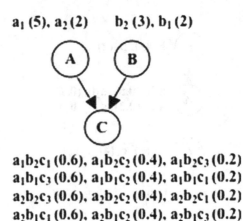

a$_1$ (5), a$_2$ (2)   b$_2$ (3), b$_1$ (2)

a$_1$b$_2$c$_1$ (0.6), a$_1$b$_2$c$_2$ (0.4), a$_1$b$_2$c$_3$ (0.2)
a$_1$b$_1$c$_3$ (0.6), a$_1$b$_1$c$_2$ (0.4), a$_1$b$_1$c$_1$ (0.2)
a$_2$b$_2$c$_3$ (0.6), a$_2$b$_2$c$_2$ (0.4), a$_2$b$_2$c$_1$ (0.2)
a$_2$b$_1$c$_1$ (0.6), a$_2$b$_1$c$_2$ (0.4), a$_2$b$_1$c$_3$ (0.2)

Fig. 9. UCP-net for Player 3.

In this case study, the acceptable probability from Player 1's preferred string a_1, b_1, c_1 to Player 2's preferred string a_2, b_2, c_1 is 0.8 and to Player 3's preferred string a_1, b_2, c_1 it is 0.9 on Player 1's induced graph (see Fig. 2). For Player 2, probability from his string a_2, b_2, c_1 to Player 1's proposed string a_1, b_1, c_1 is 0.8 and probability to Player 3's proposed string a_1, b_2, c_1 is 0.9 (see Fig. 5). For Player 3, probability from his string a_1, b_2, c_1 to Player 1's proposed string a_1, b_1, c_1 is 0.9 and probability to Player 2's proposed string a_2, b_2, c_1 is 0.9 (see Fig. 7). According to this example, a_1, b_2, c_1 is jointly optimal for all players because it obtains reachable probability 0.9 from their maximum preference strings. Therefore, the mediator proposes a_1, b_2, c_1 as a first jointly optimal negotiation text.

After receiving a new negotiation text from the mediator, all players check their utility outcomes (see Table 1) of the text to make a decision "accept" or "reject". Player 1 rejects the proposal a_1, b_2, c_1 because the difference between her maximum utility and the utility of the current text is greater than the threshold ($maxU - a_1, b_2, c_1 = 6.2 - 5.5 = 0.7$) according to Algorithm 1 (p. 177). We assume that the starting threshold is 0.4 in Algorithm 1 (p. 177). The threshold in the algorithm can be changed according to the type of utility values. Player 3 strongly accepts the current proposal because he gets his maximum utility. Player 2 also accepts because the difference between his maximum utility and the current text is less than the threshold ($maxU - a_1, b_2, c_1 = 6.1 - 5.8 = 0.3$).

The negotiation process continues until the agreement is achieved by the mediator acting according to Algorithm 2 and the players acting according to Algorithm 1. Finally, in this case, the mediator proposes $a_1b_2c_3$ as a jointly optimal negotiation text. Player 1 accepts the proposal because the difference between her maximum utility and the current text is less than the threshold ($maxU - a_1, b_2, c_3 = 6.2 - 5.9 = 0.3$). Player 2 and 3 also accept the proposal because the difference between their maximum utilities and the current text is

equal to threshold ($maxU - a_1, b_2, c_3 = 6.1 - 5.7 = 0.4$ and $maxU - a_1, b_2, c_3 =$
$8.6 - 8.2 = 0.4$, respectively). All players achieve a jointly optimal outcome,
which is greater than their average outcomes (see Table 1), although they do not
achieve their maximum outcomes.

Finally, a few words on the complexity issues for this approach instantiating
what we discussed in Sect. 3.1. It is evident that the time required for constructing the induced preference graphs depends on the number of variables and the
cardinality of the variable domains. For instance, if we consider 10 issues (variable
A to J) with the numbers of the domain variables being 2, 2, 3, 2, 2, 3, 2, 2, 2, 4,
respectively, the total number of combinations of possible strings becomes 4608.
The computation time for constructing the induced preference graphs from the
CP-nets grows linearly. However, the mediator works on searching the joint optimal agreement until the average acceptable probability, 0.5 is reached, which is
the worst case. Thus, it is not needed to construct the full induced graph because
the algorithm processes mostly the bottom half part of the graph in many cases.
Most real-world cases do not have thousands of different issues of negotiation.
Therefore, the proposed approach can provide the interactive negotiation within
reasonable time bounds. A detailed technical study is left for future work.

3.4 Cyclic CP-nets

In addition, our approach can achieve a negotiation outcome even when players'
CP-nets are cyclic as shown in Fig. 10(a). Let us show a simple example of
negotiation between two players. Player 1's preferences and induced graph are
shown in Fig. 10(b) and (c). Player 1's private utilities are: a_1b_1 (4), a_2b_2 (4),
a_2b_1 (2) and a_1b_2 (2). Player 2's preferences and induced graph are shown in
Fig. 10(d) and (e). Player 2's private utilities are: a_1b_1 (3), a_2b_2 (3), a_2b_1 (3) and
a_1b_2 (3). Actually, player 2's preference utilities are all the same and its induced
graph is not satisfiable [5].

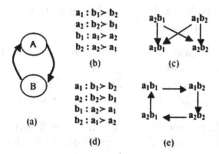

Fig. 10. Examples of cyclic CP-nets and their induced preference graphs.

In our negotiation process, Player 1 proposes a_1b_1 as her maximum preferred
string and Player 2 proposes a_2b_2. When the mediator computes the acceptable

probability, a_2b_2 has the same probability as a_1b_1 for Player 1 and a_1b_1 has 0.8, an acceptable probability for Player 2. If there is no backward edge from the maximum preferred string to a particular string, the two strings may have the same probability. For instance, if two strings, a_1b_1 and a_2b_2 (see Fig. 10(c)) have a backward edge from the same string (a_2b_1), then a_1b_1 and a_2b_2 have the same probability. This reasoning can easily be applied to search on the preference graphs given from the cyclic CP-nets. In our example, the mediator proposes a_2b_2 which is Player 2's proposed string. It also has the same acceptable probability as Player 1's proposed string a_1b_1. Both players accept the mediator's proposal because it meets their maximum preference utility.

3.5   Negotiating International Conflict: Camp David

Our approach can be applied to international conflict resolution as well. As a reminder, Camp David was a well-known negotiation process that happened between Egypt and Israel in 1978. The negotiation process lasted for 13 days and the United States acted as a mediator. U.S mediators had already known deeply about the preferred solutions of Egypt and Israeli and the impossibility of the countries' teams negotiating directly face to face. Therefore, they decided to use a single negotiation text (SNT). The U.S started by offering its first SNT-1 but was not trying to push this first proposal. It was meant to serve as an initial SNT; a text to be criticized by both sides, then modified, and remodified in an iterative manner. These modifications would be made by the U.S based on the recommended changes by both sides. After six rounds, a satisfactory agreement, the Camp David accord, was reached [19]. We can simulate this negotiation using the proposed approach. In Camp David, there are two players, Egypt and Israel, and four basic negotiation issues [16,22]:

A A peace treaty and normalization of relations between Egypt and Israel;
B Demilitarization and removal of Israeli settlements from Sinai;
C The future of the West Bank and Gaza;
D A statement of principles on Israeli withdrawal from occupied territories and the right of Palestinians to self-determination.

Our considerations are meant for illustrative purposes and do not exactly fit the details of actual Egyptian and Israeli preferences. Let us consider the following as domains of the four issues A, B, C, D: $D(A) = a_1, a_2$; $D(B) = b_1, b_2$; $D(C) = c_1, c_2, c_3$; and $D(D) = d_1, d_2, d_3$. The descriptions of the alternatives are as follows:

a_1: Egyptian armed forces are present around Israeli sovereignty;
a_2: Egypt guarantees freedom of passage through the Suez Canal and nearby waterways and normal relations are established between Egypt and Israel;
b_1: Israeli armed forces withdraw from the Sinai;
b_2: Israeli armed forces are present in the Sinai;
c_1: Israel sovereignty exists in the West Bank and Gaza;
c_2: Israel withdraws from West Bank and Gaza and closes the airfields there;

c_3: Israel withdraws from West Bank and Gaza and the airfields there are transferred to civilian purposes only;

d_1: Israeli armed forces withdraw from all occupied territories and no promise for Palestinians to self-determination;

d_2: Israeli armed forces withdraw from all occupied territories and Palestinians gain right to self-determination;

d_3: Israel does not withdraw from occupied territories and keeps its military government there.

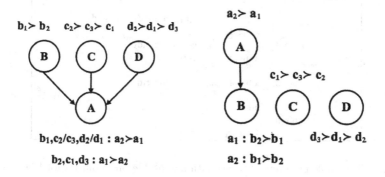

Fig. 11. CP-Nets for Player I (Israel, left) and Player E (Egypt, right).

The CP-nets for both players are shown in Fig. 11. For the above preferences, there is a total of $2 \times 2 \times 3 \times 3 = 36$ possible agreements, presented in Table 2. We show all possible preference strings for both players with acceptable probabilities (see Figs. 12 and 13) instead of preference graphs.

Both players also prepare their utility CP-nets (see Fig. 14). Moreover, we define the total utility values of all possible strings for both players as shown in Table 2. The negotiation process continues according to Algorithm 1 (see p. 177) and Algorithm 2 (see p. 178). Let us sketch the main steps.

First, both players privately present their maximum preferred strings to the mediator (line 4 of Algorithm 2). Thus, Player E proposes string $a_2b_1c_2d_2$ with utility value 20, while Player I proposes string $a_2b_1c_1d_3$, also with utility value 20 (see Table 2). These proposals correspond to the bottommost strings of their induced preference graphs (lefthand columns in Figs. 12 and 13).

The mediator searches the acceptable probability for both players based on their proposals according to line 11 of Algorithm 2 (see p. 178). Player E's proposal $a_2b_1c_2d_2$ is calculated for acceptable probability of player I and it gets the value 0.6. Player I's proposal $a_2b_1c_1d_3$ is reached with probability 0.6 from the bottommost string of player E's graph. If there exists an acceptable probability which is equal to the maximum probability (0.9), the mediator chooses this string as a joint optimal outcome for proposing the single negotiation text (SNT). But, there is no such probability that equals 0.9. So, the mediator searches for an alternative

bottommost	0.9	0.8	0.7	0.6	0.5	0.4
				$a_1b_2c_1d_2$	$a_1b_2c_1d_1$	$a_1b_2c_1d_3$
			$a_1b_2c_3d_2$	$a_1b_2c_3d_1$	$a_1b_2c_3d_3$	
		$a_1b_2c_2d_2$				
	$a_1b_1c_2d_2$			$a_1b_2c_2d_1$	$a_1b_2c_2d_3$	
			$a_1b_1c_3d_2$	$a_1b_1c_1d_2$	$a_1b_1c_1d_1$	$a_1b_1c_1d_3$
				$a_1b_1c_3d_1$	$a_1b_1c_3d_3$	
$a_2b_1c_2d_2$			$a_1b_1c_2d_1$	$a_1b_1c_2d_3$		
				$a_2b_2c_1d_2$	$a_2b_2c_1d_1$	$a_2b_2c_1d_3$
		$a_2b_2c_3d_2$				
	$a_2b_2c_2d_2$			$a_2b_2c_3d_1$	$a_2b_2c_3d_3$	
		$a_2b_2c_2d_1$	$a_2b_2c_2d_3$			
	$a_2b_1c_3d_2$		$a_2b_1c_1d_2$	$a_2b_1c_1d_1$	$a_2b_1c_1d_3$	
			$a_2b_1c_3d_1$	$a_2b_1c_3d_3$		
	$a_2b_1c_2d_1$					
		$a_2b_1c_2d_3$				

Fig. 12. All possible preference strings with acceptable probabilities for Player Egypt.

bottommost	0.9	0.8	0.7	0.6	0.5	0.4
				$a_1b_2c_2d_3$		
			$a_1b_2c_1d_3$		$a_1b_2c_2d_1$	$a_1b_2c_2d_2$
		$a_1b_2c_1d_3$		$a_1b_2c_3d_1$		
					$a_1b_2c_3d_2$	
	$a_1b_1c_1d_3$		$a_1b_2c_1d_1$	$a_1b_2c_1d_2$		
			$a_1b_1c_2d_3$	$a_1b_1c_2d_1$	$a_1b_1c_2d_2$	
		$a_1b_1c_3d_3$				
			$a_1b_1c_3d_1$	$a_1b_1c_3d_2$		
$a_2b_1c_1d_3$			$a_1b_1c_1d_1$	$a_1b_1c_1d_2$		
			$a_2b_2c_2d_3$	$a_2b_2c_2d_1$	$a_2b_2c_2d_2$	
		$a_2b_2c_3d_3$				
	$a_2b_2c_1d_3$		$a_2b_2c_3d_1$	$a_2b_2c_3d_2$		
		$a_2b_2c_1d_1$	$a_2b_2c_1d_2$			
			$a_2b_1c_2d_3$	$a_2b_1c_2d_1$		
	$a_2b_1c_3d_3$					
			$a_2b_1c_3d_1$	$a_2b_1c_3d_2$	$a_2b_1c_2d_2$	
	$a_2b_1c_1d_1$					
		$a_2b_1c_1d_2$				

Fig. 13. All possible preference strings with acceptable probabilities for Player Israel.

Table 2. Table of utilities of all 36 possible proposals for Egypt and Israel.

Strings	Utility for Egypt	Utility for Israel
$a_1b_1c_1d_1$	12	10
$a_1b_1c_1d_2$	13	8
$a_1b_1c_1d_3$	7	12
$a_1b_1c_2d_1$	18	6
$a_1b_1c_2d_2$	19	4
$a_1b_1c_2d_3$	13	8
$a_1b_1c_3d_1$	17	8
$a_1b_1c_3d_2$	18	6
$a_1b_1c_3d_3$	13	10
$a_1b_2c_1d_1$	9	12
$a_1b_2c_1d_2$	10	10
$a_1b_2c_1d_3$	4	14
$a_1b_2c_2d_1$	15	8
$a_1b_2c_2d_2$	16	6
$a_1b_2c_2d_3$	10	10
$a_1b_2c_3d_1$	14	10
$a_1b_2c_3d_2$	15	8
$a_1b_2c_3d_3$	9	12
$a_2b_1c_1d_1$	13	18
$a_2b_1c_1d_2$	14	16
$a_2b_1c_1d_3$	8	20
$a_2b_1c_2d_1$	19	14
$a_2b_1c_2d_2$	20	12
$a_2b_1c_2d_3$	14	16
$a_2b_1c_3d_1$	18	16
$a_2b_1c_3d_2$	19	14
$a_2b_1c_3d_3$	13	18
$a_2b_2c_1d_1$	10	17
$a_2b_2c_1d_2$	11	15
$a_2b_2c_1d_3$	5	19
$a_2b_2c_2d_1$	16	13
$a_2b_2c_2d_2$	17	11
$a_2b_2c_2d_3$	10	15
$a_2b_2c_3d_1$	15	15
$a_2b_2c_3d_2$	16	13
$a_2b_2c_3d_3$	10	17
Average	13.33	12.25

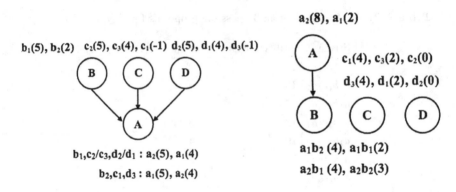

$a_2(8),\ a_1(2)$

$b_1(5),\ b_2(2)$ $c_2(5),\ c_3(4),\ c_1(-1)$ $d_2(5),\ d_1(4),\ d_3(-1)$

B   C   D

A

$c_1(4),\ c_3(2),\ c_2(0)$

$d_3(4),\ d_1(2),\ d_2(0)$

A

B   C   D

$b_1,c_2/c_3,d_2/d_1 : a_2(5),\ a_1(4)$

$b_2,c_1,d_3 : a_1(5),\ a_2(4)$

$a_1b_2\ (4),\ a_1b_1(2)$

$a_2b_1\ (4),\ a_2b_2(3)$

Fig. 14. UCP-net for Player E (Egypt, left) and Player I (Israel, right).

optimal according to line 21 of Algorithm 2 (see p. 178) which cannot be found in this case. This process continues for probability 0.8 (see Algorithm 2, line 15 to 30, p. 178). Now the mediator finds one acceptable probability (0.8) as the alternative optimal for both players (see Algorithm 2, line 21 to 23, p. 178). Therefore, the mediator proposes the jointly optimal string $a_2b_1c_2d_3$ as the first SNT.

After receiving the mediator's proposal, both players check whether the proposal can be accepted or not according to line 10 and 11 of Algorithm 1 (see p. 177). As we mentioned above, the threshold value can vary according to the types of the utility values. Here, we assume that the threshold (Algorithm 1, line 4, see p. 177) is 3. Both players reject the proposal because the difference between the maximum utility (see Table 2) and the utility of the proposal is greater than the threshold value ($20 - 14 = 6 > 3$ and $20 - 16 = 4 > 3$).

The mediator asks for new proposals from the players. Player E proposes $a_1b_1c_2d_2$ and player I proposes $a_2b_2c_1d_3$. Then, the mediator searches for the acceptable probabilities. Once again, there exists no such acceptable probability that is equal to the maximum probability. The mediator continues the searching process to get an alternative optimal outcome and finds one with the acceptable probability 0.8.

In the second round, the mediator proposes $a_2b_1c_3d_1$ to the players. Player E accepts the proposal because the difference between his maximum utility and the utility of the proposal ($20 - 18 = 2$) is less than the threshold value (3). Player I also accepts the proposal as he gets the utility difference ($19 - 16 = 3$), which is equal to the threshold (3). Note that these utility values are greater than their average utility values and they are quite close to the utility values of their maximum expected outcomes, which were 20 for both the players.

Therefore, we find that indeed, a final agreement is achieved within a limited number of rounds, and this algorithmic approach to negotiation via mediator provides a simulation of the historical Camp David Accords. Summing up, Egypt guarantees freedom of passage through the Suez Canal and nearby waterways and normal relations are established between Egypt and Israel; Israeli armed forces withdraw from the Sinai. They also withdraw from the West Bank and

Gaza, and the airfields there are used for civilian purposes only. Finally, Israeli armed forces withdraw from all occupied territories. However, Israel makes no promise for Palestinians about their self-determination.

4 Discussion on Related Work

This paper presents an approach for negotiation over multiple players on multiple issues with the support of a mediator. To achieve a jointly optimal agreement, the mediator offers a single negotiation text based on all players' preference graphs given from their CP-nets. Every player can decide to accept or reject the offer by checking the negotiation text's utility on his or her private UCP-nets. We proposed two algorithms for the mediator and the players. For successful negotiation between players, they often need to give up their maximum expected preferences because otherwise the negotiation process may not achieve a satisfactory agreement within a finite number of rounds. The proposed approach is appropriate for players who are willing to accept a jointly optimal choice.

M. Li and colleagues presented a protocol for negotiation in combinatorial domains [13], which can lead rational agents to reach optimal agreements under an incomplete information setting. They proposed POANCD (Protocol to reach Optimal Agreement in Negotiation over Combinatorial Domains), which has two phases. The first phase of POANCD consists of distributed formation of a negotiation tree by the participating agents, based on CP-nets of agents. After the first phase, the agents make a few initial agreements. In the second phase, the agents act cooperatively to achieve best possible agreement by exploring possible mutually beneficial alternatives. Li and colleagues also proved their approach to dominance testing in CP-nets [12]. Their approach did not have a solution on cyclic CP-nets yet in [13]. Recently, however, Li and colleagues proposed an approach called MajCP (Majority-rule-based collective decision-making with CP-nets) that can work with cyclic CP-nets as well [14].

The purpose of the proposed approach in this paper is to deal with similar situations, players do not only have preference orderings in their CP-nets, but they also have their private utility values (possibly different utilities for the same preference order). Our approach provides negotiation in an interactive way, with mediator and players as a game where the mediator proposes a single negotiation text and players can decide about agreement themselves.

K. Purrington and E. H. Durfee also proposed an algorithm to find social choices of two agents by exploiting the CP-net structure [18]. Their algorithm searches agents' outcome graphs from the top down, using the satisfaction interval associated with each tier, and it proceeds for each agent. A set of candidate outcomes is maintained for each agent. It contains all the outcomes that an agent is willing to accept. For each agent, the algorithm examines the highest tier of outcomes that are not currently in its candidate set, and for the agent(s) with the highest minimum for this next tier, adds those outcomes to the candidate set(s). If the intersection of the agents' candidate sets is non-empty, one of the outcomes in the intersection has maximin optimality. Their algorithm considers only the level of the preference graphs. Our framework provides not only the mediator's joint choice, but also the players' decisions based on their private UCP-nets.

R. Aydogan and colleagues developed a negotiation approach using heuristics for CP-nets with partial preferences [2]. They observed three negotiation strategies: depth-based, ranking-based and utility-based. They showed an example of negotiation between a producer and a consumer agent over a service. Negotiation takes place in a turn-taking fashion, where the consumer agent starts the negotiation with a particular service request. A service request can be considered as a vector of issues (discrete or continuous), which represents the service. If the producer agent does not prefer to supply this service, then the producer generates an alternative service. The consumer agent can accept this alternative service or continue negotiation to pursue a better one. This process continues until reaching a consensus or a deadline. Aydogan and colleagues focus only on one player's preferences and do not mention the other player's preferences. They do not deal with negotiation for multiple (more than two) players. The purpose of our approach is to deal with multi-player, multi-issue negotiation via a mediator.

M. Chalamish and S. Kraus presented AutoMed, an automated mediator for bilateral negotiation under time constraints, which uses a qualitative model. AutoMed produces the negotiators' preferences using Weighted CP-networks (WCP-nets). Each disputant specifies her preferences by creating her WCP-net using a graphical interface. Next, AutoMed sorts all possible agreements according to the WCP-nets and removes all non-optimal sets. During the negotiation process, AutoMed searches for an optimal offer by finding all agreements preferred to the offer made by the opponent in each list [7]. In our approach, the mediator does not use weighted or utility CP-nets but only CP-nets based on partial preferences of the players, because the players do not want to show their private utility values.

5   Conclusion and Future Work

In this paper, we present a simple negotiation approach that is useful in a practical way for negotiations. The mediator offers jointly optimal negotiation texts based on CP-nets over a finite number of rounds and the rest of the players are willing to adjust their private interests at each round using UCP-nets. In this interactive framework, the mediator and the players can play on different machines by sending messages. The framework can deal with negotiation for multiple issues, and with multiple players who have different preferences even when their preference graphs are cyclic. The proposed approach provides a satisfactory agreement for all players with their optimal outcomes, which are not less than average utility. In what follows we list some future avenues for investigation.

Performance testing through experiments. The algorithms provide us with certain outcomes which are acceptable to all the players (in the case studies provided in Sects. 3.3 and 3.5). But to test how these algorithms work in real life scenarios, some more empirical studies are necessary. We plan to test the performance of this approach and hope to construct a more efficient search algorithm on preference graphs.

Formal investigations. We have described two algorithms, Algorithms 1 and 2 for the players and the mediator, respectively. Applying these, a jointly optimal outcome could be agreed upon by all the players. The formal treatment of this approach could be a valuable contribution which would provide solid grounding for these algorithms. We would need a proof of the statement that the reached agreement found by the algorithm is indeed a jointly optimal outcome. If this is not always the case, it would also be interesting to investigate the conditions under which the reached agreement would become a jointly optimal outcome. Some conditions on the threshold value might be needed.

Moreover, the way the mediator searches for the acceptable probabilities of the players towards the outcomes is an ad hoc treatment solely focusing on the distance of an outcome from the most preferred outcome (in terms of edges in the induced graph). Several variants could be considered, introducing some other parameters, e.g. transforming the graph into some linear order. A comparative study of the different resulting algorithms could provide interesting new insights into multi-player, multi-issue negotiations.

Information, costs and incentives. In this approach we have made several assumptions regarding the players and the mediator, which include the following:

- The individual partial CP-nets are known to the mediator only, whereas the UCP-nets are assumed to be private information.
- Individuals do not procure any costs while rejecting the outcomes proposed by the mediator.
- Related to the previous condition, no incentives were provided to the players that could have led them to accept non-optimal outcomes.

Changing the choices on these issues could lead to interesting further studies on obtaining agreeable outcomes through negotiation. For example, common knowledge of CP-nets and UCP-nets among the players would make the role of the mediator redundant, and it would be interesting to check the effect of the mediator for different levels of knowledge among the players. Incurring costs on individual players for possible rejections of the mediator's proposal would give a whole new dimension to Algorithm 1, the procedure which the players follow towards accepting or rejecting proposals put forward by the mediator. When the individual UCP-nets become known to other players, these may also act as incentives for their behaviors, and once again, effects of different knowledge levels in different players could be investigated.

Acknowledgements. We gratefully acknowledge the anonymous reviewers of ICAART 2013 as well as of Transactions CCI whose comments helped us to improve this paper. We also acknowledge NWO research grant 600.065.120.08N- 201, Vici grant NWO 227-80-001, and a Lotus II grant from the EU.

References

1. Apt, K.R., Rossi, F., Venable, K.B.: CP-nets and Nash equilibria. In: Proceedings of the 3rd International Conference on Computational Intelligence, Robotics and Autonomous Systems (CIRAS), pp. 13–16 (2005)
2. Aydogan, R., Baarslag, T., Hindriks, K., Jonker, C., Yolum, P.: Heuristic-based approaches for CP-nets in negotiation. In: Proceedings of the 4th International Workshop on Agent-based Complex Automated Negotiations (ACAN) (2011)
3. Bacchus, F., Grove, A.: Graphical models for preference and utility. In: Proceedings of the 11th Conference on Uncertainty in Artificial Intelligence, UAI'95, pp. 3–10 (1995)
4. Boutilier, C., Bacchus, F., Brafman, R.I.: UCP-networks: A directed graphical representation of conditional utilities. In: Proceedings of the 17th Conference on Uncertainty in Artificial Intelligence (UAI-01), pp. 56–64 (2001)
5. Boutilier, C., Brafman, R.I., Hoos, H.H., Poole, D.: CP-nets: a tool for representing and reasoning with conditional ceteris paribus preference statements. J. Artif. Intell. Res. **21**, 135–191 (2004)
6. Boutilier, C., Brafman, R.I., Hoos, H.H., Poole, D.: Preference-based constrained optimization with CP-nets. Comput. Intell. **20**, 137–157 (2004)
7. Chalamish, M., Kraus, S.: Automed: an automated mediator for multi-issue bilateral negotiations. Auton. Agent. Multi-Agent Syst. **24**(3), 536–564 (2012)
8. Ehtamo, H., Kettunen, E., Hamalainen, R.P.: Searching for joint gains in multi-party negotiations. Eur. J. Oper. Res. **130**(1), 54–69 (2001)
9. Fatima, S.S., Wooldridge, M., Jennings, N.R.: Bargaining with incomplete information. Ann. Math. Artifi. Intell. **44**(3), 207–232 (2005)
10. Fisher, R.: International Mediation: A Working Guide. International Peace Academy, New York (1978)
11. Korhonen, P., Oretskin, N., Teich, J., Wallenius, J.: The impact of a biased starting position in a single negotiation text type mediation. Group Decis. Negot. **4**, 357–374 (1995)
12. Li, M., Vo, Q.B., Kowalczyk, R.: Efficient heuristic approach to dominance testing in CP-nets. In: Proceedings of 10th International Conference on Autonomous Agents and Multiagent Systems (AAMAS), pp. 353–360 (2011)
13. Li, M., Vo, Q.B., Kowalczyk, R.: An efficient protocol for negotiation over combinatorial domains with incomplete information. In: Proceedings of the 27th Conference on Uncertainty in Artificial Intelligence (UAI), Barcelona, Spain. pp. 436–444 (2011)
14. Li, M., Vo, Q.B., Kowalczyk, R.: Majority-rule-based preference aggregation on multi-attribute domains with CP-nets, In: Tumer, K., Yolum, P., Sonenberg, L., Stone, P. (eds.) Proceedings of 10th International Conference on Autonomous Agents and Multiagent Systems (AAMAS), pp. 659–666 (2011)
15. Liu, Z., Li, X., Guo, S., Liu, J.: A game tree algorithm for optimal outcome of CP-nets. Int. J. Digital Content Technol. Appl. (JDCTA) **6**(4), 173–179 (2012)
16. Oakman, J.: The Camp David Accords: A case study on international negotiation. Princeton University, Woodrow Wilson School of Public and International Affairs, Technical report (2002)
17. Pearl, J.: Probabilistic Reasoning in Intelligent Systems: Networks of Plausible Inference. Morgan Kaufmann Publishers Inc, San Francisco, CA, USA (1988)
18. Purrington, K., Durfee, E.H.: Agreeing on social outcomes using individual CP-nets. Multiagent and Grid Syst. **5**(4), 409–425 (2009)

19. Raiffa, H., Richardson, J., Metcalfe, D.: Negotiation Analysis: The Science and Art of Collaborative Decision Making. Belknap Press of Harvard University Press, Cambridge (2002)
20. Rasmusen, E.: Games and Information, 4th edn. Blackwell Publishing, New Jersy (2007)
21. Rossi, F., Venable, K.B., Walsh. T.: mCP nets: Representing and reasoning with preferences of multiple agents. In: Proceedings of the 19th National Conference on Artificial Intelligence (AAAI), pp. 729–734 (2004)
22. Telhami, S.: Evaluating bargaining performance: the case of Camp David. Polit. Sci. Q. **107**, 629–653 (1993)

Genetic Algorithm and Firefly Algorithm Hybrid Schemes for Cultivation Processes Modelling

Olympia Roeva[✉]

Institute of Biophysics and Biomedical Engineering, BAS,
105 Acad. G. Bonchev Str., 1113 Sofia, Bulgaria
olympia@biomed.bas.bg

Abstract. In this paper two hybrid schemes using Firefly Algorithm (FA) and Genetic Algorithm (GA) are introduced. The novel hybrid meta-heuristics algorithms are realized and applied to parameter identification problem of a non-linear mathematical model of the *E. coli* cultivation process. This is a hard combinatorial optimization problem for which exact algorithms or traditional numerical methods does not work efficiently. A system of four ordinary differential equations is proposed to model the growth of the bacteria, substrate utilization and acetate formation. Parameter optimization is performed using a real experimental data set from an *E. coli* MC4110 fed-batch cultivation process. In the considered non-linear mathematical model five parameters are estimated, namely maximum specific growth rate, two saturation constants and two yield coefficients. Based on the numerical and simulation result, it is shown that the model obtained by the proposed hybrid algorithms are highly competitive with standard FA and GA. The hybrid algorithms obtain similar objective function values compared to pure GA and FA, but using four times less population size and seven times less computation time. Thus, the hybrids have two advantages – take much less running time and required much less memory compared to standard GA and FA.

Keywords: Meta-heuristics · Genetic algorithms · Firefly algorithms · Hybrid · Cultivation process · Identification · Model parameters

1 Introduction

Microorganisms have been a subject of particular attention as a biotechnological instrument, and are used in so-called cultivation processes. Numerous useful bacteria, yeasts and fungi are widely found in nature, but the optimum conditions for growth and product formation in their natural environment are seldom discovered.

Cultivation of recombinant microorganisms, e.g. *E. coli*, in many cases is the only economical way to produce pharmaceutic biochemicals such as interleukins, insulin, interferons, enzymes and growth factors. Research on *E. coli* has accelerated even more since 1997, when its entire genome was published. Some recent researches and developed models of *E. coli* can be found in [12,13,18].

© Springer-Verlag Berlin Heidelberg 2014
N.T. Nguyen (Ed.): TCCI XVII 2014, LNCS 8790, pp. 196–211, 2014.
DOI: 10.1007/978-3-662-44994-3_10

Modelling approaches are central in system biology and provide new ways towards the analysis and understanding of cells and organisms. A common approach to model cellular dynamics is by using sets of non-linear differential equations. Real parameter optimization of cellular dynamics models has become a research field of particularly great interest. Such problems have widespread application. The parameter identification of a non-linear dynamic model is more difficult than that of a linear one, as no general analytic results exist. The difficulties that may arise are, for instance, convergence to local solutions if standard local methods are used, over-determined models, badly scaled model function, etc. Due to the non-linearity and constrained nature of the considered systems, these problems are very often multimodal. Thus, traditional gradient-based methods may fail to identify the good solution. Although a lot of different global optimization methods exist, the efficacy of an optimization method is always problem-specific.

While searching for new, more adequate modeling metaphors and concepts, methods which draw their initial inspiration from nature have received the early attention. During the last decade a large class of meta-heuristics has been developed and applied to a variety of areas. The three best known heuristics are the iterative improvement algorithms, the probabilistic optimization algorithms, and the constructive heuristics [24,25]. In this paper, the attention is focused on two effective population-based algorithms, namely Genetic algorithms (GA) [8] and Firefly algorithm (FA) [30].

Holland's book [10], published in 1975, is generally acknowledged as the beginning of the research of GA. The GA is a model of machine learning which derives its behavior from a metaphor of the processes of evolution in nature [8]. Since their introduction and subsequent popularization, the GA have been frequently used as an alternative optimization tool to the conventional methods and have been successfully applied to a variety of areas, and find increasing acceptance [23].

The meta-heuristic algorithm, namely FA, which idealizes some of the flashing characteristics of fireflies, has been recently developed by Xin-She Yang [30]. Although the FA has many similarities with other swarm intelligence based algorithms, it is indeed much simpler both in concept and implementation [32]. There are already several applications of FA to different optimization problems [2,5,15,20,22,31–33]. The authors reported that the FA is powerful and very efficient novel population-based method and can outperform other meta-heuristics, such as GA, in solving many optimization problems and particularly NP-hard problems.

In recent years, it has become evident that the concentration on a sole meta-heuristic is rather restrictive. A skilled combination of a meta-heuristic with other optimization techniques, a so called hybrid meta-heuristic, can provide a more efficient behavior and a higher flexibility when dealing with real-world and large-scale problems. This is because hybrid meta-heuristics combine their advantages with the complementary strengths of, for example, more classical optimization techniques such as branch and bound or dynamic programming.

In general, hybrid meta-heuristic approaches can be classified as either "collaborative combinations" or "integrative combinations" [4].

In the other hand, We may distinguish between two categories [26]: the first consists in designing a solver including components from a meta-heuristic into another one, while the second combines meta-heuristics with other techniques typical of fields such as operations research and artificial intelligence. A prominent represent of the first category is the use of trajectory methods into population based techniques or the use of a specific local search method into a more general trajectory method such as iterated local search.

The second category includes hybrids resulting from the combination of meta-heuristics with constraint programming, integer programming, tree-based search methods, data mining techniques, etc. [26].

Recently, different meta-heuristic methods have been combined to overcome some disadvantages that appear in real applications and their effectiveness have been proved in several high dimensional and non-linear problems [1,6,7,9,17, 21,27–29]. For example, the superiority of the hybrid algorithms between meta-heuristics ACO and GA is shown in applications in different areas and problems [9,14,16].

Following these results, in this paper, two hybrid meta-heuristic algorithms, based on GA and FA, are proposed for parameter identification of an *E. coli* fed-batch cultivation process. The algorithms performances are compared to the pure GA and FA and the results are analyzed.

The paper is organized as follows. The problem formulation – parameter identification of the non-linear dynamic model of an *E. coli* cultivation process – is given in Sect. 2. In Sect. 3 the hybrid schemes between GA and FA are presented. The numerical results and discussion are presented in Sect. 4. Conclusion remarks are done in Sect. 5.

2   Problem Formulation

There is an increasing interest in technologies that maximize the production of various essential enzymes and therapeutic proteins based on *E. coli* cultivation. The costs of developing mathematical models for bioprocesses improvements are often too high and the benefits are too low. The main reason for this is related to the intrinsic complexity and non-linearity of biological systems. The important part of model building is the choice of a certain optimization procedure for parameter estimation. The estimation of model parameters with high parameter accuracy is essential for successful model development.

The application of the general state space dynamical model to the *E. coli* fed-batch cultivation process leads to the following non-linear differential equation system [22]:

$$\frac{dX}{dt} = \mu_{max}\frac{S}{k_S + S}X - \frac{F_{in}}{V}X \tag{1}$$

$$\frac{dS}{dt} = -\frac{1}{Y_{S/X}}\mu_{max}\frac{S}{k_S + S}X + \frac{F_{in}}{V}(S_{in} - S) \tag{2}$$

$$\frac{dA}{dt} = -\frac{1}{Y_{A/X}}\mu_{max}\frac{A}{k_A + A}X - \frac{F_{in}}{V}A \tag{3}$$

$$\frac{dV}{dt} = F_{in} \tag{4}$$

where X is biomass concentration, [g/l]; S is substrate concentration, [g/l]; A is acetate concentration, [g/l]; F_{in} is feeding rate, [l/h]; V is bioreactor volume, [l]; S_{in} is substrate concentration in the feeding solution, [g/l]; μ_{max} is maximum value of the specific growth rate, $[h^{-1}]$; k_S and k_A are saturation constants, [g/l]; $Y_{S/X}$ and $Y_{A/X}$ are yield coefficients, [-].

The model consists of a set of four differential Eqs. (1)–(4) thus represented: three dependent state variables $x = [X\ S\ A]$ and five unknown parameters $p = [\mu_{max}\ k_S\ k_A\ Y_{S/X}\ Y_{A/X}]$.

Parameter estimation problem of the presented non-linear dynamic system is stated as the minimization of the distance measure J between the experimental and the model predicted values of the considered state variables:

$$J = \sum_{i=1}^{n}\sum_{j=1}^{m}\{[\mathbf{y}_{\exp}(i) - \mathbf{y}_{\mathrm{mod}}(i)]_j\}^2 \to min \tag{5}$$

where m is the number of experimental data; n is the number of state variables; $\mathbf{y}_{\exp}$ is the known vector of experimental data for X, S, and A; $\mathbf{y}_{\mathrm{mod}}$ is the vector of model predictions for X, S, and A with a given set of parameters (μ_{max}, k_S, k_A, $Y_{S/X}$ and $Y_{A/X}$).

The cultivation experiments are performed in the Institute of Technical Chemistry, University of Hannover, Germany during the collaboration work with the Institute of Biophysics and Biomedical Engineering, BAS, Bulgaria, granted by DFG. The process conditions of the E. coli MC4110 fed-batch cultivation are presented in details in [3].

3   Hybrids Between Firefly Algorithm and Genetic Algorithm

Since, the hybrids are composed of standard GA and FA below is presented a brief description of the pure meta-heuristics.

3.1   Firefly Algorithm

The FA is a meta-heuristic algorithm which is inspired from flashing light behaviour of fireflies in nature. The pattern of flashes is often unique for a particular species of fireflies. The two basic functions of such flashes are to attract mating partners or communicate with them, and to attract potential victim. Additionally, flashing may also serve as a protective warning mechanism.

Based on [30] the basic steps of the FA can be summarized as the pseudo code presented in Fig. 1.

begin

        Define light absorption coefficient γ

        initial attractiveness β_0

        randomization parameter α

        objective function $f(x)$, where $x = (x_1, ..., x_d)^{\mathrm{T}}$

        Generate initial population of fireflies x_i $(i = 1, 2, ..., n)$

        Determine light intensity I_i via $f(x_i)$

            while (t ¡ MaxGeneration) do

                for $i = 1 : n$ all n fireflies **do**

                    for $j = 1 : i$ all n fireflies **do**

                        if $(I_j > I_i)$ then

                        Move firefly i towards j based on Eq. (8)

                        end if

                        Attractiveness varies with distance r via $\exp[\gamma r^2]$

                        Evaluate new solutions and update light intensity

                    end for j

                end for i

                Rank the fireflies and find the current best

            end while i

        Postprocess results and visualization

end

Fig. 1. Pseudo code for FA

In FA, each firefly has a location $y = (y_1, ..., y_d)^{\mathrm{T}}$ in a d-dimensional space and light intensity $I(y)$ or attractiveness $\beta(y)$, which are proportional to an objective function $f(y)$. Attractiveness $\beta(y)$ and light intensity $I(y)$ are relative and these should be judged by the rest fireflies. Thus, attractiveness will vary with the distance $r_{i,j}$ between firefly i and firefly j. So, attractiveness β of a firefly can be defined by Eq. (6) [30, 31]:

$$\beta(r) = \beta_0 e^{-\gamma r^2}, \tag{6}$$

where r (or $r_{i,j}$) is the distance between the i-th and j-th of two fireflies. β_0 is the initial attractiveness at $r = 0$ and γ is a fixed light absorption coefficient that controls the decrease of the light intensity.

The initial solution is generated based on:

$$y_j = rand(Ub - Lb) + Lb, \tag{7}$$

where $rand$ is a random number generator uniformly distributed in the space $[0, 1]$; Ub and Lb are the upper range and lower range of the j-th firefly, respectively. When firefly i is attracted to another more attractive firefly j, its movement is determined by:

$$y_{i+1} = y_i + \beta_0 e^{-\gamma r_{i,j}^2}(y_i - y_j) + \alpha(rand - \frac{1}{2}), \tag{8}$$

where the first term is the current position of a firefly, the second term is used for considering a firefly's attractiveness to light intensity seen by adjacent fireflies

$\beta(r)$ (Eq. (6)), and the third term is used to describe the random movement of a firefly in case there are no brighter ones. The coefficient α is a randomization parameter determined by the problem of interest. The distance $r_{i,j}$ between any two fireflies i and j at y_i and y_j, respectively, is defined according to [30,31]:

$$r_{i,j} = \|y_i - y_j\| = \sqrt{\sum_{k=1}^{d} (y_{i,k} - y_{j,k})^2},\tag{9}$$

where $y_{i,k}$ is the k-th component of the spatial coordinate y_i of the i-th firefly.

3.2   Genetic Algorithm

The structure of the GA is shown by the pseudo-code in Fig. 2.

```
begin
    i = 0
    Initial population P(0)
    Evaluate P(0)
    while (not done) do (test for termination criterion)
    begin
        i = i + 1
        Select P(i) from P(i − 1)
        Recombine P(i)
        Mutate P(i)
        Evaluate P(i)
    end
end
```

Fig. 2. Pseudocode for GA

The population at time t is represented by the time-dependent variable P, with the initial population of random estimates being $P(0)$. Here, each decision variable in the parameter set is encoded as a binary string (with precision of binary representation). The initial population is generated using a random number generator that uniformly distributes numbers in the desired range. The objective function (see Eq. (4)) is used to provide a measure of how individuals have performed in the problem domain.

Selection Function. A common selection approach assigns a probability of selection, P_j, to each individual, j based on its fitness value. A series of N random numbers is generated and compared against the cumulative probability, $C_i = \sum_{j=1}^{i} P_j$ of the population. The appropriate individual, i, is selected and copied into the new population if $C_{i-1} < U(0,1) \leq C_i$. Various methods exist to assign probabilities to individuals: roulette wheel, linear ranking and geometric ranking. Roulette wheel, developed by Holland [10] is the first selection method. The probability, P_i, for each individual is defined by:

$$P[\text{Individual } i \text{ is chosen}] = \frac{F_i}{\sum\limits_{j=1}^{PopSize} F_j}, \tag{10}$$

where F_i equals the fitness of individual i and $PopSize$ is the population size.

The fitness function, is normally used to transform the objective function value into a measure of relative fitness. A commonly used transformation is that of proportional fitness assignment.

Genetic Operators. The genetic operators provide the basic search mechanism of the GA. The operators are used to create new solutions based on existing solutions in the population. There are two basic types of operators: crossover and mutation. The crossover takes two individuals and produces two new individuals. The crossover can be quite complicated and depends (as well as the technique of mutation) mainly on the chromosome representation used. The mutation alters one individual to produce a single new solution. By itself, mutation is a random walk through the string space. When used sparingly with reproduction and crossover, it is an insurance policy against premature loss of important notions.

Let $\overline{X}$ and $\overline{Y}$ be two m-dimensional row vectors denoting individuals (parents) from the population. For $\overline{X}$ and $\overline{Y}$ binary, the following operators are defined: binary mutation and simple crossover.

Binary mutation flips each bit in every individual in the population with probability p_m according to Eq. (11) [11]:

$$x_i = \begin{cases} 1 - x_i, & \text{if } U(0,1) < p_m \\ x_i, & \text{otherwise.} \end{cases} \tag{11}$$

Simple crossover generates a random number r from a uniform distribution from 1 to m and creates two new individuals $\overline{X'}$ and $\overline{Y'}$ according to Eqs. (12) and (13) [11].

$$x_i' = \begin{cases} x_i, & \text{if } i < r \\ y_i, & \text{otherwise,} \end{cases} \tag{12}$$

$$y_i' = \begin{cases} y_i, & \text{if } i < r \\ x_i, & \text{otherwise.} \end{cases} \tag{13}$$

In proposed genetic algorithm fitness-based reinsertion (selection of offspring) is used [19].

3.3   Hybrid Schemes Firefly Algorithm - Genetic Algorithm

The proposed FA-GA and GA-FA algorithms are collaborative combinations of the FA and GA techniques. In these hybrids, in the first step, FA (or GA) explores the search place in order to either isolate the most promising region of the search space. In the second step, to improve global search and get rid of trapping into several local optima, it is introduced GA (or FA) to explore search space (starting with the solution obtained by FA (or GA)) and find new better solutions.

The structure of the hybrid FA-GA is shown by the pseudo-code in Fig. 3.

begin FA
Define
    algorithm parameters and operators
    objective function $f(y)$, where $y = (y_1, ..., y_d)^{\mathrm{T}}$
Generate initial population of fireflies y_i, $(i = 1, 2, ..., n)$
Determine light intensity I_i at y_i via $f(y_i)$
    while $(t < FA_{MaxIteration})$ **do**
      for $i = 1 : n$ all n fireflies **do**
        for $j = 1 : i$ all n fireflies **do**
          if $(I_j > I_i)$ **then**
          Move firefly i towards j
          end if
          Attractiveness varies with distance r via $\exp[-\gamma r^2]$
          Evaluate new solutions and update light intensity
        end for j
      end for i
      Rank the fireflies and find the current best
    end while
    Final best population of fireflies
end begin FA
begin GA
    $i = 0$
    Initial population $P(0)$ = Final best population of fireflies
    Evaluate $P(0)$ fitness
      while $(t < GA_{MaxGeneration})$ **do**
        $i = i + 1$
        Select $P(i)$ from $P(i-1)$
        Recombine $P(i)$ with crossover probability p_c
        Mutate $P(i)$ with mutation probability p_m
        Evaluate $P(i)$ fitness
      end while
      Rank the chromosomes, find the current best and save
      Postprocess results and visualization
end begin GA

Fig. 3. Pseudo-code for hybrid FA-GA

In analogical manner the hybrid GA-FA is introduced – in the first step, GA explores the search place in order to generate solutions and then uses them as an initial population for FA. Thus, the FA will start with a population, which is closer to optimal solution. Further, FA will be obtained the best model parameters vector.

4   Results and Discussion

4.1   Tuning of the Meta-Heuristic Algorithms Parameters

Each algorithm has its own influential parameters that affect its performance in terms of solution quality and computational time. In order to increase the performance of the FA and GA, it is necessary to provide the adjustments of the parameters depending on the problem domain. With the appropriate choice of the algorithm settings the accuracy of the decisions and the execution time can be optimized. Parameters of the FA and GA are tuned on the basis of a large number of pre-tests according to the parameter identification problem, considered here.

Firefly Algorithm Parameters. After tuning procedures the main FA parameters are set to the following optimal settings:

- Attractiveness, $\beta_0 = 1$,
- light absorption coefficient, $\gamma = 1$,
- randomization parameter, $\alpha = 0.2$,
- number of fireflies, nffs $= 100$,
- number of iterations, maxiter $= 100$.

Genetic Algorithm Parameters. For the considered here model parameter identification, the type of the basic operators in GA are as follows:

- encoding – binary,
- fitness function – linear ranking,
- selection function – roulette wheel selection,
- crossover function – simple crossover,
- mutation function – binary mutation,
- reinsertion – fitness-based.

The values of GA parameters are:

- generation gap, ggap $= 0.97$,
- crossover probability, xovr $= 0.75$,
- mutation probability, mutr $= 0.01$,
- number of individuals, nind $= 100$,
- maximum number of generations, maxgen $= 100$.

Hybrid Algorithms Parameters. Some of the hybrid FA-GA (or GA-FA) parameters are tuned based on several pre-tests according to the problem considered here. As a results the GA and FA populations are decreased in times. The results are presented as follows:

The values of FA-GA parameters are:

- nffs = 25, maxiter = 10,
- nind = 25, maxgen = 40.

The values of GA-FA parameters are:

- nind = 25, maxgen = 10,
- nffs = 25, maxiter = 40.

The rest of the hybrid algorithm parameters are the same as the above listed algorithm parameters for GA and FA.

4.2   Numerical Computations

A series of parameter identification procedures for the considered model Eqs. (1)–(4), using FA, GA, FA-GA and GA-FA, are performed. Because of the stochastic characteristics of the applied algorithm, the algorithms have been run at least 30 times in order to carry out meaningful statistical analysis.

For fair and realistic comparison, the pure GA and FA are run for the same number of function evaluations $(N_{FE}) - 10000$. The hybrid meta-heuristic algorithms are run for $N_{FE} = 1250$.

All computations are performed using a PC/Intel Core i5-2320 CPU @ 3.00 GHz, 8 GB Memory (RAM), Windows 7 (64 bit) operating system and Matlab 7.5 environment.

Five model parameters are represented in the solutions - maximum specific growth rate (μ_{max}), two saturation constants $(k_S$ and $k_A)$, and two yield coefficients $(Y_{S/X}$ and $Y_{A/X})$. The following upper and lower bounds are considered:

$$0 < \mu_{max} < 0.8,$$

$$0 < k_S < 1,$$

$$0 < k_A, Y_{S/X}, Y_{A/X} < 30.$$

The mean results of the parameters estimates, total time for the solver to run (T) and objective function value J (Eq. (5)) are observed. The obtained results are summarized in Table 1.

The results about pure GA and FA are closed to the reported ones in [22]. In this work, the algorithms are run with 100 chromosomes/fireflies in contrast to [22] – 60 chromosomes/fireflies. Thus, objective function evaluations are slightly more – 10000, and the corresponding running time is about 220 s (see Table 1). This is the reason for more accurate values for J (especially for GA) obtained here – $J^{GA} = 6.0953$ vs. $J^{GA} = 6.2007$ in [22]. In the case of FA the obtained results are similar: $J^{FA} = 6.0251$ [in this work] vs. $J^{FA} = 6.0259$ in [22].

Table 1. Algorithms performance

Model parameters	Meta-heuristic algorithm			
	FA	GA	FA-GA	GA-FA
μ_{max}	0.5042	0.5050	0.4927	0.4908
k_S	0.0235	0.0239	0.0199	0.0184
k_A	47.7390	45.0182	46.8121	44.9195
$1/Y_{S/X}$	2.0134	2.0106	2.0132	2.0142
$1/Y_{A/X}$	6.3800	6.1935	7.2700	7.9459
J	6.0251	6.0953	6.0479	6.0502
N_{FE}	10000	10000	1250	1250
T, s	208.2145	222.5042	29.9210	24.9758

This is an confirmation of the better performance of the FA compared to GA for considered model parameter identification problem.

The results from the FA-GA and GA-FA (see Table 1), show that the proposed hybrid schemes achieve very close to pure FA and pure GA solutions, but the running time is about seven times less – for example, $T^{FA} = 208.2145$ s vs. $T^{FA-GA} = 29.9210$ s. For example, in the case of the FA-GA algorithm, the pure FA starts from randomly generated initial solutions (population) which can be very fare from the optimal one. The FA is run for 10 iterations only and thus the initial solutions for GA, which are closer to the optimal, is generated. The GA starts from solutions which are not fare from the optimal and thus the convergence of the algorithm is increased. More over in hybrid schemes the populations (chromosomes and fireflies) are very small, only 25 individuals (vs. 100 individuals in pure GA and FA). Such small population considerably decreases the used memory.

A graphical representation of the convergence of the objective function J (mean values of the 30 runs) for both pure GA and FA algorithms with time is shown (in logarithmic scale) in Fig. 4. The results about the hybrid GA-FA and FA-GA are shown (in logarithmic scale) in Fig. 5.

As can be seen form Fig. 4 the FA algorithm shows a little bit better convergence performance in the beginning of the optimization process, compared to the GA. The FA converges faster than the GA and achieves lower value for J in the end of the optimization.

The FA better performance is more clear in the hybrid algorithms (see Fig. 5). For the hybrid FA-GA it is clearly visible that FA converges faster than the GA for the first 10 iterations (10 iterations and 25 chromosomes/fireflies – 250 objective function evaluations). Then GA with initial population – FA final solution – faster achieves accurate solution (40 iterations and 25 chromosomes/fireflies – 1000 objective function evaluations). In the other case, hybrid GA-FA, even the more inaccurate initial population FA convergence fast and achieved similar to FA-GA hybrid solution – $J^{GA-FA} = 6.0502$ vs. $J^{FA-GA} = 6.0479$. Total

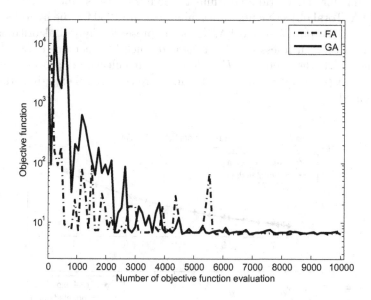

Fig. 4. Improving the objective function during the time – pure GA and FA

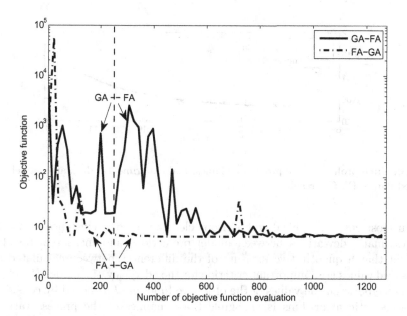

Fig. 5. Improving the objective function during the time – hybrid GA-FA and FA-GA

running time for the hybrid algorithms is about 25–30 s vs. about 220 s for pure GA and FA. Total objective function evaluations are 1250 for the hybrid schemes vs. 10000 for the pure GA and FA. Thus the presented hybrid algorithms have two advantages - much less running time and much less memory usage.

In the Fig. 6 the modelled *E. coli* fed-batch cultivation process variables (biomass, substrate and acetate) and the measured ones (real experimental data) are presented.

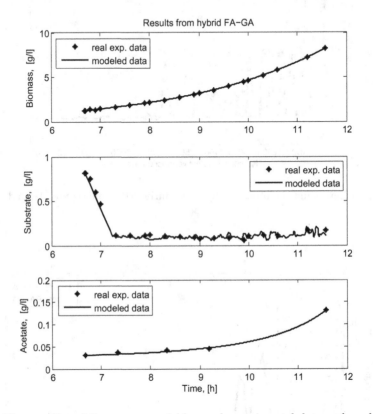

Fig. 6. Time profiles of the process variables: real experimental data and models predicted data – FA-GA result

In most cases, graphical comparisons clearly show the existence or absence of systematic deviations between model predictions and measurements. It is evident that a quantitative measure of the differences between calculated and measured values is an important criterion for the adequacy of a model. Hence, the difference between the values of the objective function J achieved by considered meta-heuristic algorithms is negligible the dynamics of the process variables (experimental data and modeled data) for FA-GA result, are presented only.

Figure 6 shows that there is a very good coincidence between the measured estimates and those modelled with FA-GA hybrid. The model obtained on the basis of FA-GA predicts in a high degree of accuracy the biomass, substrate and acetate dynamics.

5   Conclusion

In this paper, a hybrid meta-heuristic approach, which is a combination between two meta-heuristics, FA and GA is applied to the problem of parameter identification of an *E. coli* fed-batch cultivation process model. The proposed hybrid FA-GA and GA-FA algorithms are collaborative combinations of the FA and GA techniques.

The non-linear mathematical model is considered as a system of four ordinary differential equations, describing the three considered process variables biomass, substrate and acetate.

A comparison of pure FA, pure GA and hybrids FA-GA and GA-FA were done. Some adjustments of the considered meta-heuristics, according to the regarded problem, were performed to improve the optimization capability and the decision speed. Numerical and simulation results from model parameter identification based on the proposed algorithms reveal that correct and consistent results can be obtained using the discussed meta-heuristics.

Combining the advantages of both approaches – FA and GA, better performance of the hybrid algorithms was achieved in terms of computational time and memory usage, yet preserving the precision of the calculation. As shown in the presented numerical results, in the hybrid algorithms about seven times less computational time was consumed (220 s vs. 30 s). Moreover, four times (100 vs. 25 individuals) smaller populations were required to achieve solution. Thus, the hybrid algorithms use in times less memory for the computation.

Acknowledgments. This work has been partially supported by the Bulgarian National Science Fund under the Grants DID 02/29 "Modelling Processes with Fixed Development Rules (ModProFix)" and DMU 02/4 "High quality control of biotechnological processes with application of modified conventional and metaheuristics methods".

References

1. Abdullah, A., Deris, S., Mohamad, M.S., Hashim, S.Z.M.: A new hybrid firefly algorithm for complex and nonlinear problem. In: Omatu, S., et al. (eds.) Distributed Computing and Artificial Intelligence, pp. 673–680. Springer-Verlag, Heidelberg (2012)
2. Apostolopoulos, T., Vlachos, A.: Application of the firefly algorithm for solving the economic emissions load dispatch problem. Int. J. Comb. **2011** (2011). Article ID 523806
3. Arndt, M., Hitzmann, B.: Feed forward/feedback control of glucose concentration during cultivation of Escherichia coli. In: 8th IFAC International Conference on Computer Applications in Biotechnology, Canada, pp. 425–429 (2001)

4. Atanassova, V., Fidanova, S., Popchev, I., Chountas, P.: Generalized nets, ACO algorithms and genetic algorithms. In: Karl, K., Sabelfeld, I.D. (eds.) Proceedings in Mathematics Monte Carlo Methods and Applications, De Gruyter, pp. 39–46 (2012)

5. Chai-ead, N., Aungkulanon, P., Luangpaiboon, P.: Bees and firefly algorithms for noisy non-linear optimisation problems. In: Proceedings of International Multiconference of Engineers and Computer Scientists, vol. 2, pp. 1449–1454 (2011)

6. Fidanova, S.: Hybrid heuristic algorithm for GPS surveying problem. In: Boyanov, T., Dimova, S., Georgiev, K., Nikolov, G. (eds.) NMA 2006. LNCS, vol. 4310, pp. 239–246. Springer, Heidelberg (2007)

7. Ganesan, T., Vasant, P., Elamvazuthi, I.: Hybrid neuro-swarm optimization approach for design of distributed generation power system. Neural Comput. Appl. **23**(1), 105–117 (2013). doi:10.1007/s00521-012-0976-4

8. Goldberg, D.E.: Genetic Algorithms in Search, Optimization and Machine Learning. Addison Wesley Longman, London (2006)

9. Guangdong, H., Qun, W.: A hybrid ACO-GA on sports competition scheduling. In: Ostfeld, A. (ed.) Ant Colony Optimization - Methods and Applications, pp. 89–100. InTech, Rijeka (2011)

10. Holland, J.H.: Adaptation in Natural and Artificial Systems, 2nd edn. MIT Press, Cambridge (1992)

11. Houck, C.R., Joines, J.A., Kay, M.G.: A Genetic Algorithm for Function Optimization: A Matlab Implementation. Genetic Algorithm Toolbox Toutorial (1996). http://read.pudn.com/downloads152/ebook/662702/gaotv5.pdf

12. Jiang, L., Ouyang, Q., Tu, Y.: Quantitative modeling of Escherichia coli chemotactic motion in environments varying in space and time. PLoS Comput. Biol. **6**(4), e1000735 (2010). doi:10.1371/journal.pcbi.1000735

13. Karelina, T.A., Ma, H., Goryanin, I., Demin, O.V.: EI of the phosphotransferase system of Escherichia coli: mathematical modeling approach to analysis of its kinetic properties. J. Biophys. **2011** (2011). Article ID 579402, http://dx.doi.org/10.1155/2011/579402

14. Li, N., Wang, S., Li, Y.: A hybrid approach of GA and ACO for VRP. J. Comput. Inf. Syst. **7**(13), 4939–4946 (2011)

15. Nasiri, B., Meybodi, M.R.: Speciation-based firefly algorithm for optimization in dynamic environments. Int. J. Artif. Intell. **8**(S12), 118–132 (2012)

16. Nemati, S., Basiri, M.E., Ghasem-Aghaee, N., Aghdam, M.H.: A novel ACO-GA hybrid algorithm for feature selection in protein function prediction. J. Expert Syst. Appl. Int. J. Arch. **36**(10), 12086–12094 (2009)

17. Olabiyisi, S.O., Fagbola, T.M., Omidiora, E.O., Oyeleye, A.C.: Hybrid metaheuristic feature extraction technique for solving timetabling problem. Int. J. Sci. Eng. Res. **3**(8), 1–6 (2012). http://www.ijser.org

18. Petersen, C.M., Rifai, H.S., Villarreal, G.C., Stein, R.: Modeling Escherichia coli and its sources in an Urban Bayou with hydrologic simulation program - FORTRAN. J. Environ. Eng. **137**(6), 487–503 (2011)

19. Pohlheim, H.: Genetic and Evolutionary Algorithms: Principles, Methods and Algorithms. Genetic and Evolutionary Toolbox (2003). http://www.geattb.com/docu/algindex.html

20. Han, T.A.: Intention recognition promotes the emergence of cooperation: a Bayesian network model. In: Han, T.A. (ed.) Intention Recognition, Commitment and Their Roles in the Evolution of Cooperation. SAPERE, vol. 9, pp. 101–114. Springer, Heidelberg (2013)

21. Rodriguez, F.J., Garcia-Martinez, C., Lozano, M.: Hybrid metaheuristics based on evolutionary algorithms and simulated annealing: taxonomy, comparison, and synergy test. IEEE Trans. Evol. Comput. **16**(6), 787–800 (2012)
22. Roeva, O., Trenkova, T.: Genetic algorithms and firefly algorithms for non-linear bioprocess model parameters identification. In: Proceedings of the 4th International Joint Conference on Computational Intelligence (ECTA), Barcelona, Spain, 5–7 October 2012, pp. 164–169 (2012)
23. Roeva, O.: Real-World Application of Genetic Algorithms. In Tech, Rijeka (2012)
24. Syam, W.P., Al-Harkan, I.M.: Comparison of three meta heuristics to optimize hybrid flow shop scheduling problem with parallel machines. In: WASET, vol. 62, pp. 271–278 (2010)
25. Tahouni, N., Smith, R., Panjeshahi, M.H.: Comparison of stochastic methods with respect to performance and reliability of low-temperature gas separation processes. Can. J. Chem. Eng. **88**(2), 256–267 (2010)
26. Talbi, E.G.: Hybrid Metaheuristics. Studies in Computational Intelligence, vol. 434, p. 458. Springer, Heidelberg (2013)
27. Vasant, P.: Hybrid LS-SA-PS methods for solving fuzzy non-linear programming problems. Math. Comput. Model. **57**(1–2), 180–188 (2013)
28. Vasant, P., Barsoum, N.: Hybrid pattern search and simulated annealing for fuzzy production planning problems. Comput. Math. Appl. **60**(4), 1058–1067 (2010)
29. Wang, G., Guo, L., Duan, H., Wang, H., Liu, L., Shao, M.: A hybrid metaheuristic DE/CS algorithm for UCAV three-dimension path planning. Sci. World J. **2012**, 1–11 (2012). doi:10.1100/2012/583973
30. Yang, X.S.: Nature-Inspired Meta-Heuristic Algorithms. Luniver Press, Beckington (2008)
31. Yang, X.-S.: Firefly algorithms for multimodal optimization. In: Watanabe, O., Zeugmann, T. (eds.) SAGA 2009. LNCS, vol. 5792, pp. 169–178. Springer, Heidelberg (2009)
32. Yang, X.S.: Firefly algorithm, stochastic test functions and design optimisation. Int. J. Bio-Inspired Comput. **2**(2), 78–84 (2010a)
33. Yousif, A., Abdullah, A.H., Nor, S.M., Abdelaziz, A.A.: Scheduling jobs on grid computing using firefly algorithm. J. Theor. Appl. Inf. Technol. **33**(2), 155–164 (2011)

Color Quantization with Magnitude Sensitive Competitive Learning Algorithm

Enrique Pelayo[✉], David Buldain, and Carlos Orrite

Aragon Institute for Engineering Research, University of Zaragoza, Zaragoza, Spain
epelayoc@gmail.com, {buldain,corrite}@unizar.es
http://www.unizar.es

Abstract. In this paper we introduce a competitive neural model called Magnitude Sensitive Competitive Learning (MSCL) for Color-Quantization. The aim is to obtain a codification of the color palette taking into account some specific regions of interest in the image, such as salient area, center of the image, etc. MSCL algorithm allows distributing color vector prototypes in the desired data regions according to a magnitude function. This magnitude function can allocate the code-words (colors of the palette) not only in relation to their frequency but also in response to any other data-dependent magnitude tailored to the specific goal. As we show in five different examples in this paper, MSCL is able to surpass the performance of other standard Color Quantization algorithms.

Keywords: Color · Vector quantization · Competitive learning · Neural networks · Saliency · Binarization

1 Introduction

With the huge development of informatics in the modern society, large amount of scanned documents and images are transmitted and stored daily. Therefore, some kind of image processing to reduce storage and transmission is necessary. This is generally achieved by means of Vector Quantization (VQ) techniques. The idea behind VQ is the selection of a reduced number of prototypes that accurately represent the whole data set. When each data sample is a vector representing the color of a pixel, it is denoted as Color Quantization (CQ). This kind of algorithms are useful in certain applications related to segmentation, compression, and transmission of images.

A subset of VQ algorithms comprises Competitive Learning (CL) methods, where a neural network model is used to find an approach of VQ calculation in an unsupervised way. Their advantage over other VQ algorithms is that CL is simple and easily parallelizable. Well known CL approaches are K-means [13] (including

---

This work is partially supported by Spanish Grant TIN2010-20177 (MICINN) and FEDER and by the regional government DGA-FSE.

N.T. Nguyen (Ed.): TCCI XVII 2014, LNCS 8790, pp. 212–231, 2014.
DOI: 10.1007/978-3-662-44994-3_11

some of its variants as Weighted K-Means and improvements [5]), Frequency Sensitive Competitive Learning (FSCL) [1], Rival Penalized Controlled Competitive Learning [22], the Self-Organizing Map (SOM) [11], and Neural Gas (NG) [14].

Some of these methods, or their variants, have already been used in CQ and Color Segmentation tasks. Uchiyama and Arbib [20] developed Adaptive Distributing Units (ADU), a CL algorithm used in Color Segmentation that is based on a simple cluster splitting rule. More recently, Celebi [4] demonstrated that it outperforms other common algorithms in a CQ task. Fuzzy C-Means (FCM), is a well-known clustering method in which the allocation of data points to clusters is not hard, and each sample can belong to more than one cluster [3]. Celebi presented a relevant work using NG [6].

SOM has also been used in color related applications: in binarization [16], segmentation [12] and CQ [7–9,15] where author presents FS-SOM a frequency sensitive learning scheme including neighborhood adaptation that achieves similar results to SOM, but less sensitive to the training parameters. One variant of special interest is the neural network Self-Growing and Self-Organized Neural Gas (SGONG) [2], an hybrid algorithm using the GNG mechanism for growing the neural lattice and the SOM leaning adaptation mechanism. Author proved that it is one of the most efficient Color Reduction algorithms, closely followed by SOM and FCM.

Methods based in traditional competitive learning are focused on data density representation to be optimal from the point of view of reducing the Shannon's information entropy for the use of codewords in a transmission task. However it is not always desirable a codebook representation with direct proportion between its codeword density and the data density. For example, in the human vision system, the attention is attracted to visually salient stimuli, and therefore only scene locations sufficiently different from their surroundings are processed in detail. A simple framework to think about how Saliency may be computed in biological brains has been developed over the past three decades [10,19].

In a previous work [18], we introduced a new neural method for unsupervised learning denoted as Magnitude Sensitive Competitive Learning (MSCL), which has the property of distributing the unit centroids following any magnitude calculated from the unit parameters or the input data inside its Voronoi region. This controlled behavior allows to outperform standard Competitive Learning algorithms that only tend to concentrate neurons according to the input data density.

In this work we expand the previous paper [17], where we used a MSCL neural network in a CQ task. We add to the previous saliency examples, a methodology to achieve CQ avoiding dominant colors in the image. As a result, final color palette will enhance interesting areas of the image according to a user-specified magnitude (using different definitions of saliency).

1.1 Problem Formulation

Given an image I of size (x_{max}, y_{max}), we define a data sample $\mathbf{x}(t)$ from the pixel I(x,y) as the color vector of that pixel in the coordinates in the corresponding color space:

$$\mathbf{x}(t) = Color(I(x,y)), \quad x = 1..x_{max} \quad \text{and} \quad y = 1..y_{max} \tag{1}$$

$$t = 1..N, \quad \text{where} \quad N = x_{max} * y_{max}. \tag{2}$$

Each pixel receives an additional value coming from a magnitude function, $mf(t)$. This function is proposed as to weight each pixel with a value of interest. As higher is the value of this magnitude, more relevant is the pixel. The goal is to train a neural network to get units representing the colors of the interesting pixels in higher detail. To do it, feature vectors $\mathbf{x}(t)$ are fed to the neural network with M units. The prototype of unit i ($i = 1 \ldots M$) is represented by a vector of weights $\mathbf{w}_i(t) = (w_{i1}, w_{i2}, w_{i3})$ in the 3-dimensional color space. The associated value of the magnitude in that unit, $mu_i(t)$, can be calculated from the values of $mf(t)$ at samples in its Voronoi region, or can be introduced to the network as the rest of input data.

Figure 1 shows this process. From one image (tiger example), we get a dataset with the 3-D color coordinates of each pixel. The dataset is presented to the

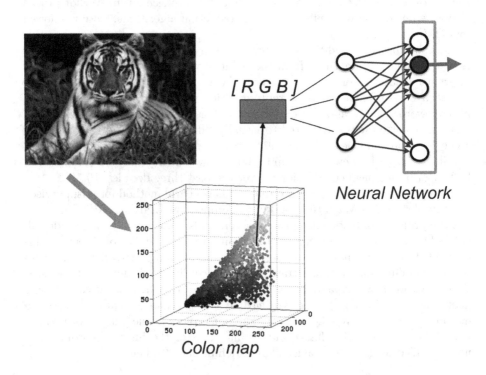

Fig. 1. Problem formulation of Color Quantization: pixels are considered 3-dimensional vectors that are processed as inputs for a competitive neural network with many units as colors in the palette. Magnitude value can be associated to the pixel, as another input to the network, or be associated to the units, as an internal parameter (Color figure onlline).

competitive neural network to generate the color palette with as many colors as units in the network. We paint the color distribution of the image using a [R G B] color space.

1.2 Proposed Approach

We propose the use of MSCL neural network, to train this 3-D dataset, taking into account the magnitude function, that can be defined to lead the training process of the palette to accomplish the desired task. This algorithm follows the general *Competitive Learning* steps:

Step 1. *Selecting the winner prototype.* Given an input data vector, the competitive units compete each other to select the winner neuron comparing their prototypes with the input. This winner unit, also called Best Matching Unit (BMU) is selected in MSCL as the one that minimizes the product of a user-defined Magnitude Function and the distance of the unit prototypes to the input data vector. This differs from other usual competitive algorithms where BMU is determined only by distance. MSCL is implemented by a two-step competition: global and local, as it is explained in next section.

Step 2. *Updating the winner and the unit magnitude.* Both winner's weights and magnitude (if the unit has an associated magnitude) are adjusted iteratively for each training sample, with a learning factor forced to decay with training time.

The idea behind the use of the magnitude term is that, in the case of a sample placed at equal distance from two competing units, the winner will be the unit with lower magnitude value. So, the result of the training process is that units will be forced to move from the data regions with low magnitude values to regions where the magnitude function is higher.

1.3 Paper Description

The remainder of this paper is organized as follows:

Section 2 describes the *Magnitude Sensitive Competitive Learning (MSCL)* method.

Section 3 shows the comparison of the new method with some of the well known algorithms mentioned in the introduction of this article, using five different examples of applications. The first proposed example gets a color quantization that we call homogeneous quantization (Subsect. 3.1). The second example gets a color quantization focused in the image center (Subsect. 3.2). The third example is focused on getting a color palette avoiding the dominant colors usually found in image background (Subsect. 3.3). Fourth example returns a color palette according with a certain image saliency (Subsect. 3.4). Last example shows the use of MSCL in a document image binarization (Subsect. 3.5).

Section 4 concludes with a brief discussion and ideas for future work.

2 The MSCL Algorithm

The next subsections describe the algorithm, which flowchart is shown in Fig. 2.

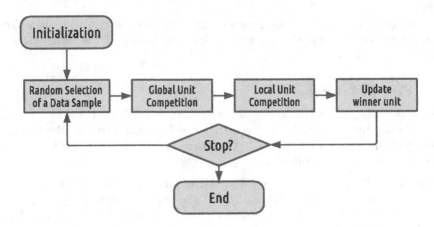

Fig. 2. MSCL flowchart

2.1   Initialization

M unit weights are initialized with data inputs randomly selected from the dataset, and their initial value of its magnitude is equal to the magnitude function at these samples. We also initialize to ones the value of a counter n_i of the number of times that each unit has been the best matching unit.

$$\mathbf{w}_i(1) = \mathbf{x}(1) \tag{3}$$
$$mu_i(1) = mf(1) \tag{4}$$
$$n_i(1) = 1. \tag{5}$$

2.2   Random Selection of Data Samples

A sample data $\mathbf{x}(t) = (x_{t1}, .., x_{td}) \in \Re^d$ (with N samples) is randomly selected at time t from the dataset, and its associated magnitude, $mf(t)$, is calculated. This process will be repeated until every data has been presented to the MSCL neural network. It is important to mention that it is recommended to retrain the neural network with the whole dataset several cycles, along T input data presentations (iterations), to make results independent of data-presentation ordering.

2.3   Global Unit Competition

K units with minimum distance from their weights to the input data vector are selected as winners in this first step. In all the simulations of this work it was used $K = 2$. These units form the S set ($size(S) = K$):

$$S = \{\mathbf{w}_k\} \vee \|\mathbf{x}(t) - \mathbf{w}_k(t)\| < \|\mathbf{x}(t) - \mathbf{w}_i(t)\| \ \forall i \notin S. \tag{6}$$

2.4   Local Unit Competition

In the second step, winner unit j is selected from units belonging to S as the one that minimizes the product of its magnitude value with the distance of its weights to input data vector, following:

$$j = argmin(mu_k(t) \cdot \|\mathbf{x}(t) - \mathbf{w}_k(t)\|) \ \forall k \in S. \tag{7}$$

2.5   Winner and Magnitude Updating

Only winner's weights, counter and magnitude are adjusted iteratively for each training sample, following:

$$n_i(t+1) = n_i(t) + 1 \tag{8}$$

$$\alpha = \left(\frac{1}{n_i(t+1)}\right)^{\beta} \tag{9}$$

$$\mathbf{w}_j(t+1) = \mathbf{w}_j(t) + \alpha\left(\mathbf{x}(t) - \mathbf{w}_j(t)\right) \tag{10}$$

$$mu_j(t+1) = mu_j(t) + \alpha\left(mf(t) - mu_j(t)\right) \tag{11}$$

where α is the learning factor calculated for the winner and forced to decay with iteration time and β is a scalar value between 0 and 1. Using this definition, when β is equal to one, the value of the magnitude at each unit becomes the moving average of the magnitude of the data samples belonging to its Voronoi region.

2.6   Stopping Condition

Training is stopped when a termination condition is reached. It may be the situation when all data samples has been presented to the MSCL neural network along certain number of cycles (if a limited number of samples is used), or the condition of low mean change in unit weights, or any other function that could measure the training stabilization.

2.7   The Magnitude Function

As it has been mentioned before, $mf(t)$ is a function that associates a positive scalar value to the input sample at time t. There are three ways to define this function:

1. As a magnitude map, where each sample has a fixed magnitude value obtained by an user defined function of the data. An example of magnitude map is the one used in the saliency section. The saliency function provides a value for each pixel of the image proportional to its interest. In this case, magnitude is like a data input for modulating the competitive behavior of the unit.

2. A function calculated depending on the unit weights and/or the values of data samples belonging to its Voronoi region. An example of this function is the used for Homogeneous Color Quantization. In that case $mf(t)$ is the value of the mean quantization error of the best matching unit of $\mathbf{x}(t)$.

3   Applications

In the following examples, data samples are 3D vectors corresponding to the RGB components of the image pixels. We have used the RGB space in order to have comparable results to other works, in spite that it is a non-uniform color space (instead of using this one, we could have used other color models as $L*a*b$ whose suitability has been demonstrated for interpreting the real world).

The goal is to get a reduced color palette to represent the colors in the image focused on different objectives. The next five examples show that, adequately selecting the magnitude function, it is possible to get an optimal palette according to the desired application.

3.1   Homogeneous Color Quantization

This example shows the case we call Homogeneous Color Quantization. The mean quantization error (q_{err}) for all samples within the Voronoi region of unit i is used as magnitude function. The q_{err} for sample $\mathbf{x}(t)$ is the distance between $\mathbf{x}(t)$ and the prototype (weights) of its corresponding best matching unit. This magnitude forces the palette colors to be uniformly distributed over the data distribution in the RGB space, independently of its data density, and giving as result Voronoi regions that present similar mean q_{err}.

We use the known Tiger, Lena and Baboon images for performance comparison in CQ tasks (marked in the table as T^*, L^* and B^*, where * is the number of colors in the palette). Homogeneous MSCL (M-h) and Centered MSCL (M-c, explained in next subsection) are compared against the most successful neural models used in different papers: SOM, FSCL, FCM, FS-SOM, ADU and SGONG. Training process applied learning rates between (0.7-0.01) along three cycles, except in ADU whose algorithm parameters selection follows [20]. The threshold for adding/removing a neuron used in SGONG was (0.1/0.05).

Figure 3 shows the color reduction effects for tiger image with ADU, Homogeneous MSCL and Centered MSCL. The upper part of Table 1 shows the mean of MSE (Mean Squared Error) in 10 trials with different number of palette colors (8, 16 and 32) calculated in all the images. Peak Signal-to-Noise Ratio (PSNR) measure can be easily calculated from MSE value. In general, ADU outperforms all other models, closely followed by SOM and FS-SOM. However, it is clear that ADU (top-right image in Fig. 3) paints the tiger skin with greenish color as an effect of the over-representation of green colors. Both MSCL results (bottom images in Fig. 3) tend to maintain orange colors in the tiger skin, as they are not focused in data density representation. Similar results are obtained in the Lena and Baboon images, as it can been seen in the table.

Fig. 3. Original Tiger image (*top-left*) and its reconstruction using 8 colors applying: ADU (*top-right*), Homogeneous MSCL (*bottom-left*) and Centered MSCL (*bottom-right*) (Color figure onlline).

3.2   CQ Focused on the Image Center

Previous example provides a CQ task giving equal importance to every pixel of the image, and not distinguishing between pixels of the foreground or the background. However the more interesting image regions are usually located in the foreground center. Using MSCL with the adequate magnitude function, it is possible to get a palette with colors mainly adapted to pixels located in the foreground, or any other desired point in the image. In this example we use the following magnitude function:

$$mf(t) = 1 - d(\mathbf{x}(t)) \tag{12}$$

where $d(\mathbf{x}(t))$ is the normalized distance, in the plane of the image (x, y), calculated from the corresponding pixel position to the center of the image. This magnitude function is normalized by the maximum.

We compare the performance of centered MSCL, with the same methods used in previous example. Number of colors and training parameters were also the same.

Prototypes of centered MSCL tend to focus on colors in the central part of the image. Therefore, MSE for the whole image is worse than those obtained using

Table 1. MSE calculated in the whole image and in the image center.

Pixels	Image	Som	FSCL	M-h	FCM	FSSom	ADU	M-c	Sgong
Whole img.	T8	987	1016	1037	1005	**985**	990	1095	987
	T16	566	596	577	606	564	**562**	667	570
	T32	334	343	341	357	328.1	**327.8**	409	574
	L8	401	416	424	451	**400.2**	406	406	400.9
	L16	216	234	215	234	216	**214**	217	218
	L32	121	126	122	141	120	**119**	125	222
	B8	1120	1126	1138	1151	**1117**	1126	1227	1121
	B16	633	641	633	693	**632.4**	632.8	751	635
	B32	380	389	380	440	**375.2**	375.9	479	442
Img. center	T8	1223	1311	1207	1263	1214	1244	**1151**	1226
	T16	626	710	596	735	631	608	**485**	655
	T32	361	381	356	408	353	355	**283**	407
	L8	445	472	436	552	440	447	**423**	447
	L16	265	294	273	301	262	266	**254**	267
	L32	161	167	160	187	159	159	**149**	163
	B8	1346	1354	1210	1421	1343	1338	**1062**	1321
	B16	708	740	683	833	705	689	**602**	714
	B32	381	412	387	515	372	374	**354**	539

other methods, as background is under-represented. However, when repeating the measures in the central area of the image (150×170 pixels), this algorithm (column M-c in the table) outperforms the others (as it can be seen in Table 1 in the three used images), because its color palette models in more detail the central region of the image.

3.3   CQ Avoiding Dominant Colors

Many natural images present few dominant background colors. That means that the majority of the image pixels are represented with these limited set of colors, while other small chunks of the image use a wider palette. By this reason, when it is applied traditional Competitive Learning algorithms on those kind of images for color quantization, color palette usually over-represent these dominant colors, and other secondary colors tend to disappear. In this example we will use MSCL to get a reduced color palette avoiding the color dominance.

To do it we use a two-step method. First we find the dominant colors of the image, and then, we apply MSCL to avoid these dominant colors by defining a magnitude function that gives higher values to the pixels that are more distant from them. We tested this methodology with 4 images (shown in Fig. 4: fish, flower, tower, goat) and compared it with the results of 5 neural models used in different papers: FSCL, FCM, Neural Gas (NG), K-Means and SOM.

Following we describe in detail the two-step method and the experimental results.

Fig. 4. Original images used in the example of MSCL avoiding dominant colors and one example of the corresponding dominant color palettes considering from 1 to 8 colors (*Left to right:* Fish, Flower, Tower, Goat.) (Color figure onlline).

Determination of Dominant Colors. First step is the determination of the dominant colors in the image. One simple way to do it, frequently used in the literature, is using some type of competitive learning algorithm to cluster pixel colors. Weights of units after training the neural network will be the dominant colors. A good candidate for this approach is FSCL method. FSCL can be considered a particular case of MSCL where $mf(t)$ is the number of hits of the best matching unit in sample $\mathbf{x}(t)$. We use this definition to implement FSCL as a data-density sensitive method that can cluster the data colors.

It is possible to use a unique simulation of FSCL to obtain the dominant colors. However, this method is dependent of the goodness of the unit initialization. So, in order to smooth this 'noisy' initialization in the results of the analysis, we use an ensemble of 50 FSCLs for each number of dominant colors (except for the case of one dominant color, calculated as the mean of the image colors). After generating the 50 networks of each ensemble, their prototypes are used to train the final FSCL to get the 'averaged' dominant colors. We call $\mathbf{pal}_k$ with $k \in \{dominants\}$ to the final dominant-colors palette.

Bottom of Fig. 4 shows the resulting palettes from 1 to 8 dominant colors in the four test images. The evolution of these palettes shows that, in the fish dominant-color palette, orange does not appear until using 5 dominant colors. The flower needs 4 dominant colors to show a good red color, and the tower needs 8 dominant colors to include the red in the roof. The goat dominant-color palette shows that the palette is quite monochromatic.

MSCL Avoiding Dominant Colors. The magnitude function $mf(t)$ used in this example needs to present higher values as the pixel color is more distant from the dominant-color palette. So, for each palette of dominant colors, we define a function $(distcol(t))$ for each pixel as the distance in the color space of that pixel to the closest color in the palette $\mathbf{pal}_j(t)$:

$$j = argmin(\|\mathbf{pal}_k(t) - \mathbf{x}(t)\|) \quad k \in \{dominants\} \tag{13}$$
$$distcol(t) = \|\mathbf{pal}_j(t) - \mathbf{x}(t)\|. \tag{14}$$

Figure 5 shows how this magnitude function works in the case of the fish image using an 8-color palette that avoids two dominant colors. A fraction of the pixels in the color distribution is depicted jointly with the closest regions of the dominant colors (large red circles) and the prototypes generated with MSCL (8 blue circles). MSCL uses three palette-colors for the orange colors of the fish, two colors for the white tones, one stronger black and only two colors dedicated to the background colors with the anemone. One of these colors almost coincide with one of the dominant color (in the center of the graph). This result appears because a large amount of the pixels are in this zone, and MSCL also is forced to move a prototype to this zone to reduce quantization error in (7).

The reconstructed images in this example, with 8-color palettes, for comparing the different methods, appear in Fig. 6, showing from left to right and top to bottom: MSCL avoiding two dominant colors, NG, FSCL, FCM, K-MEANS and SOM. It can be appreciated that MSCL obtained a more vivid color representation for the fish, losing the detail in the anemonae, while other algorithms tend to concentrate the units in the most common colors, showing a lot of greyish tones of the anemone.

Results of Experiments Avoiding Dominant Colors. The main problem of the method is to determine what should be the optimum number of dominant colors. So, we propose to calculate the amount of pixels in High Magnitude Regions (HMR) as a measure of the level of detail that the MSCL method has to deal with. The HMR in the image can be estimated with a threshold of the magnitude function that we chose at the 50 % of the maximum magnitude value. Figure 10 shows this process for the fish example in an 8-color palette. Images from top to bottom in each column correspond to number of dominant colors from 1 to 8. The first column of images in this figure represents the value of $distcol(t)$ in form of image (the magnitude map). The second column shows the

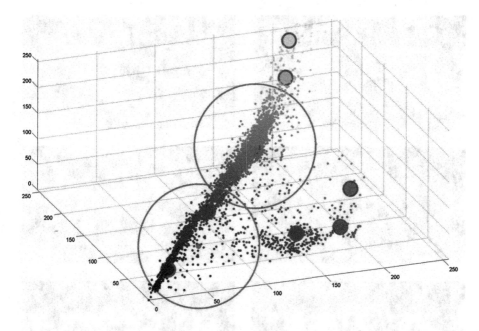

Fig. 5. Representation of a fraction of the pixels in the color distribution for the fish image. The large red circles represent the regions close to the two dominant colors of the image. The 8 blue circles represent the 8-color palette obtained for MSCL avoiding those dominant colors. MSCL uses three palette-colors for the orange colors of the fish, two colors for the white tones, and only three colors dedicated to the background colors (Color figure online).

HMR as the corresponding binarization of the magnitude maps. In this column it is possible to see that, considering only one dominant color, there are still quite a lot of pixels in HMR (corresponding to the fish and the darker areas in the background of the image). However, when two dominant colors are used, HMR extension is quite reduced and corresponds only to certain areas in the fish. Therefore the use of two dominant colors would be a good option for the fish image. The third column of images in this figure shows examples of the MSCL reconstruction for the corresponding number of dominant-colors avoidance.

As comparison, Fig. 11 shows in three columns the resulting HMRs for the other three images. In the first column, the flower image presents an interesting behavior for four dominant colors. In the tower image we have a similar situation, but for three colors (white, blue and dark grey). However, the goat image tends to keep similar HMR extensions. The reason of this behavior is possibly because it is a quite monochromatic image.

In order to visualize the effect of the number of dominant colors, we define the HMR-ratio as the number of pixels in HMR divided by the number of pixels in the image. We generated 50 palettes of dominant colors for each number of colors that varied from 1 to 20. The evolution of the averaged HMR-ratios are shown if the bottom graph of Fig. 9. The curves in the graphs have been smothered.

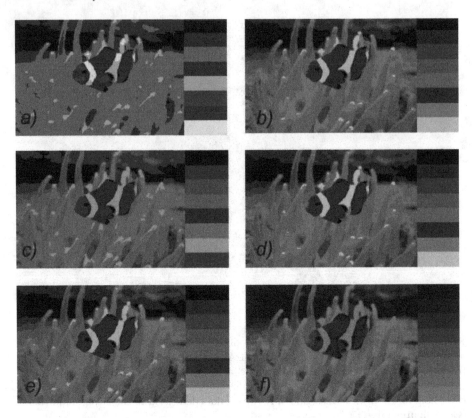

Fig. 6. Results of color quantization for the fish example using an 8-color palette with different methods: *(a)* MSCL avoiding two dominant colors, *(b)* NG, *(c)* FSCL, *(d)* FCM, *(e)* K-MEANS, *(f)* SOM. The corresponding color palettes are shown in the right of each image. As can be appreciated, MSCL gets a more vivid palette for the fish and presents a lower number of colors in the palette dedicated to the background with the anemone (Color figure onlline).

The abscissa shows the different number of dominant colors analysed in the four images. The ordinates show the mean value of the HMR-ratio. A lower value in this ratio means that there are fewer pixels in the image far from the dominant colors. Therefore that palette is a good representative of the dominant colors in the image.

The evolution of HMR-ratio for the fish image shows that there is an abrupt fall in this value from using one dominant color to the use of two. This value tends to keep in similar values until they are used 7 dominant colors. An explanation of this behavior can be visualized in Fig. 10 (image in row 7 and second column) where the dark band in the background is far from any dominant color, which makes the HMR-ratio to grow considerably in the bottom graph of Fig. 9.

It would be possible to detect the optimum number of dominant colors by analysing the HMR-ratio behavior, like detecting relative minimums or thresholding its variation, however we will left open this possibility, as it is out of the scope of this work.

In order to evaluate the performance of the methods in the HMR, we propose to calculate the Sum Square Error of quantization (SSE) in the HMR, divided by the total SSE in the image, that we will call the SSE-ratio. Graphically this can be appreciated in Fig. 9 (top four graphs corresponding to the four example images). The abscissas in the graphs show several numbers of dominant colors, from 1 to 5, when dealing with generation of 8-color palettes. The different algorithms (FSCL, FCM, NG, K-MEANS, SOM and MSCL) were simulated 50 times to show the averaged SSE-ratio. As it can be seen, MSCL always presents the smallest SSE-ratio, for all the images and different number of dominant colors. That means that MSCL with dominant-color avoidance is able to maintain a reduced amount of error in the HMR, while the others methods tend to concentrate their SSE reduction in the rest of the image.

3.4   CQ Focused in Salient Colors

The aim of salient feature detection is to find distinctive local events in images. Some works [21] exploit the possibilities of color distinctiveness in salient detection. This example shows the MSCL algorithm generating a color palette focused on those salient regions. To achieve that, the chosen magnitude function is the mean computational global saliency (defined as in [21]). The magnitude is normalized by the maximum, and varies from one to values near zero in zones with low saliency (see image in Fig. 7 in the middle of the top row). We used 8 colors with decreasing learning rates between 0.7 and 0.01 for every algorithm.

Figure 7 shows the results. The first two algorithms (SOM, FS-SOM) only obtain a red color and present higher MSE values (SOM: 103.21 and FS-SOM: 103.07) in those pixels belonging to the white mask region of saliency (third top image of Fig. 7). However, using the global saliency (second top image of Fig. 7) as the magnitude for MSCL, the resulting image shows three red variants and the MSE error is lower (87.5). A drawback is that other colors are underrepresented, what means a minor problem if we want to detail the salient regions of the image.

3.5   Image Binarization

Binarization of a text grey-scale image is the process of assigning each pixel of a text image depending of its grey-scale value to one of two classes, one corresponding to the text and the other one to the background. First row of Fig. 8 shows the image of a badly illuminated document (image a), and the results of applying classical binarization algorithms: Otsu method (b), filtering of original image with Laplacian operator (c) and its binarization with Otsu (d). Otsu Method definitely fails to get an adequate binarization because of the dark grey values in the right margin of the paper. Filtering with Laplacian operator provides a better result, because it is an edge extraction mask. However, this method does not fill the letters.

Fig. 7. Saliency example. *Top row, from left to right*: Original image, saliency map (clearer values for high saliency), the mask binary image used for MSE measurement and (*bottom row, from left to right*) the reconstructed image with an 8-colors palette from: SOM, FS-SOM and MSCL focused on the saliency (Color figure onlline).

Competitive learning can be used for this application by training 2 units to represent two levels of gray-scale, which should correspond to the background and foreground classes. Second row of Fig. 8 shows the results with: (e) SOM, (f) MSCL in homogeneous grey quantization, (g) MSCL with two features (explained below), and (h) Otsu binarization of last example. The MSCL

Fig. 8. Binarization example: in *top row* (a) original image, (b) Otsu method, (c) filtering with Laplacian operator, and (d) its binarization with Otsu; in *bottom row* (e) SOM, (f) MSCL in homogeneous grey quantization, (g) MSCL with two features, and (h) Otsu binarization of (g).

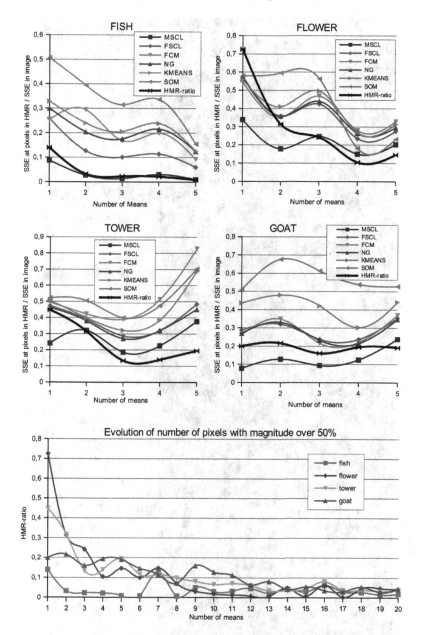

Fig. 9. The top four graphs correspond to each example image, when dealing with generation of 8-color palettes. The averaged Sum Square Error in the High Magnitude Region (HMR), divided by the total SSE in the image (SSE-ratio) is represented for the different algorithms (FSCL, FCM, NG, K-MEANS, SOM and MSCL). The abscissas in the graphs show several numbers of dominant colors, from 1 to 5. MSCL always presents a smaller SSE-ratio, for all the images and different number of dominant colors. The bottom graph represents the evolution of the averaged HMR-ratios (number of pixels in HMR divided by total number of pixels) when using from 1 to 20 dominant colors (Color figure onlline).

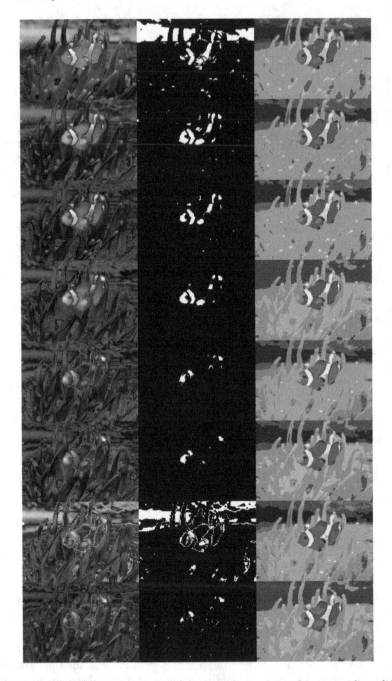

Fig. 10. Results of CQ of the Fish example in a 8 color palette, avoiding different number of dominant colors: (from top to bottom) with 1 to 8 dominant colors. (*In columns*): magnitude map, pixels with magnitude value over 50 % of the maximum (High Magnitude Region), and MSCL reconstruction for the corresponding number of dominant colors (Color figure onlline).

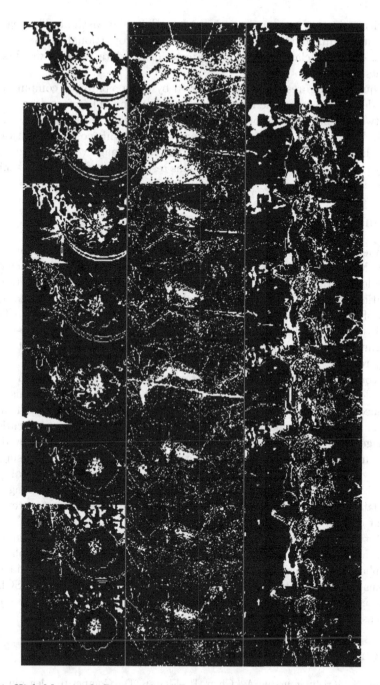

Fig. 11. High Magnitude Regions for different number of dominant colors. Images in rows correspond, from top to bottom, with 1 to 8 dominant colors. Images in the left column correspond to the flower example, the column in the middle for the tower and the right column for the goat image (Color figure onlline).

in (f) with only two neurons is equivalent to the Otsu Method. The reason is that the mean quantization error for each unit is proportional to the standard deviation of a data class when using as mean of the data the unit weights that represents the class.

The quantization result can be improved by using as input a combination of the gray-level values and the result of Laplace filtering. Therefore data samples will be two dimensional vectors combining the values of both features. Then if we apply MSCL using homogeneous quantization to this combined dataset we will get the two-level image (g) in Fig. 8 (the same image with binarized pixel intensity can be seen in next image (h)). This result is better than those achieved by other classical methods.

4   Conclusions

This paper has shown the capabilities of MSCL algorithm for Color Quantization. MSCL is a neural competitive learning algorithm, which includes a magnitude function as a modulation factor of the distance used for the unit competition. As other competitive methods, MSCL accomplishes a vector quantization of the data. However, unlike most of the competitive methods who are oriented to represent in more detail only those zones with higher data-density, the magnitude function in MSCL can address the competitive process to represent any region.

We compare MSCL with other vector quantization approaches in several image color quantization examples for different targets, such as focusing on homogeneous mean quantization error, focusing on image foreground, avoiding dominant colors, focusing on a saliency function and finally, application in text image binarization. As a result of these experiments we have showed that MSCL is more versatile than other competitive learning algorithms focusing only on density representations. MSCL forces the units to distribute their color prototypes following a tailored property, expressed by the appropriate magnitude of the data image. In this way, the palette exhibits more colors to accurately represent certain interesting zones of the image.

As future work we intend to use MSCL for vector quantization in multi-channel satellite images. In this application, the number of colors is replaced by the number of channels, thus the dimension of the data increases considerably. By means of a magnitude map obtained from labelled image zones MSCL will allow to orient the vector quantification to the regions of interest such as specific crop areas.

References

1. Ahalt, S., Krishnamurthy, A., Chen, P., Melton, D.: Competitive learning algorithms for vector quantization. Neural Netw. **3**(3), 277–290 (1990)
2. Atsalakis, A., Papamarkos, N.: Color reduction and estimation of the number of dominant colors by using a self-growing and self-organized neural gas. Eng. Appl. Artif. Intell. **19**(7), 769–786 (2006)

3. Bezdek, J.: Pattern Recognition with Fuzzy Objective Function Algorithms. Plenum Press, New York (1981)
4. Celebi, M.: An effective color quantization method based on the competitive learning paradigm. In: Proceedings of the International Conference on Image Processing, Computer Vision, and Pattern Recognition, IPCV, vol. 2, pp. 876–880 (2009)
5. Celebi, M.: Improving the performance of k-means for color quantization. Image Vision Comput. 29(4), 260–271 (2011). (Rochester, N.Y.)
6. Celebi, M., Schaefer, G.: Neural gas clustering for color reduction. In: Proceedings of the International Conference on Image Processing, Computer Vision, and Pattern Recognition, IPCV, vol. 1, pp. 429–432 (2010)
7. Chang, C., Xu, P., Xiao, R.: New adaptive color quantization method based on self-organizing maps. IEEE Neural Netw. 16(1), 237–249 (2005)
8. Cheng, G., Yang, J., Wang, K., Wang, X.: Image color reduction based on self-organizing maps and growing self-organizing neural networks. In: 2006 Sixth International Conference on on Hybrid Intelligent Systems (HIS'06) (40572082), 24 Dec 2006 (2006)
9. Dekker, A.: Kohonen neural networks for optimal colour quantization. Netw. Comput. Neural Syst. 3(5), 351–367 (1994)
10. Itti, L., Koch, C.: Computational modeling of visual attention. Nat. Rev. Neurosci. 2(3), 194–203 (2001)
11. Kohonen, T.: Self-Organizing Maps. Springer, Heidelberg (2001)
12. Lazaro, J., Arias, J., Martin, J., Zuloaga, A., Cuadrado, C.: SOM segmentation of gray scale images for optical recognition. Pattern Recogn. Lett. 27(16), 1991–1997 (2006)
13. Lloyd, S.: Least squares quantization in PCM. IEEE Trans. Inf. Theor. 28(2), 129–137 (1982)
14. Martinetz, T., Berkovich, S., Schulten, K.: 'Neural-gas' network for vector quantization and its application to time-series prediction. IEEE Trans. Neural Netw. 4(4), 558–569 (1993)
15. Nikolaou, N., Papamarkos, N.: Color reduction for complex document images. Int. J. Imaging Syst. Technol. 19(1), 14–26 (2009)
16. Papamarkos, N.: A neuro-fuzzy technique for document binarisation. Neural Comput. Appl. 12(3–4), 190–199 (2003)
17. Pelayo, E., Buldain, D., Orrite, C.: Focused image color quantization using magnitude sensitive competitive learning algorithm. In: IJCCI, pp. 516–521 (2012)
18. Pelayo, E., Buldain, D., Orrite, C.: Magnitude sensitive competitive learning. In: 20th European Symposium on Artificial Neural Networks, Computational Intelligence and Machine Learning. vol. 1, pp. 305–310 (2012)
19. Treisman, A., Gelade, G.: A feature integration theory of attention. Cogn. Psychol. 12, 97–136 (1980)
20. Uchiyama, T., Arbib, M.: Color image segmentation using competitive learning. IEEE Trans. Pattern Anal. Mach. Intell. 16(12), 1197–1206 (1994)
21. Vazquez, E., Gevers, T., Lucassen, M., van de Weijer, J., Baldrich, R.: Saliency of color image derivatives: a comparison between computational models and human perception. J. Opt. Soc. Am. A: Opt. Image Sci. Vision 27(3), 21–613 (2010)
22. Xu, L., Krzyzak, A., Oja, E.: Rival penalized competitive learning for clustering analysis, RBF net and curve detection. IEEE Trans Neural Netw. 4, 636–649 (1993)

A Subset-Based Ant Colony Optimisation with Tournament Path Selection for High-Dimensional Problems

Emmanuel Sapin[✉] and Ed Keedwell

College of Engineering, Mathematics and Physical Sciences, University of Exeter, Harrison Building, Exeter, England, UK
{e.sapin,e.c.keedwell}@exeter.ac.uk

Abstract. The analysis of big data, particularly from the biosciences, provides unique challenges to the methods used to analyse such data. Datasets such as those used in genome-wide association studies can have a very high number of variables/dimensions (e.g. 400,000+) and therefore modifications are required to standard methods to allow them to function correctly.

A variety of methods can be used for such problems, among them ant colony optimisation is a promising method, inspired by the way in which ants find the shortest path in nature. The selection of paths traditionally uses a roulette wheel which works well for problems of smaller dimensionality but breaks down when higher numbers of variables are considered. In this paper, a subset-based tournament selection ACO approach is proposed that is shown to outperform the roulette wheel-based approach for operations research problems of higher dimensionality in terms of the performance of the final solutions and execution time on problems taken from the literature.

Keywords: Subset-based ant colony optimisation · High dimensional NP-hard problems · Tournament selection · Roulette wheel selection · Knapsack problem

1 Introduction

NP-hard combinatorial problems are an important class of problems in theoretical and real-world tasks. For these problems no algorithm can solve them in polynomial time. Examples of such problems in operations research are the bin packing problem and the knapsack problem.

Some recent approaches to solve these problems are to use stochastic algorithms including nature inspired algorithms that are known to have delivered good results for this class of problems. Ant Colony Optimisation (ACO), as one such algorithm is inspired by the way in which ants in the wild find a short path from the nest to food using pheromones. Ant colony optimisation

© Springer-Verlag Berlin Heidelberg 2014
N.T. Nguyen (Ed.): TCCI XVII 2014, LNCS 8790, pp. 232–247, 2014.
DOI: 10.1007/978-3-662-44994-3_12

has been shown to deliver excellent results on discrete combinatorial test problems (Dorigo and Caro 1999) and has been widely applied to real-world problems ranging from water distribution system optimisation (Zecchin et al. 2007) to robotics (Mohamad 2008) or scheduling (Blum 2002; Merkle et al. 2000).

Recently, there has been considerable interest in the use of ant colony optimisation to the discovery of gene-gene interactions in genomic data (Moore 2005; Christmas et al. 2011; Greene et al. 2008; Sapin et al. 2013b). The problem is to search a large database (up to 400,000) of small DNA changes known as single nucleotide polymorphisms (SNPs), and find SNPs or combination of SNPs that best discriminates between diseased and healthy individuals (for a more in-depth discussion of the problem, readers are directed to Christmas et al. (2011) and Sapin et al. (2013a)). The sheer size of the data presents a unique challenge to ant colony optimisation as there are many thousands of possible choices for each ant to select from at each decision point. Modifications to the algorithm are therefore required to enable it to process this data effectively. Ant paths in ACO are usually chosen through the use of a roulette wheel which weights decisions based on the level of pheromone for each SNP. This procedure works well for small numbers of decision variables, but as we will show the performance of the roulette wheel breaks down when many thousands of path choices are included and a new method based on a tournament is investigated.

The selection procedure in evolutionary algorithms is closely related to path choices in ant colony optimisation as both procedures are required to provide a stochastic decision but one that is weighted towards individuals with the greatest fitness, or paths with the greatest pheromone. Tournament selection is often preferred over the roulette wheel in evolutionary computing for a number of reasons, including its comparative ease of implementation, computational efficiency, the ease with which selection pressure can be modified and perhaps most importantly, its robustness with respect to the distribution of the fitness function. Roulette wheels do not function well where the distribution of fitness (pheromone) is highly skewed or where negative fitness values exist. Although negative pheromone is not a concern in ant colony optimisation, the remaining benefits to evolutionary computing should translate to ant colony optimisation with the use of a tournament in place of the roulette wheel for path selection. Here it is shown how Tournament Ant Colony Optimisation (T-ACO) can replace the roulette wheel with a tournament in path selection in ant colony optimisation.

The following sections describe the implementation of the algorithm, experimentation with knapsack problems and multiple parameter settings, and concluding remarks.

2 Previous Work

Previous work concerning ant colony optimisation are presented here.

2.1   Standard Ant Colony Optimisation

The standard ant colony optimisation algorithm (Dorigo and Caro 1999) creates a population of agents ants that traverse a topology. The topology can reflect the underlying topology of the problem (e.g. with the travelling salesman problem) or can make use of a construction graph where each variable choice is aligned with connections between variable choices forming the set of paths for the algorithm to traverse. Construction graphs are used for problems that do not have a native topology and in this way, any discrete combinatorial problem is solvable with an ant colony optimisation approach. Ants make path choices at each junction in the graph based on the level of pheromone (and occasionally local heuristic values) on the paths leading to the next variable selection. However, a further modification is desirable where the selection of subsets of variables is required and the order of variable selection is not important (e.g. in the knapsack and genomics problems). In this case, a full construction graph is not required and pheromone can be deposited on the variables themselves, using the subset-based approach described in (Leguizamon and Michalewicz 1999), which is used here.

The probability of selecting a variable can be calculated thus:

$$P_i^k(t) = \frac{[\tau_i(t)]^\alpha \cdot [\eta_i(t)]^\beta}{\sum_{h \in J^k} [\tau_h(t)]^\alpha \cdot [\eta_h(t)]^\beta} \tag{1}$$

Where $\tau_i(t)$ is the pheromone on the variable i at time t and $\eta_i(t)$ is the local heuristic value (optional) on the same variable. α and β coefficients allow the balance between the two components to be adjusted.

Once an ant reaches its destination, it leaves pheromone on the chosen variables that reflect the quality of the solution that the variables represent. Pheromone is then evaporated by a fixed percentage across all variables and the algorithm iterates again. The updated pheromone can therefore be calculated thus:

$$\tau_i(t+1) = (1-\rho) \cdot \tau_i(t) + \Delta_i(t) \tag{2}$$

Where ρ is the pheromone evaporation rate (typically between 1 and 10 %) and $\Delta_i(t)$ is the additional pheromone laid by the ants traversing the graph.

2.2   Subset and Ordering Problems

A traditional ACO topology-based approach would usually require variables and their selections to be optimised in a specific order (e.g. an ant will visit variable 1, then variable 2 etc. until the path through the topology is complete). However, subset selection based problems such as those in genomics where a small number of variables from the total number available should be selected, do not require this ordering of ant visitation. This is also the case for the well-known knapsack problem where the order of items in the bag is irrelevant in terms of fitness.

Early experiments with ant colony optimisation algorithms were about ordering problems such as the Quadratic Assignment Problem or the Traveling Salesman Problem. The latter was used as example to illustrate the basic concepts of the original ant system (Dorigo et al. 1991).

Leguizamon and Michalewicz showed that ant colony optimisation can be apply to subset problems (Leguizamon and Michalewicz 1999). Ordering problems and subset problems differ in the way pheromone trail is laid on the topology of the problem. For ordering problems, the connections between elements of the problem receive pheromone whereas the components themselves receive pheromone in subset problems. The ACO algorithm here makes use of the subset-based approach described in the work of Leguizamon and Michalewicz but crucially adds tournament selection to allow for the application of the algorithm to very large datasets.

3   Knapsack Problem

The Knapsack problem was chosen for experimentation as it is an NP-hard combinatorial problem which has the required flexibility in terms of the number of decision variables. This problem has been studied for more than a century (Mathews 1897) and it was introduced by the mathematician Tobias Dantzig (Dantzig 1930).

The problem is described as follows: given a set of items, each with a weight and a value, determine the count of each item to include in a collection so that the total weight is less than or equal to a given limit and the total value is as large as possible. It derives its name from the problem faced by someone who is constrained by a fixed-size Knapsack and must fill it with the most useful items.

In the Knapsack problem that was chosen for experimentation, each item s has two attributes:

- a weight $s.weight$ between 0 and 100.
- a value $s.value$ between 0 and 100.

The knapsack capacity is 1000. A solution is a set of n items $\{S\}_i$ such that:

$$\sum_{i=1}^{n} S_i.weight < 100 \tag{3}$$

The fitness function is the sum of the values of the selected items:

$$Fitness = \sum_{i=1}^{n} S_i.value \tag{4}$$

The level of pheromone of the items corresponding to the highest fitness are increased by the value of the fitness.

4   Method

The algorithms of the roulette wheel and tournament ant colony optimisation are described here.

4.1   Ant Colony Algorithm

T-ACO uses the standard equations (without local heuristic) of Sect. 2.1 as the basis for its algorithm. The key difference between T-ACO and ACO is how the variable is selected for a given set of probabilities. Traditionally this is achieved by summing the probabilities as calculated in Sect. 2.1 and selecting randomly from these summed probabilities to determine the next variables chosen by the ant. This process allows the ant to choose randomly but with a decision weighted towards those variables with greater pheromone values. Here the algorithms of a Tournament-ACO and Roulette Wheel-ACO are described.

Roulette Wheel Ant Colony Optimisation. Roulette wheel ant colony optimisation runs as follows:

```
Initialise pheromone;
Repeat
  For all the nbant ants:
   Do
      Select an item according to the roulette wheel;
      Put the item in the Knapsack;
    While the Knapsack is not full;
    Store the items the ant has chosen;
    Calculate the fitness depending of the value of the chosen
    items;
  For the ant with the best fitness:
    Update pheromone of the chosen items;
  For all items: apply evaporation rate of 1 %;
End
```

Where:

– *nbant*: the numbers of ants of the algorithm;

Tournament-ACO. T-ACO differs in that a tournament selection is used.

In this process, T variables are randomly chosen from the set of possible variable choices and the variable with the highest pheromone value is selected. T is the size of the tournament. By varying T the greediness of the algorithm can be modified, lower values of T approximate random search as the competition element of the tournament is lessened and the influence of paths with high pheromone is reduced. Higher values of T increase the greediness of the search.

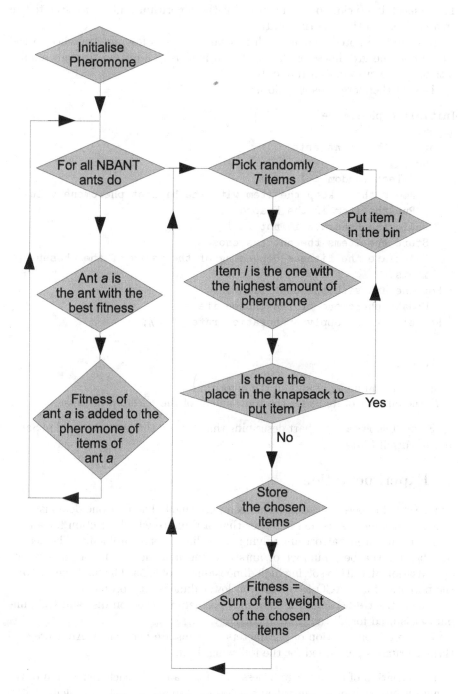

Fig. 1. Flow chart describing the method.

This aspect is crucial to the function of the algorithm and is investigated in greater depth in the experimentation.

It should be noted that no such mechanism exists for roulette wheel based search and the greediness of the algorithm is usually adjusted through modifications of the evaporation rate only.

T-ACO therefore runs as follows:

```
Initialise pheromone;
Repeat
  For all the nbant ants:
    Do:
      Select randomly T items;
      Among them, keep the item with the highest pheromone value;
      Put the item in the Knapsack;
    While the Knapsack is not full;
    Store the items the ant has chosen;
    Calculate the fitness depending of the value of the chosen
    items;
  For the ant with the best fitness:
    Update pheromone of the chosen items
  For all items: apply evaporation rate of 1 %;
End
```

Where:

- *nbant*: the numbers of ants of the algorithm;
- *T*: the number of items for the tournament of the selection process;

Figure 1 shows a flow chart describing this method that was also used in Sapin and Keedwell (2012).

5   Experimentation

Three sets of experimentation have been performed. The first one demonstrates that a tournament selection is better than a roulette wheel selection for an ant colony optimisation algorithm solving high dimensional problems. The second searches for the best number of ants and tournament size for an ant colony optimisation algorithm solving high dimensional problems. The final one explores the potential for T-ACO to operate on lower dimensional problems.

The dataset describing the knapsack problem is saved on disc and the same dataset is used for all the experiments.

For every combination of parameters, 10 runs are performed. An average of these 10 runs is performed for the following data:

- The variation of the average fitness fit of the ants. At each generation of the algorithm, each of the *nbant* ants chooses a solution to the problem that is evaluated by a fitness value. An average of the fitness value of the solutions of each ant is performed.

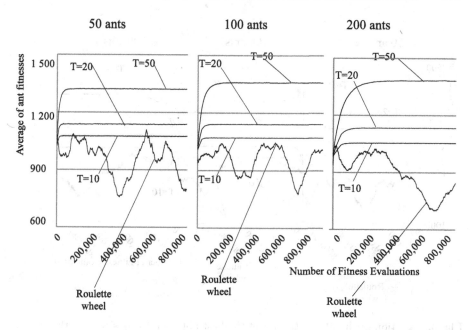

Fig. 2. Variation of the average fitness fit of the ants over 10 runs with T the size of the tournament.

- The variation of the fitness $bestfit$ of the best ant. At each generation of the algorithm, the pheromone amounts of the items of the solution with the highest fitness value are updated. An average of these highest fitness values are performed.
- The variation of the highest fitness $highestfit$ found throughout the run. The highest fitness values that have been found during each run are stored. An average of these is then computed.

For each experiment, 1,000,000 evaluations of the fitness function are performed before the experiment is stopped.

5.1   Tournament Versus Roulette Wheel

This experiment demonstrates that tournament selection outperforms roulette wheel selection for an ant colony optimisation algorithm solving high dimensional problems. In this experiment, the roulette wheel and tournament selection methods are compared on the knapsack problem of size 500,000. The experiment investigates the performance of the roulette wheel method against the T-ACO approach with varying tournament sizes (20, 50 and 100), using the general experimental conditions shown above and various numbers of ants (50, 100 and 200).

The results in Figs. 2, 3 and 4 show the dominance of the T-ACO approach for knapsack problems of this size. The size of the tournament clearly has an

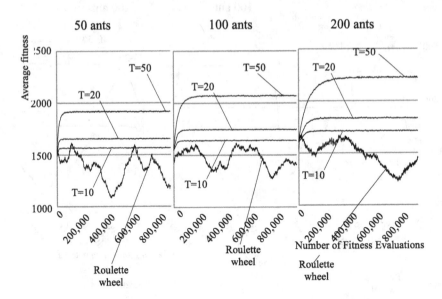

Fig. 3. Variation of the fitness *bestfit* of the best ant over 10 runs with T the size of the tournament.

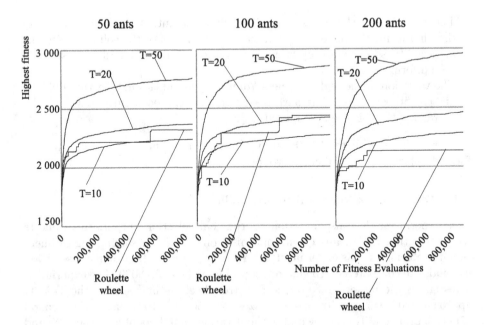

Fig. 4. Variation of the highest fitness *highestfit* found through the run over 10 runs with T the size of the tournament.

effect on the performance of the algorithm and in particular it's convergence properties. As expected, greater tournament sizes increase the speed of convergence and limit the ability for exploration but it is clear that the tournament outperforms the roulette wheel for this problem size. The results suggest that the best tournament size has not yet been found for this problem. Increasing the tournament to 50 has the effect of improving mean performance. This is to be expected when one considers the size of the problem of 500,000 variables, even a tournament size of 50 is a vanishingly small percentage of the total number of variables. In evolutionary algorithms a tournament size of approximately 10 % is favoured suggesting an optimum tournament size for this problem of 5 000. However the application of the tournament here in ACO path selection is somewhat different to the standard evolutionary algorithm application and will depend to a certain degree on the number of ants used in the population. In the next set of experiments, tournaments of larger size have been used along with variations in the population to ascertain reasonable parameter settings for this large problem.

5.2   Number of Ants and Size of Tournament

The best number of ants and tournament size for an ant colony optimisation algorithm solving high dimensional problems are investigated here. This experiment investigates the performance of the T-ACO approach with varying tournament sizes (50 and 500) and number of ants (50, 100 and 200), using the general experimental conditions shown above on the knapsack problem of size 500,000. Sizes of tournament greater than the ones investigated in the previous section are chosen as the previous section shows that greater tournament sizes increase the speed of convergence.

The results in Fig. 5 show the effect of the number of ants for the T-ACO approach for knapsack problems of size 500,000 and the tournament selection of size 50. The highest fitness for 100 ants is better than the highest fitness for 50 or 20 ants. It is interesting noting that the highest fitness is better for 50 ants during the first 100,000 evaluations of the fitness function. For 100 ants, the pheromones are updated only every 100 evaluations of the fitness function that makes the convergence slower that with 50 ants.

The results in Fig. 6 show the effect of the number of ants for the T-ACO approach for knapsack problems of size 500,000 and the tournament selection of size 500. The highest fitness for 50 ants is better than the highest fitness for 100 or 20 ants. It seems that 50 ants allow a good trade-off of the algorithm between exploration and exploitation for this problem and this size of tournament.

The results in Figs. 5 and 6 clearly show the number of ants and the size of the tournament are not independent in the T-ACO approach for knapsack problems of size 500,000. In this experimentation, the fitness is the highest for 50 ants and 500 items. 500 items is 0.1 % of the total number of items therefore 0.1 % of the total number of items and 50 ants are the chosen parameters of the algorithm for further experiments.

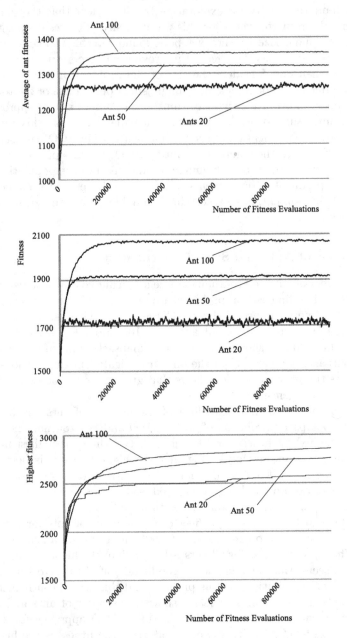

Fig. 5. Variation of the average fitness *fit*, the fitness *bestfit* of the best ant and the highest fitness *highestfit* found through the run over 10 runs for a tournament size of 50.

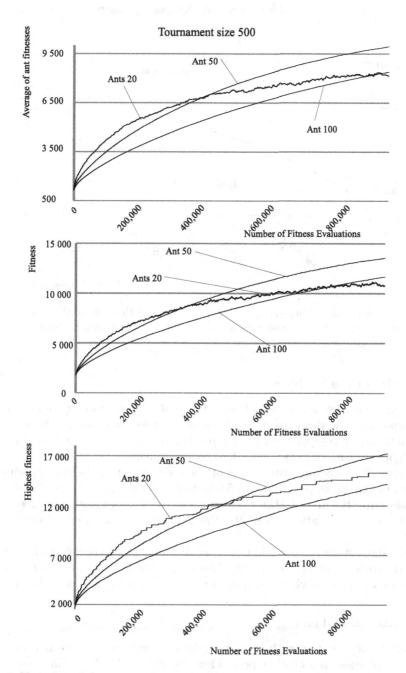

Fig. 6. Variation of the average fitness fit, the fitness $bestfit$ of the best ant and the highest fitness $highestfit$ found through the run over 10 runs for a tournament size of 500.

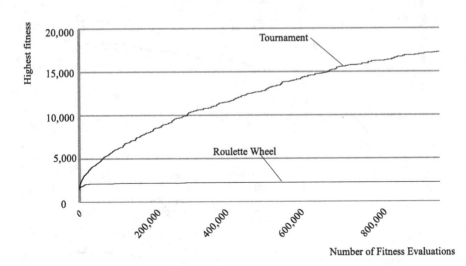

Fig. 7. Variation of the highest fitness *highestfit* found throughout the run, over 10 runs, with 50 the size of the tournament and 50 ants for a knapsack problem of 50,000 items.

5.3 Size of the Problem

This experiment explores the potential for T-ACO to operate on lower dimensional problems. In this experiment, the roulette wheel and tournament selection of size 0.1 % are compared on the knapsack problem of sizes 50,000 and 5,000. An algorithm with 50 ants is used for this experiment.

Figures 7 and 8 show the results of these experiments. For the experiment solving the knapsack problem with 5,000 items only the variation of the highest fitness during the first 500,000 evaluations of the fitness function is presented. This because no variation arises after the 500,000 first evaluations of the fitness function.

For 50,000 items as shown in Fig. 7, the tournament selection performs better than the roulette wheel but for 5,000 items Fig. 8 the roulette wheel is better. It shows that a roulette wheel selection is better for smaller sizes of problems.

5.4 Execution Time

A further consideration with large-scale data is the time taken to perform the selection process. As a highly repeated function within the algorithm, even small differences in execution time will make a large difference to the overall execution time of the algorithm.

Figure 9 shows the comparison between runtimes for roulette wheel and a tournament size of 10 % of the problem size based on the experimentation

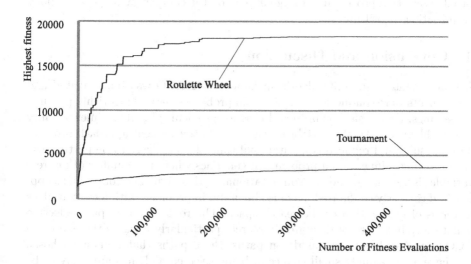

Fig. 8. Variation of the highest fitness *highest fit* found throughout the run, over 10 runs, with 5 the size of the tournament and 50 ants for a knapsack problem of 5,000 items.

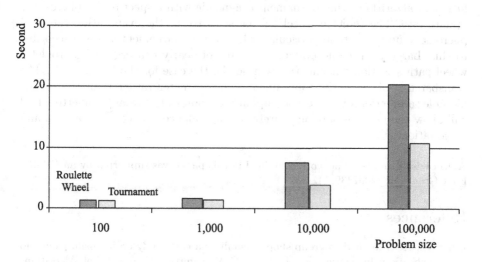

Fig. 9. A comparison of execution times on four different problem sizes.

described in Sapin and Keedwell (2012). This is the complete execution time, including the calculation of the objective function, so it can be seen that the variable selection process has a large impact on the complexity of the ant colony optimisation algorithm.

6   Conclusion and Discussion

A tournament-based ACO algorithm known as T-ACO was implemented and experiments were conducted on a variety of problem sizes and algorithm parameter settings. From this it is proposed that for problems of higher dimensionality (i.e. problems of 50,000+ variables), the use of a tournament approach provides better results and reduced computational time. This is likely to be particularly useful for high-dimensional problems in genomics where the number of discrete variables is very large and the computational load is high. The tournament approach, if correctly configured may also be useful in problems with fewer variables in terms of exploration of the search space. The roulette wheel path selection is naturally biased towards a greedy search, particularly towards the end of an ACO run. As pheromone builds on paths, those paths that remain unchosen will have a vanishingly small chance of being selected and thus are likely to be ignored for the remainder of the optimisation. The tournament, particularly one with a small percentage of variables allows for all paths to be considered regardless of the status of the optimisation. Of course there is a trade-off here, if the tournament is too small then progress is slow, a process seen quite clearly in Fig. 7, too large and the progress becomes too greedy. However, the ability for the tournament size to be modified provides the user with a mechanism to modify the exploitation/exploration trade-off, in addition to the evaporation rate. One final advantage of the tournament path selection is that, similarly to evolutionary algorithms, the tournament is agnostic with respect to the pheromone update rate. The roulette wheel will be sensitive to the evaporation rate and pheromone update rate in particular, whereas the tournament is less susceptible to this. Large pheromone updates will promote early convergence for roulette wheel path selection whereas this will not be the case for the tournament. The transparency of using the tournament size parameter rather than the unpredictable interaction of pheromone update, evaporation rate and roulette wheel will allow the user to more accurately set the balance between exploration and exploitation.

Acknowledgments. The work contained in this paper was supported by an EPSRC First Grant (EP/J007439/1).

References

Blum, C.: ACO applied to group shop scheduling: a case study on intensification and diversification. In: Dorigo, M., Di Caro, G.A., Sampels, M. (eds.) Ant Algorithms 2002. LNCS, vol. 2463, pp. 14–27. Springer, Heidelberg (2002)

Christmas, J., Keedwell, E., Frayling, T., Perry, J.: Ant colony optimisation to identify genetic variant association with type 2 diabetes. Inf. Sci. **181**, 1609–1622 (2011)

Dantzig, T.: Numbers: The Language of Science. Macmillan, New York (1930)

Dorigo, M., Caro, G.D.: New Ideas in Optimization, pp. 11–32. McGraw-Hill Ltd., Maidenhead (1999)

Dorigo, M., Maniezzo, V., Colorni, A.: Positive Feedback as a Search Strategy (1991)

Greene, C.S., White, B.C., Moore, J.H.: Ant colony optimization for genome-wide genetic analysis. In: Dorigo, M., Birattari, M., Blum, C., Clerc, M., Stützle, T., Winfield, A.F.T. (eds.) ANTS 2008. LNCS, vol. 5217, pp. 37–47. Springer, Heidelberg (2008)

Leguizamon, G., Michalewicz, Z.: A new version of ant system for subset problems. In: Angeline, P.J., Michalewicz, Z., Schoenauer, M., Yao, X., Zalzala, A. (eds.) Proceedings of the Congress on Evolutionary Computation, Mayflower Hotel, Washington, vol. 2, pp. 1459–1464. IEEE Press (1999)

Mathews, G.B.: On the partition of numbers. Proc. London Math. Soc. **28**, 486–490 (1897)

Merkle, D., Middendorf, M., Schmeck, H.: Ant colony optimization for resource-constrained project scheduling. IEEE Trans. Evol. Comput. **6**, 893–900 (2000)

Mohamad, M.M.: Articulated robots motion planning using foraging ant strategy. J. Inf. Technol. **20**, 163–181 (2008). Special Issues in Artificial Intelligence

Moore, J.H.: A global view of epistasis. Nat. Genet. **37**, 13–14 (2005). (Nature Publishing Group)

Sapin, E., Keedwell, E.: T-aco - tournament ant colony optimisation for high dimensional problems, pp. 81–86, SciTePress (2012)

Sapin, E., Keedwell, E., Frayling, T.: Ant colony optimisation for exploring logical gene-gene associations in genome wide association studies (2013a)

Sapin, E., Keedwell, E., Frayling, T.: Subset-based ant colony optimisation for the discovery of gene-gene interactions in genome wide association studies (2013b)

Zecchin, A., Maier, H., Simpson, A., Leonard, M., Nixon, J.: Ant colony optimization applied to water distribution system design: comparative study of five algorithms. J. Water Resour. Plan. Manage. **133**, 87–92 (2007)

An Analysis of the Local Optima Storage Capacity of Hopfield Network Based Fitness Function Models

Kevin Swingler$^{(\boxtimes)}$ and Leslie Smith

Computing Science and Maths, University of Stirling, Stirling FK9 4LA, Scotland
kms@cs.stir.ac.uk

Abstract. A Hopfield Neural Network (HNN) with a new weight update rule can be treated as a second order Estimation of Distribution Algorithm (EDA) or Fitness Function Model (FFM) for solving optimisation problems. The HNN models promising solutions and has a capacity for storing a certain number of local optima as low energy attractors. Solutions are generated by sampling the patterns stored in the attractors. The number of attractors a network can store (its capacity) has an impact on solution diversity and, consequently solution quality. This paper introduces two new HNN learning rules and presents the Hopfield EDA (HEDA), which learns weight values from samples of the fitness function. It investigates the attractor storage capacity of the HEDA and shows it to be equal to that known in the literature for a standard HNN. The relationship between HEDA capacity and linkage order is also investigated.

1 Introduction

A certain class of optimisation problem may be solved (or an attempt at solving may be made) using metaheuristics. Such problems generally have the following qualities: the search is for an optimal (or near optimal) pattern of values over a number (often many) of random variables; any candidate solution, which is an instantiation of each of those variables, has an associated score, which is its quality as a solution; a fitness function exists that takes a candidate solution and produces a score. The function (or algorithm) for calculating the score may be evaluated for any input vector, but may not be inverted to produce an input vector that would maximise the score. For this reason, the process of optimisation may be viewed as a directed search. Metaheuristics are methods for making use of the score returned by the fitness function to speed the search for good solutions when an exhaustive search would not be practical.

Most metaheuristic algorithms maintain a memory of some kind that reflects the input patterns previously chosen and the scores they received. In general such algorithms proceed by generating one or more new candidate solutions based on their memory of previous trials. Each new solution is then given a score using the fitness function and the memory is updated. The new memory is then used to

© Springer-Verlag Berlin Heidelberg 2014
N.T. Nguyen (Ed.): TCCI XVII 2014, LNCS 8790, pp. 248–271, 2014.
DOI: 10.1007/978-3-662-44994-3_13

produce new (hopefully improved) solutions and the process continues until some stopping criterion is met. One simple way to divide metaheuristic algorithms is between those that develop an explicit model and those that maintain a population of 'good' solutions in place of a model. Perhaps the best known population based method is the Genetic Algorithm (GA) [1]. A GA maintains a population of good solutions and uses them to produce new solutions that are combinations of two (sometimes more) existing solutions. Combination is performed by picking values for each variable from one or other parent to instantiate the variables in a new child solution. Better solutions have a higher probability of producing offspring than poorer ones and some offspring may be altered slightly (a process called mutation) to extend the search space. In a GA the population and the recombination process are the memory and the generative process respectively.

An alternative to maintaining a population of solutions is to build a model of some aspect of the fitness function and use that to guide the search. One well studied method is to model the probability of each variable taking each of its possible values in a good solution. As the model evolves, new candidate solutions are drawn from the model's distribution, which in turn cause the model to be updated. This approach is known as an Estimation of Distribution Algorithm (EDA) and is described in more detail in Sect. 2.

A problem that many metaheuristic algorithms face (GAs and EDAs included) is that of local optima. Local optima are globally sub-optimal points that are optimal in a local neighbourhood. That is, points from which a small change in the variables' values will not lead to an improvement in score. In terms of metaheuristic algorithms local optima are points from which the chosen algorithm will not move, even when there are better scoring solutions in other parts of the search space. For example, a population in a GA may reach a state where neither recombination nor any small mutation will produce a sufficient improvement to generate a candidate solution that is better than any in the existing population. When sampling from an EDA, a local optimum is a solution that has a high probability of being sampled, but which is not the best solution. An EDA can contain two types of local optima. Firstly, if none of the patterns that it produces are the true global optimum, then they are all local optima. Secondly, an EDA can contain many local optima — all of the high probability patterns — and one of those will score more than the others, making those others local optima compared to the model's own global optimum. In a perfect model, the EDA's global optimum will be the global optimum of the problem being tackled. In less than perfect models, it may well be a local optimum itself.

The number of local optima a fitness function contains is one measure of the difficulty of finding the global optimum. Another related measure is the size of the field of attraction around each optima. The field of attraction for an optimum is the sub-space of points from which an algorithm will make a series of steps leading to that optimum. For a simple hill climbing algorithm, the field of attraction for a local optimum, x is the set of points from which a hill climb will lead to x. So called *deceptive* functions are those in which the fields of attraction of local optima are large and that for the global optimum is small [2].

A fundamental aspect of GA research considers the role played by subsets of the variables being optimised. These subsets are often called building blocks [1] or analysed as schemata [3]. For example, in a vector $\mathbf{x} = x_1 \dots x_n$, it may be that variables x_2, x_3 and x_4 all interact in a non-linear fashion and that the effect of changing the value of any one of them can only be understood in terms of the values of the other two. This interdependency between variable subsets and the fitness function output is known as the linkage problem [4] or, sometimes in the GA literature, epistasis [5]. The number of variables in a building block is known as its order and we can talk about a problem being of order m if the order of its highest meaningful building block is m. This introduces the question of how to discover the linkage order of a function.

One way in which researchers have addressed the question of linkage order is with the use of Walsh functions [6,7]. These are described in detail in Sect. 3 and summarised here. The Walsh functions form a basis for functions over $f :$ $\{0, 1\}^n \rightarrow \mathbb{R}$. Any such function can be decomposed into a weighted sum of Walsh functions. The Walsh functions that contribute to the weighted sum are of differing orders, defined by the number of bits they contain that are set to 1. The process of performing a Walsh decomposition of a function produces the weights (known as the Walsh coefficients) associated with each Walsh function and many have values of zero. Consequently, the order of the functions with non-zero coefficients tells us about the order of interactions in the function.

These two measures of problem difficulty — fields of attraction to local optima and linkage order — are related. This paper addresses the relationship between local optima attractors and linkage order for a particular type of EDA implemented using a Hopfield Neural Network (HNN). The HNN is described in detail in Sect. 4. It can be understood variously as a neural network using an adjusted Hebbian learning rule and McCulloch-Pitts neurons, or as a Markov random field or as a second order EDA. It is well known [8] that HNNs have a certain capacity for storing patterns in memory and this capacity holds for the number of local optima a network can learn. The important point to note is that in the standard HNN, only second order linkages are learned. It is not the case, however, that the HNN can only find all the attractors in problems of order 2 or below. We show that a HNN can discover the local optima of functions with higher order linkages, up to some capacity, and investigate the relationship between linkage order, network capacity and local optima count.

The main contributions of this paper are the adaptation of a Hopfield network to learn functions with real valued outputs and an analysis of the number of local optima such networks can represent at one time. An algorithm for improving the capacity of a Hopfield network is also adapted and its capacity analysed. Several functions are analysed in terms of their linkage order and the number of local attractors they contain. These results are then related to the capacity of Hopfield networks and their ability to capture the local optima in higher order functions. The paper suggests a parallel between the number of attractor states in the network and population diversity in a GA. This should be of interest to researchers developing multi-variate EDAs as it highlights the need to manage the attractors of an EDA and demonstrates how all attractors in a model degrade once capacity is exceeded. The main focus of the paper is on the second of these contributions—the analysis of attractor capacity. An analysis of the ability of the method to improve optimisation requires the study of algorithms for evolving models and solutions and a large number of experiments, which are all the focus of a future paper.

The paper is organised as follows. Sections 2, 3 and 4 introduce EDAs, Walsh functions and Hopfield networks respectively. Sections 5 and 6 describe a Hopfield EDA (HEDA) and presents two learning rules: one based on a standard Hebbian update and one designed to improve network capacity. Section 7 describes a set of experiments and an analysis of network size, capacity and the time taken during learning. Section 8 analyses the weights of a HEDA and Sect. 9 offers some conclusions and discusses future work.

1.1 Scope

The functions discussed in this paper are real valued functions of binary vectors, that is:

$$f : \{-1, 1\}^n \to \mathbb{R} \tag{1}$$

A single candidate solution is a point in n-dimensional binary space defined by a vector **c** of elements c_i that can take binary values:

$$\mathbf{c} = c_1, \ldots, c_n \qquad c_i \in \{-1, 1\} \tag{2}$$

The function $f(\mathbf{c})$ that guides the search is known as the fitness function.

2 Estimation of Distribution Algorithms

A common class of model based optimisation methods are the Estimation of Distribution Algorithms (EDAs). Rather than maintain individual searches, an EDA attempts to model the probability of a value or sub-pattern appearing in a high scoring candidate solution. Reasons for building a fitness model include the advantages gained from being able to analyse the model to better understand the problem to be optimised [9] and the improved speed of estimating fitness function output rather than making a time consuming calculation for every required evaluation.

The simplest EDA models the marginal probability of each variable taking each of its possible values in the optimal solution. Population Based Incremental Learning (PBIL) [10] is an example of such a method. PBIL works by sampling from the set of possible solutions and maintaining a marginal probability distribution for each variable. PBIL is a population based search as the probabilities are updated based on the best scoring members of each generation of the population. Subsequent populations are generated based on the probabilities in the distribution. PBIL makes use of a learning rate to smooth the evolution of the probabilities. For solving problems with binary valued variables, PBIL's update rule is:

$$P(p_i = 1) \leftarrow (1 - \alpha)P(p_i = 1) + \alpha\rho(p_i = 1) \tag{3}$$

where ← indicates assignment, $P(p_i = 1)$ is the probability that $p_i = 1$ in the model, and $\rho(p_i = 1)$ is the probability that $p_i = 1$ amongst the best of the current population. α is the learning rate.

PBIL is a first order method as it models each variable independently. It will solve first order problems as they have no local optima to trap it. For higher order problems, it may find the global optimum or it may become trapped in a local optimum. The evolutionary aspect of PBIL ensures that it converges on an optimum of some kind (local or global). Other univariate algorithms include the compact Genetic Algorithm (cGA) [11] and the Univariate Marginal Distribution Algorithm (UMDA) [12].

Early attempts at capturing second order interactions included the Mutual Information Maximising Input Clustering algorithm (MIMIC) [13]. This algorithm imposes an ordering on the variables and links them in a chain so that each variable (except the last in the chain) is linked to exactly one other. The ordering is discovered using a greedy algorithm (a full search for the correct ordering is NP-complete), and so is not guaranteed to find the optimal chain. Another pairwise method is the Bivariate Marginal Distribution Algorithm (BMDA) [14], which models second order linkage in a forest (a set of independent dependency trees). Higher order interactions are learned by the Bayesian Optimisation Algorithm (BOA) [15], which builds a Bayesian network to attempt to capture the joint distribution of values in a population of promising solutions. Again, building a correct Bayesian network is an NP-complete problem, so heuristics are needed to build the network in sensible time. More recently, the Distribution Estimation Using Markov networks (DEUM) algorithm [16] has modelled second and higher order interactions using Markov random fields. DEUM models conditional probabilities and generates new samples using Gibbs sampling.

Most EDA approaches consist of a method for representing the distribution and a method for evolving a solution. The evolution of a solution generally follows a pattern of generating a population of candidate solutions from the current model, updating the model based on the quality of those candidates by either learning only the most fit or by learning them all with a weight that depends on the fitness score. The process is then repeated until the algorithm finds a good solution or converges. There are a number of choices to be made when designing the evolutionary algorithm: whether to learn a subset of the population or use the score of every member; the size of each generation, which effects the accuracy of the model; whether to start a new model at each generation or to add to the existing one; and what schedule, learning rate or forgetting factor to use if a model persists from generation to generation. These factors greatly affect the quality of an EDA optimisation algorithm, but they are not the subject of this paper, which demonstrates how a second order EDA can be built from a HNN and then makes use of the fact that much is understood of the capacity and function of such networks.

These methods all share a common feature: they do not attempt to model the distribution of values in all good solutions, just a small number of them. In the case of the univariate methods, it should be clear that the number of solutions the distribution can model is just one: the pattern produced by picking the value with the highest probability from each variable. In multivariate models, the number of different promising patterns that can be stored at any one time is greater than one. This paper investigates this capacity for bivariate models.

3   Walsh Functions

Walsh functions [17] form a basis for functions of binary vectors. Any function $f : \{0,1\}^n \rightarrow \mathbb{R}$ can be represented as a weighted sum of Walsh functions. The contribution of each Walsh function to the sum is determined by its Walsh coefficient.

3.1   Generating the Walsh Functions

To decompose a function of n variables, Walsh functions of length 2^n are used, denoted ψ_j where $j = 0 \ldots 2^n - 1$. There are 2^n such functions, each represented by a string of 2^n bits: $\psi_j(c)$ where $c = 0 \ldots 2^n - 1$. $\psi_j(c)$ is the cth bit in the jth Walsh function. They are calculated in a bit wise fashion from the binary representation of their indices, c and j. Note the slight abuse of notation: j is an integer index, $\mathbf{j}$ is the binary representation of j and j_i is the ith bit of $\mathbf{j}$, counting from the right. For example, $j = 3$, $\mathbf{j} = 011$, $j_3 = 0$. The same applies to c. To calculate $\psi_j(c)$, first re-code the binary representation of c so that 1 becomes -1 and 0 becomes 1. This slightly counter-intuitive re-coding allows multiplication to perform the XOR function. This can be done bitwise using:

$$y_i \leftarrow -(2c_i - 1) \tag{4}$$

Then use the recoded vector $\mathbf{y}$ and the binary representation of $\mathbf{j}$ to calculate each bit $\psi_j(y)$ as

$$\psi_j(y) = \prod_{i=1}^{n} y_i^{j_i} \tag{5}$$

where $j_i \in \{0,1\}$ so $y_i^{j_i} = y_i$ when $j_i = 1$ and $y_i^{j_i} = 1$ when $j_i = 0$. The binary word $\mathbf{j}$ acts as a mask to determine which values $y_i \in \{-1,1\}$ are included in the product. Figure 1 shows a pictorial representation of the order 3 Walsh functions.

3.2   Calculating the Walsh Coefficients

The Walsh transform of an n-bit function produces 2^n Walsh coefficients, ω_j where $j = 0 \ldots 2^n - 1$. Each coefficient is calculated as follows:

$$\omega_j = \frac{1}{2^n} \sum_{c=0}^{2^n-1} f(\mathbf{c})\psi_j(c) \tag{6}$$

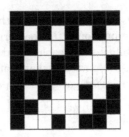

Fig. 1. A pictorial representation of the third order Walsh functions with black squares representing 1 and white squares −1.

where $f(\mathbf{c})$ is the real valued output of the fitness function when the input variables are instantiated with the values from the binary representation of c. Note that for $f : \{-1, 1\}^n$, each 0 in the binary word must first be converted to −1.

3.3 Stating the Fitness Function as a Walsh Function

The function $f(\mathbf{c})$ can now be restated as a Walsh sum:

$$f(\mathbf{c}) = \sum_{j=0}^{2^n} \omega_j \psi_j(c) \tag{7}$$

where c is the integer represented by the binary word $\mathbf{c}$, with the same allowance for converting $0 \leftarrow -1$ if required when converting from $\mathbf{c}$ to the bit index c.

3.4 Analysis of Walsh Coefficients

We can now directly introduce the concept of linkage order with respect to Walsh functions. A Walsh decomposition of an n-bit function leads to 2^n Walsh coefficients, $\omega_i (i = 0 \ldots 2^n - 1)$. The index i determines how the coefficient ω_i is calculated (see Eq. 6). It also determines the linkage order of the coefficient. Let the binary equivalent of the index i of ω_i be $\mathbf{i}$, which acts as a mask, selecting bit positions where there is a 1 in $\mathbf{i}$. Counting the number of 1s in $\mathbf{i}$ tells you the linkage order of ω_i. For example, ω_0 is of zero order and ω_3 (011) is second order. Consider the full results of a Walsh analysis of a first order binary problem over three bits where the target pattern is 101 and the fitness function is an inverse Hamming distance such that $f(101) = 1$ and $f(010) = 0$. The first order coefficients, ω_1, ω_2 and ω_4 all have none-zero values and the higher order coefficients are all zero.

Table 1 shows how to extract the first order optimum from the Walsh coefficients directly. The location of the 1 bit in the first order index, $\mathbf{i}$ of ω_i corresponds to the location in the optimum whose value is determined by ω_i. If ω_i is positive, the optimum contains a zero at that location and if it is negative,

Table 1. Walsh Coefficients and linkage order for $f(\mathbf{c}) = 1 - Hamming(c, 101)$

Coefficient	Index	Order
$\omega_0 = 0.5$	000	0
$\omega_1 = -0.167$	001	1
$\omega_2 = 0.167$	010	1
$\omega_4 = -0.167$	100	1
$\omega_3 = 0$	011	2
$\omega_5 = 0$	101	2
$\omega_6 = 0$	110	2
$\omega_7 = 0$	111	3

the optimum contains a 1. Looking at Table 1, we see that ω_1 is negative, ω_2 is positive and ω_4 is negative, so the optimum must be at 101.

A full Walsh decomposition requires 2^n function evaluations and so is not a practical method for solving large optimisation problems. It is, however, a useful tool for understanding concepts of linkage on small, toy problems.

4   Hopfield Networks

Hopfield networks [18] are able to store patterns as point attractors in n dimensional binary space and recall them in response to partial or degraded versions of stored patterns. For this reason, they are known as content addressable memories where each memory is a point attractor for nearby, similar patterns. Traditionally, known patterns are loaded directly into the network (see the learning rule 10 below), but in this paper we investigate the use of a Hopfield network to discover point attractors by sampling from a fitness function. A Hopfield network is a neural network consisting of n simple connected processing units. The values the units take are represented by a vector, $\mathbf{u}$:

$$\mathbf{u} = u_0, \ldots, u_{n-1} \qquad u_i \in \{-1, 1\} \tag{8}$$

The processing units are connected by weighted connections:

$$W = [w_{ij}] \tag{9}$$

where w_{ij} is the strength of the connection from unit i to unit j. Units are not connected to themselves, i.e. $w_{ii} = 0$ and connections are symmetrical, i.e. $w_{ij} = w_{ji}$. The values of the weighted connections define the point attractors and learning in a standard Hopfield network takes place by setting the pattern to be learned using formula 11 and applying the Hebbian weight update rule:

$$w_{ij} \leftarrow w_{ij} + u_i u_j \quad \forall i \neq j \tag{10}$$

A single pattern, $\mathbf{c}$ is set by

$$\forall i \quad u_i \leftarrow c_i \tag{11}$$

Pattern recall is performed by allowing the network to settle to an attractor state determined by the values of its weights. The unit update rule during settling is

$$a_i \leftarrow \sum_{j=0}^{n-1} w_{ji} u_j \tag{12}$$

where a_i is a temporary activation value, following which the unit's value is capped by a threshold, θ, such that:

$$u_i \leftarrow \begin{cases} 1 & \text{if } a_i > \theta \\ -1 & \text{otherwise} \end{cases} \tag{13}$$

In this paper, we will always use $\theta = 0$. The process of settling repeatedly uses the unit update rule of formulae 12 and 13 for a randomly selected unit in the network until no update produces a change in unit values. At that point, the network is said to have settled. The symmetrical weights and zero self-connections mean that the network is a Lyapunov function, which guarantees that the network will settle to one of its fixed points from any starting point. With the above restrictions in place, the network has an energy function that determines the set of possible stable states into which it will settle. The energy function is defined as:

$$E = -\frac{1}{2} \sum_{i,j} w_{ij} u_i u_j \tag{14}$$

Settling the network, by formulae 12 and 13 produces a pattern corresponding to a local minimum of E in Eq. 14. Hopfield networks have been used to solve optimization tasks such as the travelling salesman problem [19] but weights are set by an analysis of the problem rather than by learning. Other examples of hand built Hopfield optimisers include [20], in which the authors comment on the lack of a method for finding the right set of weights for an arbitrary optimisation problem. In the next section, we show how random patterns and a fitness function can be used to train a Hopfield network as a search technique.

5   Hopfield EDAs

We define a Hopfield EDA (HEDA) as an EDA implemented by means of a Hopfield neural network. This section describes the training and use of a HEDA. Figure 2 shows a four neuron HEDA with the units labelled u_i and weights in one direction labelled $W_{i,j}$.

5.1   Training a HEDA

In this section we describe a method for training a HEDA. The principles apply equally to HEDAs of higher order. During learning, candidate solutions are generated randomly one at a time. Each candidate solution is evaluated using the

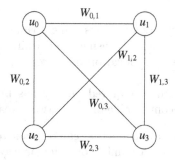

Fig. 2. A four neuron HEDA with units u_i and weights $W_{i,j}$. Due to weight symmetry, only half the weights are shown as each $W_{i,j} = W_{j,i}$.

fitness function and the result is used as a learning rate in the Hebbian weight update rule (see update rule 15). Consequently, each pattern is learned with a different strength, which reflects its quality as a solution.

5.2 The New Weight Update Rule

Hopfield networks have a limited capacity for storing patterns. If a number of patterns greater than this capacity are learned, patterns interfere with each other producing spurious states, which are a combination of more than one pattern. To learn the point attractors of local optima without ever sampling those points, we need to create spurious states that are a combination of lower points. We do this by over-filling a Hopfield network with samples and introducing a strength of learning so that higher scoring patterns contribute more to the new spurious states. This yields a simple modification to the Hebbian rule:

$$w_{ij} \leftarrow w_{ij} + f(\mathbf{c})u_i u_j \quad i \neq j \tag{15}$$

where $\mathbf{c}$ is the candidate solution to be learned and $f(\mathbf{c})$ is the output of the fitness function given $\mathbf{c}$. This has the effect of learning high scoring second order sub-patterns more than lower scoring ones. Note that due to the symmetry of the weight connections, each attractor has an associated inverse pattern that is also an attractor. The means that both the pattern and its inverse may need to be scored to tell the solutions apart from their inverse twins.

5.3 The Learning Algorithm

The simplest version of the learning algorithm simply builds the network from samples of $\mathbf{c}$ and $f(\mathbf{c})$ and proceeds as follows:

1. Set up a Hopfield network with $W_{ij}=0$ for all i,j
2. Repeat the following until one or more stopping criteria are met
   (a) Generate a random pattern, $\mathbf{c}$, where each c_i has an equal probability of being set to 1 or -1

(b) Calculate $f(\mathbf{c})$
(c) Load $\mathbf{c}$ into the network's neurons using formula 11
(d) Update the weight matrix W using the learning rule in formula 15
(e) Sample attractor states (local optima) from the network and keep the best found
(f) Stop when a pattern of required quality has been found or when the attractor states become stable or the network reaches capacity.

There are a great many improvements that can be made to this simple algorithm. The sampling can be done in a number of different ways, for example. Rather than sample after each single weight update, sampling could occur less frequently. Also, the sampled 'good' solutions from local optima could be used to drive the choice of new candidate solutions in a number of ways (as it does in an EDA). A degree of forgetting could also be introduced, either by starting a new HEDA with zeroed weights for each new set of candidate solutions, or by something less drastic such as dividing the weights by a constant. These questions are outside the scope of this paper, but may be informed by an understanding of the capacity of the HEDA to store a number of local attractors. In particular step 2e will be limited by the number of attractors the HEDA contains.

5.4   Sampling a HEDA Model

During the search process, new candidate solutions are generated by sampling the HEDA. The sampling process may be carried out in a number of ways. This paper is more concerned with network capacity than with the details of sampling methods, but some concepts are outlined here. Local optima can be sampled by picking a random pattern or a pattern from the current population if a population based search is being used and loading it into the network using Eq. 11. The network is then settled to a local optima by repeatedly applying the update rule 12 to neurons picked in random order until no neuron produces a change in its output value over an exhaustive sweep of the network. Neurons can be treated stochastically by replacing the activation function with a probability based calculation. This turns the HNN into a Boltzmann machine [21] and allows simulated annealing to be used as the search technique.

6   A Learning Rule for Improving Capacity

Storkey [22] introduced a new learning rule for Hopfield networks that increased the capacity of a network compared to using the Hebbian rule. The new weight update rule is:

$$w_{ij} \leftarrow w_{ij} + \frac{1}{n} u_i u_j - \frac{1}{n} u_i h_{ji} - \frac{1}{n} u_j h_{ij} \tag{16}$$

where

$$h_{ij} \leftarrow \sum_{k \neq i,j} w_{ik} u_k \tag{17}$$

The new terms, h_{ji} and h_{ij} have the effect of creating a local field around w_{ij} that reduces the lower order noise brought about by the interaction of different attractors.

To use this learning rule in a HEDA, we make the following alterations to the update rules:

$$w_{ij} \leftarrow w_{ij} + \frac{1}{n}(u_i u_j - u_i h_{ji} - u_j h_{ij})f(p) \tag{18}$$

and

$$h_{ij} \leftarrow \sum_{k \neq i,j} w_{ik} u_k \beta \tag{19}$$

where $\beta < 1$ is a discount parameter that controls how much damping is applied to the learning rule and which keeps the weights at reasonable values.

7   Experimental Results

This paper investigates the effects of the number of local optima in a fitness function and the capacity of a HEDA to represent them, rather than the effectiveness of the HEDA as an optimisation tool in its own right. The following experiments reflect this focus.

7.1   Experimental Functions

We build functions with a fixed number of local attractors using a method based on nearest Hamming distance. In this method, a number of target patterns are chosen as the local optima and the function is evaluated by calculating the Hamming distance to the closest of the set of target patterns. Consequently, the number of local optima equals the number of target patterns. The set of target patterns are denoted as the set $\mathbf{T}$:

$$\mathbf{T} = \{t_1, \ldots, t_s\} \tag{20}$$

We then define the fitness function as one minus the normalised Hamming distance between $\mathbf{c}$ and each target pattern t_j in $\mathbf{T}$:

$$f(\mathbf{c}, t_j) = 1 - \sum_{i=1}^{n} \frac{\delta_{c_i, t_{ji}}}{n} , \tag{21}$$

where t_{ji} is element i of target j and $\delta_{c_j, t_{ji}}$ is the Kronecker delta function between pattern element i in t_j and its equivalent in $\mathbf{c}$. We take the score of a single pattern to be the maximal score of all the members of the target set.

$$f(\mathbf{c}, \mathbf{T}) = max_{j=1\ldots s}(f(\mathbf{c}, t_j)) \tag{22}$$

This method of building the fitness function relates to existing research on HNN capacity, which is often based on the capacity for storing random patterns.

7.2   HEDA Capacity Experiments

This section investigates the capacity of the HEDA, which is the number of distinct attractors it can model. As each attractor is a single local optimum, the capacity of the network determines the number of local optima a HEDA can represent at any one time. Depending on how the HEDA is being used, this has a number of consequences. Most EDA approaches to optimisation try to model the distribution of 'promising solutions'. A local optima in the search space represents a single neighbourhood of promising solutions. Consequently, the ability to model a number of different local optima requires the EDA to hold a number of local attractors. A univariate EDA has a single attractor and multivariate EDAs have higher capacities.

The literature on the capacity of a Hopfield network has generally concentrated on the capacity for storing random patterns. A pattern is deemed to be successfully stored in a Hopfield network if the pattern of activity corresponding to that pattern is an attractor point in the network. This is tested by setting the chosen pattern as a starting point using Eq. 11 and then settling the network using Eq. 12. If the network does not move away from the attractor point, then the pattern is still in its memory. Other nearby points will also cause the network to settle to the same attractor point, depending on the size of its basin of attraction. In terms of storing random patterns, [8] states that the capacity of a HNN is $n/(2 \ln n)$ where n is the number of neurons in the network. This is the figure we will be using for our analysis in this paper.

This set of experiments compares the capacity of a normally trained Hopfield network with the search capacity of a HEDA. We will compare two learning rules (Hebbian and Storkey). The experiments are repeated many times, all using randomly generated target patterns where each element has an equal probability of being +1 or −1.

7.3   Experiment 1: Hebbian HEDA Capacity

Experiment 1 compares Hebbian trained Hopfield networks with their equivalent HEDA models. The aim is to discover whether or not the HEDA model can achieve the capacity of the Hopfield network. Hopfield networks were trained on patterns using standard Hebbian learning, with one pattern at a time being added until the network's capacity was exceeded. At this point, the learned patterns were set to be the targets for the HEDA search using Eqs. 21 and 22 and the network's weights were reset.

100 repeated trials were made training HEDA networks ranging in size from 10 to 100 units in steps of 5. For each trial, the capacity of the trained network, the number of those patterns discovered by global searching and the time taken to find them all (or give up short) were recorded.

Results. Regardless of the capacity or size of the Hopfield network, the HEDA search was always able to discover every pattern learned during the capacity filling stage of the test. From this, we conclude that the capacity of a HEDA for

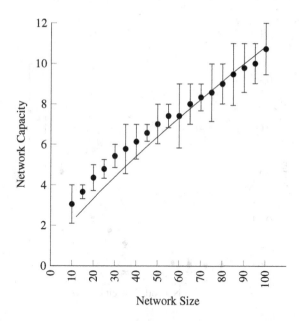

Fig. 3. The mean and inter-quartile range of the capacity of HEDA networks of varying sizes and the theoretic capacity of similar HNNs (single line).

storing local optima when searching for a set of random targets is the same as the capacity of the equivalent Hopfield network.

Figure 3 shows the relationship between HEDA network size and capacity. The spread of capacity values is wide, varying with the level of interdependence between the random patterns. The chart shows the mean and the inter-quartile range of capacity for each network size. The solid line shows the theoretical capacity of HNNs by size.

In these simple examples, no evolution takes place; the network is not used to generate new populations. This paper is not concerned with algorithms to improve search performance, it is concerned with memory capacity in EDAs (specifically the HEDA). However, it is instructive to investigate the relationship between the number of local optima a HEDA can store and the number of uniform random samples required to model them. To that end, the number of samples that were required to allow the HEDA to identify all of the local optima in the experiments above was recorded. Figure 4 shows the number of samples required to find all the local optima of a function plotted against network capacity. By curve fitting the data shown, we find that the number of samples required to find all local optima is quadratic with number of such optima.

In fact, as the search space grows, the number of iterations required to model every local optima, as a proportion of the size of search space diminishes exponentially. For networks of size 100, the search space has 2^{100} possible states and the HEDA is able to find all of the targets in an average of around 355,000 samples. That is a sample set consisting of 2.8×10^{-25} of all possible patterns.

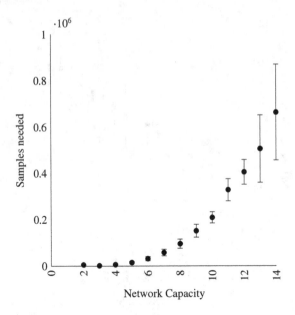

Fig. 4. The mean and inter-quartile range of the number of samples needed to find all local optima in a HEDA filled to capacity, plotted against the number of patterns to find.

Experiment 2: Storkey HEDA Capacity. As mentioned above, [22] suggest an alternative to the Hebbian learning rule that increases the capacity of a Hopfield network. This new learning rule can be used to increase the number of attractors in a HEDA and so increase the number of local optima it is able to model. A Hopfield network trained with Storkey's learning rule has a capacity of $n/\sqrt{2\ln n}$. In experiment 2 we repeat experiment 1 but use the Storkey learning rule rather than the Hebbian version. The experimental procedure is the same.

Results. As with the Hebbian learning, the Storkey trained HEDA search was always able to discover every pattern learned during the capacity filling stage of the test. This shows that the improved learning rule will deliver the increased capacity for capturing local optima that we sought. The cost of this capacity is a far slower learning algorithm, however as Eqs. 18 and 19 have more terms to evaluate. Figure 5 shows the relationship between Hopfield network size and capacity for the Storkey trained network.

Figure 6 shows the number of samples required to find all the local optima plotted against network size when using the Storkey rule. Again, we see that search iterations increase quadratically with network capacity.

7.4   Linkage Order and Network Capacity

Section 7.2 described how a HNN and a HEDA have a capacity for storing a number of attractors, or local optima. In this section, we investigate the relationship between network size, network capacity (in terms of attractor states),

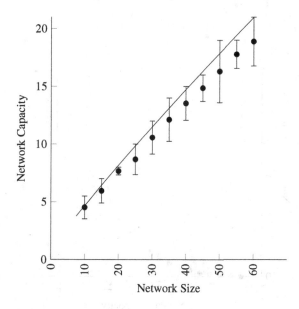

Fig. 5. The mean and inter-quartile range of the capacity of Storkey trained HEDA models and their theoretical limit (single line).

and the highest order of linkage interactions in the fitness function. In these experiments, a standard Hopfield network is trained incrementally on patterns until the addition of a new pattern causes one of the previous patterns to be forgotten, that is, the pattern is no longer an attractor state. This is tested by setting each target pattern as an input to the network, and then settling the network to a local attractor. If the network moves away from its starting point, then that point is no longer an attractor.

Once the network has reached capacity, the set of patterns that it has learned are used as the local optima in a Hamming function as in Eq. 22. The Walsh decomposition of this function is calculated and the highest order weight is recorded. This process generates pairs of numbers: the network capacity and the highest order of the function whose local optima are the patterns that fill that capacity.

Figure 7 shows the results of these experiments as a set of histograms, one for each network capacity from 2 to 5. A Hopfield network with capacity m has learned all the attractors in a function with m local optima using the standard Hebbian rule. This function undergoes a Walsh decomposition and the resulting coefficients have a maximal order at which the coefficient is non-zero. This highest order is recorded and counted for representation in the histograms. None of the networks of order m had a highest order below m and the larger the capacity, the more often the function had a larger highest order of interaction. It is clear from the histograms that many high order functions may have their attractors represented by a second order Hopfield network.

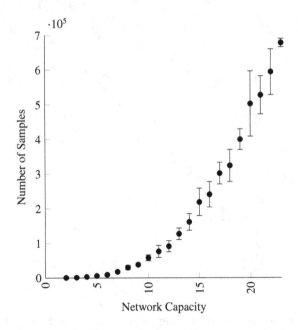

Fig. 6. The mean and inter-quartile range of the number of samples needed to find all local optima in a Hopfield network filled to capacity using the Storkey learning rule, plotted against the number of patterns to find.

8   Analysis of Network Weights

This section describes an analysis of the weights of a trained HEDA. Section 3 introduced Walsh functions and in Sect. 7.3 they were used in the analysis of fitness function linkage order. This section describes the equivalence between the weights of a HEDA and the second order Walsh coefficients. The important finding is that the weights of an exhaustively trained HEDA, $\mathbf{W}$ are equal to the second order Walsh coefficients, as stated in Eq. 23.

$$W_{ij} = \omega_c \tag{23}$$

where c is the integer obtained by constructing a binary word of n bits, setting every bit to zero except the two at indices i and j, and converting the resulting word to an integer with the standard place encoding method. The binary word, $\mathbf{b}(i,j)$ is constructed one bit at a time where $b_k(i,j)$ is the kth bit (least significant first) of the word constructed for weight W_{ij}.

$$b_k(i,j) = \begin{cases} 1, & \text{if } k = i \text{ or } k = j \\ 0, & \text{otherwise} \end{cases} \tag{24}$$

Then c is calculated as

$$c \leftarrow \sum_{k=0}^{n-1} 2^{b_k} \tag{25}$$

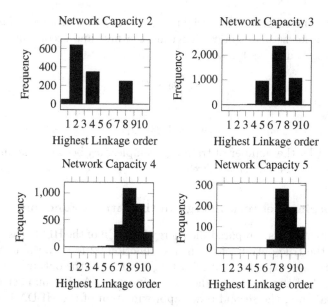

Fig. 7. Histograms showing the frequency of the highest linkage order across 10,000 trials, organised by Hopfield network capacity. Networks are trained with the standard Hebbian rule. Networks with capacity greater than 5 require a number of units greater than that for which it is possible to run multiple Walsh decompositions.

An exhaustively trained HEDA is built by generating every possible pattern across the input space, scoring each one, and training the HEDA on the resulting input/output pairs. After training, the weights are all divided by the number of patterns learned (i.e. 2^n), so the learning rule for each weight, given every sample is

$$W_{ij} \leftarrow \frac{1}{2^n} \sum_{\mathbf{c} \in \{-1,1\}^n} f(\mathbf{c}) c_i c_j \qquad (26)$$

There is a clear parallel between Eqs. 26 and 6 and between Eqs. 14 and 7, which shows that the HEDA's energy function is a second order approximation of the learned function. Section 7.3 showed that second order HEDAs can capture the local optima of higher order functions, but Eq. 7 suggests that the inclusion of lower order weights in the HEDA might also be of use. First order weights are the equivalent of adding bias weights to each neuron in a Hopfield network. Let the first order weights be a vector, $\mathbf{v}$ of size n. To introduce ω_0 requires the addition of a zero order weight to the HEDA, w_0, which has the rather un-neural quality of being connected to no neurons. However, if these weights are included in the HEDA energy function, then the approximation to the fitness function becomes more accurate. Now, an approximation to $f(\mathbf{c})$ can be calculated as

$$f(\mathbf{c}) = w_0 - \sum_i v_i u_i + \sum_{i,j} w_{ij} u_i u_j \qquad (27)$$

where w_{ij} are the second order weights, v_i are the first order weights and w_0 is the single order zero weight. Calculating the first and second order weights during learning is done as follows.

$$w_0 \leftarrow w_0 + f(\mathbf{c}) \tag{28}$$

and

$$v_i \leftarrow v_i + f(\mathbf{c})u_i \tag{29}$$

After dividing by the number of training examples, w_0 becomes the mean of all the function outputs, i.e. $w_0 = \langle f(\mathbf{x}) \rangle$.

8.1   Comparing Network Energy to the Fitness Function

A series of experiments compared the energy function of the HEDA, as calculated in Eq. 27 to the true output of the fitness function 22 for a variable number of target patterns. As expected, with few target patterns, the output of the energy function matched the output of the fitness function. As the number of targets (local optima) rose, the second order approximation of the HEDA became less accurate and its capacity for correctly scoring local optima above other patterns diminished. Figure 8 shows some results of these experiments. Each graph shows the energy output from a HEDA calculated using Eq. 27 plotted against the target output from Eq. 22. Each graph in Fig. 8 was produced with a different set of target patterns. It is clear from the figures that the HEDA's ability to model the function and capture the optima reduces as the number of optima increases.

The graphs showing functions with one and two local optima demonstrate that the function output calculated using Eq. 27 is equal to the true function output for every different input pattern. The graph for four local optima shows that three of those optima have been captured by the network, and that there is some difference between the network output and the function output. The last plot, with eight local optima, shows the network performance degraded past the point where it is useful. The plot shows a number of spurious optima — maximal in the network output but not in the function and also shows that the true optima have not been recorded. This illustrates a central point to this paper: if the population of attractors being modelled is too large, the ability of the HEDA (and other similar EDAs) degrades quickly to the point where all the local optima are lost. The number of quality of the attractors needs careful management.

8.2   Comparing HEDA Weights to HNN Weights

A number of sampling methods for training a HEDA have been mentioned in this paper. The simplest is uniform random sampling. A more directed evolutionary approach is to let the current attractors of the HEDA guide the sampling of the next generation of candidate solutions. The exhaustive method used above

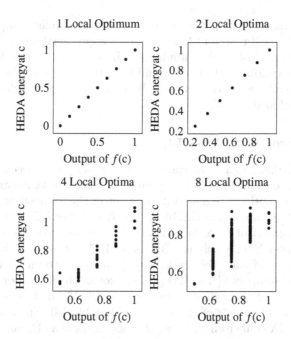

Fig. 8. HEDA energy plotted against fitness function output for functions with different numbers of local optima

trains the HEDA on every possible candidate solution, which is not of interest in terms of optimisation, but is useful in revealing structure in the weights.

A standard HNN can be viewed as an extreme example of the second method: an evolutionary approach where only the local optima of the fitness function are sampled and learned. In the simplest case, a HNN with a single pattern in its memory has learned a function where $f(\mathbf{c}) = 0$ everywhere except where $\mathbf{c}$ equals the single learned pattern, where $f(\mathbf{c}) = 1$. In this case, Eq. 10 differs only from Eq. 15 by the constant term $\frac{1}{2^n}$ as nothing is learned where $f(\mathbf{c}) = 0$ and the pattern is learned once when $f(\mathbf{c}) = 1$. In terms of the attractors, only the relative magnitude and the sign of the weights are important. Scaling all the weights in a network by dividing by a constant (in this case, 2^n) makes no difference to the location of the attractors. The function described here has interactions all the way up to order n, so although the network can model the attractor correctly, it cannot reproduce the function correctly. Adding further attractors, up to the capacity of the network, maintains the equivalence. The HEDA weights are simply a multiple of the HNN weights.

Now consider a similar function, where the Hamming measure of Eq. 21 is used with a single target pattern. When sampling $f(\mathbf{c})$ at random and updating the HEDA weights using Eq. 15 the first pattern sampled will become an attractor point instantly, regardless of its score. Subsequent samples will first add and then move the attractor points until the weights combine to produce a 'spurious' attractor that happens to be the global optimum (this will happen without the input pattern that leads to that optimum being sampled). At this point, the weights will represent a second order approximation to the first order Hamming function - just as they would in a HNN trained on the single pattern. In this example, continuing to train would eventually move all the second order weights to zero and the solution would only remain in the first order bias weights (if they were included).

8.3   Comparison with Other EDAs

The purpose of this paper is to consider the capacity of a second order EDA for storing local optima as attractor points. It is not to demonstrate that one EDA structure or optimisation algorithm is better than any other. It is instructive, however, to compare the HEDA approach to other EDAs to demonstrate that the measurement of capacity generalises across methods. Starting with the simplest first order EDA (such as PBIL or UMDA), it is clear that such models have a capacity of one—the single most probable pattern, which maximises $\prod_{i=1}^{n} P(c_i)$. The compact GA (cGA) [11] overcomes the limitation of a univariate EDA by building a marginal probability model (MPM) that is a product of joint probabilities of subsets of variables (building blocks). The name and motivation for the cGA come from the idea that members of a GA population might be modelled by an area of high probability (the attractors) in the MPM. This leads to the observation that there is a strong relationship between the capacity of a probabilistic model and the diversity of the population of a GA it is able to replace, which is one reason why it is important to study the capacity of EDAs.

The Bivariate Marginal Distribution Algorithm (BMDA) [14] is an example of a second order model. It does not build a fully connected model like the HEDA, but discovers a sparse set of second order dependencies between variable pairs. The sparse nature of the connections means that subsets of variables may be completely separate from the rest, meaning that a set of graphs (known as a forest) is produced. The more sparse the network, the lower its capacity for storing attractors. The connections in the BMDA are conditional probabilities, making the model more akin to a Bayesian network, whereas the HEDA structure is more like that of a Markov Random Field.

A recent example of a high order EDA can be found in the multi-variate DEUM model, [23]. DEUM performs distribution estimation using Markov random fields (MRF). The HEDA shares its structure with a second order MRF but differs in the way it represents the fitness function. An MRF attempts to model the probability distribution of highly fit patterns as a product across cliques in the graph, which is equivalent to a Gibbs distribution, in which the probability of a pattern across the inputs is calculated as the exponential of the energy state.

$$P(\mathbf{x}) = \frac{1}{Z} e^{-Tu(\mathbf{x})} \tag{30}$$

where u is the energy function, equivalent to Eq. 14 and Z is the normalising constant, which can be ignored in the context of network capacity as dividing the energy by a constant has no effect on the location or number of attractor

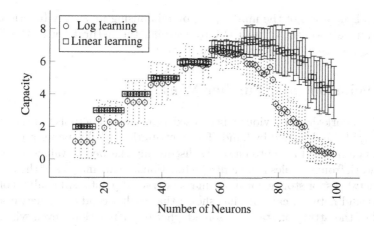

Fig. 9. Number of attractors correctly discovered from the same random set by a HEDA with a standard linear learning rule (square markers and solid error bars) and a HEDA trained with the log-Hebbian rule. In both cases, the target function contained $n(2\ln n)$ attractors and the graph shows how many of them were found.

states. When using the MRF as an EDA, new candidate solutions are sampled by a stochastic probability hill climb such as the Metropolis Hastings algorithm [24] or simulated annealing. Attractor points have an exponentially higher probability of appearing in a sample due to Eq. 30 so the number of attractors (and hence, the capacity of the network) is an important consideration. The similarity between a MRF based EDA and a HEDA is clear. The HEDA models the fitness function rather than the probabilities explicitly, but differs from the probability distribution in that the estimate of the fitness is the natural log of the estimate of the probability of a pattern. The HEDA can be made to learn the probability distribution in the same way as the MRF by changing the learning rule to become a log-Hebbian rule:

$$w_{ij} \leftarrow w_{ij} + \ln(f(\mathbf{c}))u_i u_j \tag{31}$$

Testing the log-Hebbian rule on the Hamming distance function revealed it to have a lower capacity than the standard HEDA rule, which is to be expected because the Hamming function is based on a sum rather than a product across variables. Figure 9 shows the results of testing the capacity of a number of differently sized HEDAs trained on both the Hebbian and the log-Hebbian rule. The models were tested on Hamming distance functions with m random attractors where m was set to be the theoretical capacity for the size of the network. In these experiments, capacity is defined as the number of attractors from the target list successfully found. As the networks pass 70 neurons in size (6 patterns) higher order interactions begin to damage stored memories and the number of patterns correctly stored starts to fall.

It might be argued that the HEDA is not an EDA at all, but a fitness function model as its energy function is a second order model of the fitness function. Its use in optimisation, however, is akin to that of an EDA as it can be used to sample from promising areas of the input space by minimising its energy function. The HEDA can be used as a true EDA by learning the natural log of the fitness function rather than the function itself.

9   Conclusions and Further Work

Hopfield networks have previously been used as optimisation tools but the weights have always been designed by hand. The contributions of this paper are twofold. It presents a method for automatically discovering the weight values for a Hopfield network from samples from a fitness function and an analysis of the capacity of such networks for storing local optima as attractor points. An analysis of linkage order and network capacity has shown that such second order networks can learn all of the attractor states of some higher order functions, even when they cannot reproduce the function output reliably.

The attractors of a HEDA can be viewed as diverse members of a GA population. They are a set of current best points in the search. The capacity of the network limits the number of such points that can be stored at any one time and exceeding the capacity damages all the other existing memories held in the network. For this reason, some form of attractor management may be required to ensure that newly emerging attractors have higher scores than the ones they are destroying.

The next step in this research is to develop an evolutionary algorithm that can store an evolving set of attractor states and sample from them to produce a model of a small quantity of high fitness solutions. The role played by spurious states needs further investigation, as does the effect of adding higher order weights. [25] states that the capacity of order m associative memories over n neurons is $O(n^m / \ln n)$ but the trade-off between network capacity, network size and model overfitting needs careful management. Work on discovering useful heuristics for sampling the space of possible weights to optimise the multiple goals of model accuracy and small network size is ongoing, for example [26] describes some work on the use of higher order versions of the HEDA to learn and sample from distributions.

References

1. Goldberg, D.E.: Genetic Algorithms in Search, Optimization, and Machine Learning. Addison-Wesley Professional, Upper Saddle River (1989)
2. Goldberg, D.E.: Genetic algorithms and walsh functions: Part II, deception and its analysis. Complex Syst. **3**, 153–171 (1989)
3. Holland, J.: Adaptation in Natural and Artificial Systems: An Introductory Analysis with Applications to Biology, Control, and Artificial Intelligence. University of Michigan Press, Ann Arbor (1975)
4. Pelikan, M., Goldberg, D.E., Cantú-paz, E.E.: Linkage problem, distribution estimation, and bayesian networks. Evol. Comput. **8**(3), 311–340 (2000)
5. Davidor, Y.: Epistasis variance: a viewpoint on ga-hardness. In: Rawlins, G.J.E. (ed.) Foundations of Genetic Algorithms, pp. 23–35. Morgan Kaufmann, San Mateo (1990)

6. Goldberg, D.E.: Genetic algorithms and walsh functions: part I, a gentle introduction. Complex Syst. **3**, 129–152 (1989)
7. Bethke, D.: Genetic algorithms as function optimizers (1978)
8. McEliece, R., Posner, E., Rodemich, E., Venkatesh, S.: The capacity of the hopfield associative memory. IEEE Trans. Inf. Theory **33**(4), 461–482 (1987)
9. Santana, R.: Estimation of distribution algorithms: from available implementations to potential developments. In: Proceedings of the 13th Annual Conference Companion on Genetic and Evolutionary Computation, pp. 679–686. ACM (2011)
10. Baluja, S., Caruana, R.: Removing the genetics from the standard genetic algorithm. In: ICML, 38–46. Morgan Kaufmann (1995)
11. Harik, G., Lobo, F., Goldberg, D.: The compact genetic algorithm. IEEE Trans. Evol. Comput. **3**(4), 287–297 (1999)
12. Mhlenbein, H.: The equation for response to selection and its use for prediction. Evol. Comput. **5**(3), 303–346 (1997)
13. Bonet, J.S.D., Isbell Jr., C.L., Viola, P.: Finding optima by estimating probability densities. In: Mozer, M., Jordan, M., Petsche, T. (eds.) Advances in Neural Information Processing Systems, p. 424. The MIT Press, Cambridge (1996)
14. Pelikan, M., Mühlenbein, H.: The bivariate marginal distribution algorithm. In: Roy, R., Furuhashi, T., Chawdhry, P.K. (eds.) Advances in Soft Computing - Engineering Design and Manufacturing, pp. 521–535. Springer, London (1999)
15. Pelikan, M., Goldberg, D., Cant-Paz, E.: Linkage problem, distribution estimation, and bayesian networks. Evol. Comput. **8**(3), 311–340 (2000)
16. Shakya, S., McCall, J., Brownlee, A., Owusu, G.: Deum - distribution estimation using markov networks. In: Shakya, S., Santana, R. (eds.) Markov Networks in Evolutionary Computation. Adaptation, Learning, and Optimization, vol. 14, pp. 55–71. Springer, Berlin (2012)
17. Walsh, J.: A closed set of normal orthogonal functions. Am. J. Math. **45**, 5–24 (1923)
18. Hopfield, J.J.: Neural networks and physical systems with emergent collective computational abilities. Proc. Nat. Acad. Sci. USA **79**(8), 2554–2558 (1982)
19. Hopfield, J.J., Tank, D.W.: Neural computation of decisions in optimization problems. Biol. Cybern. **52**, 141–152 (1985)
20. Caparrós, G.J., Ruiz, M.A.A., Hernández, F.S.: Hopfield neural networks for optimization: study of the different dynamics. Neurocomputing **43**(1–4), 219–237 (2002)
21. Ackley, D., Hinton, G., Sejnowski, T.: A learning algorithm for Boltzmann machines. Cogn. Sci. **9**(1), 147–169 (1985)
22. Storkey, A.J., Valabregue, R.: The basins of attraction of a new hopfield learning rule. Neural Netw. **12**(6), 869–876 (1999)
23. Shakya, S., Brownlee, A., McCall, J., Fournier, F., Owusu, G.: A fully multivariate deum algorithm. In: IEEE Congress on Evolutionary Computation, CEC '09, pp. 479–486 (2009)
24. Chib, S., Greenberg, E.: Understanding the metropolis-hastings algorithm. Am. Stat. **49**(4), 327–335 (1995)
25. Kubota, T.: A higher order associative memory with Mcculloch-Pitts neurons and plastic synapses. In: International Joint Conference on Neural Networks, IJCNN 2007, pp. 1982–1989 (2007)
26. Swingler, K., Smith, L.S.: Mixed order associative networks for function approximation, optimisation and sampling. In: Proceedings of 21st European Symposium on Artificial Neural Networks, ESANN 2013 (2013)

On the Alzheimer's Disease Diagnosis: Automatic Spontaneous Speech Analysis

K. Lopez-de-Ipiña[1(✉)], J. Solé-Casals[2], J.B. Alonso[3], C.M. Travieso[3],
M. Ecay[4], and P. Martinez-Lage[4]

[1] System Engineering and Automation Department,
University of the Basque Country, 20008 Donostia, Spain
karmele.ipina@ehu.es
[2] Data and Signal Processing Research Group, University of Vic,
Barcelona, Spain
jordi.sole@uvic.cat
[3] Universidad de Las Palmas de Gran Canaria, IDeTIC, Las Palmas, Spain
[4] Neurology Department CITA-Alzheimer Foundation, Donostia, Spain

Abstract. Alzheimer's disease (AD) is the most prevalent form of progressive degenerative dementia and it has a high socio-economic impact in Western countries therefore is one of the most active research areas today. Its diagnosis is sometimes made by excluding other dementias and definitive confirmation must be done through a post-mortem study of the brain tissue of the patient. The purpose of this paper is to contribute to the improvement of early diagnosis of AD and its degree of severity from an automatic analysis performed by non-invasive intelligent methods. The methods selected in this case are Automatic Spontaneous Speech Analysis (ASSA) and Emotional Temperature (ET) that have the great advantage of being non invasive low cost and without any side effects. The developed system obtains hopeful results for early diagnosis.

Keywords: Alzheimer's disease diagnosis · Spontaneous speech · Emotion recognition

1 Introduction

Alzheimer's disease (AD) is the most common type of dementia among the elderly people and it is characterized by progressive and irreversible cognitive deterioration with memory loss, impaired judgment and language together with other cognitive deficits and behavioral symptoms. Cognitive deficits and behavioral symptoms are severe enough to limit the ability of an individual to perform professional, social or family activities of daily living. As the disease progresses patients develop severe disability and full dependence. An early and accurate diagnosis of AD helps patients and their families to plan for the future and offers the best opportunity to treat the symptoms of the disease. According to current criteria the diagnosis is expressed with different degrees of certainty as possible or probable AD when dementia is present and other possible causes have been ruled out. The diagnosis of definite AD requires the demonstration of the typical AD pathological changes at autopsy [1–3]. This paper presents a new approach for early AD diagnosis based on two non-invasive and low

© Springer-Verlag Berlin Heidelberg 2014
N.T. Nguyen (Ed.): TCCI XVII 2014, LNCS 8790, pp. 272–281, 2014.
DOI: 10.1007/978-3-662-44994-3_14

cost automatic methods: the Automatic Spontaneous Speech Analysis and the Emotional Temperature.

This paper is organized as follows: some aspects of Alzheimer's disease are analyzed in the next section. Section 3 is devoted to non-invasive methodologies oriented to early diagnosis. The used methods and resources are described in Sect. 4. In Sect. 5, experimental results are presented. Finally, Sect. 6, is devoted to conclusions and future work.

2 Alzheimer's Disease (AD) Diagnosis

The clinical hallmark and earliest manifestation of AD is episodic memory impairment. At the time of clinical presentation other cognitive deficits are present in areas such as language, executive functions, orientation, perceptual abilities and constructional skills. Associated behavioral and psychological symptoms include apathy, irritability, depression, anxiety, delusions, hallucinations, disinhibition, aggression, aberrant motor behavior as well as eating or sleep behavior changes. [3, 4]. All these symptoms lead to impaired performance in family, social or professional activities of daily living as the disease progresses from mild to moderate to severe dementia.

The diagnosis of AD is made on clinical grounds and requires the confirmation of a progressive dementia syndrome as well as the exclusion of other potential causes by clinical history and examination, complete blood workup and a brain imaging test such as CT or MRI. This diagnosis of "exclusion" has changed in the last years as the interpretation of neuroimaging tests, including also functional imaging with SPECT and PET has focused on the "positive" findings of typical AD changes (medial temporal atrophy on CT or MRI, temporoparietal hypometabolism in PET). Nonetheless, the diagnosis of the early stages of not only mild cognitive impairment but also mild dementia remains problematic. On one hand, patients and relatives tend to ignore the first clinical manifestations or may ascribe them to the expectable cognitive changes related to age. It usually takes 2 to 3 years to seek medical advice after the onset of symptoms. On the other hand, physicians may feel uncertain and uncomfortable to establish a diagnosis until the whole picture of dementia is fully present. Otherwise they might need to apply long neuropsychological batteries, expensive neuroimaging techniques or invasive tests such as a lumbar puncture to reach a diagnosis. In this context, it is not surprising that most patients are diagnosed when they have already reached the moderate stage of the disease and have become substantially dependent. At this stage it is very difficult for any treatment strategy to show significant efficacy to stop or even delay the disease process.

In the approach of early diagnosis of AD significant advances in the development of reliable clinical biomarkers have been accomplished in the last years. However, the cost and technology requirements make it impossible to apply such biomarkers to any patient with memory complaints. First patients should be clinically selected so that only those with a high suspicion of an underlying AD pathology would be amenable to have an invasive lumbar puncture or a very expensive PET performed. In this setting non-invasive Intelligent Techniques of diagnosis may become valuable tools for early detection of dementia. Non-technologists people in the habitual environments of patient could use these methodologies, without altering or blocking their abilities. ASSA and ET are some of them. In these techniques, the patient does not perceive the spontaneous speech as a stressful test. Moreover, the cost is really low, they do not require extensive infrastructure or the availability of medical equipment. They provide fostering information easily, quickly and inexpensively.

3   Non-invasive Diagnostic Techniques Based on the Analysis of Spontaneous Speech and Emotion Response

After the loss of memory, one of the major problems of AD is the loss of language skills, reflected in difficulties both to speak and to understand others, which makes more difficult the natural communication process with the environment. This inability to communicate already appears in the early phases of the diseases. We can meet different communication deficits in the area of language, including [5, 6] aphasia (difficulty in speaking and understanding) and anomia (difficulty for recognizing and naming things). The problems that the patients encounter to communicate are dependant on the stage of the disease [3, 4] and are:

1. *First Stage or Early stage (ES):* difficulty in finding the right word in the spontaneous speech. Often remains undetected.
2. *Second Stage or intermediate stage (SS):* impoverishment of language and vocabulary in everyday use.
3. *Third Stage or advance stage (TS):* the answers are sometimes very limited and with very few words.

Moreover, the emotional response in Alzheimer's patients becomes impaired and seems to go through different stages. In the early stages, social and even sexual disinhibition appear and behavioral changes are also observed (for example, being angry and not being able to perform common tasks, express themselves or remember) [7–10]. However, the emotional memory remains, and they cry more easily. The Alzheimer's patient reacts aggressively to things that for healthy people are harmless and perceives a threat or danger where it does not exist. In more advanced stages of Alzheimer's disease, patients may often seem shy and apathetic, symptoms often attributed to memory problems or difficulty to finding the right words and some responses are likely to be magnified due to an alteration in perception. Other research suggests that patients in advanced stages of AD may also display a reduced ability to feel emotions due to loss of memory and this may in turn induce the appearance of apathy and depression.

Emotions arise in intelligent natural or artificial systems when they become necessary to survive in a changing and partially unpredictable world [11–13]. Emotions are cognitive processes related to the architecture of the human mind (such as decision making, memory or attention) closely linked to learning and understanding. Human interaction includes emotional information about partners that is transmitted through language explicitly and implicitly through nonverbal communication. The non-verbal information, which often includes body-language, attitudes, modulations of voice, facial expressions, etc., is essential in human communication and on the intelligibility of speech [11–13].

Human emotions are affected by the environment, the direct interaction with the outside world and also by the emotional memory that emerges from the experience of individual and cultural environment, the so called socialized emotion. Thus, emotions use the same components subjective, cultural, physiological and behavioral that the individual's perception express with regard to the mental state, the body and how it interacts with the environment. Specifically in this work, speech features for the automatic selection of emotional speech will be analyzed: shimmer, jitter, intensity, energy or/and RMS [14].

Moreover the development of non-invasive intelligent diagnosis techniques would be very valuable for the early detection and classification of different types of dementia. Particularly, because they do not require specialized personnel or laboratory equipment, so that anyone in the habitual environment of the patient could perform (after proper training) without altering or blocking the patient's abilities. Automatic Spontaneous Speech Analysis (ASSA) and Emotional Response Analysis (ERA) on speech are two of them [15, 16].

4 Materials and Methods

4.1 Materials

The research presented here is in the nature of a preliminary experiment; its aim is to define thresholds for a number of biomarkers related to spontaneous speech. It forms part of a broader study focused on early AD detection. Feature search in this work aims at pre-clinical evaluation so as to formulate useful tests for AD diagnosis.

In an effort to develop a new methodology applicable to a wide range of individuals of different sex, age, language and cultural and social background, we have built a multicultural and multilingual database with video recordings of 50 healthy subjects and 20 AD patients (with a prior diagnosis of AD) recorded for 12 and 8 hours, respectively (Table 1). The age span of the individuals in the database was 20–98 years and there were 33 males and 37 females. This database is called AZTIAHO. All the work was performed in strict accordance with the ethical guidelines of the organizations involved in the project [14].

The recordings consisted of videos of Spontaneous Speech – people telling pleasant stories or recounting pleasant feelings as well as interacting with each other in friendly conversation. The recording atmosphere was relaxed and non-invasive. The shorter recording times for the AD group are due to the fact that AD patients find speech more of an effort than healthy individuals: they speak more slowly, with longer pauses, and with more time spent on looking for the correct word and uttering speech disfluencies or break messages. In the advanced stage of the disease, they find this effort tiring and often want to stop the recording; in such cases, we always complied with their requests.

The video was processed and the audio extracted in wav format (16 bits and 16 Khz). The first step was removing non-analyzable events: laughter, coughing, short hard noises and segments where speakers overlapped. Next, background noise was removed using denoiser adaptive filtering. After the pre-processing, about 80 % of the material from the control group and 50 % of the material from the AD group remained suitable for further analysis. The complete speech database consists of about 60 minutes of material for the AD group and about 9 hours for the control. The speech was next divided into consecutive segments of 60 seconds in order to obtain appropriate segments for all speakers, resulting finally in a database of about 600 segments of Spontaneous Speech.

Finally, for experimentation from the original database, a subset of 20 AD patients was selected (68–96 years of age, 12 women, 8 men) with a distribution in the three stages of AD as follows: First Stage [ES = 4], Secondary Stage [IS = 10] and Tertiary stage [AS = 6]. The control group (CR) was made up of 20 individuals (10 male and 10 female, aged 20–98 years) representing a wide range of speech responses. This subset of the database is called AZTIAHORE.

4.2   Methods

On the one hand spoken language is one of the most important elements defining an individual's intellect, his/her social life, and personality; it allows us to communicate with each other, share knowledge, and express our cultural and personal identity. Spoken language is the most spontaneous, natural, intuitive and efficient method of communication among people. Therefore, the analysis by automated methods of Spontaneous Speech (SS, which is the freer and more natural expression of communication), possibly combined with other methodologies, could be a useful non-invasive method for early AD diagnosis. The analysis of the spontaneous speech fluency is carried out by measuring: voice segment length, pause length, short time energy and centroid, Voiced/unvoiced segment average, voiced/voiceless percentage and spontaneous speech evolution along the time.

On the other hand the method we wish to develop, called "emotional temperature", is intended to give an estimate of the severity of AD in the patient. This method proposes a new strategy based on a few prosodic and paralinguistic feature sets obtained from a temporal segmentation of the speech signal. The speech signal $\{s(n)\}$ is windowed by a hamming window of 0.5 seconds overlapped 50 %. In each frame $\{x(n)\}$ the DC component is removed and a z-normalization of the frame is made. From each frame 2 prosodic features and 4 paralinguistic features related to pitch and energy, respectively, are estimated. These features were chosen for several reasons: first, they are quickly and easily calculated; second, their robustness in emotion recognition has been proven; and, finally, they are independent of linguistic segmentation, which means that problems in real-time applications in real environments can be avoided [17–21]. Then Emotional Temperature is calculated as in [22].

At last but not least, the main goal of the present work is feature search in spontaneous speech and in emotional response aiming at pre-clinical evaluation in order to define tests for AD diagnosis. These features will define the control group (CR) and the three AD levels (ES, IS and AS). A secondary goal is the optimization of computational cost with the aim of making these techniques useful for real-time applications in real environments. Thus automatic classification will be modeled with this in mind. We have used a Multi Layer Perceptron (MLP) with neuron number in hidden layer (NNHL) of max(Attribute/Number + Classes/Number) and training step (TS) NNHL*10.

The WEKA software suite [23] has been used in carrying out the experiments. The results were evaluated using Accuracy (Acc). For the training and validation steps, we used k-fold cross-validation with k = 10. Cross-validation is a robust validation method for variable selection [24]. Repeated cross-validation (as calculated by the WEKA environment) allows robust statistical tests. We also use the measurement provided automatically by WEKA "Coverage of cases" (0.95 level).

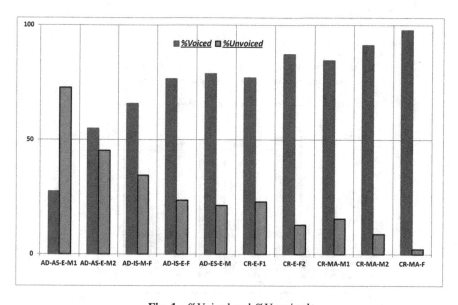

Fig. 1. %Voiced and %Unvoiced

5 Experimental Results

In the first stage, we carried out preliminary experimentation on the AZTITXIKI subset, analyzing the direct characteristics of spontaneous speech(SS) involved in AD symptoms. The experiment was designed to detect changes and features in SS characterizing the control group, on the one hand, and each of the different groups of AD levels, on the other. The first set of tests consisted of ASSA experiments. Patients suffering from AD manifested a lower voiced percentage and a higher voiceless percentage (see Fig. 1) in their spontaneous speech than healthy subjects. The first set of tests consisted of ASSA experiments. Patients suffering from AD manifested a lower voiced percentage and a higher voiceless percentage in their spontaneous speech than healthy subjects (see Fig. 1). This indicates a significant loss of fluency in the speech of AD-suffering subjects. In the data-base there is control people of middle age (ME) (males and females) and elderly people (E). 5 people with different levels of AD (E) diagnosis. They will be used to analyze direct characteristics of SS. The analysis shows that people with AD tend to decrease the number and fluency of voiced segments by increasing the voiceless segment length and decreasing the length of voiced segments

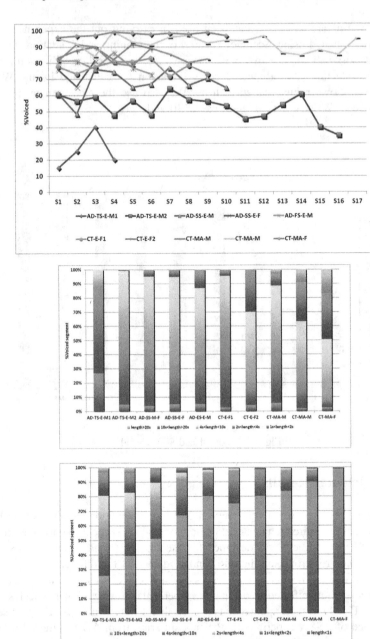

Fig. 2. (a) Spontaneous Speech Evolution with regard to the Speech Percentage along the time, for the consecutive segments (S2:S6). (b) Voiced segment analysis with regard to segment length (c) Voiceless segment analysis with regard to segment length

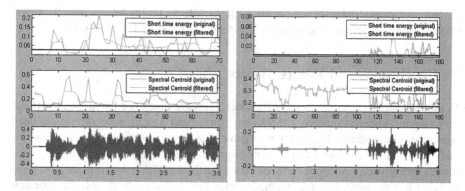

Fig. 3. Plots of speech signal, short time energy and spectral centroid for a control person (CR) and a person with AD

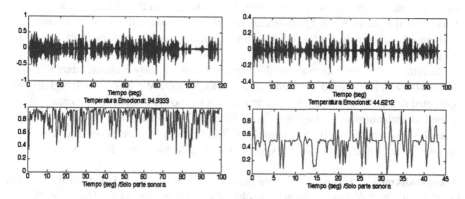

Fig. 4. Emotional Temperature for healthy people (left) and people with AD (right)

(see Fig. 2). Figure 2 (a) shows the evolution of spontaneous speech with regard to the speech percentage along the time axis for consecutive segments (S1:SN): it can be observed that for people with AD the voiced percentage along the time axis decreases. Moreover people with AD also displayed a decreasing slope in the evolution of their spontaneous speech, and a decreasing slope is evident in the analysis of their voiced and voiceless segments with regard to length segments. Figure 2 (b and c) displays the tendency to use an increased number of short voiced segments and long voiceless segments. The speech of AD sufferers is fluent only for short periods of time, and segments longer than 20 seconds seldom appear in their spontaneous speech. The results also show a higher Short Time Energy for members of the control group than for AD sufferers and a higher Spectral Centroid for the AD group (see Fig. 3).

Finally the "Emotional Temperature" is calculated over AZTIAHORE and is normalized in order to have ET = 50 as the threshold; that threshold indicates the limit between pathological and non-pathological frames. This normalization will make it substantially easier for medical specialists to interpret the data. Figure 4 shows the results of Emotional Temperature. For healthy elderly people (59.66, 54.62), healthy middle age people (94.93), and people with AD (46.1, 41.29, 36.31). The Accuracy (%) for global result with the selected MLP and AZTIAHORE is of 93.02.

6 Conclusions and Future Works

In this paper new approaches for Alzheimer's disease diagnosis based on Automatic Spontaneous Speech Analysis (ASSA) and Emotional Temperature (ET) have been presented. The purpose of the work is to contribute to improve clinical grounds and for early diagnosis of dementia and severity from automatic analysis, performed by non-invasive automated intelligent methods. These methodologies have the great advantage of being non-invasive, low cost methodologies and have no side effects. The research on multicultural and multilingual population shows some encouraging results both in terms of the ASSA and the Emotional Temperature, showing tendencies to explore with a broader population. The performance of the approach is very satisfactory, and the results are promising for new diagnosis tests. The goal of the new tests is to provide a tool for the analysis of spontaneous speech and emotional response oriented to Alzheimer's diagnosis, independent with regard to social, cultural and language environment.

In future work, we will evaluate this approach with an early diagnosis database and new tests oriented toward semantic and memory tasks. We will also integrate the described methodologies with automatic analysis methods of drawing and handwriting as well as with automatic analysis of facial features. We will also extend the population of analysis as well as the type of pathology. The first step will be developed with new samples of controlled spontaneous speech from CITA Alzheimer Foundation.

Acknowledgements. This work has been partially supported by SAIOTEK from the Basque Government. Dr. Solé-Casals also acknowledges the partial support of the University of Vic under the research grant R0904 and by the Spanish Ministerio de Ciencia e Innovación TEC2012-38630-C04-03.

References

1. Mc Kahn, G., Drachman, D., Folstein, M., Katzman, R., Price, D., Stadlan, E.M.: Clinical diagnosis of Alzheimer's disease: report of the NINCDS-ADRDA Workgroup on Alzheimer's disease, **24**, pp. 939–944 (1984)
2. McKhann, G.M., Knopman, D.S., Chertkow, H., Hyman, B.T., Jack Jr., C.R., Kawas, C.H., Klunk, W.E., Koroshetz, W.J., Manly, J.J., Mayeux, R., Mohs, R.C., Morris, J.C., Rossor, M.N., Scheltens, P., Carrillo, M.C., Thies, B., Weintraub, S., Phelps, C.H.: The diagnosis of dementia due to Alzheimer's disease: Recommendations from the National Institute on Aging-Alzheimer's Association workgroups on diagnostic guidelines for Alzheimer's disease (PDF). Alzheimers Dement. **7**(3), 263–269 (2011)
3. Van de Pole, L.A., et al.: The effects of age and Alzheimer's disease on hippocampal volumes, a MRI study. Alzheimer's Dement. **1**(1, Supplement 1), 51 (2005)
4. Morris, J.C.: The Clinical Dementia Rating (CDR): current version and scoring rules. Neurology **43**, 2412b–2414b (1993)

5. American Psychiatric Association: Diagnostic and Statistical Manual of Mental Disorders, 4th edn., Text Revision. American Psychiatric Association, Washington DC (2000)
6. Cristian, B.: Evaluación y tratamiento de los trastornos del lenguaje, Psicóloga. Gerontóloga. Unidad de Memoria y Alzheimer. Matia Fundazioa, Donostia (2010)
7. Martinez, F., Garcia, J., Perez, E., Carro, J., Anara, J.M.: Patrones de Prosodia expresiva en pacientes con enfermedad de Alzheimer. Psicothema 24(1), 16–21 (2012)
8. Shimokawa, A., Yatomi, N., Anamizu, S., Torii, S., Isono, H., Sugai, Y., Kohno, M.: Influence of deteriorating ability of emotional comprehension on interpersonal behaviour in Alzheimer-type dementia. Brain Cogn. 47, 423–433 (2001)
9. Goodkind, M.S., Gyurak, A., McCarthy, M., Miller, B.L., Levenson, R.W.: Emotion regulation deficits in frontotemporal lobar degeneration and Alzheimer's disease. Psychol Aging., 25(1):30–37, Mar 2010. PMID, 20230125, PMCID: PMC2841311
10. Cadieux, N., Greeve, K.: Emotion processing in Alzheimer's disease. J. Int. Neuropsychol. Soc. 3, 411–419 (1997). The International Neuropsychological Society. DOI: (About DOI) Published online: 2000
11. Knapp, M.L.: Essentials of Nonverbal Communication. Holt, Rinehart & Winston, New York (1980)
12. Cowie, E., et al.: Emotion recognition in human-computer interaction. IEEE Signal Process. Mag. 18(1), 32–80 (2001)
13. Plutchnik, R.: Emotion: A Psychoevolutionary Synthesis'. Harper and Row, New York (1980)
14. Lopez-de-Ipiña, K., Alonso, J.B., Travieso, C.M., Solé-Casals, J., Egiraun, H., Faundez-Zanuy, M., Ezeiza, A., Barroso, N., Ecay, M., Martinez-Lage, P., Martinez-de-Lizardui, U.: On the selection of non-invasive methods based on speech analysis oriented to Automatic Alzheimer Disease Diagnosis. Sensors 13(5), 6730–6745 (2013)
15. Faúndez Zanuy, M., Sesa-Nogueras, E., Monte-Moreno, E., Garre-Olmo, J., Lopez-de-Ipiña, K., Viñals, F., Luz Puente, M.: Aplicaciones biométricas más allá de la seguridad. In: VI Jornadas de reconocimiento biométrico de personas, Las Palmas de Gran Canaria, pp. 25–43, 26–27 January 2012. ISBN 978-84-695-0695-0
16. López de Ipiña, K., Alonso, J.B., Solé-Casals, J., Barroso, N., Faundez, M., Ecay, M., Travieso, C., Ezeiza, A., Estanga, A.: Alzheimer disease diagnosis based on automatic spontaneous speech analysis. In: Proceedings of NCTA 2012, Barcelona (2012)
17. Pao, T.L., Chien, C.S., Yen, J.H., Chen, Y.T., Cheng, Y.M.: Continuous tracking of user emotion in mandarin emotional speech. In: Proceedings, 3th International Conference on International Information Hiding and Multimedia Signal Processing (IIH-MSP'07), pp. 1:47–1:52 (2007)
18. Petrushin, V.A.: Emotion in speech: recognition and application to call centers. In: Proceedings, Conference on Artificial Neural Networks in Engineering (ANNIE), pp. 7–10 (1999)
19. Lee, C.M., Narayanan, S.: Emotion recognition using a data-driven fuzzy interference system. In: Proceedings, 8th ECSCT, pp. 157–160 (2003)
20. Kwon, O.W., Chan, K., Hao, J., Lee, T.W.: Emotion recognition by speech signals. In: 8th European Conference on Speech Communication and Technology, 125–128 (2003)
21. De Cheveigné, A., Kawahara, H.: YIN, a fundamental frequency estimator for speech and music. J. Acoust. Soc. Am. 111(4), 1917–1930 (2002)
22. Alonso, J., De León, J., Alonso, I., Ferrer, M.A.: Automatic detection of pathologies in the voice by HOS base parameters. Journal on Applied Signal Processing 4, 275–284 (2001)
23. WEKA. http://www.cs.waikato.ac.nz/ml/weka/
24. Picard, R., Cook, D.: Cross-validation of regression models. J. Am. Stat. Assoc. 79(387), 575–583 (1984)

Synthesis of Multicomponent Reuse Water Networks by PSO Approach

Mauro A.S.S. Ravagnani[1(✉)], Daniela E.G. Trigueros[2],
Aparecido N. Módenes[2], and Fernando Espinoza-Quiñones[2]

[1] State University of Maringá, Av.Colombo 5790, Maringá, PR, Brazil
ravag@deq.uem.br, mauro.ravagnani@hotmail.com
[2] State University of Paraná West, Rua Da Faculdade 645, Toledo, PR, Brazil

Abstract. In the present paper the problem of reuse water networks (RWN) have been modeled and optimized by the application of a modified Particle Swarm Optimization (PSO) algorithm. A proposed modified PSO method lead with both discrete and continuous variables in Mixed Integer Non-Linear Programming (MINLP) formulation that represent the water allocation problems. Pinch Analysis concepts are used jointly with the improved PSO method. Two literature problems considering mono and multicomponent problems were solved with the developed systematic and results has shown excellent performance in the optimality of reuse water network synthesis based on the criterion of minimization of annual total cost.

Keywords: Reuse water networks · PSO · MINLP · Optimization

1 Introduction

In the last decades the studies in the minimization of primary water consumption in industrial processes and in the wastewater reduction from such processes have contributed to the minimization of environmental impacts. The traditional approach to the minimization of the environmental impacts consists in the Water/Wastewater Allocation planning (WAP) whose main objective is the minimization of the fresh water consumption and, consequently, the effluents minimization in industrial processes. One of the pioneers papers focusing this problem was presented by Takama *et al.* 1980 and in the last decades several process integration methodologies related to this theme has been proposed, as Pinch Analysis, Mathematical Programming or a combination of both of them (Wang and Smith 1994; Dhole and Smith 1997; Huang *et al.* 1999; Alva-Argáez *et al.* 1999; Mann and Liu 1999; Bagajewicz *et al.* 2000; Gómez *et al.* 2001; Hallale 2003; El-Halwagi *et al.* 2003; Manan *et al.* 2004; Tan *et al.* 2007; Liu *et al.* 2009; Iancu *et al.* 2010; Trigueros *et al.* 2012).

Instead of applying graphic and algebraic technologies to solve the problems of process integration, mathematical programming has been used as a very convenient alternative method when the subject can be formulated as an optimization problem. The great advantage of mathematical programming against graphical or algebraic methodologies like Pinch Analysis is in the flexibility of incorporating network design constraints and in the facility of treating multicomponent systems with a large number

© Springer-Verlag Berlin Heidelberg 2014
N.T. Nguyen (Ed.): TCCI XVII 2014, LNCS 8790, pp. 282–294, 2014.
DOI: 10.1007/978-3-662-44994-3_15

of process streams. Its application allows incorporating other strategies like conceptual ideas, optimality necessary conditions, good initial estimative and heuristics in the models formulation to achieve a better solution. Generally such formulations result in NLP (Non Linear Programming) and complex MINLP (Mixed Integer Non Linear Programing) models, considering the structural optimization including discrete/binary variables and parametric optimization including continuous variables in the industrial plant. The problem of Water/Wastewater Allocation Planning can also consider both discrete and continuous variables. A large group of WAP problems have MINLP and NLP formulations and a great variety of algorithms has been proposed, developed and improved.

In this context, a great variety of metaheuristic algorithms have been developed, easily implemented and widely applied in different areas of science, showing high quality and performance (Lin and Miller 2004; Tan *et al.* 2008; Ravagnani *et al.* 2009; Tudor and Lavric 2010; Poplewski *et al.* 2011; Trigueros *et al.* 2012). Such algorithms have appeared to lead with optimization problems in which classical heuristics have not reliably solved, because they have frequently provided not suited solutions, demanding thus new approaches on the global solution searching. In this regard, approaches on global solutions searching have been properly implemented in metaheuristic algorithms in order to not become trapped in local solutions and achieve efficiently and reliable solution by specifying suited parameters. In spite of not performing formal proves as commonly performed by deterministic methods for assessment of solutions in optimization problems, metaheuristic algorithms have shown strong evidences of achieving good solutions by empirical tests at relatively lesser times than deterministic methods.

In this work, the PSO algorithm was properly modified in order to satisfy the requirements of leading with discrete type variables and other strategies were also included to solve MINLP-based models. In addition, as criteria for obtaining the synthesis of the reuse water network, the minimization of the total cost was applied. At first, the WAP problem definitions and its mathematical formulation are presented. Then, the proposed modified PSO is shown, and finally applied in two literature case studies, mono and multicomponent problems, considering the minimization of annual total cost as optimization criteria.

2 Wap Problem Definitions and Model Formulation

With regard to the total possible configurations of mass transfer between the water streams and the process streams and all the possibilities for reuse water, a super-structure was built, as reported by, Trigueros *et al.* (2012) in order to attain optimization of the mass exchange network design in a simultaneous analysis procedure. A reduction in the high contaminant loads of the process streams is essentially performed by transferring mass to a cleaner water stream, with the possibility of reusing it in the other $(N - 1)$ process units.

In this work, maximum inlet and outlet pollutant concentration data were used in the synthesis of the reuse water network, calculating the maximum water flowrate (Eq. 1) and demanding a global mass balance (Eq. 2). The superstructure was fractioned into small components corresponding to each process unit, mixing and splitting nodes in which their individual mass balances are defined by Eqs. (3)–(5), respectively. In addition, pollutant mass balances in the process streams are also performed in Eqs. (6) and (7), and the maximum allowed pollutant concentration constraints for the inlet and outlet of each process unit, is given by two inequalities (Eqs. 8 and 9). A necessary condition to warrant no violation of the minimum ΔC_i, (see Eq. 10) was demanded in each process unit. In addition, the pinch point freshwater flowrate value was introduced in the modeling as a physical constraint variable (Eq. 11), among other non-negativity constraints (Eqs. 12–17).

$$f_i = \frac{\dot{m}_i}{(C_j^{out^{max}} - C_j^{in^{max}})} \tag{1}$$

$$\sum_{i=1}^{N} f_i^{freshwater} + \sum_{i=1}^{N}\sum_{j=1}^{J} \dot{m}_{i,j} - \sum_{i=1}^{N} f_i^{wastewater} = 0 \tag{2}$$

$$f_i^{out} - f_i^{in} - \sum_{j=1}^{J} \dot{m}_{i,j} = 0 \quad \forall i \in N \tag{3}$$

$$f_i^{freshwater} + \sum_{\substack{k=1 \\ k \neq i}}^{K} f_{i,k} - f_i^{in} = 0 \quad \forall i \in N \tag{4}$$

$$f_i^{wastewater} + \sum_{\substack{k=1 \\ i \neq k}}^{K} f_{k,i} - f_i^{out} = 0 \quad \forall i \in N \tag{5}$$

$$f_i^{freshwater} C_j^{freshwater} + \sum_{\substack{k=1 \\ i \neq k}}^{K} f_{i,k} C_{k,j}^{out} - f_i^{in} C_{i,j}^{in} = 0 \quad \forall i \in N; \forall j \in J \tag{6}$$

$$f_i^{in} C_{i,j}^{in} + \dot{m}_{i,j} - f_i^{out} C_{i,j}^{out} = 0 \quad \forall i \in N; \forall j \in J \tag{7}$$

$$C_{i,j}^{in} \leq C_{i,j}^{in^{max}} \quad \forall i \in N; \forall j \in J \tag{8}$$

$$C_{i,j}^{out} \leq C_{i,j}^{out^{max}} \quad \forall i \in N; \forall j \in J \tag{9}$$

$$f_i^{in} - f_i^{max} \leq 0 \quad \forall i \in N \tag{10}$$

$$\sum_{i=1}^{N} f_i^{freshwater} - f^{Pinch} \leq 0 \tag{11}$$

$$f_i^{freshwater}, \quad f_i^{wastewater}, \quad f_i^{in}, \quad f_i^{out}, \quad f_{i,k}, \quad f_{k,i} \geq 0 \quad \forall i \in N \tag{12–17}$$

Finally, the total cost of the industrial plant according to Eq. (18) was considered as an optimization criterion of the reuse water network synthesis. The network total cost considers the cost of the final treatment, the operational cost, the fresh water cost and piping costs. Parameters A, B, C, D, E, F and α were extracted from the literature (Wang and Smith 1994; Lee and Grossmann 2003; Gunaratnam *et al.* 2005).

$$
z = AB \sum_{k=1}^{N} \left(\sum_{\substack{i=1 \\ i \neq k}}^{N} f_{i,k} + f_i^{freshwater} \right)^{\alpha} + CD \sum_{k=1}^{N} \left(\sum_{\substack{i=1 \\ i \neq k}}^{N} f_{i,k} + f_i^{freshwater} \right)
$$

$$
+ CE \sum_{i=1}^{N} f_i^{freshwater} + \ldots \ldots + F \left(\sum_{k=1}^{N} \sum_{\substack{i=1 \\ i \neq k}}^{N} y_{i,k} + \sum_{i=1}^{N} y_i^{freshwater} + \sum_{i=1}^{N} y_i^{wastewater} \right)
$$

(18)

The solutions of the non-linear models, having non-convex characteristics in the suitable search space region, are commonly driven and trapped in local optima regions. However, in the case of linear type models, all suitable search spaces are convex and the global optimum solutions are thus always attained. Thus, some analysis strategies such as the modified PSO method and the concepts of pinch analysis are suitable for application in order to lead with the nonlinearity of the WAP problem models and consequently attain their optimized solutions.

2.1 PSO Proposed Algorithm

In the framework of programming methodologies for processes optimization, PSO is essentially based on two approaches related to mimic evolutionary and genetic patterns, commonly seen, for instance, in bird flocking and other collective animal behavior (Kennedy and Eberhart 2001; Clerc and Kennedy 2002). As reported by others researchers (Yiqing *et al.* 2007; Espinoza-Quiñones *et al.* 2009; Trigueros *et al.* 2010a, b; 2012; Módenes *et al.* 2012), the basic principle of PSO method is to seek a set of potential solutions located in a wide search hyperspace that is randomly scanning at different kinematic conditions of bird flocking, according to some considerations based on local (c1) and global (c2) accelerations and swarm inertia (ω).

By performing an approach of collective cooperation and group memory into a chaotic movement of particles, complex equations might be solved and achieved near-optimum solutions. In this regard, an initial particle swarm is defined as well as an iteration number in order to scan a wide search hyperspace where potential solutions are identified and stored. Meanwhile, it is expected to improve the probability of attaining the near-global solution by choosing suited algorithm parameters as well as increasing the particle densities in the domain; i.e., choosing a great number of iterations or swarm size. In PSO method, each particle moving into the swarm is described by two kinetic parameters (**X** and **V**), which are defined by Eqs. 19 and 20, being iteratively updated (Eq. 21). Thereby, regarding suitable PSO parameters related to local and global collective acceleration (c1 and c2) and swarm inertia range (ω), further two random weightings (λ_1 and λ_2), the near-optimal solution with a large probability and high convergence rate could be attained, reducing efficiently the running time. Each particle flies through the problem space following the current optimum particles, adjusting constantly its flying by searching the best position, according to its own flying experience, namely better visited position ($\mathbf{X}_{ibest}$), and flying experience of other particles, namely global solution ($\mathbf{X}_{gbest}$).

$$\mathbf{X}_i^{(k)} = \mathbf{X}_{min} + \lambda(\mathbf{X}_{max} - \mathbf{X}_{min}) \tag{19}$$

$$\mathbf{V}_i^{(k+1)} = \omega^{(k)}\mathbf{V}_i^{(k)} + c_1\lambda_1(\mathbf{X}_{ibest}^{(k)} - \mathbf{X}_i^{(k)}) + c_2\lambda_2(\mathbf{X}_{gbest}^{(k)} - \mathbf{X}_i^{(k)}) \tag{20}$$

$$\mathbf{X}_i^{(k+1)} = \mathbf{X}_i^{(k)} + \mathbf{V}_i^{(k+1)}. \tag{21}$$

A PSO algorithm that was applied by Trigueros *et al.* (2010) to solve problems with continuous variables was modified to consider also discrete variables. A numeric generator function in the 0–1 range and a cut-off value condition were introduced in the PSO algorithm (Eqs. 22 and 23). In addition, the modified PSO algorithm applied for synthesis of reuse water networks included a complementary binary attribution test (Eqs. 24 and 25).

$$sig(\mathbf{x}_i^k) = \frac{1}{1 + e^{(-\mathbf{x}_i^k)}} \tag{22}$$

$$\text{If} \quad \mathbf{x}_i^k > sig(\mathbf{x}_i^k) \quad \text{then} \quad \mathbf{x}_i^k = 1 \quad \text{else} \quad \mathbf{x}_i^k = 0 \tag{23}$$

$$\text{If} \quad y_{i,k} = 0 \quad \text{then} \quad f_{i,k} = 0 \quad \text{else} \quad f_{i,k} = rand() \tag{24}$$

$$\text{If} \quad f_{i,k} = 0 \quad \text{then} \quad y_{i,k} = 0 \quad \text{else} \quad y_{i,k} = 1 \tag{25}$$

To avoid non-viable solutions, the original objective function (see Eq. 18) was penalized by adding the inequality and equality constraints that were previously violated as well as assigning weights to each type of violation, according to Eqs. (26–28). In order to avoid the constrain search space and the increasing computational time, two strategies were considered: dependent and independent variables were defined in the mathematical model and adopting the fundamental concepts of pinch analysis in order to achieve feasible or very near feasible solutions.

$$\mathbf{H}(\mathbf{x}, \mathbf{y}) = \begin{cases} \mathbf{h}(\mathbf{x}, \mathbf{y}) & \text{se} \quad |\mathbf{h}(\mathbf{x}, \mathbf{y})| - \varepsilon > 0 \\ 0 & \text{se} \quad |\mathbf{h}(\mathbf{x}, \mathbf{y})| - \varepsilon \le 0 \end{cases} \tag{26}$$

$$\mathbf{G}(\mathbf{x}, \mathbf{y}) = \begin{cases} \mathbf{g}(\mathbf{x}, \mathbf{y}) & \text{se} \quad \mathbf{g}(\mathbf{x}, \mathbf{y}) > 0 \\ 0 & \text{se} \quad \mathbf{g}(\mathbf{x}, \mathbf{y}) \le 0 \end{cases} \tag{27}$$

$$z_p = z + \left[\sum_{i=1}^{m} b_i G_i + \sum_{j=1}^{n} c_j H_j \right] \tag{28}$$

The performance of each particle is related to the expected global minimum value for a specific test-function, saving better solutions (group memory) and allowing assigning the near-global solution among all better ones. Such algorithm was coded in Maple® software, running in Windows 7 OS by using an Intel® CoreTM i7-930 processor (2.8 GHz clock speed, 8 GB cache).

3 Case Studies

3.1 Monocomponent Problem

An early proposition of Olsen and Polley (1997), summarized in Table 1, was used as a modified PSO method testing system in the optimization procedure. Firstly, the pinch point flow rate was estimated (157.14 ton h^{-1}) and required as a physical criterion in the optimization procedure. A set of 51 equations (38 equality constraints and 12 inequality constraints and one objective function), 73 continuous and 48 binary decision variables are required to represent the WAP problem. By redefining some variables as dependent in the PSO algorithm, decision variables were reduced (23 continuous and 42 binary variables). All financial parameter values were obtained from literature (A = US$ 34,200.00 ton$^{-0.7}$, α = 0.7, B = 0.10 year^{-1}, C = 8600 h year^{-1}, D = US$ 1.0067 ton^{-1}, E = US$ 0.3 ton^{-1}, and F = US$ 10 year^{-1}).

Table 1. Problem data - Olesen and Polley (1997)

Process	C_{max}^{in} (ppm)	C_{max}^{out} (ppm)	mass (g h^{-1})
1	25	80	2000
2	25	100	5000
3	25	200	4000
4	50	100	5000
5	50	800	30000
6	400	800	4000

The RWN were synthesized during 30 runs of the MINLP model optimization, assuming 3000 particles and 25 iterations. Both local (c_1) and global (c_2) collective accelerations were chosen to be equal to 1.5 and swarm inertia (ω) from 0,9 to 0,4. The runs required on average 1800 seconds in achieving the final results. The reuse water networks (RWN) synthesized are shown in Fig. 1. As some situations that are expected for the minimization of the total cost, two strategies were applied, being a fixed pinch point flow rate as first strategy (results in Fig. 1a), whereas no constraint on the consumption of freshwater was considered as second strategy (results in Fig. 1b). PSO algorithm convergence during the models optimization was pointed in the 20th iteration for the first MINLP, and in the 3rd iteration for the second MINLP.

When applying the first strategy, a minimum water flowrate of 157.16 ton h^{-1} and an annual total cost of US$ 2,217,101.70 were attained. The network contains 5 freshwater, 4 reuse water and 5 wastewater streams (see Fig. 1a). Table 2 shows the results for the annual cost in both reuse networks synthesized, and for the initial scenario without the integration process. Reductions are 32 and 34 %, respectively. In addition, by considering a variation on the fresh water flowrate near to the Pinch point, other reuse network synthesis were obtained with different annual total cost as shown in Fig. 2, where its behavior is depending on the total fresh water (see Fig. 2) and reuse water flowrate (see Fig. 3).

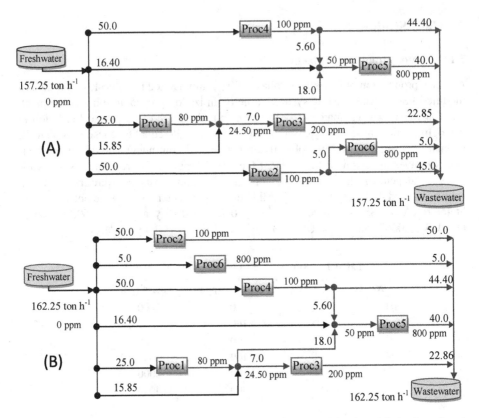

Fig. 1. Reuse water network (RWN) synthesis by the PSO method for the minimization of total cost, considering (A) as the first and (B) as the second strategies

Table 2. Results for the total annual cost in (A) and (B) strategies, and scenario without integration

Network	Freshwater flow-rate (t h^{-1})	Total water flow-rate (t h^{-1})	Total annual cost (US$ year^{-1})	% reduction
Without integration	–	275.88	3,275,237	–
Reuse A (first strategy)	157.15	193.48	2,217,101	32.30
Reuse B (second strategy)	162.25	192.86	2,175,815	33.60

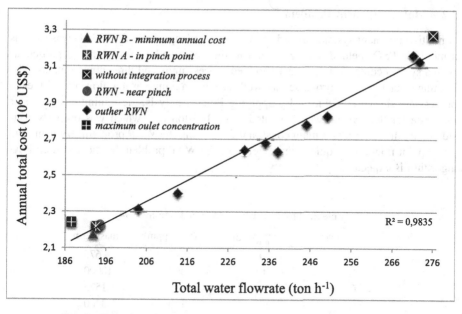

Fig. 2. Behavior of the total cost as a function of total water flow rate

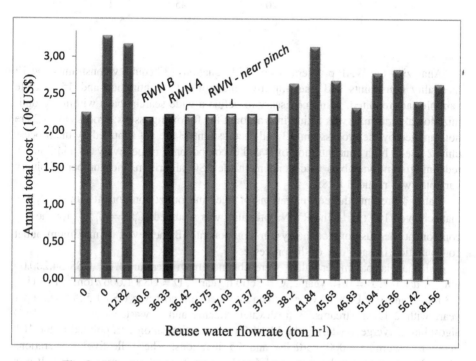

Fig. 3. Behavior of the total cost as a function of reuse water flow rates

3.2   Multicomponent Problem

A multi-component system, an early proposal by, Wang and Smith (1994) was used as a modified PSO method testing system in the optimization procedure. In particular, such a system contains three water supplied process units and three contaminants. The limiting data for these processes as well as the maximum water flow rate for each process are shown in Table 3. By applying Pinch Analysis, the minimum freshwater flow rate for this system was estimated to be 105 ton h^{-1}, which was properly considered by the criteria as a main constraint for solving the WAP problem. By using the pinch point flow rate, a quick convergence of the WAP problem by the modified PSO algorithm is expected.

Table 3. Problem data - Wang and Smith (1994)

Process	Component	C_{max}^{in} (ppm)	C_{max}^{out} (ppm)	mass (g h^{-1})
1	A	0	15	675
	B	0	400	18000
	C	0	35	1575
2	A	20	120	3400
	B	300	12500	414800
	C	45	180	4590
3	A	120	220	5600
	B	20	45	1400
	C	200	9500	520800

Analyzing the WAP problem, a set of 51 equations (38 equality constraints and 12 inequality constraints and one objective function), 10 continuous and 15 discrete variables are required, being necessary to define a wide search space within the optimization algorithm. It was taking into account the following issues: process units 2 are not supplied by the process units 3 and process units 3 are not supplied by the process units 2 due to high concentration of B and C components, respectively. In addition, by redefining some variables as dependent in the PSO algorithm, the number of binary variables was reduced to 8.

Table 4 presents the concentrations of inlet and outlet components for the RWN that achieved 105 t h^{-1}. The RWN optimality was assumed ($C_{i,j}^{out} = C_{i,j}^{out\,max}$ for the key component) because one of the system components (B) achieved its maximum outlet concentration in each one of the processes.

All financial parameter values were obtained from literature (A = US\$ 34,200.00 ton$^{-0.7}$, α = 0.7, B = 0.10 year^{-1}, C = 8600 h year^{-1}, D = US\$ 1.0067 ton^{-1}, E = US\$ 0.3 ton^{-1}, and F = US\$ 10 year^{-1}). The total network cost was US\$ 1,525,967.20 per year, with 2 reuse streams, 3 freshwater streams and 3 wastewater streams. PSO algorithm convergence during the MINLP model optimization was pointed in the 16th iteration, assuming 2000 particles and 25 iterations. The collective accelerations c1 = c2 were chosen to be equal to 1.5 and swarm inertia (ω) from 0,9 to 0,4. It was

Table 4. Results for the concentrations of inlet and outlet components

Process	C_i^{in} (ppm)		C_i^{out} (ppm)	
1	A	0	A	15
	B	0	B	400
	C	0	C	35
2	A	11.25	A	111.139
	B	300	B	12499.84
	C	26.25	C	160.963
3	A	0.737	A	102.861
	B	19.656	B	45
	C	1.72	C	9499.907

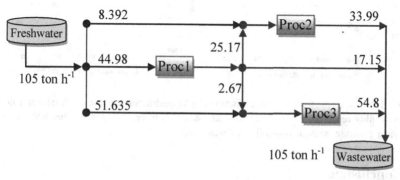

Fig. 4. Reuse water network (RWN) synthesis by the PSO method for the minimization of total cost

necessary 10 runs to achieve the final results, and it was required in average 2500 s CPU. The RWN synthetized is present in Fig. 4.

The annual total cost was analyzed considering 3 variables: (i) total water flowrate (see Fig. 5a, b); (ii) freshwater flowrate (see Fig. 5c) and (ii) water reuse flowrate (see Fig. 5d). This evaluation was done considering the total annual cost variation respect to the total flowrate into two steps. First, an interval of water reuse possibilities was observed, according to Fig. 5a, in which the total water flowrate varies from 132.7 to 132.85 t h^{-1}. In this interval the total cost decreased linearly until the minimum Pinch flow rate. Below the 132.7 t h^{-1} there are no viable reuse networks. In a second analysis it was observed that above 132.85 t h^{-1} the total annual cost increased, as can be observed in Fig. 5b. It means that in this interval there are no possibilities of reuse and the process operation is between the minimum necessary limits for the key component mass transfer until the maximum available value to the industrial plant operation.

Finally this analysis show that between the streams reuse possibilities interval, as less is the total water flowrate grater is the necessity of freshwater and less is the water reuse. It means that the total cost decreases as the freshwater flowrate decreases until the minimum Pinch flowrate is achieved as Fig. 5c. The contrary occurs when the reuse water flowrate decreased, increasing also the total cost, according to Fig. 5d.

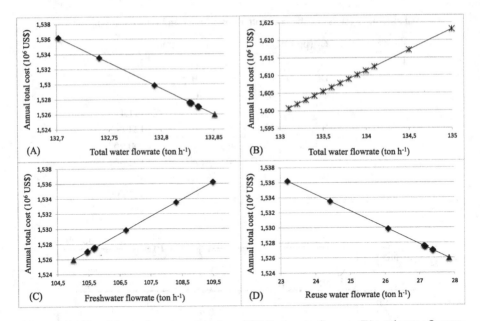

Fig. 5. Behavior of the total cost as a function of (A) freshwater flowrate (B) total water flowrate with possibility reuse (C) reuse water flowrate (▲ RWN in pinch point; ♦ other RWN) and (D) total water flowrate without possibility of water reuse

4 Conclusions

A modified PSO algorithm was proposed and tested to optimize a WAP problem. It is possible to achieve different RWN synthesis by demanding the minimum annual total cost as criterion and requiring on fixing or assigning values near the Pinch point for the freshwater flowrate, and without any constraint in the freshwater flowrate. Two literature problems considering mono and multicomponent problems were solved with the developed systematic and results has shown excellent performance in the optimality of reuse water network synthesis based on the criterion of minimization of annual total cost. It can be concluded that the modified PSO algorithm has shown high flexibility and capability to provide optimal results for the reuse water network synthesis, being independent of initial estimative for the decision variables.

References

Alva-Argáez, A., Vallianatos, A., Kokossis, A.: A multi-contaminant transhipment model for mass exchange networks and wastewater minimisation problems. Comput. Chem. Eng. **23**, 1439–1453 (1999)

Bagajewicz, M., Rivas, M., Savelski, M.: A robust method to obtain optimal and sub-optimal design and retrofit solutions of water utilization systems with multiple contaminants in process plants. Comput. Chem. Eng. **24**, 1461–1466 (2000)

Clerc, M., Kennedy, J.: The particle swarm - explosion, stability, and convergence in a multidimensional complex space. IEEE Trans. Evol. Comput. **6**, 58–73 (2002)

Dhole, S.J., Smith, R.: Targeting water reuse with multiple contaminants. Trans. Int. Chem. Eng. **75**, 181–189 (1997)

El-Halwagi, M.M., Gabriel, F., Harell, D.: Rigorous graphical targeting for resource conservation via material recycle/reuse networks. Ind. Eng. Chem. Res. **42**, 4319–4328 (2003)

Espinoza-Quiñones, F.R., Módenes, A.N., Thomé, L.P., Palácio, S.M., Trigueros, D.E.G., Oliveira, A.P., Szymanski, N.: Study of the bioaccumulation kinetic of lead by living aquatic macrophyte Salvinia auriculata. Chem. Eng. J. **150**, 316–322 (2009)

Gómez, J., Savelski, M.J., Bagajewicz, M.J.: On a systematic design procedure for single component water utilization systems in process plants. Chem. Eng. Commun. **186**, 183–203 (2001)

Gunaratnam, M., Alva-Argaez, A., Kokosis, A., Kim, J.K., Smith, R.: Automated design of total water systems. Ind. Eng. Chem. Res. **44**, 588–599 (2005)

Hallale, N.: A new graphical targeting method for water minimization. Adv. Environ. Res. **6**, 377–390 (2003)

Huang, C.-H., Chang, C.-T., Ling, H.-C., Chang, C.-C.: A mathematical programming model for water usage and treatment network design. Ind. Eng. Chem. Res. **38**, 2666 (1999)

Iancu, P., Lavric, V., Plesu, V.: Optimisation of water networks using ranking as preprocessingstep to get equipartition driving force. Chem. Eng. Trans. **21**, 289–294 (2010). DOI:10.3303/CET1021049

Kennedy, J., Eberhart, R.: Swarm Intelligence. Morgan Kaufmann Publishers, San Francisco (2001)

Lee, S., Grossmann, I.E.: Global optimization of nonlinear generalized disjunctive programming with bilinear equality constraints: Applications to process networks. Comput. Chem. Eng. **27**, 1557–1575 (2003)

Lin, B., Miller, D.C.: Tabu search algorithm for chemical process optimization. Comput. Chem. Eng. **28**, 2287–2306 (2004)

Liu, Z.-Y., Zhang, Y., Yang, Y.: A mass-load-based procedure for minimizing total flowrate of the water systems with single contaminant. Chem. Eng. Trans. **18**, 869–874 (2009)

Manan, Z.A., Tan, Y.L., Foo, D.C.Y.: Targeting the minimum water flowrate using water cascade analysis technique. AIChE J. **50**, 3169–3183 (2004)

Mann, J.G., Liu, Y.A.: Industrial Water Reuse and Wastewater Minimization. Mcgraw-Hill, New York (1999)

Módenes, A.N., Espinoza-Quiñones, F.R., Trigueros, D.E.G., Pietrobelli, J.M.T.A., Lavarda, F. L., Ravagnani, M.A.S.S., Bergamasco, R.: Binary Adsorption of a Zn(II)-Cu(II) Mixture onto *Egeria densa* and *Eichhornia crassipes*: Kinetic and Equilibrium data modeling by PSO. Sep. Sci. Technol. **47**, 875–885 (2012)

Olesen, S.G., Polley, S.G.: A simple methodology for the design of water networks handling single contaminants. Trans. Inst. Chem. Eng. Part A, **75**, 420–426 (1997)

Poplewski, G., Jeżowski, J.M., Jeżowska, A.: Water network design with stochastic optimization approach. Chem. Eng. Res. Des. **89**, 2085–2101 (2011)

Ravagnani, M.A.S.S., Silva, A.P., Biscaia Jr., E.C., Caballero, J.A.: Optimal design of shell-and-tube heat heat exchangers using particle swarm optimization. Ind. Eng. Chem. Res. **48**, 2927–2935 (2009)

Takama, N., Kuriyama, T., Shikoko, K., Umeda, T.: Optimal water allocation in petroleum refinery. Comput. Chem. Eng. **4**, 251–258 (1980)

Tan, R.R., Col-long, K.J., Foo, D.C.Y., Hul, S., Ng, D.K.S.: A methodology for the design of efficient resource conservation networks using adaptive swarm intelligence. J. Cleaner Prod. **16**, 822–832 (2008)

Tan, Y.L., Foo, D.C.Y., Tan, R.R., Ng, D.K.S.: Approximate graphical targeting for water network with two contaminants. Chem. Eng. Trans. **12**, 347–352 (2007)

Trigueros, D.E.G., Módenes, A.N., Ravagnani, M.A.S.S., Espinoza-Quiñones, F.R.: Reuse water network synthesis by modified PSO approach. Chem. Eng. J. **183**, 198–211 (2012)

Trigueros, D.E.G., Módenes, A.N., Kroumov, A.D., Espinoza-Quiñones, F.R.: Modeling of biodegradation process of BTEX compounds: Kinetic parameters estimation by using Particle Swarm Global Optimizer. Process Biochem. **45**(8), 1355–1361 (2010a)

Trigueros, D.E.G., Módenes, A.N., Espinoza-Quiñones, F.R., Kroumov, A.D.: The evaluation of benzene and phenol biodegradation kinetics by applying non-structured models. Water Sci. Technol. **61**, 1289–1298 (2010b)

Tudor, R., Lavric, V.: Optimization of total networks of water-using and treatment units by genetic algorithms. Ind. Eng. Chem. Res. **49**, 3715–3731 (2010)

Wang, Y.P., Smith, R.: Wastewater minimization. Chem. Eng. Sci. **49**, 981–1006 (1994)

Yiqing, L., Xigang, Y., Yongjian, L.: An improved PSO algorithm for solving non-convex NLP/ MINLP problems with equality constraints. Comput. Chem. Eng. **31**, 153–162 (2007)

Author Index

Printed in the United States
By Bookmasters